Cold Rules, Hot Profits

Cold Rules, Hot Profits

How Insurance, Classification, and Law Shape Arctic Expansion

By

Nuno Valcorte

Vij Books

New Delhi (India)

Published by

Vij Books
(Publishers, Distributors & Importers)
4836/24, 3rd Floor, Ansari Road
Delhi – 110 002
Phone: 91-11-43596460
Mobile: 98110 94883
e-mail: contact@vijpublishing.com
www.vijbooks.in

ISBN: 978-93-7794-024-9 (PB)

This book was developed using advanced writing tools to support the drafting and ideation process. All content has been thoughtfully curated, refined, and reviewed to ensure quality and relevance.

Contents

Introduction		1
Chapter 1	Arctic Access and Private Governance	7
Chapter 2	Marine Insurance and Polar History	30
Chapter 3	Underwriting Arctic Risk with Thin Data	49
Chapter 4	Classification Societies and Ice Class Rules	78
Chapter 5	Polar Safety Standards and the Polar Code	103
Chapter 6	Compliance Documentation and Audit Trails	137
Chapter 7	Flag State, Port State, and Control Points	156
Chapter 8	Liability Regimes and Loss Allocation	179
Chapter 9	P&I Clubs and Reinsurance Structures	208
Chapter 10	Claims, Disputes, and Precedent Effects	225
Chapter 11	Premium Shocks and Market Withdrawal	256
Chapter 12	Ports, Terminals, and Infrastructure Risk	276
Chapter 13	Community Impacts and Social Licence Risks	292
Chapter 14	Geopolitics, Sanctions, and Security Externalities	311
Chapter 15	Scenarios for Arctic Access and Governance	334
About the Author		349

Introduction

In August 2016, the *Crystal Serenity* slipped out of Seward, Alaska, on a luxury transit through the Northwest Passage, its white hull carrying more than a thousand passengers towards New York by way of waters long treated as forbidding, seasonal, and commercially awkward. The air smelt of diesel and salt. Cameras clicked on the quay. The voyage was presented as a spectacle of access: a ship once associated with warm-water leisure moving through a geography that had, for generations, been narrated as a margin of danger and distance. Yet the real drama did not begin at the rail. It began in files, surveys, contingency plans, class records, and the quiet judgements of markets that had to decide whether such a passage was thinkable on acceptable terms. The ice was not alone.

That is the Arctic's modern paradox. As sea ice retreats and political rhetoric grows bolder, one hears a familiar language of opening: new lanes, new projects, new frontiers, new strategic possibilities. And yet every opening produces a second, less visible enclosure. A ship may have the steel, the engines, and the charted route; a project may have the concession, the financing, and the public blessing. Still, an exclusion in a policy wording, a limitation in a class notation, a deficiency on an inspection report, or a dispute over "reasonable precautions" can narrow the field more effectively than any formal prohibition. It is not only states that govern access to the Arctic. In many cases, they do not govern it most intimately.

The point is not rhetorical. On 1 January 2017, the International Maritime Organisation's Polar Code entered into force, turning years of anxiety about remote operations, limited search-and-rescue coverage, extreme weather, and environmental sensitivity into a more formal architecture of obligations. That date matters, but not because one code suddenly solved the Arctic. It matters because it made plain a larger truth: expansion in polar regions depends on the conversion of uncertainty into administrable categories. Risks must be described, measured, certified, inspected, priced, and, above all, allocated. When that conversion works, activity becomes possible. When it fails, ambition stalls. What often looks like a contest over geography is, at close range, a contest over legibility.

This is why the commanding institutions of Arctic expansion are often neither theatrical nor sovereign in the old style. They do not sail with flags in the foreground. They read submissions. They compare deficiencies. They revise terms after losses. They ask for another survey, another manual, another piece of evidence that the operator is not merely optimistic but governable. Their authority does not arrive through grand declaration. It accumulates through paperwork that bites. The Arctic has always tested endurance; now it also tests whether an enterprise can survive contact with underwriting discipline, classification requirements, port scrutiny, contractual liability, and the commercial memory of specialist markets. The decisive frontier is frequently a paper one: a field of what might be called paper ice, shifting and hardening beneath commercial feet.

Consider the Russian tanker *Christophe de Margerie*, delivered in 2017 for work connected to the Yamal LNG project and designed for independent navigation in severe ice conditions. Here was a vessel that seemed to answer the usual objections. It had a purpose-built design, a clear industrial mission, and a route embedded in a larger state-backed energy strategy. The spectacle, when it drew attention, was technological. But the deeper significance lay elsewhere. A vessel like this is not simply stronger than ordinary tonnage. It is more documentable. Its value to markets rests in part on the way its design, notation, operating limits, training expectations, and support assumptions can be translated into forms that insurers, charterers, and counterparties recognise. Strength, by itself, is mute. It must be rendered into records.

That translation is one of the book's governing concerns because it is where lofty abstractions turn practical. Trust is not a mood. It appears in a complete loss record, in a survey recommendation closed out on time, in a maintenance regime that can be evidenced rather than asserted, in a crew matrix that shows polar competence rather than vague experience, in a voyage plan that states clear thresholds for turning back. Efficiency is not merely speed. It may mean fewer deficiencies at inspection, less argumentative renewal negotiations, shorter delays at terminals, and fewer surprises in claims handling. Risk is not a cloud hovering over the Arctic. It is a deductible raised, a sublimit introduced, an escort requirement imposed, a season shortened, and a warranty tightened until a feasible voyage becomes a marginal one.

One lesson follows quickly. Operators do not enter the Arctic alone, even when only one hull appears on the horizon. They arrive trailed by insurers, brokers, reinsurers, P&I clubs, class societies, auditors, surveyors, charterers, terminal owners, flag administrations, port inspectors, lawyers, and financiers. Some have formal coercive powers. Some do not. But together they create a mesh of expectations dense enough to structure behaviour. This is not a side story to geopolitics. It is one of geopolitics' working parts. States may dream aloud about corridors, resources, and strategic presence; companies may speak the idiom of opportunity. Between the dream and the deed sits a long chain of private judgement. A voyage goes ahead because enough actors agree that the risk, while real, has been made legible and tolerable. A project fails because one or two of them decide the opposite.

Marine history helps sharpen that claim. Polar waters did not become dangerous yesterday, nor did markets only recently discover remoteness, ice, or sparse rescue capability. Older ideas of seaworthiness still cast long shadows. The language may have become more codified, the data more abundant in places, the technology more sophisticated, yet the enduring concerns are recognisable: what can break, how far help is, whether a master has enough margin, and whether operators know more than they can truly prove. The institutional answer to those old questions has shifted over time from heroic judgement and episodic subsidy towards standards, comparability, audit trails, and portfolio management. In the Arctic, that shift is especially consequential because novelty tempts overstatement. Markets answer novelty with caution.

The caution is not irrational. In September 2018, the *Venta Maersk* completed a trial container transit of the Northern Sea Route, travelling from Vladivostok towards St Petersburg. The voyage attracted global notice because it seemed to announce a future in which Arctic shipping would become routine enough to redraw trade assumptions. Yet one voyage is not a market. It is evidence of possibility under specific conditions, not proof of general viability. Seasonality still bites. Infrastructure remains uneven. Repair options are limited. Salvage can become ruinously complex. Routes that look efficient on a map can become expensive once delay, inspection intensity, convoy constraints, political uncertainty, and insurance terms are placed in the calculation. What appears from a distance as an opening lane may, from inside the file, look like a chain of dependencies.

And yet the argument is not that insurers and standards simply suppress enterprise. They also make enterprise possible. Without classification, there is no common technical language for baseline integrity. Without liability structures, there is no durable way to distribute the costs of collision, pollution, wreck, injury, or delay. Without P&I mechanisms, reinsurance, and a culture of claims documentation, many Arctic ventures would remain too opaque to finance or charter at all. Private governance constrains, but it also coordinates. It narrows improvisation in order to preserve a broader possibility of trade. That is why the sector's disciplinarians are also, in an odd way, its enablers. The cold rule is not the enemy of profit; it is often the condition under which profit stops being fantasy.

Still, the promise of rules should not be romanticised. Standardisation can conceal as much as it reveals. A vessel may be in class and yet operationally brittle. A company may carry a handsome compliance portfolio while tolerating weak onboard practice. An exemption lawfully granted can alarm an underwriter more than a plain prohibition ever would. Third-party verification reduces information asymmetry, but it never abolishes it. Nor do global standards land evenly. One flag administration may be demanding and technically confident; another may lack depth or take a lighter view. One port may treat a string of minor deficiencies as evidence of systemic weakness; another may process the same vessel with less curiosity. The resulting unevenness matters because uncertainty itself carries a price. Markets are often more comfortable with stern clarity than with permissive ambiguity.

Here, the Arctic differs from easier seas not in kind but in amplification. Everywhere, maritime commerce depends on documents, maintenance, professional judgement, and the quiet correction of small errors before they grow teeth. In the Arctic, the margin for that correction narrows. Cold slows the body, stiffens materials, narrows rescue windows, punishes delay, and turns modest faults into compounding events. Remoteness enlarges claims. A machinery problem that might be inconvenient elsewhere can become consequential where towing assets are scarce and weather windows brief. Pollution liability acquires a sharper edge where clean-up is harder, habitats politically charged, and evidentiary disputes likely to stretch over time and distance. Geography alters severity. That simple fact radiates through every institutional layer.

This is why the most revealing Arctic struggles often begin after the apparent event has passed. An incident occurs. Logs are reviewed. Statements diverge. Experts argue over causation. Was the damage truly ice-related, or did maintenance failures create the real vulnerability? Did the master follow the voyage plan, or depart from it under commercial pressure? Was the relevant condition precedent satisfied, and if not, did that failure materially increase the loss? Confidential settlements may keep formal precedent scarce, but the market learns anyway. Rumour fills gaps. Reinsurers notice patterns. A recommendation that was once advisory reappears at renewal as an expectation, then hardens into a requirement. Claims history becomes a quiet legislator. That is how governance continues after the fact, in the long afterlife of loss.

The same logic extends ashore. Ports, terminals, tugs, repair yards, emergency response arrangements, medical support, and data infrastructure all shape the insurance imagination of Arctic operations. A strong hull cannot compensate indefinitely for a weak system. Terminal operators know this, and often impose their own entry rules, indemnities, inspections, and documentary thresholds, acting as regulators by commercial contract rather than public law. Communities know it too, although they articulate the problem differently: not as accumulation exposure or claims severity, but as lived consequence, uneven consultation, environmental disturbance, and distrust of outside assurances. Social licence is not sentiment floating above the transaction. It can harden into cancellations, delays, stricter requirements, litigation risk, adverse publicity, or insurer discomfort with controversy. When activism collides with underwriting, the language changes, but the effect may be the same: access becomes more conditional.

Political risk adds another layer, and one increasingly difficult to quarantine from routine commerce. Sanctions screening, security concerns, dual-use anxieties, and contested attribution after suspicious incidents all create forms of friction that insurers and counterparties struggle to domesticate. A region described in strategic terms will sooner or later find those terms sedimented into cancellation clauses, disclosure demands, narrower appetites, or heightened scrutiny of partners and routes. Here again, the state is present but not solitary. Market actors sometimes amplify official caution; sometimes they exceed it; sometimes they behave more conservatively than governments intended. In that sense, insurers can become inadvertent foreign policy actors—not because they issue doctrines, but because they decide what can proceed on tolerable terms and what cannot.

The hard question, then, is not whether the Arctic is opening. It is opening, unevenly and contingently, and in ways that invite exaggeration from both boosters and pessimists. The harder question is who gets to decide what counts as prudent access, by what evidence, at whose cost, and with what recourse when judgement fails. A shipowner seeking passage, an energy developer planning support logistics, a charterer comparing routes, a regulator designing standards, a scholar studying non-state power: all are, in different forms, confronting the same underlying problem. They must decide whether the rules now governing Arctic expansion are producing disciplined possibility or merely shifting power into technical arenas where accountability is harder to see.

That question is not abstract. It appears whenever a promising route becomes unfinanceable after repricing, whenever a vessel technically allowed to trade cannot secure cover on workable terms, whenever a deficiency history shadows an operator longer than any formal sanction, whenever a community's objections alter the risk appetite of markets that never meet it directly, whenever a project looks feasible in engineering drawings but fragile in claims scenarios. The Arctic's future will not be settled only by thaw, technology, or state ambition. It will also be settled in the patient, unspectacular work of comparison: comparing incidents to models, models to surveys, surveys to contracts, contracts to losses, and losses to memory.

The important thing is to see the grain of power where it actually lies. Not all borders are mapped. Some are written into exclusions. Some sit inside notations, warranties, audit findings, and indemnity clauses. Some emerge only when something goes wrong and a market asks, with cold precision, whether the precautions were reasonable, the disclosure complete, the control real. By then, the paper ice is already underfoot. The central decision is never merely whether the Arctic can be entered. It is whether access can be made durable under institutions that reward evidence, punish opacity, and remember failure for longer than any press cycle. That is the pressure point on which hot profits and cold rules now meet.

Chapter 1

Arctic Access and Private Governance

What does it mean for a region to open if permission must still be sought from people who never set foot there? The Arctic invites a familiar vocabulary of movement: passage, access, expansion, reach. Yet the decisive barriers often appear long before a vessel meets ice or a project meets weather. They arise in underwriting rooms, in class files, in the small print of liability clauses, in the sober language of surveys and recommendations. The door may look open on a map. The lock sits elsewhere.

A commercial operator can possess the technical means to proceed and still find the venture slowed, narrowed, or quietly refused. Not because a navy blocks the route. Not because a border closes. Because the activity cannot be rendered acceptable to those who must absorb, certify, distribute, or price its hazards. That distinction matters. It shifts attention from the visible drama of Arctic ambition to the quieter machinery that decides which ambitions become ordinary business and which remain expensive theatre. The file matters as much as the flag.

This creates a tension that runs through nearly every serious Arctic venture. Expansion rewards speed, timing, and confidence. Risk management rewards proof, comparison, and caution. One side wants to move before rivals do, to claim commercial position while conditions permit. The other side asks whether the vessel, the crew, the operator, and the wider support system can withstand conditions that punish weak assumptions. Neither instinct is irrational. Profit seeks an opening; governance tests whether the opening can bear weight. Where those impulses meet, private authority takes shape.

That authority often escapes public notice because it does not always speak in grand political language. It speaks in terms that sound technical, narrow, even dull: warranty, condition, notation, deficiency, recommendation, due diligence. And yet these are powerful words. They decide who must prove what, who bears delay, who pays when conditions deteriorate, who may proceed only within tighter limits, and who discovers that nominal permission offers little practical freedom. A region as physically demanding as the Arctic magnifies the force of such language because the margin for improvisation is thin and the cost of misjudgement rises quickly once distance, cold, and sparse infrastructure come into play.

The stakes exceed marine administration. Private governance changes commercial geography. It influences which routes look viable, which seasons appear tolerable, which counterparties attract confidence, which operators must accept punishing terms, and which projects never advance beyond paper. It also alters political meaning. States may declare priorities, promote corridors, or invoke sovereignty, but commercial access depends on whether risk can be translated into forms legible to insurers, classification societies, reinsurers, P&I clubs, auditors, charterers, and infrastructure owners. Power does not vanish when it leaves the state. It becomes more dispersed, more contractual, and sometimes harder to contest.

That diffusion of power explains why Arctic governance cannot be understood through public law alone. Formal regulation matters, of course, but much of the working discipline of the region emerges through linked private judgements. A surveyor records a condition. An underwriter treats that condition as material. A broker reframes the submission. A class society's notation establishes one baseline while a charterer demands another. A port inspection history follows the vessel into later negotiations. Each step may appear modest in isolation. Together they form a chain of control. The cumulative effect is practical rather than theatrical: behaviour changes because the cost of resisting these expectations is too high.

And yet private conservatism is not merely obstructive. It can be enabling in the strictest sense. Without credible risk transfer, many Arctic voyages would not proceed. Without class, auditability, and predictable forms of liability allocation, commercial actors would struggle to distinguish disciplined operators from reckless ones. The same institutions that narrow the room for manoeuvre also create the minimum confidence on which trade depends. This double character gives Arctic governance its edge. The gatekeeper is also the facilitator. That is why disputes about standards and insurance terms are never only technical disagreements; they are arguments about who gets to define prudence, and on what evidence.

The pressure builds along a clear path. It begins with risk transfer, where insurance stops being an afterthought and becomes a precondition of movement. It then widens into the larger cast of non-state rule-makers whose contracts and standards travel across jurisdictions more smoothly than most public commands. From there, the friction sharpens: commercial actors chase advantage while underwriters and classifiers lean towards restraint, especially where novelty outpaces reliable comparison. Once that conflict is visible, the rest of the terrain comes into focus - the modelling of uncertain conditions, the authority of standards, the discipline of inspections, the allocation of liability, the afterlife of claims, and the way each incident feeds back into future terms.

Seen from that angle, the Arctic is not simply a harsh environment awaiting better technology or stronger political will. It is an arena where documentation, verification, and loss allocation determine the practical meaning of access. A vessel can meet a technical standard and still present an unattractive risk. A project can satisfy a legal threshold and still fail to secure workable cover. A minor deficiency can travel farther than expected because specialised markets remember, compare, and harden their judgements over time. Quiet feedback loops govern the region: incidents shape claims, claims reshape premiums, premiums reshape operations, and altered operations create new norms that soon begin to feel inevitable.

The question that matters, then, is not whether private governance exists in the Arctic. It plainly does. The harder question is where its real threshold lies. At what point does prudent caution become a hidden form of exclusion, and at what point does commercial optimism become a demand that others subsidise uncertainty they cannot properly measure? Everything turns on that line. Before any later dispute over responsibility, before any argument about precedent or pricing, there is a simpler test waiting at the start: can this risk be made legible enough, and credible enough, for someone to carry it?

Risk transfer as a gatekeeper

In August 2016, the *Crystal Serenity* left Seward, Alaska, for a transit through the Northwest Passage that drew headlines for its novelty and its symbolism. A large passenger vessel, associated with leisure rather than hardship, was moving through waters still defined by remoteness, uncertain ice, sparse infrastructure, and rescue constraints. The visible story sat on deck: passengers, cameras, the clean white hull against dark water. The decisive story sat elsewhere. Before such a voyage could become a ticketed reality, somebody had to accept the possibility of collision, machinery failure, delay, evacuation, pollution, medical emergency, and a chain of losses made harsher by cold and distance. The route had to pass through a file before it could pass through ice.

That file carried more than a premium. It carried judgement. Insurers, brokers, reinsurers, P&I interests, chartering parties and technical advisers were not simply pricing a ship in water; they were pricing a chain of operational claims about competence, restraint, support capacity, and evidence. The Arctic sharpens this point because it strips away the illusion that insurance is a clerical afterthought. In temperate trades, cover can appear routine, folded into the machinery of commerce almost unnoticed. In polar waters, the question becomes plain: who is willing to stand behind this voyage, on what terms, with what exclusions, subject to what proof? No file, no voyage.

Risk transfer is often described as a financial tool. That is true, but too mild. In Arctic operations, it acts as an entrance examination. It decides whether a proposed movement can be translated into acceptable loss-bearing terms. The practical force of that decision reaches much further than premium alone. It shapes the season in which a vessel sails, the route it takes, the qualifications expected of the crew, the maintenance work completed before departure, the support arrangements secured ashore, and even the words used to describe the venture. A market does not need to ban an operation to discipline it. It only needs to make uncertainty expensive enough, or narrow cover enough, that ambition changes shape before the lines are cast off.

This is where the language of risk transfer acquires a sharper meaning than everyday commercial speech allows. A warranty is not decorative wording. A condition is not a polite preference. A deductible is not merely a number waiting at the end of a claims process. Each converts uncertainty into behaviour. If cover depends on weather routing support, the operator buys it. If underwriters insist on demonstrated ice competence in the bridge team, crewing decisions change. If machinery reliability or hull condition draws close scrutiny, deferred maintenance becomes harder to defend. If the route threatens accumulation exposure or doubtful salvage prospects, planners look again at season, ports of refuge, escort arrangements, or whether the voyage should proceed at all. The price matters, but the terms often matter more.

A visible example sits in the difference between an operator who arrives with a disciplined record and one who arrives with aspiration. Consider two commercial entrants seeking to undertake similar Arctic voyages. The first produces a dense and orderly submission: class records up to date, survey recommendations closed out, a credible polar water operational plan, detailed maintenance history, bridge officers with relevant experience, arrangements for weather and ice information, identified emergency support, transparent claims history, and a willingness to accept prudent operating limits. The second offers broad assurances, thinner records, unresolved technical points, vague crewing claims, and a planning package that reads as though it were adapted from easier waters. Both may own capable vessels. Both may invoke market opportunity. Only one has converted capability into evidence. The first is likely to face negotiation; the second, suspicion. In Arctic risk, documentation does not merely describe prudence. It performs it.

The distinction can be felt in named voyages. When A.P. Moller-Maersk sent the *Venta Maersk* through the Northern Sea Route in 2018, the public discussion dwelt on commercial possibility and the symbolism of a container ship using an Arctic passage. Less visible, but commercially essential, was the fact that such a trial depended on an operator whose systems, technical records, and organisational discipline were legible to markets accustomed to testing large maritime risks. That did not make the route ordinary. It did not dissolve concern. But it altered the conversation from raw novelty to managed experiment. The operator was not asking the market to underwrite bravado. It was asking the market to underwrite a bounded proposition. That difference is everything.

The same logic explains why route choice is never merely geographical. On a chart, one path may look shorter. In a risk file, it may look intolerable. Underwriters do not examine route only in terms of distance; they compare ice exposure, weather volatility, communications reliability, tug and salvage availability, medical response, inspection climate, congestion at choke points, and the chance that multiple risks could crystallise at once. A route through harsher or less supported waters may save days in theory and cost months in adjustment if the terms of cover tighten, deductibles rise, exclusions multiply, or counterparties demand extra assurances. The map is not the market. In the Arctic, the shortest line can be the longest argument.

Seasonality follows the same pattern. A shipping executive may see a widening operational window; a market may see thin data at the margins of that window, greater volatility, and weaker comparability with earlier experience. Cover then becomes a way of converting seasonal doubt into discipline. Sailing later in the year may remain technically possible while becoming commercially punitive. The voyage is not forbidden. It is burdened. Additional surveys may be required. Higher retentions may apply. Ice navigator requirements may tighten. Operators may be pressed to adopt more conservative speed profiles, stronger reporting routines, or narrower decision thresholds for aborting passage. Each measure looks minor in isolation. Together they redraw the season.

Crewing offers another clear example of abstraction made visible. Markets speak often of competence, but competence in this context is not a warm sentiment about professionalism. It is evidenced through certificates, prior voyages, simulator training, bridge composition, company procedures, fatigue management, reporting discipline, and the track record of masters and chief engineers under pressure. In easier trades, some operators can hide behind general reputation. Arctic work punishes that vagueness. If the people on the vessel cannot be made legible as polar operators rather than merely seafarers, the terms of entry harden. Crewing becomes insurability in human form.

Maintenance, too, changes character once risk transfer becomes a gatekeeper. Ordinary commercial pressure always tempts delay: one more voyage before dry docking, one more season before a component replacement, one more paper explanation for a nagging deficiency. Arctic underwriting cuts against that habit because the severity of a moderate technical failure increases in remote waters. A maintenance issue that might produce inconvenience in a dense support environment can produce a major claim in an area with sparse repair options and slow rescue. Underwriters know this. P&I interests know this. Reinsurers know this. So maintenance history becomes more than a record of engineering care; it becomes a proxy for organisational honesty. What has been repaired? What remains deferred? What was recommended at survey, and what was done about it? The file remembers.

The 2017 entry into force of the IMO Polar Code sharpened this dynamic without replacing it. Formal standards gave markets a stronger common language for planning, equipment, procedures, and limits in polar operations. That mattered because risk transfer depends on comparability. Rules help markets decide what counts as ordinary prudence and what counts as hazardous deviation. But codification did not remove judgement. It intensified it. Compliance became evidence, not absolution. A vessel could meet formal expectations and still attract restrictive terms if its support arrangements looked thin, its crew weak, its history patchy, or its intended trade too ambitious for the comfort of insurers. Legality opens one gate. Insurability opens another.

A second named example makes the point from a different angle. The *Christophe de Margerie*, delivered in 2017 for Arctic LNG service, represented not a speculative flirtation with the region but a purpose-built industrial commitment. Its significance lay not only in hull strength or propulsion design. It lay in the fact that an entire operation had been organised to make extreme service intelligible to multiple risk-bearing institutions: technical classification, operational planning, industrial backing, route assumptions, and a larger commercial logic capable of sustaining specialised terms. It is tempting to say such projects prove that the Arctic ceases to be exceptional once enough money and engineering are applied. That would be too neat. What they prove, rather, is that exceptionality can sometimes be managed when evidence, infrastructure, and financial architecture move together.

And yet a limitation must be admitted. Not every Arctic operation depends on commercial insurance in the same way, or to the same visible degree. State-backed ventures, military support operations, and certain strategically favoured industrial projects may retain more risk internally, receive public backing, or proceed under political rationales that soften the disciplining force of ordinary market judgement. A sovereign can choose to absorb uncertainty that a commercial underwriter would reject or price brutally. That matters because it prevents an easy overstatement: private risk transfer does not rule everything, everywhere, all at once.

Still, even that apparent exception confirms the broader point. Risk does not disappear when it escapes commercial insurance. It is merely relocated. Someone still bears the possibility of loss, delay, liability, wreck, or pollution. Someone still decides how much uncertainty is tolerable and what evidence counts as enough. The difference is institutional form, not the end of gatekeeping. Indeed, state-backed projects often rely on highly formalised technical verification and tightly documented operating controls precisely because they need to compensate for the risks others might hesitate to assume. Retained risk demands its own bureaucracy. The gate does not vanish; it changes hands.

Once seen clearly, risk transfer appears less like a financial service appended to Arctic commerce and more like the hidden architecture of the trade itself. It tells operators which ambitions can be normalised and which remain too unruly to support. It converts weather, ice, remoteness, liability, and reputation into a disciplined sequence of choices. It forces declarations of confidence to submit to comparison. It rewards operators who can produce a persuasive record and punishes those who rely on broad assurances or heroic language. It also creates a market memory that bites long after a voyage ends. A closed recommendation, a clean inspection history, a transparent renewal discussion: these accumulate. So do evasions.

The effect is not merely conservative. It is selective. The Arctic does not simply open or close. It opens for some operators sooner than for others; on some terms, not others; in some windows, not others. That selectivity has commercial and political consequences. A well-documented company with disciplined systems may find a costly but workable path into difficult waters. A newcomer with weaker records may meet the same geography only to discover that the real barrier lies in narrower cover, broader exclusions, higher retentions, more intrusive survey conditions, and scepticism from counterparties who read those terms as warning signs. In that sense, insurance does more than spread loss. It sorts participants.

The quiet motif returns here: the file before the ice. Arctic commerce likes stories of endurance, design, strategy, and nerve. Those stories are not false, but they are incomplete. Before steel meets pressure ridge, before a master decides whether to turn or press on, before cargo owners count days saved, someone has already tested whether the proposed risk can be measured, compared, and carried. That prior test governs more than many public debates admit. The hard question is never simply whether a vessel can make the passage. It is whether the people asked to absorb the consequences believe the operator has earned the right to try.

Who sets the "rules" outside the state

In September 2018, the *Venta Maersk* completed its trial voyage through the Northern Sea Route, linking East Asia and Europe by a passage that has long attracted strategic longing and commercial caution. The public image was simple enough: a container ship, a thinning seasonal window, a route once treated as marginal now tested by a major operator. The real architecture of permission was far less visible. Before a vessel like that could move through Arctic waters under tolerable commercial conditions, a cluster of actors had already done their work: class had to accept the vessel's technical standing, insurers had to decide what risks they would assume, brokers had to present the submission persuasively, reinsurers had to tolerate the accumulation, and surveyors had to convert operational realities into language other parties could trust. The voyage needed more than a chart. It needed a stamp.

That stamp did not come from one hand. It emerged from a sequence of judgements, each formally separate and commercially entangled. A classification notation could indicate structural fitness for certain conditions without promising that insurers would like the trade. A P&I club could support third-party liabilities while still probing crew competence, voyage planning, and emergency arrangements. A broker could improve the file, but not abolish concern. A surveyor could close one question and open three more. None of this looked like legislation. Much of it carried greater practical force than legislation. A state may proclaim access. A market asks for proof.

The central fact of modern maritime commerce, especially in demanding theatres such as the Arctic, is that authority accumulates through linked private decisions. Contracts, manuals, certificates, recommendations, rules of class, club circulars, reinsurance appetites, inspection records and audit findings combine to produce a working order that no single statute fully captures. That order does not replace public law. It sits alongside it, translates it, narrows it, and sometimes hardens it. A vessel may satisfy a formal legal threshold and still find itself commercially constrained because other institutions treat legality as a starting point rather than a finish. The state draws part of the frame. Private governance fills in the room.

Insurers sit near the centre of this room because they price uncertainty and because their willingness to carry loss affects almost every other commercial relationship around the voyage. Yet insurers rarely act alone. The broker matters because underwriters do not see the vessel directly; they see a submission. A good broker does more than shop for terms. The broker organises facts, anticipates objections, identifies comparators, and decides what kind of narrative the risk will inhabit. That is not cosmetic work. It can determine whether a voyage appears as a disciplined operation with bounded uncertainty or as an expensive surprise waiting for a claims file. Trust, in this setting, takes visible form: a complete loss record, clear maintenance history, coherent route assumptions, prompt answers to technical questions, and a willingness to disclose awkward facts before others discover them.

Reinsurers make the picture still larger. Their names may never appear in public reporting of an Arctic voyage, yet their appetite shapes the outer limits of what primary insurers can tolerate. The point matters because

Arctic exposures often carry an accumulation logic. A single vessel may not threaten a market, but multiple vessels operating in the same seasonal corridor, with limited salvage options and correlated environmental hazards, can alter the background calculation. Reinsurance therefore acts as a kind of remote discipline. It does not tell the master what to do on the bridge. It influences whether the original insurer can offer broad terms, narrow terms, or no terms at all. Capital at a distance governs conduct up close.

P&I clubs add a distinct layer of authority because the liabilities they address do not behave like ordinary property damage alone. Collision, pollution, wreck removal, cargo claims, personal injury, passenger exposure, and a long tail of third-party costs all turn Arctic incidents into legal and financial entanglements rather than purely technical mishaps. Mutuality gives the clubs a particular tone. They are not only paying institutions; they are communities of risk-sharing with a strong interest in preventing one member's bad discipline from burdening the rest. That can make them quietly interventionist. A club may not write the vessel's safety management system, but it can ask hard questions, require information, support certain precautions, and react sharply when disclosure falls short or procedures look ornamental. Mutual insurance becomes collective discipline.

Classification societies operate through a different register again. They do not insure the voyage, and they are not states, even though public regulation often relies on their technical work. Their authority comes from rules, surveys, notations, and the immense commercial value of being "in class". That phrase sounds almost casual to outsiders. In practice it behaves like a passport. Banks, charterers, terminals, insurers and counterparties often treat class standing as a threshold matter, not because class guarantees safety in any absolute sense, but because it establishes a recognised baseline of design, construction and maintenance. In Arctic operations, where technical margins narrow and hull, machinery, and systems face harsher demands, class becomes more than a background credential. It becomes a language others use to begin their own judgements.

A named example shows the point. After the *Costa Concordia* casualty off Giglio, Italy, in January 2012, the immediate public focus fell on command decisions, passenger safety and the spectacle of a modern cruise ship capsized near shore. Less publicly dramatic, but institutionally important, was the wave of scrutiny that followed through insurers, P&I structures, classification review, auditing of procedures and reassessment of risk assumptions across passenger operations. One casualty, in one place, triggered a much wider hardening of expectations because the same private actors that support routine commerce also learn through loss. The lesson travels through circulars, renewal negotiations, survey emphases, audit depth and changed tolerances. Authority here is cumulative, not ceremonial.

Surveyors and auditors are often mistaken for minor characters because they do not always hold the contract that attracts the most attention. That is a mistake. They translate conditions on the ground into terms others can act on. A surveyor visiting a vessel, a terminal, or a set of support arrangements does more than record facts. The surveyor selects what counts as salient, frames deficiencies in degrees of seriousness, decides how much comfort or discomfort the evidence warrants, and converts local observations into portable judgements. An auditor performs a parallel task at the level of organisational behaviour: does the company merely possess procedures, or does it live by them when schedules tighten and uncertainty grows? Their work creates the bridge between the messy world of practice and the cleaner world of contractual response.

The language they produce deserves attention because it is where private governance often becomes tangible. A warranty can require that a condition be maintained, not admired. A condition precedent can make compliance essential before liability attaches. A survey recommendation can begin as advice and end as a practical obligation once insurers or charterers decide they will not proceed without closure. Even the vocabulary signals gradation. A note in a report may register concern. A recommendation invites remediation. A held-covered clause may preserve continuity but at a cost and on terms. Operators learn quickly that small phrases can carry large consequences. One word can delay a fixture. One unresolved point can narrow a season. The stamp returns.

Coordination across borders depends on this shared language. An Arctic voyage can involve a flag in one jurisdiction, insurance placed in another, reinsurance spread internationally, class headquartered elsewhere, a P&I club with global membership, cargo interests from several states, and ports with different inspection cultures. No single sovereign command can manage that complexity alone. Contracts and standards travel more easily. They also stabilise expectation. A charterer in one market can read class standing, survey history, club support, warranty language and audit outcome as meaningful signals without personally knowing the operator. Efficiency takes a visible form here: fewer ad hoc arguments, faster screening of counterparties, more comparable judgements across distance. The gain is real. So is the power embedded in it.

The International Association of Classification Societies, founded in 1968, offers a useful institutional anchor because it shows how private rule-making can become globally consequential without ever becoming a parliament. By coordinating technical standards among major societies, it helped create forms of comparability that commercial actors increasingly relied upon. The point is not that all societies think identically or that interpretation ceases to matter. Quite the reverse. Operators know that technical disputes still arise, survey cultures differ, and rule changes can feel like moving ground. But a common framework allows multiple markets to talk to one another. It reduces some uncertainty while creating a platform on which new distinctions can be drawn. Standardisation, then, does not end judgement. It organises it.

A credible limitation should be admitted. Private actors do not rule in a vacuum, and they do not always prevail. States still control sanctions, cabotage rules, environmental law, certification frameworks, and the broader political conditions within which Arctic ventures proceed. A strategic project backed by a determined government may advance despite obvious market unease, either because risk is retained internally, public support softens the commercial blow, or political imperatives outweigh ordinary caution. That matters because it prevents a crude inversion in which one simply swaps state sovereignty for market sovereignty and calls the matter settled.

Yet the limitation goes only so far. Even politically backed projects need technical verification, contractual allocation, operational discipline, and someone willing to absorb or carry the consequences of failure. If commercial insurers step back, retained risk expands and internal controls usually tighten rather than loosen. If external finance enters, documentary expectations return. If international partners participate, comparability becomes indispensable. Private governance may bend under political pressure, but it rarely disappears. More often it changes shape, becoming less visible precisely when its practical demands grow stricter.

What gives this non-state order its peculiar force is that it seldom announces itself as rule in the grand style. It arrives as requirement, recommendation, caveat, endorsement, exclusion, survey finding, club query, or audit trail. It sounds procedural. It decides outcomes. A vessel owner may think the decisive negotiation concerns freight, timing or access to a route. Quietly, the harder negotiation concerns whether enough dispersed institutions can align around a shared view of acceptable exposure. Each actor sees only part of the risk. Together they create a gate no single one could erect alone.

This helps explain why Arctic access often feels simultaneously open and conditional. The route exists. The technology exists. The commercial interest exists. What remains uncertain is whether the web of private institutions will permit these elements to cohere on terms that do not unravel under scrutiny. That is why apparently technical disagreements matter so much. They are not arguments at the edge of the real business. They are arguments about who has authority to define the real business in the first place.

The unresolved problem lies here. Cross-border commerce needs private standards, transferable trust and institutions able to compare unlike operators without starting from zero each time. But the more power those institutions acquire, the more consequential their blind spots, their conservatisms and their opaque judgements become. At what point does coordination become quiet legislation by contract, survey and stamp - and who gets to challenge the decision when the gate remains shut?

Commercial ambition versus safety conservatism

In August 2018, the *Venta Maersk* completed a trial voyage along the Northern Sea Route, travelling from Vladivostok towards St Petersburg through waters that had long occupied the commercial imagination as a shortcut, a symbol, and a wager. The voyage drew attention because it seemed to compress a large argument into a single image: a modern container ship moving through an Arctic passage once treated as marginal to ordinary trade. The public meaning was speed. The private meaning was hesitation. Before such a voyage could be attempted, a far less visible discussion had already taken place among underwriters, brokers, technical advisers, class interests, and cargo-facing counterparties about whether this was an experiment that could be bounded or a precedent that might be misread as routine. The route offered promise. The file demanded restraint.

That friction lies at the centre of Arctic commerce. Operators see timing, competitive edge, early positioning, and the reputational value of being first through a difficult corridor or first into a new service niche. Insurers and classification societies see thin comparators, severe loss potential, sparse infrastructure, uncertain rescue capability, and the hard lesson that novelty often flatters itself before it proves itself. Both sides read the same horizon and draw different conclusions. One reads opportunity. The other reads exposure. The green light flickers.

The tension is not a clash between courage and timidity. It is a structural disagreement about how much uncertainty commercial actors should be allowed to convert into enterprise before the evidence catches up. First-mover ambition rewards asymmetry. The early entrant hopes to gain advantage before competitors, regulators, or markets settle into a more crowded and rule-bound pattern. Safety conservatism works in the opposite direction. It discounts narrative and asks for records, comparators, survey findings, closed recommendations, demonstrated competence, and operating limits that can be defended after the fact. In the Arctic, where environmental severity punishes error and where incident response can become ruinously difficult, conservatism tends to enjoy the stronger moral position. It also imposes a commercial tax on novelty.

That tax takes visible form. It appears when a proposed voyage attracts wider exclusions than the operator expected, when a deductible rises to a level that changes the economics of a trade, when class requires further evidence before accepting a technical arrangement, when a broker asks for another revision to the risk submission, when a charterer insists on narrower operating windows, when a club wants clearer reporting lines and stronger contingency planning before extending comfort. None of these decisions looks dramatic in isolation. Together they can transform the commercial proposition. Efficiency ceases to mean the shortest route on paper; it comes to mean the route that survives institutional scrutiny at tolerable cost.

Arctic novelty intensifies this pattern because novelty does not arrive as a neutral fact. It arrives as a problem of comparison. Underwriters prefer histories that can be measured against other histories. Classification societies prefer design assumptions that can be tested against established operating experience. Reinsurers prefer loss patterns that sit within a wider and more stable field of calculation. The Arctic frustrates all three preferences. Conditions vary sharply across season and route. A successful passage may prove little beyond the prudence of that one operator in that one window. A failure may reveal systemic weakness or mere bad luck, and arguments about which is which can persist for years. Thin data does not produce open-minded pricing. It usually produces margins.

This helps explain why operators trying to establish an Arctic presence often behave less like adventurers than like litigants preparing a case.

They gather records, certify training, commission surveys, refine manuals, document drills, close out recommendations, and cultivate a reputation for procedural discipline that extends beyond any one vessel. They know that commercial trust in this setting is not atmospheric. It must be evidenced. A company earns a better hearing not by sounding confident but by looking governable. That means clean class standing, transparent loss history, credible technical support, conservative route thresholds, and a willingness to explain not only what will be done but what will not be attempted. Restraint becomes a commercial asset.

The *Crystal Serenity* voyage through the Northwest Passage in August 2016 revealed another side of the same story. Publicly, it looked like a breakthrough in luxury expedition cruising: a large passenger vessel entering waters that had long belonged to another maritime register entirely. Commercially, it was an exercise in layered reassurance. The voyage involved extensive planning, support arrangements, and a degree of preparation intended to convert a striking itinerary into something markets and counterparties could tolerate. The significance did not lie in proving that the Arctic had become ordinary. It lay in showing how much work was required to make an exceptional voyage appear sufficiently disciplined to proceed. The lesson was double-edged. Yes, such operations could be organised. No, they did not become normal simply because one well-prepared operator completed them.

A pattern emerges from cases like these. Optimism arrives first, usually attached to a visible success, a technological advance, a favourable season, or a burst of strategic enthusiasm. Commercial narratives expand quickly because the first signal is easy to misunderstand. A transit becomes a forecast. A specialist vessel becomes a template. A favourable year becomes evidence of durable change. Then comes correction. Markets compare the enthusiasm against thinner, colder facts: sparse rescue options, uncertain port support, uneven inspection regimes, legal complexity, correlated exposures, and the awkward truth that a handful of successful passages cannot produce the sort of claims history from which stable pricing confidence grows. After correction comes tightening. Terms harden, scrutiny deepens, and the threshold for acceptable proof rises. By then the green light has dimmed again.

This cycle is not peculiar to Arctic trade, but the Arctic sharpens it because the downside of error is so difficult to contain. In dense and well-supported shipping environments, a technical failure or navigational mistake may still prove expensive, yet the surrounding infrastructure limits the depth of the crisis. In polar conditions, remoteness stretches time. Repairs take longer. Assistance travels farther. Evacuation becomes more complex. Pollution response grows more politically and practically charged. Minor weaknesses become large losses because geography amplifies consequences. Conservative institutions are not merely protecting their balance sheets when they react strongly to Arctic novelty. They are responding to a context in which moderate misjudgements can become major claims.

Classification societies embody this conservative logic in a particularly revealing way. Their role is not to extinguish ambition but to force it into forms that can be tested. A design feature may look impressive in a commercial presentation; class asks what assumptions support it, what operating conditions it contemplates, what margins remain under stress, what inspection consequences follow, and how future survey practice will verify continued fitness. Underwriting asks a related but distinct set of questions: not merely whether the vessel meets a rule, but whether the operation as proposed presents a tolerable loss profile. That difference matters. A vessel may satisfy class and still attract restrictive insurance terms. An operator may cite technical compliance while markets worry about organisational overreach. Conservatism does not rely on one institution. It emerges from their overlap.

The operator's response is rarely passive. Companies seeking Arctic credibility know they must build a record that travels ahead of them. They invest in redundancies that would look excessive elsewhere, not because excess is elegant but because spare capacity reassures sceptical readers of the file. They choose more experienced crew even when labour costs rise. They accept additional survey burdens. They shape internal reporting so that anomalies appear early and can be evidenced later. They sometimes adopt more conservative routes than engineering capability alone would require, because a measured track record is worth more in renewal negotiations than a dramatic proof of daring. Reputation, here, is made of habits: what gets repaired promptly, what gets disclosed without prompting, what gets cancelled when conditions no longer fit the original assumptions.

Those habits become legible through documents, but they are not reducible to paperwork. Markets eventually distinguish between an operator that merely produces immaculate binders and one that behaves consistently under pressure. This is where reputational signals acquire unusual force. A disciplined company tends to answer difficult technical questions directly, provide supporting records quickly, and avoid grand claims about what Arctic change supposedly makes possible. A weaker entrant often does the reverse. It treats documentation as a hurdle rather than as evidence of culture. It offers broad assurances where particulars are needed. It mistakes an absence of past catastrophe for proof of competence. Underwriters notice. So do class surveyors. So do charterers who read insurance terms as a second opinion on operational maturity.

A credible limitation should be acknowledged. Commercial conservatism does not always get it right. Markets can misread changing technology, overprice uncertainty, and reward incumbents simply because incumbency generates familiarity. New designs, better forecasting, improved communications, and stronger procedural discipline can make certain Arctic operations safer than older assumptions allow. Excessive caution can therefore become its own distortion. It can delay useful adaptation, discourage capable entrants, and preserve a hierarchy in which those already trusted continue to benefit from a comfort that is not always perfectly rational. The green light can stay red too long.

And yet that limitation does not dissolve the basic pattern. Even when markets prove overly cautious, they are usually responding to a real institutional problem: the cost of being wrong in the Arctic is difficult to bound in advance, and the evidence needed to justify confidence accumulates slowly. That is why operators who eventually change market opinion seldom do so by argument alone. They change it by building a record, closing gaps, accepting constraints, and presenting a history of uneventful performance detailed enough to challenge inherited caution. Innovation still enters the system. It simply enters on probation.

The effect on strategy is profound. Commercial actors often speak as though the central contest concerns rivals: who secures a route, a customer base, a terminal slot, a seasonal niche. In practice, the rival may be time itself. The company that rushes for advantage can find that one poorly documented incident, one unresolved survey issue, or one episode of overreach shadows it for years in specialist markets where memory runs longer than public attention. The company that moves more slowly may surrender a headline but gain something harder to replace: the confidence that allows terms to soften, counterparties to relax, and future proposals to be read as extensions of demonstrated discipline rather than as isolated gambles.

This is why the Arctic repeatedly produces a peculiar spectacle. Public rhetoric announces breakthrough. Private governance asks whether the breakthrough can survive repetition. One side points to possibility; the other asks about durability. One values movement. The other values proof. Their disagreement creates the stop-start rhythm that has shaped so many Arctic ventures across shipping, support services, and offshore operations. The cycle continues because both sides are partly right. Without ambition, no new trade is attempted. Without conservatism, the price of early enthusiasm may be paid later by insurers, clubs, communities, states, and operators who discover too late that their confidence rested on thin ice.

The deeper question is not whether ambition should yield to caution or caution to ambition. That would be too simple, and commercially useless. The real test comes earlier. When an operator claims that a proposed Arctic venture deserves trust, what exactly is being offered as proof: an opportunity seized before others arrive, or a discipline strong enough to endure when the green light fails to stay green?

A research map for the chapters ahead

On 1 January 2017, the IMO Polar Code entered into force, and with it a particular kind of promise took firmer institutional shape. In London, Oslo, Singapore, St Petersburg, and ports far from polar waters, operators and insurers could point to a more recognisable framework for planning, equipment, procedures, and limitations in Arctic and Antarctic trade. The Code did not remove danger. It did something subtler. It offered a shared ledger: a way to record what counted as acceptable preparation, what had to be evidenced, and where discretion still remained. That ledger matters because Arctic governance is difficult to grasp when seen only as weather, steel, and political will. Much of its force lies in sequence.

Sequence is the real subject here. An incident rarely remains only an incident. A survey finding rarely remains only a note. A premium increase rarely remains only a financial irritation. Each enters a chain of translation in which technical facts become contractual terms, contractual terms become operating constraints, operating constraints alter behaviour, and altered behaviour then changes what markets, regulators, and counterparties come to treat as normal prudence. The Arctic looks dramatic from a distance. Up close, it often turns on administrative afterlives. Follow the paper trail.

That is why the argument ahead moves in a deliberately cumulative way. It starts where private judgement usually starts: with attempts to model and price uncertainty before a vessel sails, a project is financed, or a service commitment is made. Underwriting asks what can be known, what can only be inferred, and what must be buffered against because neither evidence nor precedent is good enough to support confidence.

Arctic risk enters the market not as one thing but as an unstable bundle of interacting exposures - ice, weather, machinery reliability, remoteness, rescue limitations, liability severity, political friction, inspection culture, reputational sensitivity. Once that bundle reaches an underwriter's desk, uncertainty begins to harden into terms. Pricing is the visible part. The deeper act is classification of doubt.

From there, the inquiry shifts to standards, because uncertainty rarely stays manageable unless institutions can compare unlike operators through shared criteria. That is where *class* becomes indispensable. In usable terms, class refers to the private technical verification of a vessel's design, construction, and continued condition against published rules maintained by a classification society. It is not the same thing as state certification, and it is not insurance. But it influences both. To say that a vessel is "in class" is to say that an important technical passport remains valid. Others then read that passport for their own purposes: insurers when assessing baseline integrity, charterers when screening counterparties, financiers when judging asset quality, and regulators when leaning on recognised organisations to perform delegated technical work. Class is a foundation stone, but not the whole building.

That distinction matters because many readers encounter maritime governance through terms that appear stable until they collide. *Flag* refers, in practical terms, to the state in which a vessel is registered and whose legal authority travels with it in matters of certification, oversight, and regulatory responsibility. The flag state is not merely a symbol painted at the stern. It provides the jurisdictional home from which much formal compliance begins. Yet a vessel's legal home does not exhaust its exposure. Once it enters a port abroad, *port state* authority appears. Port state control describes the inspection and enforcement power exercised by the state whose port the vessel enters, often through checks on certificates, equipment, operational deficiencies, and broader compliance indicators. A ship may satisfy its flag administration and still face searching treatment elsewhere. That tension matters in the Arctic because inspection culture, administrative capacity, and enforcement intensity can vary sharply, and markets notice the resulting patterns.

A parallel term demands equal clarity. *P&I*, shorthand for protection and indemnity, refers to a form of mutual marine insurance focused chiefly on third-party liabilities rather than the vessel's own physical damage. That includes a wide range of potential exposures: pollution, collision liabilities, cargo claims, personal injury, wreck removal, and other losses that tend to bloom after an incident rather than end with the initial casualty. P&I matters in Arctic governance because remoteness enlarges liability consequences. A machinery failure is not only a technical problem if it leads to collision, pollution, passenger evacuation, or a prolonged wreck response in a difficult environment. Mutual insurance therefore becomes not just a financial arrangement but a standing interest in prudent conduct. The club reads behaviour through the lens of collective exposure.

Seen together, these terms form more than vocabulary. They describe a chain of gates. Underwriters and reinsurers translate uncertainty into financial terms. Classification societies translate technical condition into recognised status. Flag administrations translate public law into certification and delegated oversight. Port states test whether that order holds when the vessel arrives under their jurisdiction. P&I clubs evaluate whether the web of liabilities around the venture remains bearable. Surveyors and auditors move between these institutions, carrying observations, recommendations, and doubts in language portable enough for others to act upon. No single actor controls the whole route. The route is controlled nonetheless.

A named case helps to show how these links tighten under stress. After the *Costa Concordia* grounded off Giglio, Italy, in January 2012, the catastrophe did not remain confined to one casualty site or one set of legal proceedings. It generated scrutiny across passenger operations, claims handling, training expectations, emergency planning, audit practice, insurance judgement, and public confidence in safety systems. The visible event was local and immediate. The institutional response was dispersed and durable. That pattern matters for the Arctic because its own incidents, even when smaller in scale, can travel in similar ways through claims files, survey cultures, renewal negotiations, and revised expectations. The casualty ends. The governance begins again.

The same sequence appears in less catastrophic form when a vessel attracts repeated minor deficiencies under port state control. Each deficiency may look manageable in isolation: a maintenance lapse here, a documentary irregularity there, an operational shortcoming judged non-catastrophic at the time of inspection. Yet those observations accumulate. Insurers see them at renewal. Charterers interpret them as evidence of culture rather than accident. Surveyors become less trusting of assurances unsupported by records. Brokers work harder to defend the account. Premium shifts follow, or terms narrow, or an extra survey appears before cover is continued. The original signal may have been small. The feedback loop magnifies it. Market memory is built this way.

That loop runs through much of what follows. An incident shapes a claim. A claim shapes an underwriter's understanding of causation, severity, and the reliability of the operator's disclosures. That revised understanding reshapes premium, deductible, exclusions, survey requirements, or the appetite to write similar voyages at all. Those altered terms then reshape operations: route choices become more conservative, seasons narrow, technical upgrades are accelerated, crewing standards rise, maintenance schedules tighten, or some ventures are abandoned. Once enough operators adapt, yesterday's exceptional precaution hardens into today's expectation. Governance rarely arrives in one grand act. It sediments through repetition.

The usefulness of a research map lies in resisting two common mistakes. One is to treat each institutional domain as self-contained: underwriting over here, standards over there, inspections somewhere else, liability disputes in another compartment altogether. The other is to flatten them into a vague story of "regulation", as though every source of discipline carried the same logic or the same authority. Neither view helps much. The important work happens in the transfers between domains. A technical concern becomes a survey recommendation. A survey recommendation becomes a condition of cover. A condition of cover becomes a charterparty demand. A charterparty demand alters onboard behaviour. A later dispute then asks whether that behaviour met a standard of due care or reasonable precaution. The chain only makes sense when followed end to end.

A second named example marks the positive side of the same logic. The *Venta Maersk* trial voyage through the Northern Sea Route in 2018 drew attention because it seemed to offer a commercial proof of concept. But its lasting significance lies less in spectacle than in institutional legibility. A trial voyage undertaken by a major operator with recognisable systems, documented planning, known technical standards, and established market relationships can be read by insurers, class interests, cargo-facing parties, and regulators as a bounded experiment rather than a leap into the dark. That does not remove caution. It organises it. Evidence enters the system in a form others can compare. The result is not certainty, but a narrower argument.

A credible limitation should be faced plainly. Not every part of Arctic activity fits neatly into this sequence. State-backed projects can retain risks that private markets would prefer to decline or price more severely. Strategic ambitions can distort ordinary commercial judgements. Confidential settlements can obscure lessons that would otherwise circulate more clearly. Data remain patchy in places. Informal market gossip can matter as much as formal precedent. A research map that pretends to total visibility would become untrustworthy at once.

And yet that limitation strengthens rather than weakens the need for structure. Where information is incomplete, following the chain of translation becomes even more important. One asks not only what happened, but how the event was recorded, who interpreted it, what institution had reason to emphasise one fact over another, where the cost reappeared, and which behaviour changed afterwards. That method is especially important in Arctic settings because opacity itself becomes a force in the market. When outcomes remain hidden, markets often compensate with caution. They widen margins, ask for more evidence, and reward operators whose documentation and discipline reduce the amount of guesswork required.

This approach also keeps the strategic picture in view. Arctic expansion is often narrated through visible drivers: melting sea ice, technological change, geopolitical rivalry, energy demand, infrastructure ambition. All of these matter. But they remain incomplete until one asks how they are filtered through quieter institutions that measure, compare, verify, insure, inspect, and contest. A route does not become commercially meaningful when a map says it exists. It becomes meaningful when a sufficient number of institutions agree on how its risks should be classified and who should bear them. The same is true of vessels, ports, terminals, offshore assets, and industrial projects. The technical and the strategic are not separate stories. They are the same story told at different distances.

What follows, then, is less a march through isolated topics than a movement along a connected chain of judgement. Underwriting turns uncertainty into terms. Standards and class turn technical condition into recognised status. Compliance systems try to prove that procedures hold under pressure. Flag and port state encounters reveal how public authority and private signals interact. Liability rules turn accidents into arguments about fault, causation, and cost. P&I structures and reinsurance spread those costs while teaching markets what to fear next time. Claims and disputes convert single events into institutional memory. Premium shocks and market withdrawal turn that memory into changed operational patterns. Ports, infrastructure, communities, sanctions, and security concerns then complicate every step by adding new sources of exposure and new reasons for caution. The ledger thickens.

The quiet motif remains useful here because so much of Arctic governance depends on what gets entered and what gets left blank. A clean record can open doors. A thin record can keep them closed. A vessel's technical standing, a flag's reputation, a port state's deficiency history, a club's claims concern, a surveyor's recommendation, an arbitrator's reading of causation - each becomes a line in a ledger that no single institution fully owns but many institutions read. The difficulty for any serious observer is not the absence of drama. The difficulty is knowing where to look once the drama passes.

That leaves a demanding question at the threshold of what comes next. When the Arctic presents a new opportunity or a new incident, which entry in the ledger matters most: the model before the voyage, the survey before the policy, the inspection before the port call, the clause before the casualty, or the claim that teaches markets what they should have feared all along?

Chapter 2

Marine Insurance and Polar History

In May 1845, Sir John Franklin sailed from Greenhithe with *Erebus* and *Terror*, carrying the old imperial confidence that skill, steel, provisions, and resolve might push uncertainty back far enough to make the Arctic yield. The ships vanished. What remained was not only grief, speculation, and legend, but a durable lesson about polar enterprise: distance alters judgement long before it produces loss. A ship can disappear into weather, ice, silence, and delay; so can the facts needed to explain what happened. The logbook goes dark.

That darkness still matters. Modern marine insurance no longer speaks in the language of heroic exploration, yet it continues to grapple with the same elemental problem Franklin's voyage exposed with brutal clarity. Polar operations stretch time, thin evidence, and magnify the price of error. When underwriters speak of remoteness, limited rescue, uncertain causation, or inadequate information, they are not indulging a taste for abstraction. They are naming a historical inheritance. The Arctic did not become commercially legible by escaping its older dangers. It became legible by teaching markets how to convert those dangers into terms, exclusions, surveys, and categories of acceptable doubt.

The real tension, then, lies between memory and ambition. Commercial actors approach polar waters with better ships, better communications, better forecasting, and stronger institutional support than their predecessors possessed. Yet insurance never begins from a blank page. It remembers earlier losses, older anxieties, and the stubborn fact that some environments resist ordinary assumptions about response, repair, and proof. That is why marine insurance history matters here. It shows that today's underwriting language did not appear fully formed from spreadsheets or conventions. It emerged from centuries of trying to price voyages whose gravest features often became visible only after something had already gone wrong.

Once that historical continuity comes into view, the stakes sharpen. Marine insurance is often treated as a reactive trade, arriving after danger to distribute costs. In polar settings it has long done more than that. It has helped decide which ventures deserved backing, which routes seemed tolerable, which forms of state support mattered, and which kinds of ignorance could be borne without paralysing commerce altogether. Strategic interest enters the picture at precisely this point. During periods of war, convoy, subsidy, or state-backed shipping ambition, marine markets do not stop being commercial; they begin to carry political assumptions inside commercial forms. Appetite shifts. Exclusions change tone. Wordings start to reflect security concerns even when they still look technical on the page.

This matters because strategic pressure rarely arrives wearing a label. It is easier to spot a naval deployment than an altered underwriting posture, easier to notice a public declaration than a clause drafted with geopolitical unease in mind. Yet maritime history repeatedly shows how security thinking seeps into insurance practice. Routes acquire significance beyond freight. Certain cargos, waters, counterparties, or operational patterns draw special scrutiny. The commercial document starts to do double duty: it allocates risk, but it also records what a market quietly believes about power, vulnerability, and state interest. Readers who miss that institutional imprint may misunderstand why two apparently similar voyages receive strikingly different treatment.

A second shift follows from that same history. Older marine insurance had to live with large pockets of ignorance and idiosyncratic judgement because the trade itself was more fragmented and the available evidence thinner. Over time, however, insurers, shipowners, classification societies, regulators, and international bodies sought something more disciplined: not certainty, which remained impossible, but comparability. The rise of formal safety management, harmonised class expectations, and convention-based compliance did not remove the sea's indifference. It altered the evidentiary culture around it. What counted as ordinary prudence could now be written down, inspected, audited, and compared across operators who would never meet one another. The logbook becomes a checklist.

That modern turn to standards deserves attention not because rules are inherently impressive, but because they changed the social texture of marine risk. A vessel no longer had to prove itself only through reputation, anecdote, or the boldness of its owner. It had to fit into a more codified world in which surveys, certificates, manuals, training records, and safety systems became portable signals of trustworthiness. This was especially consequential for polar trade. Difficult environments punish improvisation, and they punish unevenness. Standards offered a way to say that one operator's claim to competence could be measured against another's, even where direct comparators remained scarce. The promise was modest but powerful: not that risk would disappear, but that risk could be seen through a common frame.

And yet that promise carries its own friction. Standardisation clarifies some matters while obscuring others. A vessel may satisfy recognised requirements and still embody fragile assumptions about weather windows, crew judgement, or emergency support. A market may rely on formal compliance because it needs transferable benchmarks, while knowing perfectly well that documents can flatter practice. The historical movement from expedition hazard to commercial underwriting did not abolish uncertainty. It taught institutions to sort uncertainty more systematically. Some doubts became named categories. Some became known unknowns. Some remained stubbornly outside the neat grammar of policies and surveys, only to reappear later as claims, disputes, and abrupt corrections in price.

The path ahead follows that institutional deepening. Polar risk begins as an encounter with remoteness, rescue limits, and imperfect knowledge. It is then reshaped by strategic need, state backing, and the commercial after-effects of security thinking. From there it enters a more codified order in which standards, class, and compliance promise a steadier basis for trust, even as they create new arguments about what counts as ordinary, prudent, or sufficiently evidenced conduct. That movement matters because later questions about audits, inspections, liabilities, and claims cannot be understood if marine insurance history is treated as decorative background rather than as the source of its working instincts.

The Arctic has always tempted people to confuse access with mastery. Marine insurance history tells a less flattering, more useful story. It suggests that markets do not merely ask whether a ship can go north, or whether a state wants it to, but whether old uncertainties have really been reduced or simply renamed in more professional language. That is the pressure point from which the next problem emerges: when underwriters confront polar activity, which parts of the past do they actually believe have changed, and which still sit in the file like an unfinished entry?

From exploration hazards to commercial underwriting

In May 1845, Sir John Franklin sailed from Greenhithe with *Erebus* and *Terror* in search of the Northwest Passage, carrying the layered confidence of the British state, the Royal Navy, and an age that still believed discipline and design might force geography into obedience. The ships disappeared. Years of searching followed, along with fragments, rumours, relics, and a steadily darkening understanding of what the Arctic could do to plans made elsewhere. One lesson endured with unusual force. Distance eats evidence.

That lesson survives in modern marine insurance more directly than the romance of polar exploration usually allows. Franklin's expedition belongs to imperial history, naval history, and the literature of disaster, but it also belongs to the prehistory of underwriting judgement. Long before Arctic activity became commercially insurable in any meaningful sense, polar enterprise had already taught markets, states, and seafaring institutions a severe rule: some environments magnify not only the chance of loss, but the difficulty of knowing what happened, who failed, what might have prevented the event, and what response remains possible once things begin to go wrong. The logbook stops. The questions multiply.

The transition from expedition hazard to commercial underwriting did not occur because the Arctic became tame. It occurred because institutions learned, slowly and imperfectly, how to classify uncertainty rather than merely fear it. That distinction matters. Explorers entered polar waters under conditions of episodic ambition, political prestige, scientific curiosity, and often weak comparability. Their ventures were singular enough to resist ordinary actuarial habits. A failed expedition could become legend; it could not easily become a premium schedule. Commercial underwriting required something else: repeated activity, standardised records, technical categories, survey routines, and a vocabulary capable of converting remoteness, ice exposure, limited rescue, and informational gaps into terms that parties could accept without pretending the danger had vanished.

Continuity matters more than novelty here. One can point to better hulls, stronger engines, satellite communications, more capable forecasting, and denser regulatory frameworks, all of which changed the practical possibilities of polar activity. But the governing concerns remain strikingly familiar. Remoteness still delays assistance. Rescue limits still shape consequences. Information gaps still complicate causation. These are not decorative echoes of an earlier era. They are the backbone of modern underwriting caution. When an insurer asks about voyage planning, ice capability, crewing, communications, or contingency arrangements, it is not escaping history through technical sophistication. It is formalising old fears.

This continuity helps explain why ideas of seaworthiness remain so durable even as their expression changes. In older marine law and practice, seaworthiness did not mean invincibility; it meant fitness for the intended voyage, judged against conditions that ought reasonably to have been anticipated. That idea travelled well into the age of insurance because it linked technical condition, human competence, and route-specific judgement in a single practical standard. Polar waters pressed that standard hard. A vessel adequate for one trade could be plainly inadequate for another. A prudent crew in temperate service might not be a prudent crew in ice. A ship that looked sound at departure could still prove unseaworthy in a more contextual sense if its preparation failed to match the environment it was entering. Modern surveys and policy wordings retain this inheritance. They still ask, in effect, whether the ship, the crew, and the operator fit the voyage they have chosen.

A named example from the commercial era shows how that inheritance matured rather than disappeared. In 1969, the tanker *SS Manhattan* completed a highly publicised transit of the Northwest Passage as part of an effort tied to the question of Arctic oil transport. The voyage attracted attention because it fused technology, commerce, and geopolitics in a single passage. Yet what it really demonstrated was the difficulty of turning symbolic possibility into routine insurability. A reinforced tanker could traverse Arctic waters under carefully managed conditions and still leave unanswered the more mundane questions that matter to markets: how repeatable is this, at what support cost, under which escort assumptions, with what salvage prospects, and on whose balance sheet do the residual uncertainties sit? The achievement was real. So was its incompleteness. A successful transit is not the same thing as a mature underwriting class.

That gap between possibility and routine is where commercial underwriting begins its true work. Underwriters do not need a route to be impossible before they hesitate. They need only see that the available evidence does not yet support stable comparison. Polar risk has long suffered from that problem. Sparse voyages generate sparse records. Sparse records produce weak benchmarks. Weak benchmarks encourage caution, broader exclusions, tighter conditions, and a heavier reliance on surveys and operator documentation. This is how "known unknowns" become underwriting categories. Ice is a known unknown: present, variable, measurable only up to a point, never fully submissive to expectation. Rescue delay is a known unknown: one can model distance, weather, asset availability, and response plans, but not abolish the possibility that time itself will become a loss driver. Human performance in extreme cold, machinery reliability under sustained stress, communication interruptions, seasonal transitions, and legal complexity around incident response follow the same pattern. They are not mysteries. They are uncertainties stubborn enough to require their own pricing language.

The phrase sounds bloodless. Its consequences are not. Once a known unknown enters underwriting practice, it changes behaviour. An operator may face a higher deductible because a market cannot confidently separate minor from major loss outcomes in remote conditions. A policy may carry narrower territorial limits or voyage-specific conditions because uncertainty about ice severity remains wider than the operator's optimism suggests. Survey recommendations may become conditions of cover because paper confidence cannot replace physical verification. Crewing standards may rise because experience must compensate for the thinness of environmental data. In each case, the category does not merely describe uncertainty. It governs the response to it.

Commercial underwriting also required a cultural change in how maritime institutions treated evidence. Exploration narratives often turned on heroism, endurance, and the retrospective moral drama of survival or loss. Insurance has no use for romance. It asks for records that can survive dispute. Logs, maintenance histories, survey reports, class standing, repair evidence, route plans, weather information, crew qualifications, communications arrangements, and loss histories gradually became the grammar through which Arctic risk could be discussed without collapsing into anecdote. This was not only a bureaucratic development. It was a moral one. The burden shifted from proving courage to proving discipline.

The whaling trade offers an earlier bridge between exploration and commerce, though not a tidy one. Arctic and sub-Arctic whaling ventures in the eighteenth and nineteenth centuries were commercial, recurrent, and often insured, yet they did not convert polar waters into a comfortably governed market space. Instead they exposed the same recurring problem in harsher commercial form: seasonal concentration, ice damage, difficult rescue, sparse local support, and volatile information about conditions. Insurers could cover such ventures, but cover remained tied to the acceptance of severe environmental variability and the operator's capacity to absorb or survive interruption. The passage from expedition to commerce, then, was not a clean civilising arc. It was an extended process in which repeated economic use slowly taught markets which uncertainties could be normalised, which had to remain exceptional, and which demanded special treatment every time.

That slower teaching explains why surveys acquired such authority. When historical data remain thin or difficult to compare, the survey becomes a substitute for statistical comfort. A surveyor can examine hull condition, equipment reliability, maintenance practice, operational planning, and evidence of competence in ways no premium table can achieve by itself. In polar contexts, surveys often do more than verify compliance. They help convert local, technical, and behavioural facts into underwriter-facing language. A machinery issue that might appear minor in ordinary trade can carry different weight when repair options are distant and cold amplifies failure. A documentation gap that might attract tolerance elsewhere can look more serious where the cost of improvisation rises sharply. Survey culture therefore sits directly in the historical line that runs from exploration hazard to commercial underwriting: where knowledge is partial, inspection carries more power.

The continuity becomes even clearer when one looks at the persistence of rescue as a pricing problem. Franklin's fate dramatised the consequences of distance in an era of sail, wood, and limited communications. The technological setting has changed almost beyond recognition, but the institutional meaning has not changed nearly as much. Marine insurance remains acutely sensitive to the fact that some waters impose long response times, limited towing options, difficult medical evacuation, uncertain shelter, and politically charged environmental consequences if a casualty escalates into pollution or wreck. These are not merely operational inconveniences. They are severity multipliers. They transform the same initiating event into a much larger potential claim. The remoteness that once swallowed expeditions now expands loss scenarios.

A second named example helps to bring the historical thread into the present. When the *Crystal Serenity* transited the Northwest Passage in August 2016, the voyage was often presented as evidence that Arctic passage had moved from the age of heroic uncertainty into the age of managed tourism. That reading was too simple. The voyage's deeper significance lay in the extraordinary volume of preparation, planning, support, and documentation required to render a large passenger ship's Arctic itinerary acceptable to multiple institutions. The point was not that risk had disappeared. It was that risk had to be translated into a commercial file dense enough to reassure insurers, technical reviewers, and counterparties that this was not reckless novelty disguised as confidence. The old concerns remained plainly visible: remoteness, rescue limits, and information control. They had simply been absorbed into a more elaborate institutional response.

A credible limitation should be admitted. Historical continuity can be overstated if it flattens genuine advances in technology, data, and operational practice. Modern forecasting, satellite observation, improved communications, stronger ice-class design, enhanced safety management, and more formal international rules have changed what can sensibly be attempted. To say that Franklin's darkness still haunts underwriting is not to say that nothing important has changed since 1845. A serious account must resist sentimental continuity as much as naive progress.

And yet the limitation does not disturb the central argument. The reason historical memory still matters is not that modern operators face the same conditions as nineteenth-century expeditions. They do not. It matters because marine insurance does not ask only whether conditions improved; it asks how far improvement reduces uncertainty that remains costly when misjudged. Markets are rarely paid for admiring technology. They are paid for absorbing loss. As long as the Arctic continues to combine environmental severity with patchy comparators and difficult consequences after failure, underwriting will continue to inherit older habits of suspicion, however refined their language becomes.

One can see this inheritance in the persistent gap between capability and trust. Capability belongs to the ship, the crew, the operator, the support system. Trust belongs to the institutions asked to rely on them. Commercial underwriting tries to close that gap through records, categories, surveys, standards, and repeated experience. But the gap never closes completely, especially in environments where the rare event can dominate the whole calculation. That is why known unknowns are so powerful. They name the zone where uncertainty stops being romantic and starts being administratively expensive.

The history, then, is not a tale of progress from ignorance to mastery. It is a tale of translation. Exploration hazards became commercially intelligible not because the Arctic yielded its character, but because insurers, shipowners, surveyors, and states learned how to write old dangers into new forms. The logbook remains the quiet motif because the whole system still turns on what can be recorded before, during, and after exposure to difficult conditions. When the record grows thin, caution grows thick. When the evidence improves, terms may soften. But the discipline remains historical at its core.

That leaves a revealing test at the edge of every modern polar proposal. When an underwriter reads a plan for Arctic activity, what exactly counts as reassurance: the sophistication of the vessel, the confidence of the operator, the existence of formal standards, or the older and harsher question inherited from centuries of loss at the margins of the map - if something goes wrong out there, how much will we truly know, and how much will it cost not to know?

War, subsidy, and strategic shipping lanes

In August 1941, the first Allied convoy of Operation Dervish reached Archangel in northern Russia, carrying aircraft and matériel through waters already charged with military urgency, climatic severity, and the knowledge that delay at sea could become defeat on land. The ships did not travel as ordinary commercial ventures. They moved inside a security logic that reorganised everything around them: routing, escort, timing, communication, loss tolerance, and the meaning of insurability itself. A premium was no longer just a price for maritime uncertainty. It became a reading of war.

That moment matters far beyond naval history. Wartime convoys in Arctic and near-Arctic waters made brutally clear that marine markets do not remain commercially neutral when states decide certain routes or cargoes matter strategically. Security pressure changes underwriting appetite, but it also changes the underlying grammar of risk. Ordinary marine hazards do not disappear; they are absorbed into a larger field of concern that includes hostile action, secrecy, state subsidy, emergency rerouting, and the political necessity of continuing voyages that a purely commercial calculus might reject. The route acquires a shadow.

This pattern has repeated in quieter forms ever since. Strategic interest does not need open war to leave its mark on marine insurance. It can appear when states subsidise shipbuilding for northern service, support icebreaking capacity, promote corridor development, favour certain ports, or frame shipping lanes as instruments of sovereignty, energy policy, or regional leverage. The visible language is often public and grand: development, national presence, connectivity, resilience. The less visible language appears in policy wordings, exclusions, notice requirements, geographic limits, and the subtle widening or narrowing of appetite among insurers and reinsurers. Markets do not simply observe strategy from a distance. They translate it into terms.

The translation begins with a basic institutional fact. Insurance prices uncertainty, but uncertainty changes character when political stakes rise. In ordinary trade, an underwriter asks whether a vessel, cargo, route, and operator present a tolerable balance of frequency and severity. Under strategic pressure, a second question intrudes: what other forces might alter loss patterns, claims handling, sanctions exposure, state intervention, or the practical ability to assess and recover after a casualty? Security thinking enters the file through this door. It does not always arrive labelled as geopolitics. It arrives as concern about aggregation, interruption, cancellation rights, hostile environments, counterparties, disclosure, and the reliability of assumptions that would look stable elsewhere.

War-risk insurance offers the clearest example because it formalises a distinction that peacetime trade often keeps blurred. Hull and machinery cover, cargo cover, and liability arrangements are built around one family of marine perils. War-risk markets address another family, including hostile acts, capture, seizure, and related dangers. Yet the separation is never perfectly tidy. Strategic tension can alter the interpretation of ordinary marine risk as well. A route may become more heavily scrutinised not only because of direct war-risk exposure, but because the surrounding political climate affects communications, port access, repair options, legal enforcement, documentation standards, and the willingness of reinsurers to tolerate uncertainty. One category shadows the next.

A named example from the later Cold War period shows how strategic shipping ambitions reshape commercial expectations even outside declared war. In 1969, the SS *Manhattan* transited the Northwest Passage in a voyage tied to the question of Arctic oil transport and the wider strategic interest in northern resource development. Publicly, the event was presented as a technological and national demonstration. Commercially, it exposed a harder truth. A state or major industrial actor may wish to prove that a route is possible, but markets still ask whether that possibility can be made routine without extraordinary support, political commitment, and tolerance for residual uncertainty. The voyage succeeded as a spectacle of capability. It did not by itself create a settled commercial insurance class for Arctic tanker trade. Strategic ambition opened the conversation. Underwriting kept its distance.

That distance often narrows when subsidy enters. Subsidy matters not merely because it lowers cost, but because it redistributes what markets would otherwise force into the open. A state-backed icebreaker programme, a public commitment to northern infrastructure, or a financial guarantee for strategic shipping can make an operation appear more viable by absorbing part of the risk that commercial insurers might price more severely. This does not mean insurance becomes irrelevant. Quite the reverse. Subsidy changes the baseline against which insurance terms are negotiated. The market may still offer cover, but with an altered understanding of who ultimately carries exceptional exposures, who will fund rescue and infrastructure, or who can sustain losses that would cripple a purely private operator. Public money changes private posture.

That is why security thinking often leaves institutional fingerprints in documents that look merely technical. One can sometimes spot it in territorial descriptions that suddenly become exacting, in clauses requiring prompt notification of route changes, in wording that sharpens around sanctioned entities or government directions, in exclusions that carve out politically sensitive acts, in conditions tied to convoying, escort, or specific approvals. These provisions may not mention strategy in plain language. They do not need to. Their structure reveals the assumption that the voyage cannot be understood as ordinary commerce alone. A technical document becomes a quiet political map.

The history of wartime convoying reinforces this point. Convoys were not simply tactical arrangements for protecting ships. They reorganised the commercial logic of marine movement. A vessel sailing under convoy rules accepted altered timing, altered communications, altered autonomy, and a different distribution of risks between shipowner, state, and insurer. Delay, route deviation, concentrated exposure, and collective vulnerability all acquired new meanings. Insurance markets had to adjust not because ships ceased to be ships, but because the context had changed the significance of familiar perils. The same sea looked different once strategy entered it. It often still does.

Arctic and sub-Arctic shipping have long been especially susceptible to this reframing because these waters sit at the intersection of remoteness and state interest. They are difficult enough to demand support and symbolically charged enough to attract political overstatement. When governments declare a northern route commercially transformative, insurers do not merely ask whether the ice is thinner or the voyage shorter. They ask what political pressure may be driving the claim, what hidden dependence on subsidy or state service support sits underneath it, and whether today's appetite might contract sharply if strategic conditions change. Markets know that routes celebrated for national reasons can become difficult commercial propositions when the state steps back or when international conditions harden.

The institutional imprint of security thinking also appears in what insurers fear about causation and attribution. In a purely marine casualty, one asks whether weather, ice, machinery, navigation, human error, or maintenance failure best explains the loss. Strategic environments complicate that question. Interference, cyber disruption, ambiguous hostile action, state inspection practices, access denials, or politically motivated delay can enter the causal field. Even when none of these risks materialises, their mere plausibility can influence pricing and drafting. Underwriters prefer losses they can classify. Strategic tension creates losses whose classification may itself become contested. Ambiguity is expensive.

A second named example illustrates how geopolitical assumptions can settle into market language without needing open conflict. The opening of the Suez Canal in 1869 transformed global route calculations, but it also showed how strategic waterways quickly become objects of political and military concern as well as commerce. Although Suez is not an Arctic route, the institutional lesson travels well northward. Once a passage acquires strategic importance, marine markets stop seeing it as a neutral line on a map. They begin to treat it as a corridor whose significance can alter state behaviour, legal exposure, and interruption risk. Arctic lanes attract the same kind of attention whenever governments present them as national projects, strategic alternatives, or symbols of jurisdictional control. Geography enters the wording.

Still, a limitation deserves notice. Not every route with strategic rhetoric around it becomes an insurance outlier, and not every subsidy distorts underwriting judgement beyond recognition. Commercial markets can be surprisingly adept at separating spectacle from substance. A heavily advertised corridor may receive cautious treatment if infrastructure, operating records, and claims history remain weak. Conversely, some state-supported shipping systems become insurable on relatively stable terms because support capacity, technical discipline, and institutional clarity reduce uncertainty rather than merely masking it. Strategic importance alone does not dictate insurance response. Markets still look for evidence.

That concession sharpens the main point rather than weakening it. Security thinking matters not because it overrides every other factor, but because it changes what evidence is required and how it is interpreted. A route supported by icebreakers, state communications systems, and politically favoured infrastructure may attract insurer interest precisely because those supports are tangible. The same route may become less attractive if those supports depend on fragile budgets, diplomatic assumptions, or counterparties exposed to sanctions or other restrictions. Insurance appetite therefore tracks strategic credibility, not just strategic ambition. The distinction is crucial. Markets do not insure speeches.

Readers can often detect this credibility test in the treatment of state-linked operators and projects. Where security or industrial policy strongly supports a shipping ambition, insurers may probe the durability of public commitments, the legal clarity of obligations, the identity of counterparties, the quality of state-provided services, and the possibility that a wider political dispute could spill into claims, payments, or enforcement. These are not abstract fears. They shape visible decisions: whether notice periods shorten, whether exclusions widen, whether sublimits apply, whether additional declarations are demanded, whether reinsurance capacity remains comfortable, and whether the route is treated as exceptional rather than routine. The language may remain dry. The assumptions are anything but.

A subsidy adds a further wrinkle because it can produce two opposing effects at once. It may reassure markets by funding infrastructure, escort capacity, meteorological support, and emergency response that would otherwise remain too thin. It may also unsettle markets by signalling that the underlying trade cannot stand on commercial legs without political support. Both readings can be true. A state-backed northern corridor might be safer operationally because public investment improves conditions, while still being more uncertain institutionally because continued support depends on shifting strategic priorities. Underwriters read both sides. So should everyone else.

The deeper lesson is that marine insurance history cannot be divided neatly into a peaceful commercial sphere and a separate sphere of strategy. The two have always overlapped. War made that overlap obvious. Subsidy and strategic shipping ambitions make it quieter, but no less consequential. An insurance policy, a war-risk endorsement, a sanctions clause, a routing condition, or a geographic exclusion may look like a technical instrument written to tidy up exposure. Often it is that. It is also a record of what the market believes about state intention, route stability, political friction, and the likelihood that commercial assumptions will survive contact with strategic reality. Pricing carries memory. Wording carries judgement.

This is why technical documents deserve a closer reading than they usually receive. A phrase that narrows cover in a sensitive area, a requirement for heightened disclosure, an insistence on specified approvals or support arrangements, a reluctance to generalise from one successful northern season - each may reveal a strategic assumption that public narratives would rather keep in the background. The route's shadow falls across the page again. Not every reader notices it because the vocabulary remains procedural. Yet this is often where geopolitics becomes commercially real: not only in sanctions announcements or naval deployments, but in the measured caution of insurers deciding how much uncertainty they are willing to carry when commerce and state interest start to share the same channel.

The question that remains is not whether strategy shapes marine markets. It plainly does, and has for a very long time. The harder question is diagnostic. When a shipping lane is presented as commercially inevitable, how much of that confidence rests on durable operating evidence, and how much rests on public power standing nearby, ready to absorb the risks that private wording still refuses to forget?

The modern turn to standards regimes

On 1 July 1998, the International Safety Management Code entered into mandatory force for certain classes of ships under the SOLAS framework, and a quiet but far-reaching shift took hold in marine risk. In London, Piraeus, Singapore and countless port offices elsewhere, a familiar question began to change shape. It was no longer enough to ask whether a ship was well built, competently manned, or fortunate enough to avoid trouble. A second question pressed forward: could the operator demonstrate, in records and routines, that safety had been organised as a system rather than trusted to experience alone? The answer increasingly lived in manuals, audits, reports, non-conformity procedures, maintenance logs, and designated lines of responsibility. The clipboard grew teeth.

That moment did not create standards from nothing. Shipping had always relied on rules, customary expectations, class requirements, and state certification. But it did mark the consolidation of a new language of marine legitimacy. Older judgements about prudence had often been dispersed across reputation, craft knowledge, technical survey, and retrospective blame after casualty. The modern standards regime drew those elements into a more codified order. Conduct that once appeared sensible because reputable people said so now had to be demonstrated through procedures that others could inspect, compare, and challenge. A vessel still needed steel, machinery, and seamanship. It now also needed documentary coherence.

This change matters especially in difficult environments because difficult environments punish ambiguity. Arctic operations do not allow much space for the comforting fiction that good people will sort things out when pressure comes. The practical attraction of standards lies precisely here. They promise comparability. They allow an insurer, a charterer, a flag administration, a port inspector, a class surveyor, or a P&I club to look at two operators they do not know personally and ask whether each can produce evidence of disciplined conduct in recognisable form. The promise is not certainty. It is a common grammar for uncertainty.

That grammar emerged from painful lessons. Marine casualties in the late twentieth century repeatedly exposed a gap between technical compliance in the narrow sense and organisational competence in the fuller sense. A vessel could satisfy many formal requirements and still be operated by a company whose reporting lines were weak, maintenance culture lax, training uneven, or decision-making distorted by commercial pressure. Standards regimes responded by bringing management itself into the field of scrutiny. This was the real innovation. Risk would no longer be treated only as a matter of ship condition and external hazard; it would also be treated as a matter of systems, records, responsibility, and proof. Seaworthiness, in effect, became more institutional.

The International Safety Management Code is the clearest emblem of that shift because it made "safe management" auditable rather than aspirational. A company had to establish procedures for key shipboard operations, reporting of accidents and non-conformities, maintenance of the ship and equipment, emergency preparedness, internal review, and the identification of a designated person ashore. Those obligations were not philosophically ornate. They were practical, and that was the point. They turned broad notions such as care, competence, and vigilance into visible behaviours: drills conducted, defects reported, corrective actions tracked, responsibilities assigned, reviews completed. Trust stopped being something inferred solely from reputation. It became something documented.

Classification harmonisation followed a related path. Classification societies had long provided technical standards for design, construction, and maintenance, but the growing coordination of their work helped create broader comparability across fleets and jurisdictions. This mattered because modern marine commerce is irreducibly cross-border. A ship may be flagged in one state, insured in another, classed by an organisation headquartered elsewhere, and inspected in ports far from all three. Without some degree of common technical language, each participant would have to start from scratch. Harmonised rules do not eliminate disagreement, but they reduce the cost of basic recognition. A charterer reading a class notation, an underwriter reviewing a survey report, and a regulator assessing delegated oversight can proceed with a shared minimum understanding of what has been checked and what remains open.

The rise of international conventions strengthened the same logic. Conventions such as SOLAS and MARPOL did not simply add more rules to a crowded field. They stabilised expectation. They gave states, class societies, insurers, and operators a more settled baseline from which to distinguish ordinary practice from concerning deviation. Once a requirement becomes convention-backed and widely embedded in audit and certification culture, it changes the burden of explanation. An operator no longer argues merely that a particular approach is reasonable in its own eyes. The operator must explain why its conduct fits, departs from, or exceeds a recognised standard. That shift is subtle, but commercially decisive. Baselines move. Markets follow.

A named example shows how a new rule can alter the meaning of ordinary practice. After the *Exxon Valdez* grounding in Alaska in March 1989, political and regulatory responses helped propel major changes in tanker safety expectations, most famously through the Oil Pollution Act 1990 in the United States and the wider acceleration of the move towards double-hull requirements. Whatever one thinks of the exact policy mix, the institutional effect is plain. Features and operating assumptions that once sat within the broad range of accepted commercial normality began to appear insufficient. Insurers, charterers, regulators, and shipowners adjusted not simply because one casualty had occurred, but because the casualty helped reclassify what counted as tolerable. A technical expectation became a market expectation. The clipboard noted the change.

This is how standards regimes actually work in marine life. A casualty exposes a weakness. Investigations, politics, industry bodies, and international forums respond. A new rule, code, or interpretation emerges. At first it may look like one requirement among many. Soon it starts to reshape underwriting questions, survey priorities, charterparty expectations, and internal company procedures. After a time, younger operators may struggle to imagine that the earlier practice was ever normal at all. The standard does not merely govern conduct. It rewrites memory.

The Polar Code offers a more Arctic-specific example of the same mechanism. When it entered into force in 2017 under the IMO framework, it did not introduce the idea that polar operations were dangerous. Everyone already knew that. What it introduced was a more formal and portable way to present that danger in terms of planning, ship capability, operational limitations, training, and environmental protection. A polar water operational manual, risk-based planning obligations, and more explicit attention to conditions of operation helped convert long-standing prudential concerns into a recognisable compliance architecture. For insurers and counterparties, this mattered because it reduced some forms of guesswork. An operator could now be asked not merely whether it believed itself prepared, but whether its preparation matched a recognised documentary and procedural form.

That does not mean standards settle everything. A limitation needs stating clearly. Codification can create false comfort. A company may produce an immaculate safety management manual and still tolerate poor decision-making on board. A vessel may hold all necessary certificates and still operate at the edge of prudence because commercial pressure distorts how procedures are applied in real conditions. Some standards also lag practice, especially when technology changes faster than international consensus. Formal comparability can therefore conceal real differences in organisational seriousness. Two operators may look similar on paper while behaving very differently when weather narrows, schedules slip, or equipment begins to fail.

Yet this limitation is not an argument against standards. It is an argument for seeing what standards really do. They do not abolish judgement; they structure it. An auditor still decides whether procedures appear lived rather than staged. A surveyor still decides how much significance to attach to a technical deficiency. An underwriter still decides whether formal compliance deserves commercial confidence. Standards make those decisions more legible and less improvisational, but they do not remove the need for experienced interpretation. In fact, by creating a common baseline, they often sharpen the importance of deviations, omissions, and weak implementation. Once a standard exists, failure becomes easier to name.

That naming power explains why standards regimes appeal so strongly to marine markets. Insurance does not love risk; it loves categorised risk. Classification does not certify perfection; it certifies conformity to a rule set that others understand. Port state control does not prove that a vessel is safe in every circumstance; it reveals whether visible deficiencies suggest a wider problem. In each case, standards convert sprawling uncertainty into signals that can travel. A missing drill record, an overdue recommendation, an unresolved non-conformity, a mismatch between manual and practice - these become portable warnings. Efficiency here takes visible form: quicker screening, stronger comparability, fewer arguments about what basic prudence requires. The system gains discipline by multiplying paperwork with consequence.

This transformation also changes the social position of expertise. Older maritime authority often rested heavily on tacit knowledge, personal reputation, and the judgement of seasoned individuals whose competence was recognised rather than audited. Modern standards regimes do not eliminate such expertise, but they place it inside a more formal order. The experienced master still matters. So does the chief engineer, the surveyor, the superintendent, the claims handler, the class specialist. But their authority increasingly has to leave traces: signed reports, recorded drills, corrective actions, meeting minutes, closed recommendations, documentary evidence that a prudent act occurred when it should have occurred. The sea still respects skill. Institutions now ask skill to write things down.

This shift becomes especially consequential in the Arctic because difficult environments intensify the penalty for undocumented assumptions. If a vessel enters polar waters under planning that is vague, training that is generic, maintenance that is formally compliant but operationally thin, or reporting lines that obscure bad news, a later incident will not be treated as unfortunate bad luck alone. It will be read against standards that made the expectation of preparation legible in advance. Claims handling will notice. Port inspectors will notice. Charterers will notice. Standards do not only organise prevention; they organise hindsight.

A second named example makes the point from another angle. After the *Costa Concordia* casualty off Giglio in January 2012, the immediate public focus quite understandably settled on command failure, passenger safety, and the chaos of evacuation. But the institutional aftermath also reinforced a broader marine truth: once a high-profile casualty reveals organisational weakness, the response rarely stays confined to individual blame. Audit cultures harden. Training emphasis shifts. Insurers revisit assumptions. Companies review procedures that had seemed adequate until they were tested. What had counted as ordinary practice before the casualty may no longer satisfy markets or regulators afterwards. Standards regimes metabolise shock and return it as expectation.

The cumulative effect is a new kind of marine common sense. Ordinary practice no longer means what has usually been done by a respectable company. It increasingly means what can be evidenced against codified standards, class expectations, international conventions, and audited management systems. This has obvious benefits in difficult trades, where comparability and documentary discipline can reduce the room for wishful thinking. It also has costs. Smaller operators may struggle with the administrative burden. Formal compliance can crowd out attention to messy operational realities if organisations begin to serve the document rather than the hazard. And yet the historical direction remains unmistakable. Marine risk now speaks most authoritatively through standards.

For Arctic governance, that matters because later disputes over liability, inspection, and insurance terms no longer begin from raw environmental danger alone. They begin from a world in which danger has already been codified into expectations about preparation, reporting, maintenance, competence, and organisational proof. The baseline has shifted. A voyage plan is not merely prudent; it is expected. A polar capability claim is not merely impressive; it must be documented. A deficiency is not merely a technical flaw; it may be evidence of wider system failure. The clipboard returns because the standard made it meaningful.

This leaves a pressing question at the edge of every hard environment. If standards regimes have become the dominant language of marine risk because they promise comparability, what happens when comparability itself becomes the source of comfort - and the real danger lies in everything a compliant file can still fail to show?

Chapter 3

Underwriting Arctic Risk with Thin Data

In August 2018, the *Venta Maersk* completed its trial passage through the Northern Sea Route and offered the public a clean, simple image: a modern container ship proving that a once marginal corridor could be used by mainstream commerce. The underwriter's view was never so clean. A single voyage, however, carefully executed, does not become a stable category merely because it happened. It becomes a question. How much of the result belonged to ship design, how much to seasonal luck, how much to the operator's discipline, and how much to conditions too contingent to support confidence the next time? The map looked clearer. The file did not.

That gap between visible success and insurable certainty sits at the heart of Arctic underwriting. Marine markets do not price a route as a line on a chart. They price a moving bundle of hazards whose interaction matters more than any one element in isolation: hull exposure, propulsion vulnerability, crew judgement, weather volatility, ice behaviour, communications, emergency support, salvage prospects, inspection risk, and the operator's own willingness to turn back when commercial pressure says push on. None of this is abstract. Each item appears as a question in a submission, a condition in a quotation, a recommendation after survey, or a deduction from what the operator did not document.

The central tension is easy to state and hard to solve. Underwriters must make consequential decisions before they possess the kind of data they would prefer to have. Arctic activity is still too uneven, too route-specific, too dependent on shifting environmental and institutional conditions to fit comfortably inside the smoother habits of marine comparison. And yet commercial decisions cannot wait for perfect knowledge, because perfect knowledge never arrives. The work, then, lies in transforming partial knowledge into priced judgement without pretending that thin evidence has suddenly become thick. The estimate rules the voyage.

This matters because underwriting in harsh environments is never merely an accounting exercise. It governs access. A proposal judged too uncertain may still attract interest, but only at a cost or on terms that reshape the operation itself. A higher deductible can change whether a trade remains worthwhile. A narrower cover grant can shift liabilities back onto the operator or charterer. A tighter warranty can alter route choice, seasonality, maintenance timing, or crewing decisions. Insurance markets do not need to prohibit activity in order to govern it. They need only set the cost of uncertainty high enough that behaviour changes before departure.

The problem grows sharper when risks begin to correlate. One vessel in one difficult season may be manageable. Several vessels using related corridors, dependent on thin infrastructure, exposed to similar weather windows, and vulnerable to the same rescue limitations create a different picture entirely. Underwriters and reinsurers do not only see an individual ship. They see the possibility of clustered losses, delayed claims adjustment, contested causation, and a region where one disruption can push stress through multiple accounts at once. Arctic underwriting therefore operates with a double vision: close scrutiny of the single risk, and unease about the portfolio behind it.

Thin data also explains why underwriters care so much about matters outsiders sometimes dismiss as paperwork. Documentation does not sit outside the risk. It is part of the control of risk. A well-assembled submission shows more than technical facts; it shows whether the operator understands the questions likely to matter after a casualty. A complete maintenance history, a coherent route plan, credible emergency arrangements, a clear crewing profile, evidence of closed recommendations, and disciplined disclosure of awkward facts all reduce one particular danger: the danger that the market is being asked to rely on confidence unsupported by records. Trust takes visible form here. It appears in what can be produced promptly, defended consistently, and checked against independent observation.

That is why modelling alone never settles the matter. Models help structure uncertainty around ice, weather, route choice, and operating assumptions, but they do not abolish interpretation. Different markets may look at the same proposed voyage and reach different conclusions because they weight comparators differently, respond differently to sparse historical analogies, or carry different levels of comfort with ambiguity. The result is not irrationality so much as institutional character. One underwriter may read a route as bounded novelty. Another may read it as disguised accumulation risk. One may trust the operator's track record. Another may focus on what no one yet knows. Assumptions become financial terms with remarkable speed.

The human bridge between model and market lies in survey culture. Paper may describe a vessel as well found, its procedures disciplined, its equipment suitable, its plans credible. Surveyors test whether those claims survive contact with the physical world. They translate local conditions, technical quirks, maintenance realities, and organisational habits into language an underwriter can act upon. A minor deficiency can therefore stop being minor once placed in context. A deferred repair may suggest a wider culture of postponement. An untidy record may hint that the company's internal control is weaker than the glossy manual suggests. A narrow issue can widen fast. That is one reason survey findings so often become conditions rather than mere observations.

The path ahead follows this underwriting logic from inside outward. It begins with the facts underwriters need before they can even decide what sort of risk is in front of them, then moves into the uneasy role of models where comparators are sparse and the environment refuses neat averages. From there the focus shifts to survey practice, where on-the-ground judgement fills some gaps and exposes others, before widening to the larger problem of accumulation and systemic exposure that makes Arctic business a portfolio question as much as a voyage question. Only then does the financial expression of doubt come fully into view: premiums, deductibles, exclusions, sublimits, warranties, and the institutional decision about what level of uncertainty remains tolerable at a price the market will actually stand behind.

The deeper stake is not technical elegance. It is commercial reality. When underwriters price Arctic risk with thin data, they are deciding how much ignorance can be carried, by whom, and at what cost to movement, timing, and ambition. The judgement is never wholly scientific and never merely subjective. It is an organised form of caution shaped by records, models, inspections, memory, and the knowledge that a single misread season can echo through many later renewals. That leaves a hard question waiting at the threshold: when an operator says a voyage is ready, what exactly persuades the market that readiness is more than a well-written guess?

What underwriters need to know

In August 2016, the *Crystal Serenity* left Seward, Alaska, for a voyage through the Northwest Passage that was marketed as a feat of access and preparation. Passengers saw scenery, rarity, and the theatrical appeal of a large cruise ship entering waters long associated with hazard and remoteness. Underwriters saw a different object altogether. They saw a floating concentration of contingent liabilities, technical dependencies, human judgement, route assumptions, and rescue constraints compressed into a single proposal. One question governed all the rest: what exactly was being asked of the market if something went wrong far from help?

That question is deceptively simple. It does not ask merely whether a vessel can survive ice, whether a captain is competent, or whether a route looks possible in a favourable season. It asks how all the moving parts fit together under pressure. A strong hull can be undermined by weak voyage planning. A skilled bridge team can be defeated by poor maintenance culture. Redundant propulsion can still leave a vessel exposed if emergency support is distant and communications thin. Arctic risk is never one risk. It arrives bundled.

This is why underwriters begin with facts that appear technical but are never merely technical. Hull strength matters because ice contact is not a theoretical possibility in polar trade; it is part of the operating environment, and the question is not whether contact can occur but how the vessel is designed to bear it, absorb it, and recover from it. Propulsion redundancy matters because loss of manoeuvrability in remote waters changes a machinery problem into a navigational and potentially a liability problem. Crew competence matters because extreme conditions compress decision time and punish hesitation, overconfidence, and weak reporting. Voyage planning matters because the best technical platform in the world can still be sent into a bad problem by a poor assumption. Emergency support matters because remoteness changes severity. Underwriting begins by asking not what is ideal, but what fails next if the first layer fails.

Consider hull strength in its proper setting. Underwriters do not read it as an abstract design boast. They want to know what classification notation the vessel carries, what operating conditions that notation was meant to contemplate, what maintenance history supports continued confidence, whether prior damage or repairs suggest recurring stress, and how the owner's intended trade compares with the vessel's proven experience. The claim being tested is never simply "this ship is strong". It is "this ship is strong enough for this service, at this time, under this operating philosophy, with this degree of margin". That is a much narrower and more useful question. It also explains why two vessels with superficially similar technical descriptions may receive very different responses from markets.

Propulsion redundancy follows the same logic. A vessel operating in temperate, well-supported waters may be able to tolerate a lower degree of built-in resilience because towage, repair, shelter, and medical response sit comparatively close at hand. Arctic waters punish that complacency. Underwriters want to know whether the ship can sustain mobility if one system degrades, how quickly a fault can be diagnosed, what onboard competence exists to manage cascading failures, and whether power loss would create collision, grounding, besetment, or pollution exposure under the proposed route conditions. Redundancy is therefore not a box to tick. It is a narrative about what happens after the first bad event, before outside help arrives.

The human element is even harder to simplify. A market may accept a certain hull form or machinery configuration and still hesitate because the crewing profile does not persuade. Competence in Arctic trade is not a slogan about professionalism. Underwriters look for visible signs: polar or ice-navigation experience, bridge resource management that appears practised rather than aspirational, engine-room depth, familiarity with the operator's procedures, evidence of drills suited to cold conditions, and reporting cultures that do not disguise near misses as routine inconvenience. This is why a CV, a training matrix, a prior voyage record, and a clean trail of internal reporting can matter as much as a technical certificate. Experience must travel through paper before it can travel through price.

Voyage planning is where separate elements become a risk picture. Underwriters want to see intended routes, seasonal assumptions, weather and ice-information arrangements, speed expectations, abort criteria, communications plans, fuel margins, ports of refuge if any are plausible, and the operator's logic for proceeding or turning back when conditions narrow. The key word is not only capability but discipline. A plan that admits limits reassures more than one that promises seamless execution. A market knows that the Arctic punishes excessive confidence. It therefore reads restraint as evidence of maturity. A well-written voyage plan is not literature. It is a behavioural forecast.

Emergency support often decides whether an otherwise respectable proposal feels tolerable. Underwriters ask what response assets could realistically be reached, how medical evacuation would work, what salvage or towage assumptions are credible, how spare parts and repairs would be managed, what outside advisors the vessel can consult, and whether the operator has thought about passenger welfare, pollution control, or crew endurance in conditions where delay extends suffering and cost alike. This is the point at which geography moves directly into price. A casualty near developed support networks and a casualty in remote Arctic conditions may begin with the same initiating event. They do not end in the same claims environment.

A named example shows how these elements can cohere when an operator brings a persuasive file. When A.P. Moller-Maersk sent the *Venta Maersk* through the Northern Sea Route in August and September 2018, the voyage was widely discussed as a test of commercial possibility. For underwriters and counterparties, its real significance lay in legibility. A major operator with established systems, recognisable technical standards, documented planning, and a reputation for procedural seriousness was not offering a vague dream of Arctic commerce. It was offering a bounded experiment supported by evidence markets could evaluate. That did not dissolve uncertainty. It changed its quality. The question became whether the proposal was conservative enough for the circumstances, not whether the operator had mistaken theatre for discipline.

A second example points in a more specialised direction. The *Christophe de Margerie*, delivered in 2017 for Arctic LNG service connected to Yamal, represented a form of purpose-built confidence that markets tend to read differently from opportunistic entry. Here the submission was not merely about a ship entering difficult waters; it was about an integrated industrial proposition with a technical rationale, a service concept, supporting infrastructure, and institutional backing strong enough to render the vessel's intended work intelligible across class, insurance, and operations. What matters is not that the project was large or politically visible. What matters is that the operator could align technical design, operating assumptions, and documentation into a coherent risk story. The file held together.

That phrase deserves emphasis because a proposal becomes a risk submission precisely through acts of coherence. A commercial idea begins as ambition: a route, a vessel, a charter opportunity, a seasonal service, a specialist cargo movement. It becomes underwritable only when ambition is translated into documents others can test. Specifications are gathered. Class status is confirmed. Survey reports are assembled. Maintenance records are produced. Previous losses or incidents are disclosed. Crew profiles are summarised. Operating manuals, route plans, emergency arrangements, and any relevant limitations are brought into one package. The broker then shapes the submission so that the market sees not a scatter of facts but a disciplined account of what is proposed, why it is credible, where its limits lie, and what precautions support the request for cover. The file teaches the market how to read the risk.

That teaching function is why documentation itself acts as risk control rather than mere administration. A missing maintenance history may suggest deeper disorder. An evasive answer on crew experience may imply a wider confidence problem. A route description that ignores support limitations may reveal an operator who has not internalised Arctic severity. Conversely, a transparent file can prevent bad assumptions from surviving too long. It forces the company to compare its own claims with the evidence it can actually produce. It makes internal weaknesses visible earlier. It improves the quality of challenge from brokers, surveyors, and underwriters before the vessel sails. In that sense, documentation does not simply report discipline. It helps create it.

One can see the contrast by imagining two entrants seeking cover for comparable polar operations. One arrives with complete records, clearly stated limitations, recent technical evidence, precise crewing information, and a plan that admits operational thresholds beyond which the ship will not proceed. The other arrives with a capable vessel but patchy maintenance documentation, vague assertions about crew competence, unresolved survey points, and a route concept expressed more confidently than specifically. Both may believe they are fit for the trade. Only one has made that claim examinable. Markets tend to reward examinable prudence and punish unsupported confidence. The difference is not style. It is governability.

Still, a limitation must be faced honestly. A beautiful submission can flatter a mediocre operation. Companies sometimes learn the visual grammar of credibility faster than the underlying habits of safety. Underwriters know this. They know that glossy manuals can conceal weak practice, that good brokers can improve presentation without curing organisational defects, and that prior success may reflect favourable conditions rather than durable competence. Documentation therefore has limits as evidence. It reduces uncertainty; it does not abolish it.

And yet those limits do not weaken the basic argument. They sharpen it. Because documents can mislead, markets do not stop at paperwork alone. They compare records with survey findings, class history, claims experience, management responsiveness, and the plausibility of the operator's overall story. A good risk submission is not persuasive because it looks complete. It is persuasive because its parts support one another under scrutiny. The crew profile fits the route. The route fits the vessel. The vessel fits the class status and maintenance record. The emergency support assumptions fit the geography. The disclosed limitations fit the operator's apparent temperament. Coherence becomes a risk signal.

The broader point is that underwriters are not trying to discover some mystical essence of Arctic readiness. They are trying to capture enough of the interacting hazards to decide whether the risk is legible, bounded, and priced on terms that can survive later argument. That is why they ask so many operational questions. Each question probes a potential chain reaction. If ice contact damages the hull, what next? If a propulsion unit fails, what next? If communications degrade, what next? If the vessel must wait, divert, or retreat, what next? Underwriting is not a search for certainty. It is a search for credible sequences.

The quiet motif returns here because the file is never inert. It is an instrument through which the market imagines the future by reading traces of the present. A complete file does not guarantee a safe voyage. A thin one nearly guarantees a harder negotiation. The Arctic rewards operators who understand that reality early enough to build discipline into both practice and presentation. What underwriters need to know, then, is not merely whether the ship can go north. They need to know whether the operator has built a system in which technical strength, human competence, planning, and support still make sense when the first assumption fails and the file must stand up to the event it was written to anticipate.

Modelling ice, weather, and route uncertainty

In September 2018, the *Venta Maersk* completed its trial passage through the Northern Sea Route and offered a tempting image of Arctic commerce made legible: a modern container ship, a named operator, a route often described as an emerging shortcut, and an outcome simple enough to invite broad conclusions. For the public, the voyage suggested proof. For underwriters, it posed a harder question. What exactly had been proven? A route completed once under managed conditions does not become a stable risk class merely because the vessel arrived. It becomes a data point, and in Arctic underwriting a data point is never the same thing as confidence. The chart looks clean.

That difference matters because modelling Arctic risk begins not with certainty, but with disciplined incompleteness. Ice shifts. Weather compounds. Local conditions vary across a single voyage, let alone across seasons. Historical comparators remain thinner than markets would prefer, and even where records exist, they do not always describe like with like. A vessel's design may differ, a season may have opened unusually, escort arrangements may have changed, infrastructure support may have improved or deteriorated, and the operator's own conduct may have carried more of the result than the route itself. Underwriters therefore do not model an Arctic route as a fixed object. They model a moving set of contingencies.

That phrase can sound more technical than it needs to be. At a practical level, modelling asks a sequence of disciplined questions. What conditions is the vessel likely to face? How variable are they across the intended window of operation? What past voyages are sufficiently comparable to be useful? Where are the blind spots? What happens if one assumption proves too optimistic? The key point is that the model is not trying to foresee every event in detail. It is trying to establish the range within which prudent financial judgement can still operate. Once that range widens too far, pricing hardens, conditions multiply, or appetite fades altogether.

Ice sits at the centre of this problem because it resists simplification. Sea ice is not one hazard. It changes in thickness, concentration, movement, age, pressure, and interaction with wind, current, visibility, and vessel capability. Two voyages on what appears to be the same route may in practice encounter very different operational realities. A charted corridor can look passable in broad terms while still containing local conditions that alter speed, fuel use, hull stress, crew workload, and the margin available for retreat. Underwriters do not need to become ice navigators to grasp the commercial meaning of this. They need only recognise that variable ice conditions make the difference between a route that is theoretically open and a route that is reliably manageable on insurable terms.

Weather compounds the instability. Arctic weather is not just a matter of cold; it is a driver of visibility, icing, sea state, communications reliability, deck safety, machinery performance, and the practical feasibility of external support. A storm in a dense support environment may produce delay and expense. A storm in remote polar waters can change the whole character of the voyage, especially if it interacts with ice movement, navigation constraints, or delayed response. Models, therefore, treat weather not as a background condition but as a force multiplier. The question is rarely whether bad weather may occur. The question is how a voyage plan, vessel, crew, and support system absorb it when it arrives in combination with other stressors.

Route uncertainty follows from that combination. Underwriters are not only asking whether a line on the map is shorter or technically navigable. They are asking how stable the route assumptions remain once ice variability, weather disruption, communications limits, inspection exposure, choke points, support infrastructure, and legal or operational constraints are added to the picture. A route that looks efficient in a seasonal planning document may appear much less attractive when the model tests its dependence on favourable conditions holding together at several points at once. Efficiency, in this context, is not measured solely in distance saved. It is measured in how much uncertainty must be tolerated to realise the saving.

This is why historical comparators matter so much, and why they frustrate underwriters so often. Marine insurance likes repetition because repetition makes differences visible. A route run many times by similar vessels under reasonably comparable conditions begins to generate the material from which a market can infer patterns. Arctic routes rarely offer that comfort in full. Voyages may be too infrequent, too specialised, too dependent on state support or escort, too varied in timing, or too closely tied to one operator's discipline to provide a reassuring statistical base. The result is not ignorance in the crude sense. It is thin comparability. Markets can see enough to worry, but not always enough to relax.

A named example makes the point from another angle. The *Crystal Serenity* transit through the Northwest Passage in August 2016 demonstrated that a large passenger vessel could move through Arctic waters under conditions of extensive preparation and support. For markets, however, the lesson was limited. A single high-profile voyage with substantial planning discipline and unusual attention does not easily translate into a stable benchmark for more routine passenger operations in comparable waters. The model can incorporate the fact of success. It cannot simply assume that success generalises. The voyage therefore narrows one kind of uncertainty while preserving others. What proved possible did not automatically become ordinary.

This gap between event and category helps explain why the same route can be rated differently by different markets. One insurer may put greater weight on the quality of the operator's records, crew profile, and technical discipline, and conclude that the route is risky but bounded. Another may focus more heavily on sparse comparators, limited support infrastructure, or accumulation concerns, and read the same voyage plan as an invitation to unpleasant surprise. Reinsurers may influence this difference by setting their own appetite for correlated Arctic exposure. Internal claims experience matters too. A market that has seen losses or near-misses in remote waters may react more sharply than one whose book carries fewer painful memories. This is not pure subjectivity. It is institutional weighting.

Institutional weighting becomes financial constraint very quickly. If one market trusts the model more, the operator may see broader cover, lower retentions, or fewer voyage-specific conditions. If another market distrusts the underlying assumptions, the same proposal may attract tighter warranties, narrower territorial limits, higher deductibles, or requirements for additional surveys and reporting. Here, the model ceases to be an analytical background and becomes part of commercial reality. The assumptions built into the rating exercise shape whether the voyage remains attractive, whether the operator adjusts the season or route, whether the charter proceeds, and whether counterparties infer strength or weakness from the insurance terms themselves.

A useful way to understand this is to see models as translators rather than predictors. They translate environmental variability into terms financial institutions can compare, debate, and price. The translation is necessarily imperfect. It depends on data quality, on the judgement of the people using the model, on the assumptions chosen for vessel performance and operator competence, and on how much weight is given to rare but severe outcomes. A conservative market will often assume that where evidence remains thin, the burden falls on the operator to narrow the unknowns through documentation, demonstrated competence, stronger support arrangements, or reduced operational ambition. When that burden is not met, the model defaults towards caution.

That caution is not an emotional reflex. It arises from the shape of Arctic losses. In many marine trades, moderate operational uncertainty can be tolerated because the consequences of error remain bounded by dense infrastructure, accessible repairs, frequent traffic, and familiar legal or claims environments. In Arctic waters, a modest misjudgement can become materially larger because assistance is farther away, weather windows close quickly, salvage and towage options are limited, and causation may later be contested under difficult evidentiary conditions. Models, therefore, place unusual emphasis on severity as well as frequency. Even where the chance of an event is unclear, the cost of being wrong about its consequences can be stark.

One might object that this approach can become overly cautious, and the objection has force. Models can lag improvements in vessel design, forecasting, communications, and operational discipline. A route long treated as marginal may, under some conditions and with some operators, deserve less suspicion than inherited market habits allow. Excessive conservatism can penalise capable entrants, preserve incumbents' advantage, and slow useful adaptation in Arctic service. Some markets do, at times, price ignorance rather than hazard, and the difference matters.

Yet that limitation does not cancel the deeper logic. Where data remain uneven, and outcomes can escalate sharply, conservative pricing is not a failure of modelling so much as a visible sign of its boundaries. The model cannot make thin comparators thick. It cannot be assumed that one successful season secures the next. It cannot remove disagreement about how much an operator's discipline deserves weight relative to environmental variability. What it can do is show where the argument turns. It forces the market to name which assumptions it trusts, which it discounts, and where it will charge the operator for the uncertainty that remains.

This is also why modelling and documentation are inseparable. A model does not read weather and ice alone. It reads the vessel through class and technical records, the crew through qualifications and prior experience, the operation through the route plan, and the company's seriousness through the quality of its submission. Better documentation narrows some modelling uncertainty because it gives the market firmer grounds for judging how the operator will behave when conditions deteriorate. Poor documentation does the opposite. It pushes the model back towards harsher assumptions because the human part of the risk remains too opaque to support confidence. The chart returns here as a quiet motif: clean lines on paper, but only as reliable as the hands and systems asked to follow them.

The practical result is that Arctic modelling never produces a single neutral truth about risk. It produces structured disagreement. Different underwriters, brokers, reinsurers, and technical advisers may accept the same environmental data yet diverge over the operator, the support context, or the severity tail of a possible loss. Those divergences are not noise at the edge of the system. They are part of how the system governs. They determine which operators can secure workable terms, which must accept punishing conditions, and which discover that a route celebrated in public remains commercially elusive once modelled through institutional caution.

What matters most, then, is not whether models can tame Arctic uncertainty in any final sense. They cannot. What matters is how they distribute its burden. When a market looks at variable ice, volatile weather, sparse comparators, and a route still seeking stable commercial meaning, how much uncertainty will it absorb into price, and how much will it push back onto the operator in the form of tighter conditions, narrower cover, and a harder test of proof before the voyage is allowed to feel routine?

Survey culture and on-the-ground judgement

In January 2012, after the *Costa Concordia* grounded off Giglio, Italy, the world's attention was fixed on command failure, evacuation chaos, and the humiliating spectacle of a modern passenger ship lying on its side close to shore. For insurers and technical reviewers, another story began almost at once. Reports were gathered, inspections intensified, recommendations sharpened, and a familiar question returned with unusual force: what had the documents failed to reveal about the vessel's operating culture before the casualty made it impossible to ignore? The answer did not lie in statistics alone. It lay in the gap between formal assurance and observed condition. Someone had to walk the ship.

That need does not disappear in Arctic underwriting. It becomes more urgent. Where data are thin, conditions severe, and consequences amplified by remoteness, markets place unusual weight on the people who can translate local reality into language others can act on. Models can compare routes, seasons, vessel types, and historical patterns. They cannot smell hydraulic seepage in a machinery space, notice the untidy workaround that has quietly become routine, hear uncertainty in the explanation of an emergency procedure, or detect the difference between a manual that is followed and one that merely exists. The deck tells on you.

Survey culture begins with this blunt institutional fact: paper and practice rarely align perfectly, and difficult environments punish the gap between them. An operator seeking Arctic cover may present a strong submission - class records current, maintenance histories complete, crew qualifications persuasive, route planning carefully bounded. Underwriters still want to know what an experienced eye sees when the vessel, the support arrangements, or the operating culture is examined at close quarters. The surveyor becomes a translator between worlds. On one side sits the operator's account of itself. On the other sits the insurer's need for portable judgement. Between them stands observation.

That translation is more consequential than the word "survey" often suggests. Outside specialist circles, a survey can sound like routine box-ticking, an inspection of obvious items against known standards. In practice, especially in Arctic-related underwriting, it is often an exercise in contextual reading. A surveyor does not merely record whether equipment exists, whether documents are present, or whether visible damage can be found. The surveyor asks what a given condition means in relation to the intended trade. An acceptable level of wear in one service may look less tolerable where cold, delay, icing, and sparse repair options raise the cost of failure. A narrow deficiency on a local ferry might be manageable. The same deficiency on a vessel bound for remote waters can carry a different charge.

This is why survey recommendations matter so much. They are not just helpful notes for an owner's convenience. They are institutional signals. A recommendation may begin as technical advice, but once it enters the underwriting file it can change the commercial character of the risk. An underwriter may quote subject to compliance with the recommendation before sailing. A broker may warn that markets will not widen terms until it is closed out. A charterer may read its presence as evidence that the operator still carries unresolved weakness. Survey language travels. A sentence written in an engine room can reshape a voyage from afar.

The mechanism is easy to underestimate because it works through modest phrasing rather than dramatic command. A surveyor writes that a component shows signs of deterioration and should be monitored or replaced. An underwriter reads that not only as a technical point, but as a question about maintenance culture, spare parts planning, and the operator's appetite for deferral. Another note records that crew knowledge of a procedure appears uneven. That may seem minor until it is translated into insurer-facing language about emergency response reliability in difficult conditions. A condition report remarks on incomplete documentary support for a prior repair. Suddenly the issue is not only what was repaired, but whether the operator controls its own technical record to the standard the Arctic demands. Small observations accumulate fast.

A named example helps clarify the principle from a different angle. When the *Crystal Serenity* prepared for its August 2016 transit through the Northwest Passage, the voyage's visibility made preparation unusually legible. A passenger vessel entering remote Arctic waters could not rely on broad claims of competence alone. The significance of any technical or operational review in such a context lay in its power to convert general confidence into evidence others would trust. Passenger exposure, remoteness, and reputational stakes meant that even ordinary-seeming questions - equipment readiness, communications, medical contingencies, procedural clarity - carried heavier weight than they might in more forgiving trades. The lesson is not limited to cruise operations. High-consequence environments make survey judgement commercially decisive because the tolerance for vague reassurance collapses.

The surveyor's craft therefore depends on reading systems through particulars. A weak handrail, an improvised storage practice, a badly maintained door seal, a repeated delay in closing technical points, a bridge team's uncertain response to route thresholds - none proves disaster. That is not the standard. The surveyor is asked to judge whether the vessel and its operator present scattered flaws or a pattern. This is where on-the-ground judgement begins to look less like inspection and more like institutional interpretation. Underwriters cannot board every ship. They rely on people who can see whether the ship's condition and behaviour support the claims made in the risk submission. Trust becomes observational.

In Arctic trades, surveyors often bridge more than a vessel and an insurer. They bridge geography itself. A market in London or Oslo may know that a vessel intends to operate in a remote seasonal window, but it cannot feel the practical implications of that choice without localised translation. Surveyors and technical correspondents make those implications legible. They explain how a minor machinery issue becomes more serious when spare parts would be slow to reach the vessel. They explain how a narrow documentation gap becomes more serious when later claims will depend on reconstructing decisions taken far from witnesses and support. They explain how a route plan that appears credible in broad terms may understate the true constraints of available shelter, towage, or communications. Observation becomes commercial grammar.

A brief example shows how a minor deficiency can cascade. Imagine a surveyor noting that a vessel's heating arrangement for a critical deck line or valve enclosure is unreliable, though not yet failed outright. In ordinary coastal trade, the issue might attract a recommendation for repair at the next reasonable opportunity. In an Arctic submission, that same note may trigger a different chain. Underwriters worry that freezing could impair operation at precisely the wrong moment. The broker returns to the owner for clarification. Markets narrow cover pending repair or impose a condition precedent to sailing in certain temperatures. Charterers, seeing restrictive terms, question schedule reliability. A voyage window tightens.

The original problem was small in engineering scale. It became large because the environment multiplied its operational significance and the file multiplied its commercial consequences.

This cascading effect explains why survey findings so often become binding conditions for cover. Underwriters do not do this merely to appear stern. They do it because a survey provides one of the few grounded ways to narrow uncertainty before a loss occurs. A recommendation tied to a specific defect, procedure, or operational concern gives the market something concrete to require, monitor, and later point to if a dispute arises. Conditions are attractive to insurers because they transform unease into action. The owner must repair, document, confirm, retrain, inspect, or refrain. The unease does not vanish, but it becomes governable. That is often enough for a market to proceed.

The language used here deserves close attention. "Recommend" sounds soft. "Subject to" sounds routine. "To be complied with prior to sailing" sounds merely administrative. These phrases are not neutral. They allocate time, cost, and bargaining power. They can turn a survey from observation into enforcement without any public official issuing an order. In that sense, survey culture is one of the practical engines of private governance. It does not legislate. It conditions movement. A shipowner may technically be free to ignore a recommendation. Commercially, that freedom can prove useless if cover narrows, premiums rise, charterers retreat, or renewal negotiations sour.

A second named example shows how this logic resonates beyond the Arctic itself. The *Exxon Valdez* grounding in Alaska in March 1989 did not simply harden regulatory and political attitudes. It also altered the weight given to inspection, maintenance discipline, navigation culture, and the credibility of operator assurances in environmentally sensitive waters. One casualty helped teach markets and reviewers that technical adequacy on paper could not be separated from the lived quality of operating systems. Surveys and technical reviews became more than a snapshot of condition; they became instruments for discovering whether a company treated risk as a managed reality or a verbal performance. Arctic underwriting inherited that lesson with particular intensity because severity can escalate so quickly in remote waters.

Still, a limitation must be admitted. Survey culture is not infallible. Surveyors are human, time-constrained, and dependent on access, cooperation, and the quality of the information placed before them. Different surveyors may weight the same observation differently. Some may overstate caution; others may miss the significance of a local practice that looks harmless until conditions deteriorate. Surveys can also distort behaviour by encouraging performative tidiness around inspection windows rather than durable discipline throughout the year. A vessel may be cleaned for review, records polished, briefings rehearsed, and awkward practices temporarily suppressed. The deck can be coached.

Yet this limitation strengthens rather than weakens the case for taking survey culture seriously. Precisely because surveys are partial, markets do not read them in isolation. They compare them with class history, claims records, maintenance logs, crew profiles, previous recommendations, management responsiveness, and the plausibility of the operator's overall story. A single survey finding rarely decides everything. Its force lies in how it fits with other signals. If a recommendation aligns with a pattern of delayed maintenance or patchy disclosure, it gains weight quickly. If the owner responds promptly, transparently, and convincingly, the same finding may remain what it first appeared to be: a correctable issue rather than evidence of a wider disorder.

This is why response to survey findings matters almost as much as the findings themselves. Underwriters watch how operators behave once a deficiency is named. Do they acknowledge it directly or minimise it? Do they repair it promptly or negotiate for delay without strong reason? Do they provide evidence in an orderly way or force the market to chase answers? Those behaviours become risk signals because they reveal organisational temperament under pressure. An operator that deals well with an inconvenient recommendation often strengthens its standing. An operator that becomes evasive or defensive may confirm the underwriter's deeper fear: not that things go wrong, but that the company is poor at confronting what goes wrong.

One should also note that survey culture influences knowledge beyond the immediate account. Surveyors carry memory across vessels, fleets, and operators. They learn which technical claims usually mean what, which kinds of deferred repair tend to stay deferred, which paperwork gaps correlate with weak onboard discipline, which route plans feel grounded and which feel aspirational. This does not make them omniscient. It does mean their judgement often reflects a seasoned comparative sense that raw models cannot supply. In markets starved of thick Arctic data, that comparative memory becomes especially valuable. It gives texture to thin numbers.

The larger point is that surveys fill a specific institutional need. Models estimate. Submissions persuade. Surveys test. They provide the friction that stops underwriting from drifting too far into abstraction. They allow local realities - corrosion, improvisation, fatigue, cluttered maintenance culture, strong crew discipline, believable contingency planning - to enter the financial conversation in forms others can use. That is why survey culture often feels conservative. It is not designed to admire possibility. It is designed to ask what a possibility would look like after contact with steel, weather, cold, and habit.

For Arctic operations, this grounded scepticism is not a bureaucratic inconvenience attached to an otherwise technical trade. It is one of the means by which the market protects itself against the seduction of clean files and optimistic models. A recommendation can delay a voyage, narrow a route, alter a season, or harden a renewal. A condition report can quietly change the terms on which a company is allowed to proceed. A minor defect can become a major constraint because the environment gives it leverage and the market refuses to pretend otherwise. The deck tells on you again.

The unresolved question is not whether surveyors matter. They plainly do. It is whether markets know how to use their judgements without mistaking observed detail for complete truth. When a survey turns lived reality into insurer-facing language, where exactly is the line between prudent translation and commercially decisive over-reading - and who bears the cost when that line is drawn too late?

Aggregation, accumulation, and systemic exposure

In March 1989, the *Exxon Valdez* grounded in Prince William Sound, Alaska, and the immediate focus settled, understandably, on one ship, one casualty, one set of losses spreading through water, coastline, litigation, and public memory. Insurers never stop at one. They ask what else the event reveals about concentration, dependence, and the possibility that apparently separate exposures may in fact belong to the same underlying pattern. A single casualty can be large. A cluster can reorder a market. The ice does not act alone.

That habit of thinking beyond the individual ship becomes especially important in Arctic underwriting because polar risk rarely remains neatly confined to one hull or one voyage. A market may appear to be evaluating a vessel, a route, or a seasonal operation in isolation. In practice it is often evaluating a wider field of connected vulnerability: several ships using the same narrow window, relying on the same support assets, moving through the same chokepoints, facing the same weather system, or depending on the same limited salvage and emergency response capacity. What matters is not only whether one loss can occur. It is whether many losses can become plausible together.

This is the difference between ordinary exposure and accumulation. Ordinary exposure asks what might happen to this ship, this cargo, this operator. Accumulation asks what happens when multiple insured interests begin to lean on the same fragile conditions at the same time. An insurer may feel comfortable with one ice-capable vessel in a difficult trade and deeply uncomfortable with several vessels operating in related corridors during a short season of concentrated activity. The shift is not psychological. It is structural. The peril stops being a discrete event and starts to look like a common driver moving through the book of business.

Ice seasons create exactly this sort of common driver. They encourage convergence. Operators move when conditions appear most favourable, which means markets often see multiple Arctic exposures gather in similar periods rather than spread evenly across the calendar. A favourable seasonal opening that draws traffic can also draw correlated vulnerability. If conditions deteriorate quickly, or if ice behaves less predictably than expected, more than one vessel may face delay, route compression, besetment, or heightened mechanical stress at roughly the same time. Underwriters know this. They do not only ask whether a seasonal window exists. They ask how many insureds may try to pass through it together, and what happens if the same window narrows abruptly for all of them.

Chokepoints sharpen the same problem. Arctic routes often contain stretches where traffic, manoeuvring room, ice movement, escort dependence, or communications constraints create a concentration of operational stress. A chokepoint does not need to resemble a canal in order to matter. It can be any passage where geography and conditions reduce flexibility. For underwriters, chokepoints raise more than collision or grounding concerns. They raise the prospect of serial disruption: one vessel delayed, another forced to alter course, a third exposed to worsening conditions while waiting, support resources pulled thin, claims causation later tangled across multiple accounts. A narrow waterway or ice corridor can therefore behave like a portfolio risk amplifier.

Limited salvage and emergency response capacity deepen the concern. A single casualty in remote waters is serious enough. Several casualties, or one casualty combined with other vessels requiring assistance, can overwhelm the practical resources available to respond. This is where Arctic severity stops looking like a matter of ship design alone and starts to look like a systems problem. Underwriters ask not merely whether a vessel can withstand ice or weather, but whether the region can withstand a run of trouble. If towage assets are scarce, ports of refuge few, repair options distant, and medical response constrained, then losses begin to correlate through the response system itself. The same absence of support affects everybody.

Shared infrastructure produces a subtler but equally important form of systemic exposure. Several operators may depend on the same terminal, the same weather intelligence provider, the same icebreaker assistance, the same repair point, the same communications chain, or the same route advice. Each dependency may seem sensible in isolation. Collectively, they create a concentration that matters to insurers. If the terminal closes, if escort availability changes, if a key support service fails, or if a port becomes inaccessible, the problem radiates across multiple insured interests at once. A market that thought it held diverse Arctic exposures may discover it actually holds repeated versions of the same dependency.

A named example from the Northern Sea Route helps clarify the point. When the *Venta Maersk* completed its trial voyage in 2018, the commercial discussion often centred on whether a single container transit hinted at future viability. For underwriters, the more revealing question lay slightly to the side: what would the picture look like if such voyages became more common within a relatively narrow seasonal frame, relying on related support assumptions and subject to similar environmental constraints? One successful voyage can support optimism. A cluster of comparable voyages invites accumulation analysis. The significance of the passage, then, was not only that it occurred, but that it forced markets to imagine what correlated Arctic trading might mean if isolated novelty turned into patterned movement.

This is why Arctic risk is so often treated as a portfolio problem rather than merely a voyage problem. Underwriters do not hold one Arctic exposure and then stop thinking. They hold several accounts, often across hull, cargo, liability, and reinsurance layers, and they know that correlation can move across those layers faster than the initial underwriting file suggests. One ship delayed in ice may create cargo loss, charterparty friction, and knock-on claims elsewhere. One machinery issue in severe conditions may become pollution exposure, salvage cost, wreck concern, or passenger liability. One infrastructure bottleneck may touch multiple insureds. Portfolio thinking grows naturally from these entanglements because the peril is not fully contained within the hull form.

Reinsurers intensify this way of seeing. Primary underwriters may focus closely on a particular vessel or operator, but reinsurers often look across books, territories, and classes of business to judge whether concentration is creeping into areas that once looked manageable. Arctic exposures can alarm them not because every voyage is intrinsically uninsurable, but because the distribution of risk is uneven and the severity tail remains difficult to bound. A reinsurer does not need to predict simultaneous catastrophe with confidence. It need only suspect that several losses could arise from the same seasonal conditions, the same bottleneck, or the same support limitations for appetite to tighten. Once reinsurance tightens, the discipline moves back down through the market quickly.

That discipline usually appears in familiar commercial forms. Capacity becomes thinner. A market that once entertained a broader line cuts back. Terms become more exacting. Aggregation language sharpens. Underwriters ask more searching questions about route clustering, timing, escort dependence, contingency plans, and the operator's exposure to regional infrastructure constraints. Deductibles may rise. Sublimits may appear. Warranties may narrow freedom of movement or require more active reporting. The voyage is still technically possible. The conditions of entry grow harder. Capacity rarely announces its fear in grand terms. It expresses itself through restraint.

A brief example of cascade shows how this works. Imagine several vessels insured within related Arctic trades during the same late-season window. One suffers an ice-related machinery casualty and requires assistance. Another, waiting on altered routing advice, enters worsening conditions and sustains damage. A third arrives at the same support point only to find resources delayed and berthing priorities reshuffled. None of these losses may be individually extraordinary. Together they reveal systemic strain. Claims adjusters face overlapping facts. Salvage capacity is stretched. Repair delays extend business interruption or charter disputes. Underwriters reviewing the season afterwards do not merely price three incidents. They price a shared exposure pattern that had been underestimated.

This pattern also explains why underwriters can become wary of what appears, from the operator's perspective, to be good news. Better conditions, more traffic, expanding confidence, and improved route familiarity may seem to reduce risk. They can also produce crowding. More operators enter. Seasonal windows become busier. Shared infrastructure works harder. Exposure that was once sparse becomes denser. Underwriters therefore ask an awkward but necessary question: does apparent progress reduce uncertainty, or does it simply attract enough correlated activity that the consequences of a bad turn become larger across the portfolio? Growth itself can create concentration.

A second named example points to the same institutional lesson from another kind of event. The 2012 *Costa Concordia* casualty off Giglio was not an Arctic incident, but it demonstrated how one maritime loss can expose wider accumulation concerns across liability, passenger exposure, wreck removal, reputational shock, and market memory. Insurers did not read it only as a failure of one operation. They read it as a reminder that certain classes of risk can generate costs across multiple lines and over extended time horizons. Arctic underwriters bring that memory with them. They know that a casualty in remote, environmentally sensitive waters can likewise spill across hull, liability, response, reputational, and portfolio dimensions. One event seldom stays in its box.

A credible limitation deserves recognition here. Correlation is not destiny. Operators are not identical, routes are not interchangeable, and Arctic seasons do not produce uniform conditions across all corridors. Markets can overstate accumulation risk by treating distinct exposures as too alike, thereby penalising disciplined operators because others happen to trade in the same broad region. A vessel with stronger ice capability, better crew, clearer route thresholds, and firmer support arrangements may deserve a more favourable view than a crude portfolio lens allows. There is always a danger that systemic thinking becomes lazy thinking.

Yet the limitation does not undo the central logic. The task for underwriters is not to pretend every Arctic risk is interchangeable, but to recognise that some drivers of loss do not respect account boundaries. Ice movement, weather shifts, response scarcity, infrastructure dependence, and legal or operational chokepoints can affect many insureds at once even when the vessels themselves differ in quality. Portfolio analysis becomes valuable precisely because it disciplines the temptation to see every proposal as a standalone case. It forces the market to ask what else it already carries that depends on the same narrow margin.

This is where trust takes a particularly visible form. A market may accept an individual operator's discipline and still hesitate because the regional concentration behind that operator has grown too dense. The operator then encounters a frustrating truth: strong records are necessary, but not always sufficient. An underwriter may admire the file, respect the crew profile, and still reduce offered capacity because the book is already heavy with adjacent exposures. This can feel unfair from the insured's side, but it reflects an institutional reality. Markets do not only insure merit. They insure books of business.

Documentation still matters in this setting, though in a different way from the preceding discussion. Here the question is not only whether a single operator can prove competence. It is whether the operator can distinguish its own risk from the broader accumulation picture. Can it show route flexibility rather than dependence on one crowded corridor? Can it evidence independent support arrangements rather than reliance on thin common infrastructure? Can it demonstrate conservative timing rather than convergence with the most exposed seasonal cluster? Strong records can sometimes help a market believe that an apparently correlated risk is, in meaningful respects, less entangled than it first appeared. The file must now differentiate as well as reassure.

The commercial consequence of all this is straightforward and severe. Arctic insurance terms are often shaped not only by what the vessel may suffer, but by what the region may do to the insurer's whole portfolio if enough similar risks line up under similar conditions. That is why markets sometimes respond to Arctic growth not with celebration but with tightening. The more plausible the trade becomes, the more necessary it becomes to ask how much concentrated exposure is already accumulating behind the optimism. Shared routes, shared windows, shared support, shared assumptions: each one adds weight to the same side of the book.

The quiet motif returns here because the book of business is itself a kind of chart, one that shows concentration where operators may prefer to see individual enterprise. A single file can look clean. Several clean files can add up to an uncomfortable pattern. That is the underwriter's burden and the operator's irritation. Arctic commerce invites people to think in terms of access, technology, and courage. Insurance insists on a different discipline. It asks what happens when too many ventures rely on the same narrow set of favourable conditions at once.

The unresolved test is therefore larger than any one voyage. When a market weighs a proposed Arctic operation, how much of the decision truly turns on the ship in front of it, and how much turns on the invisible convoy already sitting in the underwriter's portfolio, waiting for the same season to go wrong?

Pricing, deductibles, and the cost of uncertainty

In August 2018, when the *Venta Maersk* completed its trial transit through the Northern Sea Route, the public image was one of technical possibility and commercial suggestion. A container ship had made the passage. A route long discussed in strategic and logistical terms had, for a moment, looked operationally real. The underwriter's question was colder. What does possibility cost? A voyage may succeed and still remain expensive to insure, not because markets deny the fact of passage, but because one completed transit does not settle what the next one will encounter, how claims might develop, or who will absorb the consequences if a narrow operational margin disappears.

That distinction matters because Arctic insurance pricing is not a neutral mirror held up to danger. It is an institutional judgement about what degree of uncertainty the market is willing to carry, on what terms, and with what protections against unpleasant surprise. Premium is the most visible part of that judgement, but it is only one part. Deductibles, warranties, exclusions, sublimits, territorial limits, reporting requirements, and conditions tied to surveys or route approvals all perform the same deeper function: they convert uncertainty into economic pressure. The bill tells a story.

Pricing in this setting begins with an uncomfortable truth. Underwriters are rarely asked to price a well-behaved risk with thick comparators, dense support infrastructure, and a clear record of repeatable outcomes. They are often asked to price an interaction of hazards whose consequences shift with season, route, vessel capability, operator discipline, and the quality of outside support. When markets face that kind of uncertainty, they do not simply raise premiums in an abstract way. They separate the uncertainty into parts and decide which parts they will accept, which they will narrow, and which they will push back onto the insured. That is why two quotations can differ sharply without either being irrational. One market may carry more doubt in premium. Another may carry it in warranty language, in a larger deductible, or in cover carved back so far that the nominal existence of insurance tells only part of the truth.

The premium itself is the most straightforward expression of caution, but also the least interesting. Premium says, in effect, that the market requires more money to stand behind this voyage or operation than it would require in easier waters or more familiar trades. That matters, of course. It affects viability, financing, charter negotiations, and the operator's own willingness to proceed. Yet a premium alone does not reveal how the market sees the risk. Two operators may pay broadly similar amounts while facing very different underlying protection structures. One may have relatively broad cover because the market trusts the file, the crew, the technical standing, and the operational limits. Another may face the same bill or a higher one, while also accepting stricter conditions because the market does not trust the same things. Price without structure can mislead.

Deductibles often tell the deeper story because they reveal where insurers want the insured to retain pain before the policy responds. In Arctic trades, a larger deductible does more than protect insurer balance sheets against attritional claims. It disciplines operational ambition. If the operator must absorb a meaningful share of smaller or moderate losses, its tolerance for marginal voyages, deferred maintenance, thin support planning, or optimistic route assumptions tends to shrink. The deductible functions as a behavioural hinge. It forces the insured to ask not only whether a voyage can be made, but whether it remains worthwhile once a foreseeable setback will be borne largely on its own account. Markets understand this perfectly well. They use retention to make prudence expensive to ignore.

Warranties sharpen the discipline further. A premium may express uncertainty in money, but a warranty expresses it in conduct. It may require that the vessel trade only within stated seasons, that specified ice information services be used, that certain routes or conditions be avoided without prior approval, that survey recommendations be complied with before sailing, or that particular manning or technical arrangements remain in place throughout the voyage. To outsiders, these may look like peripheral clauses. Commercially, they are often the real gate. A vessel can be insured and still find its operational freedom heavily narrowed by the conditions attached to that insurance. The market has not forbidden the voyage. It has priced freedom separately from protection.

A named example helps clarify the institutional meaning of this. The *Crystal Serenity* transit through the Northwest Passage in August 2016 did not show that Arctic passenger movement had become simply another itinerary item in global cruise commerce. It showed how much assurance had to be assembled before a visible voyage could proceed with tolerable commercial backing. A large passenger vessel in remote waters raises not merely hull questions but medical, evacuation, pollution, liability, and reputational ones. Markets responding to such a proposition do not only ask what premium is appropriate. They ask which assumptions must be backed by conditions, which contingencies require specific arrangements, and how much risk must remain with the operator if the voyage pushes into difficulty. Pricing in such cases is inseparable from judgement about organisational seriousness.

The same logic applies even where the operation is less publicly dramatic and more industrial. Consider specialised Arctic service linked to LNG or support logistics. Here, markets may be more comfortable with purpose-built tonnage, established industrial partners, and repeat operations than with one-off or prestige voyages. Yet comfort is never free-floating. It appears through sharper distinctions in terms. An operator with disciplined documentation, known technical standards, conservative route philosophy, clear support arrangements, and prompt closure of survey points may secure not merely a better premium, but a more workable insurance architecture. The difference can be decisive. A more modest deductible, fewer voyage-specific restrictions, or broader claims responsiveness may determine whether a trade is commercially tolerable over time. Affordability, in this sense, is partly a market verdict on credibility.

That word deserves precision. Affordability is often spoken of as though it were an objective economic fact waiting to be discovered. In insurance it is also an institutional decision. A market decides how much uncertainty it finds tolerable, how much capital it is willing to expose, how much confidence it places in the operator's controls, and how much of the remaining unknown it will sell back to the insured through pricing and terms. That means "too expensive" does not simply mean the hazard is inherently extreme. It can also mean that the market lacks trust, lacks comparators, dislikes the accumulation picture, or doubts the operator's ability to behave conservatively under pressure. Price, then, is not only a reflection of risk. It is an argument about risk.

A second named example shows how this argument can be reshaped by event and memory. After the *Exxon Valdez* grounding in Alaska in March 1989, marine markets did not merely process one large casualty and move on. They revised their view of environmental sensitivity, operational failure, liability severity, and the public and legal consequences of maritime loss in vulnerable waters. The effect was broader than any single policy renewal. The standards of what counted as tolerable exposure shifted. In insurance, such shifts often emerge as price first and doctrine second. Premiums harden, deductibles rise, terms narrow, exclusions or special conditions proliferate, and only later does the new severity assumption begin to feel ordinary. A casualty can therefore rewrite affordability by changing what uncertainty markets believe they are being paid to bear.

This dynamic explains why narrower cover matters so much. An operator may announce that a voyage or service remains insured, and the statement may be formally correct. Yet the meaningful question is what the insurance no longer covers, or covers only under strained conditions. Exclusions can push ice-related consequences, delay-linked costs, environmental liabilities, or support failures back onto owners, charterers, or project structures in ways that alter the economics of the whole venture. Sublimits can turn headline protection into partial comfort. Geographic restrictions can leave the most commercially interesting portion of a voyage under tighter control than the rest. Insurance remains in place. Practical freedom contracts.

That contraction is not always punitive. Markets often use price and terms to reward proven procedure as much as to punish uncertainty. An operator with a clean inspection and survey history, strong maintenance discipline, credible emergency arrangements, transparent disclosure, conservative route planning, and experienced crew can sometimes secure better terms not because the Arctic has become safe, but because the market believes this particular account is less likely to turn uncertainty into surprise. Reward here takes visible form. A quote comes back with fewer provisos. A deductible softens. A prior warranty is relaxed or narrowed. A broker receives a better hearing because the file has earned one. The operator has not escaped governance. It has satisfied it.

This is one reason documentation matters financially long after the submission stage. Records shape price not only at entry but at renewal, after survey, after minor incidents, and after market conditions change. An operator that can show how recommendations were closed, how procedures were revised after near misses, how crewing decisions reflected hard lessons rather than habit, and how route boundaries were respected under commercial pressure offers the market something rare: evidence that organisational memory exists. Insurers value that not out of sentiment, but because memory reduces one particular danger, namely that the next claim will reveal the same weakness dressed in slightly different facts. Pricing responds to organisations that learn in ways the file can prove.

Still, a limitation must be faced plainly. Pricing is not pure science. Markets can overreact, follow one another, or price reputation instead of exposure with more enthusiasm than justice requires. Thin data encourage caution, but they also encourage noise. An operator may find itself paying for regional anxiety, reinsurance pressure, or recent losses elsewhere that only imperfectly resemble its own trade. Capable entrants may be punished because they lack history rather than because they lack discipline. Affordability can therefore reflect market structure and mood as well as grounded assessment.

Yet that limitation strengthens the strategic point rather than weakening it. If price and terms contain elements of institutional judgement beyond hard hazard, then insurance becomes more visibly a mode of governance. Markets are not merely reimbursing loss after the fact. They are deciding, in advance, which operators can enter on workable terms, which must internalise more uncertainty, and which will be discouraged from entry unless they improve their technical, procedural, and documentary case. The governing effect is often subtle. No ministry announces a restriction. No public rule changes. The route remains legally open. The cost of entry rises until only some actors can pass.

This is especially clear in the relationship between underwriters and behaviour. A market that distrusts route discipline may insist on prior approval for certain deviations. A market uneasy about machinery reliability may enlarge the deductible or demand fresh surveys. A market doubtful about crew competence may narrow cover unless specified personnel or qualifications remain in place. None of these measures guarantees safety. All of them alter choices. Operators begin to invest where the pricing pain is sharpest: better maintenance, stronger crewing, more disciplined reporting, tighter route controls, clearer emergency arrangements. Insurance pricing thus acts as a dispersed but potent regulatory force. The bill instructs.

One can see, then, why commercial actors often misread the meaning of favourable or unfavourable terms. A low premium is not a universal certificate of safety. It may reflect competition, portfolio appetite, or support external to the operator. A high premium is not always a simple measure of objective danger. It may capture thin data, poor comparators, recent losses in adjacent accounts, or market unwillingness to subsidise uncertainty it cannot classify. What matters is the structure of the quote as a whole. Premium, deductible, exclusions, sublimits, warranties, territorial wording, and survey-related conditions together show how the market intends to distribute uncertainty if the voyage proceeds. The price list becomes a policy language of trust.

This is why strategic readers of Arctic expansion must resist the temptation to treat insurance as a background cost. It is closer to a pricing constitution for difficult trades. It allocates pain before loss, allocates freedom before departure, and allocates credibility before any public dispute begins. A project may appear technically ready and legally permitted while remaining commercially brittle because the price of uncertainty has been set too high or structured too harshly for the operator's balance sheet, timetable, or counterparties. Another project may proceed not because risk has vanished, but because the market has decided the operator's evidence and habits justify a less punitive distribution of that uncertainty. The outcome is commercial. The mechanism is institutional.

The quiet motif returns because the bill is never just a bill. It is a reading of the file, of the vessel, of the crew, of the route, of the support context, and of the market's own tolerance for not knowing enough. Arctic expansion often invites the language of breakthrough, access, and strategic opportunity. Insurance asks a more prosaic and more decisive question: who pays for doubt, and how much? The answer is written not only in premium, but in every retention, exception, and warranty that shapes the trade before it begins.

That leaves the central tension unresolved in exactly the right way. If markets govern Arctic entry by setting the cost of uncertainty, when does prudent pricing become a useful discipline on weak preparation, and when does it become a private veto on ventures that may be technically sound but institutionally unfashionable?

Chapter 4

Classification Societies and Ice Class Rules

In 2017, when the Polar Code entered into force through the IMO framework, many readers outside shipping might have imagined that the decisive questions about Arctic vessel fitness would now be settled by public rules alone. They were not. Long before any vessel meets a port inspector or an insurer's reservations, another judgement tends to matter whether the ship stands within a recognised technical order of design, construction, survey, and maintenance that commercial actors know how to read. The plate on the file matters.

That order is classification. It rarely attracts public drama, yet it sits close to the centre of maritime legitimacy. Shipowners need it, financiers look for it, charterers use it to screen, and insurers treat it as one of the first signs that a vessel belongs to the world of disciplined commerce rather than improvisation. But the force of classification lies partly in misunderstanding. Many outsiders treat class as though it were a universal certificate of safety or a complete licence to trade. It is neither. A vessel can be in class and still be a hard commercial proposition. It can satisfy a published rule and still leave serious doubts about route, crew, operating culture, or emergency support. The stamp opens doors. It does not finish the argument.

That gap between technical legitimacy and practical acceptability gives this subject its edge. Classification societies verify compliance against their rules; they do not insure the consequences of commercial optimism. They inspect, review, assign notations, and expect maintenance of standard. They do not promise that every vessel meeting those standards should be welcomed into every difficult trade on workable terms. Once Arctic operations enter the picture, the difference sharpens. Ice class notation can tell the market something important about hull strength and intended conditions of service. It cannot abolish the fact that ice is variable, weather compounds risk, local knowledge matters, and operational ambition often runs ahead of what a notation alone can justify.

The stakes reach further than technical housekeeping. Classification provides one of the key languages through which private governance becomes portable across borders. A ship may be owned in one state, flagged in another, insured elsewhere, financed through another legal order again, and chartered into remote waters by counterparties who have never seen it directly. Class creates a common starting point. That is why it carries such commercial weight. It lets dispersed actors compare unlike vessels without beginning from pure uncertainty every time. Yet the more power a notation acquires as shorthand, the more tempting it becomes to mistake shorthand for substance. Arctic access is especially vulnerable to that mistake because the urge to treat technical readiness as practical readiness is strong, commercially flattering, and often expensive.

Ice class intensifies the problem because it appears, at first glance, to offer exactly what markets crave: a coded signal linking a vessel's structural and technical features to difficult operating conditions. That signal matters. It helps differentiate ships built for ordinary trade from those intended for harsher service. It shapes chartering conversations, insurance screening, route planning, and even the operator's own view of where the vessel plausibly belongs. But a notation never speaks by itself. It requires interpretation. What kind of ice? What pattern of operation? What degree of escort or support? What margin remains when conditions depart from expectation? Once those questions arrive, the apparent clarity of classification gives way to the messier work of judgement.

This is where rule books stop being self-explanatory and begin to act more like instruments of negotiation. Classification societies publish rules, but rules do not apply themselves. Surveyors interpret them. Operators test their edges. Technical updates move the baseline. Similar facts can be read differently across societies or across time. What looked like settled compliance under one reading may later attract a stricter view, and what owners experience as moving goalposts may from the society's perspective look like a necessary refinement of prudent standards. The friction is not accidental. It is built into a system that must stabilise expectations while also responding to new information, new casualty lessons, and new forms of trade. The rule book moves.

That movement matters commercially because interpretation rarely stays technical for long. A disputed notation, a delayed recommendation, or a disagreement about how a rule applies to a particular operating profile can spill into charterparty negotiations, financing concerns, underwriting hesitation, and project timing. The bottleneck may not look political.

It may feel more maddening than politics because it emerges through specialist language that appears neutral while carrying large economic consequences. A vessel need not lose class to encounter trouble. It need only enter a zone where class no longer delivers the level of reassurance the commercial chain expected it to deliver.

The tension deepens when class and insurance do not align neatly. Their purposes overlap, but not perfectly. Classification aims at technical conformity and baseline integrity over the life of the vessel. Insurance asks a sharper commercial question: how likely is loss, how severe could it become, and what terms will force the operator to carry uncertainty in a way the market can tolerate? Those questions often reinforce each other. Sometimes they diverge. A ship may satisfy class rules and still look operationally exposed in a particular Arctic trade. Less commonly, an insurer may accept a vessel under tightly controlled terms while class-related issues remain in a narrower technical lane. When those regimes pull in different directions, the result is rarely philosophical disagreement. It is extra survey burden, tighter operating limits, delayed approvals, and hard bargaining over who absorbs the gap between technical sufficiency and commercial comfort.

The path ahead follows that gap carefully. It begins with the basic nature of classification as a private technical order and the limits of what it can honestly certify, then turns to the operational meaning carried inside ice class notations once vessels move from paper categories to actual routes and seasons. From there the focus shifts to rule change and interpretation, where technical text becomes commercial friction, before reaching the moments when class and insurance stop reinforcing one another and start generating mismatched signals that reshape access in practice. The thread running through it all is simple but easy to neglect: governance often happens through overlapping judgements rather than through one decisive rule.

The larger significance is strategic. Arctic expansion depends not only on stronger ships or clearer law, but on whether private institutions can agree that a vessel belongs within an acceptable zone of technical and commercial confidence. Classification societies help draw that zone. They do so through rules, surveys, notations, and interpretations that seem specialised until one notices how many other actors organise their decisions around them. If class is treated as a passport, the important question is not whether the passport exists. It is what happens when the vessel presents a valid document at one desk and still finds doubt waiting at the next.

What classification does and does not do

In April 1912, the *Titanic* struck ice in the North Atlantic and sank on her maiden voyage, a disaster so exhaustively retold that it can obscure one of its quieter lessons. A ship may be technically impressive, publicly admired, and institutionally approved, yet still meet conditions that expose the limits of what any prior system of verification could truly promise. That is not a lesson about a single vessel alone. It is a lesson about categories of confidence. The certificate is not the sea.

That distinction matters whenever classification is spoken of as though it were a master key to maritime legitimacy. In commercial life, to say that a vessel is "in class" often carries a satisfying solidity. The phrase sounds complete. It suggests a ship properly designed, competently built, maintained under recognised supervision, and accepted into the orderly world of serious shipping. Much of that implication is justified. But only much. Classification confers something powerful and necessary: a structured, private verification that a vessel meets published technical rules concerning design, construction, and continued condition. It does not certify that the ship is suitable for every trade, safe in every circumstance, or attractive to every insurer, charterer, or regulator. It opens the conversation. It does not end.

Classification works because it supplies a portable technical language. A vessel may be owned in one jurisdiction, built in another, flagged in a third, financed elsewhere, and insured by markets spread across several countries. Without some common framework for evaluating hull structure, machinery, equipment, and maintenance, each commercial actor would have to begin from scratch. Classification societies solve that problem by publishing rules, surveying compliance, assigning class notations, and monitoring whether the vessel continues to meet the standard required to remain in class. Their work reduces uncertainty by making technical integrity legible. That is why banks, charterers, insurers, flag administrations, and port authorities care about class status even when their own purposes differ. They all need a baseline they can recognise.

The importance of that baseline is easiest to see in ordinary commercial decisions. A charterer screening a vessel for service may ask at once whether the ship is in class and whether any class recommendations remain open. A financier assessing asset quality may look for uninterrupted class standing as a sign that the vessel belongs to a disciplined maintenance regime. An underwriter reading a risk submission may treat current class as a threshold issue before any finer discussion about route, crew, or operating philosophy begins. In these settings, class behaves like a passport. It does not guarantee welcome everywhere, but without it many doors do not open at all. The passport matters.

Yet a passport is not a biography. Classification does not tell the whole story of a ship, and it is crucial to be exact about what it does not do. It does not serve as insurance. It does not promise that loss will not occur, nor that claims will be limited if they do. It does not replace statutory certification issued under the authority of the flag state, even though classification societies often perform delegated work that supports statutory compliance. It does not judge whether a proposed voyage is commercially wise, politically acceptable, or financeable on workable terms. Nor does it ensure that a vessel meeting the rules for one service can prudently undertake a much harsher one merely because the notation looks reassuring. Classification verifies conformity to a technical rule set. That is a substantial achievement. It is also a bounded one.

The distinction from statutory certification deserves particular care because the two are often blurred in practice. Statutory certification concerns compliance with public legal requirements deriving from flag-state obligations and international conventions. Classification concerns compliance with the society's own technical rules governing matters such as structure, machinery, and continued condition. The two interlock because many flag administrations authorise recognised organisations, often classification societies, to perform surveys and issue or support certificates on their behalf. This arrangement can make class appear almost sovereign in effect. But the legal source of authority remains different. One rests in the state's public responsibilities. The other rests in a private technical order whose force comes from commercial reliance and institutional trust. They overlap heavily, but they are not the same thing.

The distinction from insurance is just as important. A class society asks whether the vessel meets technical rules and remains in a condition consistent with those rules. An insurer asks whether the proposed exposure - vessel, trade, route, operator, season, support arrangements, liabilities - presents a tolerable chance and scale of loss at a price and on terms the market is willing to bear. The difference in purpose shapes the difference in judgement. A vessel may be fully in class and still be treated by underwriters as a hard risk because the intended voyage, the operator's records, the crewing profile, or the remoteness of support makes the exposure commercially unattractive. Conversely, an insurer may sometimes accept a risk under narrow terms while still paying close attention to technical issues not because class is irrelevant, but because class is only one piece of the larger puzzle. Technical conformity and commercial insurability overlap without merging.

A named example helps bring that limit into focus. When the *Crystal Serenity* prepared for its August 2016 transit through the Northwest Passage, its viability did not depend on class standing alone. A vessel of that size carrying passengers in remote waters raised broader questions: route discipline, support arrangements, emergency planning, communications, medical contingencies, crew preparedness, and the management of severe consequences if something went wrong far from easy assistance. Current class was necessary because a ship lacking it would already have struggled for legitimacy. It was insufficient because neither markets nor counterparties could responsibly stop there. The voyage demanded an institutional chain longer than one technical passport.

This is why classification has such a peculiar authority. It is neither everything nor a formality. Commercial actors treat it as indispensable because it solves a real problem of comparability. A shipowner's self-description is not enough. A bank cannot rely on confidence alone. An insurer cannot assume that a vessel's claimed condition reflects reality. A charterer cannot inspect every structural detail personally. Class provides a trusted intermediary: a structured method of rule-based verification that travels across markets and over time. Trust, in this setting, appears in visible behaviours and records. Surveys are completed. Recommendations are tracked. Notations are maintained. Repairs are evidenced. Status changes are reported. The vessel remains within a living regime of oversight rather than drifting into technical obscurity.

Still, classification's power can tempt commercial overreading. Operators sometimes speak as though being in class settles arguments that it only begins. Charterers and insurers sometimes lean so heavily on class that they forget how much lies beyond it. The attraction is easy to understand. Class compresses immense technical complexity into digestible signals. It makes screening faster. It reduces transaction costs. It gives dispersed actors a basis for initial confidence. Efficiency likes shorthand. The danger begins when shorthand becomes substitute. A vessel can satisfy the baseline while still being badly matched to a proposed Arctic trade, poorly crewed for remote operations, weakly supported ashore, or managed by a company whose documentary discipline masks operational fragility. Class does not reveal all of that, because it was never designed to.

This limitation is not a flaw in the sense of institutional failure. It is a consequence of function. Classification is strong precisely because it does not try to do everything. It verifies against rules. It does not claim omniscience about every commercial or operational context into which a vessel may later be placed. The trouble arises when others demand from class more than it can honestly provide. Once that happens, disappointment sets in. Owners experience additional surveys, insurer reservations, or charterparty conditions as though class has somehow failed to deliver the comfort they expected. In truth, class delivered what it was built to deliver: baseline technical legitimacy. The rest belongs to other regimes of judgement.

A second named example illustrates this point from the world of high-profile casualty rather than polar trade. After the *Costa Concordia* grounded off Giglio in January 2012, no serious observer concluded that classification had been intended to prevent every form of navigational misjudgement, command failure, or emergency response breakdown that later became central to analysis of the loss. And yet the casualty intensified attention on the broader relationship between formal technical status and practical operational safety. It reminded markets that a ship can satisfy many technical expectations and still suffer disaster through failures of conduct, culture, or decision-making. Class remained necessary. It was plainly not sufficient. The event reinforced an old truth maritime commerce prefers to remember only after loss: integrity of structure is not the same thing as integrity of operation.

This is especially important in Arctic contexts because harsh environments punish any confusion between baseline and guarantee. A ship may carry an ice-related notation, remain in class, and still confront conditions more severe, dynamic, or operationally demanding than the notation alone can resolve. The technical rules tell outsiders something valuable about design intent and recognised capability. They do not ensure wise route choice, good timing, strong bridge judgement, reliable support arrangements, or conservative corporate decision-making under commercial pressure. In difficult waters, these surrounding questions gain commercial weight quickly. Charterers use class as a screening tool, but not the final one. Insurers treat class as a starting point, not a conclusion. Flag administrations rely on class, but still operate within a statutory frame. Each institution takes the passport and asks for more.

One can see why the misunderstanding persists. Classification appears objective in a way that human judgement often does not. Published rules, survey intervals, technical notation, and status confirmation all carry an appealing clarity. They seem to promise a stable answer to the question of whether a ship belongs in serious commerce. Compared with the more contestable language of underwriting appetite or the less tidy realities of onboard practice, class looks firm. That firmness is real, but partial. It tells us that the vessel has met and maintained compliance with a rule-governed technical order. It does not tell us whether the surrounding web of operational, contractual, environmental, and liability conditions makes the specific venture prudent.

A limitation must be admitted from the other side as well. Markets and counterparties can sometimes underuse class by treating it as mere routine, an entry ticket too ordinary to deserve analytical attention. That is also a mistake. Because classification provides the baseline on which so much else depends, changes in class status, outstanding recommendations, notation limits, or survey concerns can have disproportionate commercial effects. Something that looks technical and internal can become the hinge on which insurance, chartering, financing, or route permission turns. The passport may not tell the whole story, but its condition still matters enormously.

And yet this limitation only clarifies the central point. The right way to understand classification is neither to worship it nor to dismiss it. It is to see it as a disciplined private system for verifying design, construction, and maintenance against published rules, embedded in a wider institutional chain. It is a source of credibility, not the whole of credibility. It is a precondition of legitimacy, not legitimacy in full. It interlocks with statutory certification because states need reliable technical intermediaries. It interlocks with insurance because markets need a technical baseline before they price broader exposure. It interlocks with chartering and finance because counterparties need portable signals of order. But interlocking is not identity. Each regime asks a different question.

This difference becomes commercially decisive when operators mistake one answer for all answers. A vessel may be proudly described as in class and technically compliant, only to face insurer demands for further surveys, charterer hesitation over route suitability, or contractual restrictions reflecting concerns untouched by class status alone. Owners often experience this as duplication. Sometimes it is duplication. More often it is overlap born of different institutional purposes. The class society asks, in effect, whether the vessel conforms to the relevant rules and remains technically in order. Others ask what that conformity means for a particular voyage, at a particular time, in a particular environment, with a particular operator and consequence profile. The second question cannot be abolished by the first.

The quiet motif returns because the passport remains the right image if handled carefully. It establishes identity within a recognised order. It speeds passage through certain gates. It reassures strangers that the holder belongs to a legitimate system. But it does not guarantee admission everywhere, under every condition, or without further scrutiny. Arctic commerce especially resists such simplification. The more demanding the trade, the more other institutions insist on reading beyond the passport to the conduct, support, route, and liabilities surrounding it.

The crucial question, then, is not whether class matters. It plainly does, and no serious operator can treat it lightly. The harder question is how much other actors think they still need to know once the passport has been produced - and what happens commercially when the answer is much more than the owner expected.

Ice class categories and operational meanings

In September 2018, the *Venta Maersk* completed its trial passage through the Northern Sea Route and promptly became shorthand for a larger commercial idea: if a container ship could move through Arctic waters under controlled conditions, perhaps the route itself had crossed some threshold from specialist possibility to broader plausibility. That reading was always incomplete. What mattered to charterers, insurers, and technical reviewers was not only that the ship had made the voyage, but what kind of vessel it was understood to be, what conditions its design and class status were meant to contemplate, and how much room remained between its notation on paper and the ice it might actually meet. The notation travels first.

That is the quiet force of ice class. It compresses a great deal of technical judgement into a signal others can use quickly. A charterer scanning a fleet list, an underwriter reading a submission, a broker assembling a market approach, or a terminal operator wondering how much comfort to take from a vessel's specification will often begin with the ice-related notation because it seems to answer a simple question: what kind of ice service is this ship meant for? Yet the answer is only simple at a distance. Ice class categories encode expectations about structural strength, machinery protection, and intended operating conditions, but they do not abolish context. They indicate capability within assumptions. They do not promise safety without limit.

This distinction is the heart of the subject. Ice class belongs to a technical language of comparative confidence. It helps markets separate vessels built for ordinary service from those prepared for harsher conditions. It tells others that the ship's hull, propulsion arrangement, scantlings, and relevant supporting systems were assessed against rules designed for some defined degree of ice exposure. That matters enormously. Without such categories, every operator claiming Arctic readiness would have to invent its own vocabulary of adequacy, and commercial screening would become slower, cruder, and far more vulnerable to wishful description. Ice class makes comparison possible. It does not make judgement unnecessary.

The practical meaning of an ice class notation begins with intended operating conditions rather than with heroic imagery. A stronger notation signals that the vessel was designed with more demanding ice interaction in mind, but that interaction remains bounded by the assumptions of the relevant rules and by how the ship is actually used. Class categories are not simply medals for toughness. They are planning tools. They help define where a vessel can plausibly trade, in what season, with what support, at what speed of confidence, and with what constraints likely to follow from insurers, charterers, or public authorities. The stronger the notation, the wider the field may appear. Even then, the field is never infinite. Ice class says something serious. It never says everything.

That is why the operational meaning of ice class emerges most clearly when others begin to act on it. A charterer may treat a particular notation as the minimum threshold for considering a vessel for a northern service. An insurer may use the same notation as an initial screening device before asking whether the operator's route plan, crew, support arrangements, and maintenance record justify broader confidence. A port or terminal may rely on it when deciding whether additional conditions or assistance requirements are warranted. None of these actors' mistakes ice class for a full risk assessment. Each uses it as an organised first cut. The stamp on the file becomes a gate in the chain of access.

This first cut matters because Arctic risk punishes vague claims of capability. A vessel's brochure can praise reinforced structure, advanced propulsion, or cold-weather preparation. Ice class translates such claims into a recognised and reviewable form. It tells counterparties that a published rule set has been applied and that continued class standing depends on maintaining the relevant condition. Trust appears here as a visible administrative fact: notation assigned, surveys completed, recommendations tracked, status maintained. The value of ice class lies partly in this discipline of traceability. It gives others something firmer than marketing language and less cumbersome than a full technical dossier.

And yet the very usefulness of ice class creates a recurring misunderstanding. Because the notation is legible and portable, it is often asked to carry more meaning than it can honestly bear. A vessel with an ice class notation may be spoken of as though it were thereby fit for "the Arctic" in general, as though one harsh environment were a single operating category rather than a spectrum of changing ice regimes, seasonal patterns, support conditions, and route-specific hazards. This is the mistake. Ice class does not certify a ship for all ice in all circumstances. It links a vessel to an intended band of operating assumptions. Once the actual conditions depart materially from those assumptions, the notation still matters, but its comforting simplicity begins to dissolve.

One can see this when comparing paper capability with operational choice. A vessel may hold a respectable ice notation and still be commercially limited to certain routes, seasons, escort assumptions, or speed profiles. A charterer may accept it for shoulder-season service but not for more demanding periods. An insurer may agree to cover voyages in specified areas while insisting on prior approval for movement into heavier conditions. The notation has not failed. It has been read correctly. It has supplied a baseline from which others can define the margins within which they remain comfortable. Operational reality always adds qualifiers.

A named example helps clarify this. The *Christophe de Margerie*, delivered in 2017 for Arctic LNG service associated with the Yamal project, entered public discussion not merely as another ship with an ice notation, but as a vessel whose entire design concept was tied to demanding northern service. Its significance lay in the combination of purpose-built technical features, specialised operating context, and the institutional expectation that the vessel's notation would be read alongside route assumptions, infrastructure support, and industrial discipline. Here the notation did not stand alone as a symbol. It sat inside a wider operational proposition. That is exactly how ice class works at its most commercially meaningful: not as a self-sufficient guarantee, but as one highly important part of a larger chain of assurance.

The need for that larger chain explains why insurers and charterers treat ice class as a screening tool rather than a final answer. Screening is powerful precisely because it is preliminary. A charterer looking to reduce uncertainty in a crowded market may begin by excluding tonnage lacking the notation thought appropriate for the intended service. An underwriter may do much the same, declining to entertain proposals that fall below an internal threshold before even reaching more detailed analysis. This use of ice class is practical rather than philosophical. It saves time, imposes discipline, and narrows the field to vessels that at least begin from an accepted technical baseline. But once a ship passes the screen, more searching questions follow immediately. What crew will it carry? What season is proposed? What support is available? What prior experience exists? What happens if the ice proves less cooperative than expected? Screening opens the file. It does not close it.

This is why a higher ice class notation often improves commercial position without erasing scrutiny. The vessel may gain access to discussions from which weaker tonnage is excluded. It may secure a more serious hearing from charterers or a less sceptical initial reception from markets. It may reduce the burden of proving some aspects of technical adequacy because the notation itself already encodes a recognised level of structural and operational expectation. Yet stronger notation can also raise the commercial stakes. A ship built for more demanding service may attract bolder proposals, tighter schedules, or counterparties tempted to treat technical capability as permission for aggressive operating assumptions. In that sense, the very strength of the notation can become a source of new pressure. Capability invites ambition.

The gap between technical classification and practical safety is especially stark when ice class is confused with immunity from poor judgement. No notation can prevent an operator from choosing a bad window, underestimating support limitations, relying on weak route advice, or allowing commercial pressure to erode conservative decision thresholds. No notation can ensure that a bridge team interprets changing conditions well, that machinery remains reliable under sustained stress, or that emergency arrangements will function as hoped when distance and cold stretch every response. Ice class improves the technical basis on which a vessel enters difficult waters. It does not control all the human and environmental variables that decide what happens once the voyage begins.

A second named example shows how the shorthand can mislead when public excitement runs ahead of institutional caution. The *Crystal Serenity* transit through the Northwest Passage in August 2016 encouraged the broad suggestion that vessels beyond the traditional polar fleet might increasingly treat Arctic waters as commercially manageable. But any serious market reader would have recognised that the significance of such a voyage depended not only on the ship's technical standing but on the extraordinary density of planning, support, and contingency thought surrounding it. The lesson was not that class or notation had made the Arctic ordinary. It was that even highly visible, highly prepared voyages still had to build far beyond the notation if they were to appear tolerable to multiple stakeholders.

That is the practical meaning of ice class in commercial life: it tells others how to begin thinking, not how to stop. A vessel's notation may suggest where it can plausibly trade, but "plausibly" is doing heavy work in that sentence. Plausibility changes with the nature of the cargo, the season, the support infrastructure, the legal and insurance context, the operator's own record, and the tolerance of the counterparties involved. A notation that appears sufficient for one trade can look marginal for another. The same vessel may be welcomed by one charterer and declined by another, not because its class has changed, but because their assumptions about acceptable exposure differ. Ice class is stable in the file. Its meaning moves in the market.

A credible limitation should be admitted. Commercial actors sometimes overstate the authority of ice class, but they can also understate it. In the effort to emphasise that notation is not a guarantee, one might slide into the opposite error and treat it as little more than a formal hurdle. That would be wrong. Ice class can materially shape a vessel's operational horizon. It affects structural design, machinery arrangements, cost, maintenance demands, survey intensity, and the whole commercial envelope within which the ship is likely to be marketed and insured. It is not decorative. It is a serious technical commitment with lasting commercial consequences.

Still, that limitation only strengthens the central argument. The more important ice class is, the more important it becomes to understand its boundaries correctly. It offers recognised evidence of technical preparation for defined ice conditions. It does not certify universal prudence, universal insurability, or universal freedom to operate wherever ambition points. The classification society measures one kind of readiness. Charterers, insurers, and others then convert that readiness into operational permission, price, and constraint according to their own purposes. Multiple private regimes read the same notation and draw different practical lines from it.

This is where assumptions become commercial facts. A charterer may infer schedule reliability from a notation and later find that the ship's real operating margin in variable ice is narrower than hoped. An insurer may accept the notation as strong evidence of baseline suitability and still insist on tighter deductibles or route controls because the severity of a loss remains troubling. A broker may present the ship as appropriately classed for the trade and then spend the rest of the negotiation answering questions that the notation alone cannot quiet. The notation travels first because it is legible. The argument starts because it is incomplete.

The quiet motif returns because the stamp on the file remains the right image if handled with care. It is a compact signal, a technical shorthand, a commercial opener. It tells others that the vessel belongs in a recognisable category of preparation. But once the file is opened, the stamp must share authority with route, season, crew, support, history, and the market's own appetite for doubt. Arctic commerce repeatedly rewards those who can live with that layered reality and punishes those who mistake a category of class for a promise of consequence-free passage.

The real test, then, is not whether a vessel holds an ice class notation. It is what everyone else decides that notation means when the ship is proposed for a specific trade, in a specific window, under specific conditions - and how quickly confidence narrows when the ice turns out to be more than the category invited them to imagine.

Rule change, interpretation, and disputes

On 1 January 2017, when the Polar Code entered into force through the IMO framework, many shipowners and technical managers were reminded of an old maritime truth: rules never arrive alone. They bring interpretation with them. A new requirement may appear in published text with the reassuring firmness of print, yet its practical meaning only emerges when classification societies, surveyors, insurers, flag administrations, charterers, and operators begin to apply it to real vessels under real commercial pressure. The rule is written once. It is read many times.

That is why operators so often speak of moving goalposts even when no one has acted in obvious bad faith. From the outside, a rule change can look like a clean improvement in safety or comparability. From inside a fleet, it may feel like a shifting technical boundary with direct consequences for docking schedules, retrofit costs, charter commitments, and insurance conversations. A vessel that appeared comfortably compliant under yesterday's reading may suddenly sit in a more awkward light once the same wording is filtered through a revised class circular, a new survey emphasis, or a changed understanding of what prudent operation now requires. The margin narrows first on paper.

Classification rules must change. That is not a defect of the system but part of its purpose. Ships evolve, routes change, casualty lessons accumulate, materials and machinery improve, and operational expectations harden under the pressure of experience. A technical rule set that never moved would quickly become untrustworthy, especially in difficult environments such as the Arctic where design assumptions and actual operating practice often expose one another with unusual force. Rule change is therefore built into the life of class. The trouble lies not in change itself, but in the path between text and application. The text may suggest one level of certainty. Practice reveals how much still depends on judgement.

This dependence on judgement is easy to underestimate because classification presents itself through highly formal means: published rules, notations, survey procedures, circulars, review processes. It looks systematic because it is systematic. Yet no technical order of this scale can eliminate interpretation. Terms such as adequate protection, intended service, satisfactory condition, or compliance with the relevant requirements acquire meaning only when surveyors inspect actual equipment, when plan approvers review real designs, when owners propose particular operating profiles, and when societies decide how much weight to place on a specific feature or deficiency in context. The same vessel can therefore be understood through slightly different emphases depending on who reads the file and why. The margin lives there.

Ice-related classification sharpens this problem because harsh conditions magnify the significance of seemingly narrow technical choices. A rule about hull reinforcement, machinery protection, winterisation, or operating assumptions may sound precise until a vessel presents a hybrid service profile, a retrofit solution, or a proposed route that sits near the edge of what the notation was originally intended to support. Then the question ceases to be merely what the words say. It becomes what the words mean for this ship, in this service, with this maintenance history, under this operator's discipline. Interpretation enters not as an optional extra, but as the unavoidable core of governance.

A named example illustrates the broader mechanism, even beyond the Arctic proper. After the *Exxon Valdez* grounding in Alaska in March 1989, technical, regulatory, and commercial expectations across tanker operations did not simply shift through one statute or one set of engineering changes. They shifted because institutions re-read existing assumptions in the harsher light of catastrophe. Features and practices that had sat within the broad range of acceptability began to attract new suspicion. Rule books changed in places, but so did interpretation. Survey focus sharpened. Underwriters asked different questions. Owners encountered a more demanding reading of what prudent operation required. The text mattered. The post-casualty mood of reading mattered too.

This helps explain why operators often experience class interactions less as mechanical compliance than as a dialogue with consequences. A shipowner may point to the wording of a rule and argue that a design feature, maintenance choice, or operational arrangement falls within its terms. A surveyor or society may respond that, in the circumstances, a stricter reading is appropriate or further evidence is needed. Neither side is necessarily dissembling. The disagreement may arise because the rule was never self-executing. It needed a judgment about equivalence, adequacy, service intent, or risk concentration. The owner's frustration is understandable. So is the society's caution. In difficult trades, the cost of generous interpretation can be paid later by many parties.

A second named example helps show how these arguments become commercially real. When the *Venta Maersk* completed its trial Northern Sea Route passage in 2018, the public discussion leaned towards symbolism and future possibility. Commercial actors drew a harder lesson. As Arctic trading concepts moved from demonstration towards repetition, class-related questions became less about one ship's celebrated voyage and more about how notations, operating assumptions, and technical boundaries would be interpreted when applied to wider and more routine service. A trial can tolerate exceptional attention. A trade cannot rely on exception forever. Once repetition is proposed, societies, insurers, and charterers begin to test whether the technical classification comfortably supports the operational ambition or merely sits alongside it uneasily.

That unease often takes the form of disputes that appear technical at first and then spread outward into commercial bottlenecks. A disagreement over whether a given arrangement satisfies a rule may delay delivery. A debate over the scope of a notation may postpone fixture approval. A survey recommendation interpreted by one party as manageable may be treated by another as evidence of unresolved risk. Owners may discover that even when class is maintained, counterparties or insurers read the underlying technical discussion as a warning signal. The bottleneck emerges because commercial chains dislike ambiguity. They do not wait patiently for engineers to enjoy a principled disagreement. They tighten terms, demand clarifications, or walk away.

This is why technical disputes deserve far more attention than they usually receive in public discussions of Arctic access. They are not side-arguments among specialists while the real business occurs elsewhere. They are often the real business. A dispute over rule interpretation can determine whether a vessel sails on schedule, whether a project secures cover on workable terms, whether a charterparty is signed, whether a lender relaxes, or whether a terminal accepts the ship without added conditions. Governance happens here through timing, confidence, and administrative friction. A vessel does not need to lose class to feel the force of class interpretation. It need only enter a zone of unresolved meaning.

Surveyors play a particularly important role in this zone because they carry the burden of turning general rule language into specific technical judgement. Their work is not merely descriptive. It is translational. They decide whether observed condition, repair history, installation quality, crew knowledge, or operational practice supports the level of confidence the notation is supposed to signal. One surveyor may lean towards formal sufficiency, another towards precautionary insistence. Societies strive for consistency, but complete uniformity is unrealistic where conditions are varied and judgement is inescapable. Owners know this, which is one reason they sometimes complain that class depends too much on the person who arrives on the quay. The complaint is not always fair. It is rarely baseless.

The practical language surrounding these encounters reveals how authority accumulates. A recommendation may begin as a technical note and become a commercial obstacle once insurers or charterers treat it as material. A clarification request may appear procedural until it delays a certificate, a notation confirmation, or a renewal discussion. An interpretation note or circular may seem like modest administrative housekeeping until owners realise it alters the way existing fleet arrangements will now be read. Technical governance often feels most powerful when it refuses theatricality. It changes what can proceed by changing how text applies.

A credible limitation should be admitted. Owners are not always wrong when they complain about inconsistency or moving goalposts. Classification societies can differ in emphasis. Surveyors can read similar facts through different levels of caution. Rule changes can arrive at commercially awkward moments. In specialised trades, especially Arctic-related ones, technical standards can evolve faster than fleets or budgets can comfortably adapt. Some disputes do reflect institutional conservatism shading into overreach, or at least a poor appreciation of the commercial strain imposed by late or expansive interpretation.

And yet that limitation does not weaken the larger point. It clarifies why interpretation matters so much. If rules were entirely mechanical, disputes would reduce to simple error and correction. In reality, class operates in a world where technical adequacy, intended service, casualty memory, operator credibility, and future consequence all inform the reading of text. Societies do not only administer written standards. They guard the trust others place in those standards. That role almost guarantees some conservatism, especially when the vessel or trade sits near a difficult boundary. The owner's complaint about moving goalposts is often, from the society's perspective, a complaint that the trust function is being taken seriously.

The issue grows sharper where class interacts with other private regimes. A society may accept an owner's technical explanation, but the mere existence of the dispute can still trouble insurers or charterers. Conversely, an owner may resolve the class point formally and still find that underwriters continue to ask whether the underlying concern suggests something wider about maintenance culture or operational discipline. The disagreement therefore travels. It moves from rule book to insurance file, from survey exchange to contractual caution. This is why operators learn that winning a technical point is not always enough. They must also manage how the argument looks to everyone else.

One can think of class interpretation as a form of disciplined reading under conditions of incomplete certainty. The rule provides a framework. The surveyor reads condition. The society reads service intent. The owner reads commercial necessity. The insurer reads loss potential. The charterer reads reliability. None of these readings is fully independent. Each reacts to the others. What begins as a technical issue can therefore acquire a second life as a commercial narrative about whether the vessel is comfortably within the expected envelope or pressing against it in ways that may later matter more than anyone would like. The most expensive sentence in shipping is often not a prohibition. It is a qualified acceptance.

That fact helps explain why some of the most consequential Arctic governance happens through documents that look secondary to outsiders.

Guidance notes, survey reports, interpretation circulars, recommendations, conditions attached to notation, internal technical correspondence: these are not grand sources of law, yet they shape access with remarkable force. They tell operators what will now be expected, what remains doubtful, where extra evidence is required, and what must be altered before the market will stop asking questions. The rule book stays open on the desk. What counts is how the page is read.

The deeper lesson is that class rules do not merely constrain through their formal content. They constrain through the institutional confidence needed to apply them. That confidence depends on continuous revision, unevenly distributed judgment, and the refusal to treat difficult environments as though text alone can settle every borderline case. Operators often want a stable threshold. Classification can provide many thresholds, but it cannot abolish the boundary cases where interpretation, experience, and caution must do the harder work. Those are the places where technical governance becomes commercially visible.

The quiet motif returns because the margin remains the truest image. Owners want to know how much room the rule leaves them. Surveyors want to know how much room the condition of the vessel really deserves. Insurers want to know how much room remains before a technical uncertainty becomes a claims problem. Charterers want to know how much room exists between notation and delay. All are, in different ways, arguing over the same narrow space between text and consequence.

The unresolved question is not whether rule change and interpretation are necessary. They plainly are. The harder question is who gets to define the margin when words no longer settle the matter by themselves - and how much commercial power quietly sits with the party who can say that the rule has not changed, only its meaning in this case.

When class and insurance pull in different directions

In August 2016, the *Crystal Serenity* left Seward, Alaska, for its transit through the Northwest Passage carrying a form of reassurance that looked, to many observers, almost complete. The ship belonged to the formal world of recognised technical legitimacy. It could present a coherent documentary identity. It could point to planning, support arrangements, and the kinds of institutional preparation that distinguish managed ambition from bluff. And yet none of that meant that insurers were obliged to regard the voyage with the same level of comfort that class status might seem to imply. The vessel could be technically respectable and still commercially unsettling. The file said yes. The quote hesitated.

That hesitation reveals one of the most important frictions in Arctic governance. Classification and insurance are close neighbours, but they are not twins. They inspect some of the same evidence, care about some of the same failures, and rely on one another's signals. Still, they ask different questions for different reasons. Class asks whether a vessel's design, construction, and maintained condition satisfy a rule-governed technical baseline. Insurance asks whether a loss is likely enough, severe enough, uncertain enough, or awkward enough in consequence that cover should be priced tightly, narrowed, conditioned, or withheld. Those questions overlap. They do not coincide. The split matters.

A vessel may therefore meet class rules and still be treated as a hard risk by insurers without any contradiction in the formal sense. The classification society has verified conformity to its published technical regime and maintained oversight through survey and notation. The insurer, looking at the same vessel, may worry about the intended trade, the route, the season, the operator's record, the crew, the support network, the concentration of exposure in the region, or the practical costs of response if the voyage deteriorates. In Arctic settings, those extra concerns carry unusual force because the consequences of a moderate failure can widen quickly. Technical adequacy does not abolish severity. The stamp is not enough.

The reverse situation is less common but equally revealing. A vessel may occupy a technically awkward position in relation to class discussions - perhaps because of a survey issue, an interpretation dispute, a pending recommendation, or a design feature under closer review - and still remain insurable under carefully bounded terms because the insurer believes the wider operational picture is disciplined enough to tolerate the discomfort. This is not because insurers are less serious than class. It is because their decision horizon differs. They may be willing to proceed with tighter deductibles, narrower cover, extra reporting requirements, or voyage-specific conditions where a classification question remains contained and managed rather than structurally alarming. Insurance is not a seal of technical perfection. It is a priced decision about tolerable exposure.

That difference in purpose explains the recurring mismatch. Classification aims at baseline integrity over the vessel's life as a technical object within a recognised order of construction, maintenance, and survey. Insurance aims at loss prevention and cost control across a portfolio of uncertain events. The class society wants to preserve the credibility of its rules and the reliability of the notation others rely upon. The insurer wants to avoid unpleasant surprise, control severity, and allocate uncertainty back to the insured where confidence runs thin. One institution is organised around technical conformity. The other is organised around financial consequence. They often reinforce each other because bad ships can be expensive ships. But where the trade is harsh, the operator ambitious, or the route unusually exposed, their incentives can pull apart.

The practical result is often a second layer of scrutiny imposed on vessels that owners believe have already proved enough. A ship may be fully in class, carry the appropriate notations, and still face insurer demands for additional surveys, more restrictive navigation terms, clearer route thresholds, or specific evidence of crew competence and support arrangements. Owners frequently experience this as duplication. Sometimes it is. More often, it is a sign that multiple private regimes are each protecting a different margin. The classification society has answered one question: does the vessel meet the relevant technical standard? The insurer asks another: does that answer reduce expected loss enough for this voyage, this season, and this operator? The second question can remain difficult even when the first is settled.

A named example shows why. When A.P. Moller-Maersk sent the *Venta Maersk* through the Northern Sea Route in 2018, the voyage drew attention because it suggested that container traffic through Arctic waters might be more than speculative conversation. Yet the fact of a technically credible vessel making a managed passage did not mean that insurers were suddenly obliged to treat the route as routine. Class and technical preparation could establish that the ship belonged to a serious category of commercial tonnage. Insurance still had to ask whether repeated service, clustered seasonal exposure, support limitations, and the possibility of costly delay or casualty made the trade commercially attractive on ordinary terms. The vessel could clear one gate and still find another partly closed.

This is where operational limits enter. Insurers who do not dispute a vessel's class standing may nonetheless impose warranties about seasonality, geographic scope, ice information services, escort support, reporting obligations, or prior approval for certain waters. These limits do not accuse the vessel of technical inadequacy. They express distrust of the wider operating envelope. A ship technically capable of a difficult passage may still be insured only for narrower conditions than the owner hoped to exploit. Class says the vessel belongs in a broad technical category.

Insurance redraws the commercial version of that category according to its own appetite. The corridor shrinks.

Extra surveys often serve as the hinge between these regimes. A classification survey confirms continued conformity to class requirements. An insurer's additional survey may pursue a different emphasis: maintenance culture, evidence of cold-weather preparedness, practical reliability of emergency systems, route-specific vulnerabilities, outstanding technical points that matter less to class than to claims severity, or the operator's responsiveness to awkward findings. The existence of the second survey is itself a message. It tells the owner that class status, though necessary, has not resolved the insurer's uncertainty. It also tells counterparties the same thing if the survey becomes a prerequisite for cover or a condition reflected in the policy terms. One desk signs. Another asks for more.

Contract renegotiation often follows from this divergence. Charterers read insurance terms as signals. Financiers do the same. If a vessel is in class but only insurable under tightened conditions, the underlying contract may need to change. Delivery windows may be widened. Ice clauses may be sharpened. Delay allocation may be revisited. Responsibilities for escort, routing advice, survey costs, or off-hire consequences may be reallocated. These are not collateral adjustments. They are the commercial afterlife of a mismatch between technical legitimacy and financial comfort. A vessel owner who thought class would clear the ground may discover that the real negotiation only begins once the insurer reveals what technical compliance has failed to settle.

A second named example illustrates the broader principle from another angle. After the *Costa Concordia* casualty off Giglio in January 2012, no serious observer doubted that the issues raised went far beyond a simple class question. The loss sharpened insurer attention to operational conduct, emergency preparedness, liability severity, and the gap between formal technical status and real-world exposure. The lesson travelled well beyond passenger shipping. It reinforced the idea that a ship can stand within technical order and still generate extraordinary loss because the surrounding system of operation, response, and consequence proves weaker than the notation suggested to casual readers. Class remained central. Insurance became more sceptical about what class alone could settle. That scepticism endures most strongly in severe environments.

The mismatch can run the other way as well, though owners mention it less often in public. A vessel may satisfy insurers under a tightly structured arrangement while remaining caught in technical discussion with class over repairs, interpretations, recommendations, or notation details that have not yet matured into a loss concern of immediate commercial weight. The insurer may proceed because its wording, deductible structure, and operational conditions already confine the exposure. The class society, by contrast, may still insist that the technical matter be resolved before it is willing to confirm a particular status or notation. Here, the vessel looks commercially tolerable but technically unfinished. Again, there is no true contradiction. Each institution protects a different kind of order.

This difference becomes especially acute in Arctic service because the same notation can be read through two distinct logics. For class, an ice-related notation expresses a rule-governed view of design and intended operating conditions. For insurance, the same notation is only one input among many. It helps sort vessels into categories, but it does not decide how the market should feel about remoteness, rescue, pollution exposure, seasonal clustering, infrastructure scarcity, or the operator's willingness to respect limits when commercial pressure mounts. Owners sometimes mistake ice class for a financial argument. It is not. It is a technical fact that financial institutions then interpret.

A credible limitation should be acknowledged. The divergence between class and insurance can be overstated if every additional insurer question is treated as evidence of deep institutional conflict. Much of the time, the systems work in rough harmony. A vessel with sound class standing, clean surveys, disciplined maintenance, strong crew, and a conservative operating profile often finds that class and insurance reinforce one another quite effectively. The owner experiences not contradiction but layering: the technical baseline supports commercial confidence, and the commercial confidence rewards the technical discipline. In such cases, the regimes do not pull apart. They lock together.

And yet the very existence of those easier cases makes the harder ones more instructive. Where a voyage is ambitious, the environment harsh, the route thinly proven, the support structure sparse, or the operator's records less persuasive, the gap between class and insurance reveals how private governance really works. No single institution holds a monopoly on permission. Access depends on alignment across several regimes, each carrying its own vocabulary of caution. A vessel can satisfy one and still be slowed by another. To the owner, this feels like friction. To the system, it is the point. Multiple lines of judgement reduce the chance that one comfortable answer will be asked to do too much work.

This layered caution explains why private governance can constrain access more effectively than formal prohibition. A state need not ban a route. A classification society need not withdraw class. An insurer need not refuse cover outright. It is enough that the vessel remains technically legitimate while becoming commercially awkward: more expensive to insure, more tightly bound by conditions, more costly to charter, more closely watched by surveyors, and more exposed to counterparty renegotiation. The ship can sail in theory and still find that theory has become expensive. Constraint often arrives by accumulation rather than decree.

The operator's response usually reveals whether the mismatch is temporary or structural. Some companies accept the extra surveys, close the technical points, improve the evidence, narrow their ambitions, and gradually bring class and insurance back into more comfortable alignment. Others complain, negotiate, and hope the market's anxiety will soften before their own practices need to change. The first group often learns that institutions can be exacting but persuadable. The second learns that formal technical legitimacy does not force financial comfort into existence. One passport at one desk does not guarantee passage through the next.

The deeper significance of this mismatch is strategic rather than procedural. Arctic access depends on more than building stronger ships or securing the right notation. It depends on whether several private systems, each with distinct incentives, can be persuaded to treat the same vessel and the same voyage as tolerably bounded. Class guards the integrity of the technical baseline. Insurance guards against losses that make that baseline look insufficient in hindsight. Charterers, financiers, and operators then adjust around the space between those judgements. What appears from outside as one commercial decision is often the negotiated product of several partially misaligned regimes.

The quiet motif returns because the stamp remains useful only if one remembers that more than one desk can mark the file. A vessel may present excellent technical credentials and still encounter insurer caution. It may satisfy the insurer under harsh terms and still remain unsettled in class. The important question is not which institution is right in the abstract. It is how their combined caution shapes what the operator can actually do, at what cost, and under what narrowing of practical freedom.

That leaves a harder test than simple compliance. When a vessel is good enough for class but still troubling to insurers, or tolerable to insurers while class remains uneasy, which judgment will the market treat as decisive - and how much Arctic access is really determined in the uncomfortable space where both are only partly satisfied?

Chapter 5

Polar Safety Standards and the Polar Code

On 1 January 2017, the Polar Code entered into force through the IMO framework and changed something more significant than the formal status of a regulatory text. It changed the presumption under which polar operations could be discussed. A voyage north could no longer rely so comfortably on broad claims of seamanship, strong steel, or general marine competence. It had to be explained through a more specific language of planning, equipment, procedures, limitations, and evidence. The manual gained weight.

That shift mattered because the Arctic had already exposed the limits of generic seaworthiness. Ordinary marine concepts could describe a vessel's broad fitness for service, but they struggled to capture what remoteness, sparse search and rescue, severe cold, environmental sensitivity, and delayed external support do to the meaning of an incident. A machinery fault near dense infrastructure and rapid response is one kind of problem. The same fault in polar waters can become something else entirely: slower, larger, harder to contain, and more politically charged. Polar operations therefore did not simply need tougher ships. They needed a distinct institutional grammar.

The central tension lies there. Standards promise order, comparability, and a common threshold for prudent conduct in difficult waters. At the same time, polar conditions resist any fantasy that a written rule can eliminate judgement. Ice shifts. Weather compounds. Human performance changes in cold. Machinery behaves differently under sustained environmental stress. Rescue assumptions remain thin by comparison with easier trades. A standard can force these facts into view, but it cannot fully mechanise the decisions they demand. The manual opens. Someone still has to read the weather.

That is why polar standards matter as governance rather than as good housekeeping. They do not merely advise operators to behave well. They organise what counts as credible preparation, what kinds of evidence must exist before departure, how limitations should be stated, and where responsibility sits when conditions deteriorate. They shape the terms on which flag administrations, port authorities, classification societies, auditors, insurers, and charterers evaluate the same voyage. A planning document, a training record, an operational limitation, or an exemption is never just internal paperwork in this setting. It becomes a signal read by multiple institutions at once.

The stakes are commercial as much as technical. A polar standard can widen access by giving markets a recognisable way to compare operators who would otherwise look opaque or improvisational. It can also narrow access by exposing how much of an operator's confidence depends on assumptions that others do not accept. A company may be legally entitled to proceed yet still find that the evidence demanded by insurers, counterparties, or inspectors has become more exacting because the standard made weak preparation easier to spot. Standards therefore do not sit outside market power. They become one of its main instruments. They reduce information asymmetry, but they also sharpen the consequences of falling short.

This double character explains why compliance in polar trades so often means more than satisfying a checklist. It means producing records that convince sceptical readers that the ship, the crew, the operator, and the support system can function coherently under cold, delay, and uncertainty. A credible polar water operational approach is not valuable because it looks tidy in an audit file. It is valuable because it shows how the operator thinks when the easy assumptions have been removed. Training, drills, maintenance practice, route thresholds, equipment choices, reporting routines, and emergency arrangements all become visible traces of organisational seriousness. If those traces are weak, formal permission may do very little to secure workable commercial terms.

The path ahead follows that seriousness through its most important forms. It begins with the reasons polar operations required a distinct regime at all, then turns to the structure and intent of the Polar Code as the clearest current expression of how risk is made legible in these waters. From there the focus moves into safety management in cold environments, where paperwork either proves itself in practice or reveals its emptiness, before tightening around the practical force of limitations and exemptions once documents start to govern real movement. The argument then widens to the unevenness of enforcement across institutions and jurisdictions, and ends where all such standards eventually arrive in commercial life: as signals to markets and regulators that both enable entry and constrain it.

What makes this especially consequential is that polar standards never operate in a perfectly even field. Harmonisation is the aspiration. Fragmentation remains part of the reality. The same code may be read through different administrative cultures, different levels of technical capacity, different inspection habits, and different appetites for caution. One authority may treat a limitation as a serious operational boundary. Another may treat it more loosely. One market may see an exemption as a bounded and manageable deviation. Another may see it as a warning sign that the legal permission is commercially less reassuring than it looks. Uneven enforcement therefore becomes a source of uncertainty in its own right, and uncertainty is quickly translated into price, conditions, and distrust.

This is why standards in the polar context have a peculiar strategic importance. They are meant to create comparability, but they also create new grounds for differentiation. Operators with disciplined systems, coherent evidence, and a reputation for taking cold-environment limits seriously can turn compliance into a form of reputational capital. Others may satisfy the formal minimum and still struggle because markets, auditors, or charterers suspect that the paper runs ahead of the practice. The manual returns here as a quiet motif. In one company it records a living method. In another it records an aspiration that may not survive pressure.

The real question, then, is not whether the Polar Code and related polar standards matter. They plainly do. The harder question is how much weight should be placed on compliance once every serious actor knows that a respected standard can reveal discipline without ever guaranteeing it. When a voyage is technically allowed, carefully documented, and formally within the rules, what still counts as enough evidence that the operator can live inside the standard rather than merely cite it?

Why polar operations needed a distinct regime

On 1 January 2017, the Polar Code entered into force through the IMO framework, but the real significance of that date had been building for years. By then, it had become increasingly difficult to pretend that ordinary marine concepts, drafted for broader and more forgiving conditions, could carry the full weight of polar operations without strain. Ships were going north with stronger hulls, better communications, and more elaborate support arrangements than earlier generations had known. Yet the institutional grammar surrounding them remained too generic in crucial places. A ship could be seaworthy in the old broad sense and still be dangerously under-prepared for what cold, remoteness, and delay do to ordinary assumptions. The chart was not enough.

That is the central problem. Polar waters do not merely add difficulty to ordinary shipping. They rearrange it. A machinery failure, a navigational error, a communications interruption, or a medical emergency in temperate service may be serious without becoming existential. In polar regions the same initiating event often acquires a longer tail: assistance is farther away, weather windows narrow, evacuation is harder, pollution response is slower, and the environment itself punishes hesitation. A standard framed around general marine competence can recognise danger at a high level. It struggles when the real question is what happens after the first thing goes wrong.

This is why a distinct regime became necessary. The issue was never simply that polar seas were colder, more remote, or more politically sensitive than other waters. The issue was that these features changed the institutional meaning of risk. Generic seaworthiness concepts had been built to assess whether a vessel was fit for an intended voyage judged against hazards reasonably within contemplation. That idea remains powerful. But in polar operations the range of what must be contemplated expands sharply, while the consequences of getting that contemplation wrong grow harder to contain. The standard therefore needed to move from broad fitness towards demonstrable preparedness. A different threshold had to be named.

Remoteness sits at the centre of that threshold because it transforms both prevention and consequence. It is not merely a matter of distance on a chart. It is a practical condition that alters maintenance philosophy, medical planning, route discipline, crew endurance, spare-parts logic, and the credibility of emergency procedures. A ship operating where help is slow cannot rely on the surrounding system to absorb its mistakes in the way a ship in denser maritime corridors often can. This means standards must demand more from the ship and its operator before the voyage begins. They must force planning to carry some of the burden that infrastructure cannot carry later. A remote voyage is judged twice: once before departure, once by whatever happens when support fails to arrive quickly.

Search and rescue limitations make the same point with harsher clarity. Polar operations did not require a distinct regime because rescue in those regions was impossible. They required one because rescue was constrained enough that the ordinary mental shortcuts of shipping became unreliable. In more developed maritime spaces, operators can quietly rely on dense traffic, proximate aviation assets, nearby ports, tugs, hospitals, and layered response systems. In polar waters, those assumptions become fragile. The result is not only slower help. It is a different safety logic altogether. Crew training, passenger planning, equipment choices, communications protocols, and the very decision of whether to proceed under marginal conditions must be shaped by the knowledge that external support may be late, limited, or itself endangered by the environment. Rescue scarcity changes the standard of prudence.

Environmental sensitivity sharpens the case still further. Pollution is always serious. In polar regions it acquires a particular institutional charge because response is difficult, ecosystems are vulnerable, and political scrutiny is intense. A release that might be contained more quickly elsewhere can become a prolonged logistical and reputational crisis in remote cold waters. The consequence is not only ecological. It is legal, financial, and administrative. Standards therefore had to speak more explicitly to prevention and planning in these conditions because the cost of treating the environment as one concern among many had become too high. Sensitivity is not sentiment here. It is a severity multiplier that changes how regulators, insurers, and the public read the same casualty.

A named example shows why broad marine concepts had begun to feel insufficient. The *Exxon Valdez* grounding in Alaska in March 1989 did not occur in high Arctic pack ice, yet it burned into institutional memory a lesson about severe northern environments that later shaped broader thinking. The casualty showed how a maritime loss in cold, environmentally exposed waters could cascade beyond ordinary property damage into long-lived disputes, public outrage, legal change, and a reclassification of what prudent tanker operation should mean near vulnerable coastlines. Its importance here is not that it single-handedly produced polar-specific standards. It is that it revealed, with brutal force, how conventional assumptions about consequence and response could prove inadequate where geography and environment amplify the cost of error. A casualty can redraw the rule.

The move towards polar-specific standards was therefore not a flourish of bureaucratic tidiness. It was a response to a failure of fit. Generic concepts such as seaworthiness, due diligence, prudent seamanship, and proper maintenance remained necessary, but they no longer gave enough guidance where the environment multiplied both hazard and uncertainty. Regulators and markets needed a way to make polar risk more legible through planning, equipment expectations, training, operational limitations, and documentary proof. Legibility matters because without it, private and public actors struggle to compare operators, enforce expectations, or decide whether a voyage deserves to proceed on workable terms. A distinct regime turns vague concern into actionable criteria.

This is the point at which standards stop looking like best practice and start looking like governance. Best practice suggests aspiration. Governance imposes consequences. Once a polar-specific standard exists, it does not merely advise operators to think carefully about cold, ice, or remoteness. It determines what must be documented, what may trigger survey concern, what counts as an adequate operational plan, what training and drills appear credible, how limitations should be expressed, and what insurers or charterers may reasonably expect before they commit. Standards govern because they organise the terms on which other institutions judge the same voyage. A requirement in one document becomes a screening tool in another. The manual leaves the shelf.

That governance function becomes especially visible in the role of evidence. Polar regulation could not rely only on the existence of sound intentions because intentions are difficult to audit and worthless after a casualty unless they left traces in advance. Operators were therefore pushed towards showing rather than merely claiming preparedness. The quality of planning, the coherence of route limitations, the plausibility of emergency arrangements, the specificity of maintenance procedures, the realism of crew drills, and the clarity of decision thresholds all became legible signs of organisational seriousness. A distinct regime was needed because the older generic language often allowed too much to remain implicit. In polar operations, the implicit becomes dangerous quickly.

The role of operator judgement complicates this story in precisely the way that matters most. A polar-specific regime was necessary not because every decision could now be reduced to a rule, but because difficult environments make judgement more consequential and therefore more in need of structure. No code can decide when weather, ice movement, vessel condition, crew fatigue, and commercial pressure combine to make turning back the wiser course. No standard can foresee every local variation in route conditions or every chain of minor problems that produces a major one. Operator judgement remains indispensable. The purpose of the regime is to discipline that judgement: to require that it be trained, documented, bounded, reviewed, and made visible enough that others can trust it without mistaking it for instinct alone.

A second named example helps clarify this point. When the *Crystal Serenity* transited the Northwest Passage in August 2016, the voyage attracted attention because it seemed to compress the age-old dream of polar passage into the idiom of premium travel. Yet the deeper significance lay in how much planning, support logic, and organisational discipline had to be assembled to make the operation appear credible at all. The voyage did not prove that a code could replace judgement. It proved the opposite. It showed that a distinct regime works by forcing judgement into recordable form: route thresholds, support arrangements, contingency planning, medical preparation, and the willingness to acknowledge limitation rather than conceal it beneath spectacle. Standards do not eliminate judgement. They expose whether it has been done properly.

This is also why limitations and operator discretion must be understood together rather than as opposites. Polar standards typically operate by combining general requirements with context-specific judgement. They define the need for planning, capability, training, and environmental protection, but they often leave room for the operator to determine how those needs are met within the actual voyage profile. That flexibility is not a weakness. It is a recognition that polar conditions vary too widely for one-size-fits-all command. Yet flexibility creates its own challenge. The more room left for operator judgement, the more critical it becomes that supporting evidence be persuasive. Standards rely on discretion, then compensate for that reliance by demanding stronger proof that discretion has been exercised seriously.

A credible limitation should be admitted here. One can overstate the novelty of polar-specific regulation by implying that general marine law and practice had nothing useful to say before such regimes emerged. That would be false. Earlier concepts of seaworthiness, prudent navigation, proper manning, and due diligence already contained resources for thinking about harsh environments. Good operators had long understood that cold, ice, and remoteness demanded special care even before those demands were codified more explicitly. The maritime world was not blind until a new code arrived.

And yet the limitation only sharpens the main argument. The problem was not total blindness. It was unevenness. Generic concepts left too much room for inconsistent interpretation, too much dependence on informal culture, and too little comparability across operators and jurisdictions once polar activity became more commercially varied and institutionally visible. A distinct regime became necessary when the costs of leaving those matters implicit began to outweigh the convenience of broad standards. Codification did not invent prudence. It made prudence more portable, more testable, and more enforceable.

This portability matters greatly because polar operations are judged by multiple audiences at once. Flag administrations, port authorities, classification societies, insurers, charterers, auditors, and financiers all need some basis for comparing operators without starting from zero. Polar-specific standards create that basis. They reduce information asymmetry by telling outsiders what evidence to look for and what omissions to treat as warning signs. This does not eliminate disagreement. It narrows the field of plausible argument. An operator can no longer say merely that it has thought carefully about the voyage. It must show what that careful thought produced and how it maps onto recognised expectations.

The strategic significance follows naturally. A distinct regime enables access by making polar risk legible enough for institutions to engage with it. It constrains access by making weak preparation easier to detect and harder to excuse. Those are not contradictory outcomes. They are the two sides of serious governance. Standards allow commercial and regulatory systems to say yes more confidently in some cases and no more clearly in others. The operator who sees only burden has missed half the picture. The operator who sees only opportunity has missed the other half.

The quiet motif returns because the chart remains a useful image of what changed. Before polar-specific standards, a chart and a capable ship could too easily stand in for a fuller argument about what the voyage demanded. After the rise of a distinct regime, the chart still matters, but it must sit inside a thicker record of planning, support, competence, and limitation. Geography has not become less real. It has become institutionally denser.

The harder question, then, is not whether polar operations deserved their own regime. They clearly did. The more difficult question is what should happen when the rule has done all it can do - when the documents are in order, the ship is technically allowed, the plan is credible on paper, and the remaining uncertainty lies exactly where no standard can fully settle it: in the operator's judgement when the polar environment begins to punish the assumptions that made departure seem reasonable.

Structure and intent of the Polar Code

On 1 January 2017, the Polar Code entered into force through the International Maritime Organization framework and altered the practical meaning of a simple question: what does it take for a ship to be considered prepared for polar waters? Before that date, operators, insurers, class societies, and flag administrations could draw on existing conventions, technical rules, and a growing body of specialised practice, but the institutional picture remained uneven. The problem was not a total absence of safety logic. It was the absence of a single recognisable grammar through which polar risk could be described, compared, and challenged across very different vessels, operators, and jurisdictions. The file gained a spine.

That change matters because the Polar Code is often mistaken for something narrower than it is. It is not best understood as a manual for hardy ships in cold places, nor as a decorative add-on to general maritime regulation. Its deeper function is to make polar risk legible. It asks operators to convert claims of readiness into evidence about planning, equipment, training, procedures, environmental protection, and operational limitations. In other words, it takes conditions long treated as difficult but somewhat exceptional and turns them into categories that can be inspected, audited, priced, and contested. The rulebook does not abolish judgement. It organises it.

The Code's structure reflects that purpose. Rather than imagining polar danger as one undifferentiated threat, it separates the challenge into linked fields of concern that serious operators must make visible in advance. Some of these are plainly about ship capability: whether the vessel's design and equipment fit the conditions it may face. Some are about operations: whether the voyage has been planned with realistic limits, contingencies, communications, and support assumptions. Some are about human performance: whether training, procedures, and drills acknowledge what cold, isolation, fatigue, and delay do to ordinary maritime routines. Some are about pollution prevention: whether the environmental consequences of failure have been considered not as an afterthought but as part of the design of the operation itself. This is what makes the Code more than technical tidiness. It distributes responsibility before the voyage begins.

Its intent is therefore preventive in a very specific way. The Code does not promise that polar operations will become safe in any absolute sense. It tries to reduce the space in which operators can rely on broad confidence unsupported by detailed preparation. It presses for a mode of maritime governance in which a vessel's entry into polar waters is not justified by generic seaworthiness alone, but by an account of fitness tailored to severe conditions. That distinction is crucial. A ship can be well run in ordinary service and still be badly prepared for a route where help is thin, ice uncertainty remains high, and environmental sensitivity multiplies the consequence of mistakes. The Code exists to make that gap harder to hide.

Planning sits at the centre of this effort because planning is where environmental uncertainty becomes institutional evidence. The Code's logic assumes that a polar voyage is not simply a route with colder air and more difficult charts. It is a sequence of decisions that must be justified against known hazards, limited support, and the possibility that conditions will change faster than relief can reach the vessel. This is why planning obligations matter so much. They force operators to think not only about intended passage, but about operating limits, abort points, survival conditions, support arrangements, communications, and response scenarios. A good plan does not signal optimism. It signals disciplined pessimism.

That planning function is one reason the Polar Water Operational Manual became such a significant feature of the regime. The manual matters not because paperwork has some intrinsic moral dignity, but because it turns a company's internal assumptions into a form others can interrogate. A route plan, a set of ice assumptions, procedures for machinery operation in cold conditions, emergency measures, and the boundaries of permissible conduct become more than private knowledge held by a few experienced people. They become portable. Surveyors can inspect them. Flag administrations can require them. Auditors can compare them against practice. Insurers and charterers can read them as signs of organisational seriousness or its absence. The manual speaks on shore.

A named example makes the point more concrete. When the *Crystal Serenity* transited the Northwest Passage in August 2016, the voyage attracted public attention as a symbol of Arctic access. But its deeper significance lay in the density of planning and support logic required to make the operation institutionally credible. A passenger vessel carrying large numbers of people into remote waters could not be defended by general confidence alone. The route, the contingencies, the support assumptions, the thresholds for proceeding, and the practical consequences of medical or navigational difficulty all had to be thought through in much sharper detail than ordinary cruise itineraries would demand. The voyage showed, even before the Code's formal entry into force, how planning obligations reshape design choices in practice: the voyage that can be explained is not always the voyage first imagined.

This helps explain why compliance under the Polar Code so often means producing credible evidence rather than merely asserting adherence. Compliance is not a mood. It appears in records, manuals, training matrices, maintenance procedures, equipment specifications, and the coherence with which these pieces support one another. A company that claims to understand polar operations but cannot show realistic limitations, relevant crew preparation, cold-weather maintenance adaptations, or a believable strategy for communications and support is not truly offering compliance in the sense that matters. The Code's practical force lies in this evidentiary demand. It narrows the gap between saying and showing.

Equipment expectations serve the same purpose. The Code does not merely ask whether a vessel has gear on board. It asks whether the ship's equipment, systems, and arrangements are suited to the conditions contemplated. Cold affects machinery, deck operations, lifesaving arrangements, communications, visibility, and the physical endurance of people as much as the structural endurance of steel. By requiring operators to confront these interactions explicitly, the Code shifts equipment from a static inventory to an operational argument. A heating arrangement, a navigation aid, a communications system, or a survival provision matters because it links the ship's technical profile to a credible picture of what happens when conditions deteriorate. Equipment becomes evidence of a thought process.

That thought process extends to pollution prevention, which is one of the Code's defining intents even when commercial readers focus mainly on navigation and ship capability. Polar waters raise environmental stakes because clean-up is harder, response slower, and reputational and legal scrutiny fiercer. A regime concerned only with survival and safe passage would therefore be incomplete. The Code treats the environment not as an external policy concern floating beside maritime risk, but as part of the risk itself. That approach has commercial consequences. Operators who can show that they have reduced certain pollution exposures, or planned sensibly for environmental contingencies, often appear more governable to the wider chain of insurers, counterparties, and regulators who must decide whether the trade is tolerable.

The Code also changes what counts as ordinary practice. Before formal codification, much specialised polar competence lived in company culture, local knowledge, flag expectations, class rules, or the habits of a relatively small circle of operators. Codification does not erase those sources of knowledge, but it changes their standing. A practice that once seemed optional, admirable, or niche may become an expected element of credible polar readiness once it is anchored in a formal regime. This is how standards acquire quiet power. They do not always announce new obligations with drama. They rearrange the burden of explanation. The operator who omits what the Code treats as essential must now explain that omission to multiple audiences, not just to itself.

A second named example shows how this wider institutional reading matters. The *Venta Maersk* transit through the Northern Sea Route in 2018 was publicly discussed as evidence of commercial possibility. Yet what gave such a voyage significance in market and regulatory terms was not the bare fact of completion. It was the extent to which the voyage could be read as a bounded, planned, and procedurally disciplined operation rather than as a leap of confidence. The Polar Code did not itself create that discipline, but it strengthened the framework through which others could evaluate whether a proposed route, seasonal window, crew arrangement, and support concept formed a credible whole. A completed passage becomes a better piece of evidence when there is a recognised standard against which its preparation can be measured.

Still, a limitation deserves honest admission. The Polar Code does not eliminate ambiguity, and it was never capable of doing so. Some provisions depend on interpretation. Some rely heavily on operator judgement. Some become more meaningful only when filtered through flag-state administration, class practice, port-state scrutiny, or insurer appetite. Compliance can therefore be formal without being wise, and wisdom can sometimes exceed formal compliance. A vessel may satisfy the documentary expectations of the regime while still being run by a company whose real operational culture is weaker than its papers suggest. The rulebook can require evidence. It cannot guarantee depth of character.

And yet this limitation is precisely why the Code's structure matters. Because it cannot mechanise judgment, it must shape the conditions under which judgement is exercised and later evaluated. It does this by insisting that key decisions leave traces before the voyage begins. If an operator chooses a route, it must articulate the basis. If it relies on certain support assumptions, those assumptions must be legible. If it claims equipment suitability, training adequacy, or emergency preparedness, those claims must be capable of scrutiny. The regime therefore governs by making hindsight less comfortable for those who would rather rely on vague competence than on demonstrable preparation.

This is also why exemptions and limitations become so important under the Code, even though they can appear secondary at first glance. A standard gains much of its real force from how it marks boundaries. Seasonal restrictions, route limitations, capability assumptions, and recognised exceptions do more than tidy the regulatory field. They define the edge of ordinary permission. Once that edge is defined, insurers, charterers, auditors, and regulators can begin asking whether a proposed operation sits comfortably within it or leans against it in ways that deserve caution. The Code does not by itself decide all those later judgments, but it creates the architecture within which they are made.

For intelligent commercial readers, the most important lesson is that the Polar Code works as a translation device between physical danger and institutional response. It allows environmental severity, operational complexity, and organisational competence to be expressed in forms that other actors can compare. That comparison reduces some kinds of opacity and increases some kinds of discipline. It also creates a new threshold for reputational credibility. A company that can show serious compliance gains more than legal standing; it gains a language with which to reassure insurers, charterers, and regulators that it belongs inside the circle of acceptable polar operators. The Code thus enables and constrains at once.

The quiet motif returns because the file remains central. A polar voyage enters the commercial and regulatory world not as a romantic encounter with ice but as a bundle of claims made legible through plans, records, procedures, and limitations. The Polar Code gives shape to that bundle. It tells outsiders what to look for and gives operators a framework through which to show that they have thought seriously about consequences that cannot be managed by confidence alone. But that same structure also sharpens scrutiny. Once the evidence is demanded, its absence or thinness becomes harder to excuse.

The unresolved question, then, lies exactly where the Code is strongest and weakest at once. If it succeeds by making polar risk legible through planning, equipment expectations, and procedural discipline, what should markets and regulators do when the file is exemplary, yet the voyage still depends on forms of judgment, timing, and restraint that no written standard can fully verify before the ship leaves the berth?

Safety management systems in cold environments

In January 2012, after the *Costa Concordia* casualty off Giglio, Italy, attention turned quickly from the visible drama of evacuation to the quieter question that follows nearly every serious maritime failure: what did the organisation believe it was prepared to do, and what could it actually do once events moved faster than the paperwork? That question becomes sharper in polar waters. A procedure that looks adequate in a temperate office can become slow, clumsy, or dangerously thin when hands stiffen, visibility falls, equipment ices, and help is far away. Cold reveals the gap.

That is why safety management systems matter so much in Arctic and near-Arctic operations. They are not simply archives of corporate caution or formal obligations carried to satisfy auditors. They are attempts to turn a company's claims about competence into repeatable behaviour under pressure. In cold environments, that burden grows heavier because the environment does not merely add one more hazard to an otherwise familiar voyage. It changes the tempo of response, the reliability of machinery, the stamina of crew, and the consequences of delay. A system that depends on speed, dexterity, spare capacity, or cheerful improvisation may prove weaker than it looks once the temperature drops and the margin for recovery narrows.

The phrase "safety management system" can sound more bloodless than the reality it governs. In practice it refers to the organised body of procedures, responsibilities, reporting routines, maintenance disciplines, emergency planning, and internal checks through which a company tries to ensure that the ship does not rely on memory, bravado, or luck when things begin to go wrong. In ordinary trades, weak systems can sometimes hide behind experience or benign operating conditions. Cold strips away that indulgence. It forces companies to answer harder questions in advance. How long does a task take when dexterity falls? What fails first when equipment is exposed to freezing spray or severe low temperatures? How does fatigue change when every deck task becomes physically heavier? Who decides to turn back, and on what threshold? The manual must meet the weather.

Training is where this becomes most visible. A company may declare its people competent, but cold competence is not an abstract virtue. It appears in drills that reflect actual operating conditions, in bridge teams that have practised decision-making under narrowing margins, in engineering crews who understand how low temperatures affect systems they might otherwise treat as routine, and in deck personnel who know how emergency procedures change when clothing, icing, wind, and darkness slow everything down. Training in this context is not merely instructional. It is adaptive. It teaches people to expect that ordinary tasks will take longer, that communication may degrade, that physical stress will affect judgement, and that rescue assumptions must remain conservative because the environment will not forgive overconfidence.

Drills matter for the same reason. A drill in benign conditions can flatter a company. It can suggest that procedures are clear, roles understood, and timing acceptable. Cold-weather drills test something more demanding: whether the procedure still works when equipment is stiff, surfaces dangerous, visibility compromised, and participants physically constrained by protective gear and environmental stress. This is why polar safety management cannot rely on generic emergency exercises alone. The question is not whether people know the script. It is whether the script survives contact with cold. A company that drills for cold conditions is not performing bureaucracy. It is discovering whether its own assumptions are false early enough to correct them.

Maintenance also changes character in cold environments. In broad commercial language, good maintenance often means keeping machinery within expected operational condition, closing defects in a timely way, and preserving class and statutory compliance. In polar service, those same duties take on sharper edges because cold affects materials, lubricants, seals, sensors, heating arrangements, exposed systems, and the speed with which a manageable fault can become a serious casualty. A maintenance regime suited to easier waters may be technically respectable and operationally inadequate in severe conditions. Safety management therefore has to translate generic maintenance responsibility into cold-specific vigilance: winterisation, pre-departure checks shaped by temperature exposure, monitoring of vulnerable systems, conservative treatment of minor anomalies, and a willingness to repair earlier rather than later because later may come with much higher consequences.

A named example shows how this logic became commercially visible before many outside shipping paid much attention to it. When the *Crystal Serenity* prepared for its August 2016 Northwest Passage transit, the significance of the voyage did not lie only in passenger spectacle or route novelty. It lay in the degree to which a large passenger ship entering remote waters had to convert safety management from general marine good order into a cold-environment operating discipline. Passenger welfare, medical contingencies, evacuation assumptions, route limitations, communications, and procedural coherence all had to be reconsidered through the practical fact that cold and remoteness stretch time. The voyage was not meaningful because the ship had a manual. It was meaningful because the manual had to become operational design.

Decision thresholds are one of the most revealing features of a serious polar safety management system. Every company likes to say it empowers masters to make prudent decisions. The real test is whether the organisation has defined, taught, and supported the conditions under which prudence means slowing, diverting, waiting, or turning back. Cold makes this difficult because it raises the cost of hesitation while also increasing commercial pressure to press on when a weather window appears usable. A weak system leaves these decisions vague, effectively telling the ship to exercise judgement without clarifying what evidence should trigger retreat. A stronger system does the opposite. It identifies route boundaries, weather tolerances, machinery warnings, communications failures, crew fatigue signals, or support limitations that should move the operation out of routine mode. Thresholds turn prudence from sentiment into conduct.

This matters because Arctic and sub-Arctic risk is compounding risk. Cold affects human performance, which affects response quality. Cold affects machinery, which increases the chance of technical interruption. Remoteness slows external support, which makes human and machinery problems more severe. Environmental sensitivity raises the consequence of pollution or prolonged casualty management. Each factor amplifies the others. Safety management systems are meant to interrupt that chain before the compounding becomes irreversible. They do so by organising foresight: training that anticipates degraded performance, drills that expose hidden delays, maintenance that treats minor technical weaknesses as serious in context, and decision rules that prevent the company from mistaking momentum for control.

Auditors read these systems as proxies for organisational competence because they cannot directly observe every future decision the company will make. They therefore examine the traces of seriousness. Do procedures fit the actual trade, or do they read like generic text pasted into a polar file? Do drill records show repetition and adaptation, or mere completion? Are non-conformities treated as useful signals or as irritants to be cleaned away before inspection? Does maintenance evidence suggest early correction or habitual deferral? Are route limitations and emergency procedures specific enough to guide action, or so broad that they offer comfort without discipline? The audit is not just a hunt for missing signatures. It is an attempt to infer whether the organisation behaves as though cold changes reality rather than merely atmosphere.

Insurers read the same material for related but slightly harsher reasons. They are not primarily asking whether the company satisfies a management ideal. They are asking whether the system reduces the chance that a claim will reveal a culture of weak preparation, poor escalation, untested emergency logic, or deferred technical concern. In that sense, safety management systems function as reputational evidence long before a loss occurs. A well-constructed and well-lived system can make a market more willing to believe the operator's account of itself. A generic or poorly evidenced system does the opposite. It tells the market that the company may be relying on the appearance of order rather than the substance of it. Insurers know the difference often becomes visible only after the casualty. That is why they ask for clues beforehand.

A second named example, though not polar, illuminates the point precisely because it exposed the boundary between formal order and operational reality. After the *Costa Concordia* casualty in January 2012, one of the most enduring institutional lessons concerned the inadequacy of treating documented procedure as proof of effective emergency practice. Passenger shipping everywhere was reminded that systems, drills, command culture, and evacuation logic cannot be evaluated only by the existence of manuals. The lesson travels north with even greater force. In polar waters, the distance between a written emergency procedure and a workable one can become catastrophic far more quickly because cold, darkness, response scarcity, and environmental severity punish any mismatch between script and capacity.

This is why paperwork and practice must match so closely in cold environments. The phrase is easy to utter and hard to achieve. Matching means more than keeping records tidy. It means that the people on the vessel recognise the procedures as realistic; that the equipment assumed by the procedure exists, functions, and remains usable in the conditions contemplated; that the timeline implied by emergency actions survives cold-weather testing; and that the organisation ashore responds to warning signs in ways consistent with what the safety management system claims it values. A mismatch can take many forms: drills that omit the hardest conditions, maintenance regimes that satisfy minimum cycles but ignore temperature-specific stress, route thresholds written bravely and ignored quietly, reports that soften near misses into routine inconvenience. Any of these can turn a good-looking system into a dangerous fiction.

One should also note that cold has a political effect inside organisations. It redistributes authority, often without anyone saying so. When conditions become harsher, junior crew may be less willing to challenge assumptions if the culture prizes toughness over caution. Masters may feel more exposed to commercial pressure because the cost of aborting a voyage appears larger. Engineers may normalise small technical compromises to keep schedules intact. Safety management systems are meant to counter these tendencies by clarifying escalation routes, protecting conservative decisions, and making it harder for bravado to masquerade as professionalism. In cold environments, culture is part of engineering.

A limitation deserves honest admission. No safety management system, however carefully built, can script every meaningful decision in polar operations. Conditions change too quickly, local realities vary too much, and the quality of human judgement still matters too deeply. There is also a real danger that systems become performative: manuals are polished, drills are documented, checklists are completed, and audits are survived, while the deeper habits of careful operation remain inconsistent. Some companies are better at writing systems than at living them. A mature reader should never confuse administrative elegance with actual readiness.

And yet this limitation is exactly why safety management matters. Because discretion cannot be eliminated, it must be disciplined. Because cold reveals weakness quickly, organisations need structures that make weak assumptions visible before they become casualties. Because outsiders cannot board every ship every day, they need documented evidence that the operator has thought seriously about how procedures, people, and machines behave under polar stress. A good safety management system does not replace judgement. It makes better judgement more likely, poorer judgement more visible, and retrospective excuse more difficult.

Seen this way, the value of safety management in cold environments is not only preventive but interpretive. It gives auditors, insurers, charterers, and regulators a way to read the organisation through its routines. Training records show whether competence is cultivated or merely assumed. Drill reports show whether emergency practice is adapted or ceremonial. Maintenance logs show whether the company repairs ahead of trouble or behind it. Decision thresholds show whether retreat is treated as failure or as disciplined seamanship. Each record is a small piece of evidence. Together they form an institutional portrait.

The quiet motif returns because the manual is never just a manual. In one company it is an instrument that shapes behaviour, sharpens maintenance, informs route choice, protects conservative decisions, and teaches people how cold alters the ordinary. In another it is a polished object that says all the right things while the real organisation continues to rely on habit, speed, and optimistic interpretation. The distinction matters because cold will eventually adjudicate between them. Auditors and insurers know this. They read the file accordingly.

The unresolved question, then, is not whether safety management systems are necessary. They plainly are. The harder question is how to recognise the moment when a system has stopped being a living discipline and become a persuasive artefact - especially in polar service, where the difference may remain invisible until cold slows the body, stiffens the ship, lengthens the response, and asks whether the procedure ever truly belonged to the voyage it claimed to govern.

The operational meaning of limitations and exemptions

In August 2018, the *Venta Maersk* completed its trial passage through the Northern Sea Route and invited a familiar misunderstanding. A voyage had been made. A route had proved navigable under defined conditions. A large commercial operator had shown that Arctic movement could be organised without collapsing into spectacle or crisis. For many observers, that seemed to answer the central question. For insurers, charterers, and technical reviewers, it merely sharpened another one: under exactly what limits had this become possible, and how far beyond those limits was anyone entitled to infer freedom? The small print governs.

This is the hard lesson of polar regulation and private risk control alike. Permission in harsh environments is rarely absolute. It arrives qualified: by season, by route, by anticipated ice conditions, by ship capability, by support assumptions, by reporting obligations, by the continuing validity of plans made before departure. These qualifications are sometimes treated as administrative clutter surrounding the real business of movement. They are closer to the opposite. In polar operations, the limitation often *is* the real business. It tells the operator where ordinary confidence stops and conditional tolerance begins.

A distinct polar regime made this clearer by forcing operators to articulate boundaries they might previously have held only in practice, custom, or quiet internal caution. That was one of its great institutional achievements. It turned what had often been treated as tacit prudence into visible operational conditions. A route is not merely available; it may be available in a certain window, under certain assumptions, with certain retreat thresholds, in association with certain equipment, support, crew competence, and planning obligations. Once those limits are written down, they can be compared, enforced, priced, and argued over. They become part of governance rather than background seamanship.

This matters because limitations do not merely reduce freedom. They define usable freedom. A vessel's commercial life in polar waters is not determined only by its technical capability or formal eligibility to enter a region. It is determined by the overlap between what its documents permit, what its operator can credibly sustain, what insurers will support, and what counterparties regard as workable. A route limitation in a manual, an ice-condition threshold in an operational plan, a seasonal condition in a policy wording, and a charterer's risk tolerance may all point in slightly different directions. The operator's real freedom lies in the narrow space where they align.

Seasonal limitations make this plain. In ordinary shipping language, a season can sound like a planning convenience, a broad commercial parameter that helps organise schedules and expectations. In polar practice, a seasonal limit is often an argument about uncertainty expressed as time. It reflects what institutions believe about ice variability, weather stability, available support, daylight, human endurance, and the difficulty of recovering from problems as conditions harden. To say that a vessel may operate only within a specified seasonal frame is not simply to note a calendar preference. It is to declare that outside that frame, the margin for safe and insurable operation becomes too thin or too poorly evidenced to justify confidence. The season is a verdict.

Route limitations carry similar force. A vessel may be authorised, classed, and well prepared in general terms while still being restricted to specific corridors, support assumptions, or areas of operation. This does not necessarily imply weakness. It often reflects discipline. A route limitation states that capability is meaningful only in relation to context. A ship suitable for one corridor under one pattern of support may become a materially different proposition if diverted into less supported waters or more severe ice conditions. The limit protects against a common commercial temptation: the belief that one successful passage or one capable season justifies broader operational ambition than the evidence can sustain.

Ice-condition limitations are perhaps the clearest expression of this logic because they tie permission directly to an environment that refuses stable interpretation. Ice class notation, ship design, and operator planning all help define the envelope of acceptable operation, but the actual state of the ice remains dynamic and partly resistant to neat categories. A limitation tied to anticipated or observed ice conditions therefore functions as a moving boundary. It requires judgement, but not unbounded judgement. The operator must decide whether actual conditions remain within the contemplated envelope. Others then decide whether they trust that decision. This is where document and discretion meet under pressure.

A named example helps bring these abstractions into practical focus. When the *Crystal Serenity* transited the Northwest Passage in August 2016, the voyage was not meaningful simply because a large passenger vessel had entered Arctic waters. It was meaningful because so much of its viability rested on boundedness. Route planning, support arrangements, contingency thinking, and the whole structure of preparation depended on accepting that the voyage was possible only within a carefully defined operational frame. The public image was dramatic. The institutional reality was disciplined. That distinction matters because many later commercial ambitions in polar waters fail precisely when operators try to inherit the symbolism of success without inheriting the limits that made it manageable.

Exemptions complicate the picture in a different but equally revealing way. A formal exemption can suggest flexibility, pragmatism, or technical accommodation within a rule-bound system. Sometimes it is exactly that. Maritime regulation must leave some room for reasoned deviation where the underlying safety objective can still be achieved by another means or where strict compliance would be unnecessarily rigid in a particular case. The problem is that an exemption, even when lawfully granted, does not erase the fact that something ordinarily expected is absent, altered, or replaced. That absence becomes visible to insurers very quickly.

Why should insurers care if an exemption is formally valid? Because insurers do not price legality alone. They price uncertainty and consequence. An exemption may be technically justified and still signal to underwriters that the operation depends on a narrower set of assumptions or on a substitute measure whose effectiveness they find harder to compare with ordinary practice. It may indicate that the vessel or operation sits nearer the edge of what the regulatory framework treats as ordinary prudence. The exemption therefore behaves less like a free pass than like a highlighted sentence in the file. Lawful, yes. Comforting, not necessarily.

This is where the distinction between "allowed" and "insurable on workable terms" becomes decisive. Maritime operators often discover, sometimes late and painfully, that formal permission and commercial feasibility are not the same category. A flag administration, class society, or relevant authority may accept a limitation, exemption, or operating concept within the legal framework. The insurer may still narrow cover, raise deductibles, require additional surveys, restrict routes, or ask for evidence so demanding that the operator's formal freedom becomes practically constrained. The voyage remains lawful. The economics change. Permission without workable cover is a thin kind of permission.

A second named example, though not an Arctic casualty in the strictest sense, clarifies the principle through a different angle. After the *Exxon Valdez* grounding in Alaska in March 1989, the issue was not merely that one ship had failed in one place. The event intensified scrutiny of what operators and regulators had previously treated as tolerable in environmentally exposed, difficult-response waters. Practices or assumptions that had once existed within a broad field of permissibility became harder to defend, and markets learned to read lawful operation through a sharper lens of consequence. That lesson persists in polar contexts. A technically permissible deviation or exemption may attract insurer concern not because anyone disputes its legality, but because everyone understands how brutally expensive a legally permitted misjudgement can become.

The practical importance of limitations and exemptions lies in how they travel across documents. A route limit stated in a Polar Water Operational Manual may interact with a seasonal condition in an insurance policy. A class notation may imply one operating envelope while a charterparty narrows commercial expectations further. A flag-state acceptance of a particular arrangement may sit alongside an underwriter's insistence on extra survey evidence before cover attaches. A shipowner who reads each document in isolation may think the vessel has considerable room to manoeuvre. A more careful reader traces the overlap and sees that the real operating corridor is much narrower. This is why practical constraints must be tracked, not merely noticed.

Tracking them requires a particular discipline of reading. One must ask where the boundary first appears, where it is repeated, where it is tightened, and where it quietly changes meaning. A route approved in a technical document may become subject to prior notification in the policy. An equipment-related exemption may trigger stronger reporting obligations or narrower warranty language. A limitation expressed as prudent advice in one context may become a commercial condition in another. Institutions borrow each other's caution. By the time the operator experiences the full effect, it can seem as though no one ever said no and yet everyone reduced the scope of possible action.

That is why limitations so often function as the hidden architecture of access. They shape crewing, maintenance timing, scheduling, bunker planning, charter commitments, support contracts, and contingency expenditure. A route that is theoretically open but usable only under conditions so narrow that delay becomes likely may be commercially weaker than a longer route under more stable terms. A vessel technically permitted to proceed under a specific exemption may still face such onerous insurance conditions that the voyage loses appeal. In both cases the key point is the same: freedom in polar operations is rarely measured by formal allowance alone. It is measured by the friction surrounding that allowance.

A credible limitation should be admitted. Not every exemption or operational limitation signals serious commercial difficulty. Some exist precisely because regulators understand that equivalent safety outcomes can be achieved through alternative means, and markets can recognise this where evidence is strong and the operator's record persuasive. A well-documented company with disciplined planning, transparent maintenance history, proven crew competence, and a convincing explanation of why a deviation remains safe may secure workable terms even where a formal exemption appears in the background. The presence of an exemption is not, by itself, proof of fragility.

And yet this concession reinforces the larger point. Because some exemptions are tolerable and others commercially unsettling, the real question becomes one of interpretation and trust. Insurers and counterparties ask what the exemption means about the wider operation. Does it reflect thoughtful adaptation within a strong safety culture, or does it suggest that the voyage depends on exceptions because the ordinary requirements sit uncomfortably with what is being attempted? Does the operator present the limitation as a serious boundary, or treat it as language to be managed away? The answer is rarely found in the existence of the exemption alone. It lies in how the rest of the file behaves around it.

This is also why limitations and exemptions tend to discipline operator judgement without replacing it. A seasonal or route boundary still requires human assessment in changing conditions. An exemption still requires the operator to make good on the alternative safeguards it promised. The regulatory text cannot stand on deck and decide whether deteriorating ice or weather now sits outside the contemplated envelope. But it can define the responsibility to make that judgment conservatively and leave a trail by which others later assess whether the judgment was credible. Governance here does not work by scripting every decision. It works by narrowing the space in which unreasoned improvisation can later claim legitimacy.

The strategic significance is hard to miss once seen clearly. Polar expansion is often discussed as though the main question were whether technology and climate have opened a route, a season, or a project window. The quieter and more decisive question is whether the operation remains inside a mesh of limitations that insurers, charterers, regulators, and operators can all tolerate at once. That mesh is built from clauses, thresholds, exemptions, manuals, approvals, warranties, and plans. Each looks manageable alone. Together they determine whether access is thick or thin.

The quiet motif returns because the small print really does govern. A voyage may be lawful, classed, and technically imaginable while being commercially brittle because its limitations leave too little room for delay, misjudgement, or deteriorating conditions. Another voyage may proceed more steadily precisely because its limits are narrower, clearer, and more honestly respected. The operator who treats limits as embarrassing obstacles often ends up discovering that the real obstacle is the market's memory of those who treated them lightly.

The unresolved question, then, is not whether limitations and exemptions are necessary. They plainly are. The harder question is what kind of operator can live successfully inside them: the one that sees them as technical hurdles to negotiate around, or the one that understands that in polar waters the real measure of freedom is not what the documents formally allow, but how much disciplined room remains once every condition, exception, and insurer's reservation has been read together.

Harmonisation, fragmentation, and uneven enforcement

On 1 January 2017, the Polar Code entered into force through the IMO framework with a promise that was both practical and ambitious: ships operating in polar waters would now face a more recognisable common standard, one that could travel across flags, ports, insurers, and commercial chains more reliably than the older patchwork of general rules and specialist caution. The promise was real. So was the complication. A global standard can unify text far more easily than it unifies reading. The same page travels. The same page lands differently.

That difference matters because shipping never encounters standards in the abstract. It encounters them through administrations, inspectors, surveyors, auditors, port authorities, brokers, underwriters, charterers, and company managers, each with different resources, incentives, and thresholds for concern. A rule drafted to create comparability across jurisdictions may therefore produce outcomes that are only partly comparable in practice. One operator may find the standard administered as a demanding but coherent discipline. Another may meet something looser, more discretionary, or more unpredictable. The rule looks global. The encounter stays local.

This is the central tension of harmonisation in polar governance. Maritime commerce needs common standards because without them polar activity would be far harder to compare, insure, and police. A vessel flagged in one state, classed through one institution, insured in another market, and calling at ports under different authorities cannot function smoothly if every actor must reinvent the meaning of prudent polar operation from scratch. Harmonisation answers that need by giving the trade a shared vocabulary. Yet the more valuable that shared vocabulary becomes, the more consequential its uneven application becomes. Uniform text plus varied enforcement is not neutrality. It is a structured uncertainty.

The reasons for that unevenness are mundane, which is precisely why they matter. Interpretation plays an obvious role. Even a carefully drafted polar rule cannot decide every question in advance. Someone must decide whether a planning document is truly route-specific or merely competent in broad terms, whether a crew's experience is enough for the intended service, whether an exemption has been justified with real seriousness, whether a limitation has been treated as a boundary or as a polite fiction. One authority may lean towards strict reading because severe environments punish optimism. Another may take a lighter view, satisfied that formal requirements have been met and reluctant to impose burdens beyond the text. Each may regard itself as reasonable. Operators experience them as very different worlds.

Resources matter just as much. A flag administration with deep technical capacity, experienced personnel, and strong institutional memory can review polar submissions more closely, ask sharper questions, and sustain a more consistent line across cases. Another administration may possess formal authority but thinner expertise, fewer people, or less ability to challenge what it is shown. Ports display similar variation. A well-resourced inspection culture can detect patterns, connect deficiencies to wider concerns, and treat polar documentation as a live operating instrument rather than ceremonial paper. A lighter-touch setting may move traffic efficiently while leaving more of the burden to class, company systems, and insurers. Neither outcome exists in a vacuum. Markets learn from both.

Political priorities also shape enforcement more than technical language usually admits. One administration may view polar traffic as strategically important, commercially desirable, or symbolically useful, and therefore cultivate an enforcement style that stays within the rules while avoiding unnecessary friction. Another may treat environmental sensitivity, reputational exposure, or institutional caution as overriding considerations and therefore read the same standard with sharper suspicion. The difference need not be theatrical. It may emerge in the pace of review, the depth of document requests, the seriousness attached to minor deficiencies, or the willingness to accept managerial assurances without extra proof. Politics rarely rewrites the code. It influences how much weight the code carries at the point of contact.

A named example shows how the problem appears in commercial practice. When the *Venta Maersk* completed its trial voyage through the Northern Sea Route in 2018, the public debate centred on route viability and strategic significance. Commercial readers saw something else as well. A voyage of that kind could be read quite differently depending on which institutions touched it, how they understood the surrounding support assumptions, and how much practical confidence they placed in the operator's planning discipline. The same formal polar framework could therefore sit behind distinct commercial reactions because the local enforcement and market context shaped what the voyage meant as evidence. One passage did not produce one interpretation. It produced a field of them.

This helps explain why uneven enforcement becomes a pricing issue so quickly. Insurers dislike ambiguity more than severity they believe they can classify. A demanding but predictable inspection culture may impose operational burden, yet markets can often price it more comfortably because the rules of the game appear stable. A lighter-touch environment can create the opposite problem. It may look commercially easier in the short term, but if markets suspect that scrutiny is thin, document review superficial, or official comfort less trustworthy than it appears, they may compensate through higher premiums, tighter warranties, additional surveys, or narrower cover. Ease at one desk can produce harder terms at another.

A brief contrast makes the point. Imagine two otherwise similar vessels entering polar trades under broadly similar regulatory texts. In one setting, the flag and port authorities inspect closely, challenge vague route assumptions, probe operational limitations, and build a reputation for taking polar compliance seriously. Operators may grumble about delay and administrative burden, but insurers and charterers often read the resulting paperwork with more confidence. In another setting, the official process moves quickly, accepts documentation at face value, and raises fewer searching questions. Owners may prefer the efficiency. Markets may not. The first regime imposes visible cost and may reduce hidden doubt. The second reduces visible cost and may enlarge hidden doubt. Both are forms of governance. The bill changes place.

This is why fragmentation persists inside harmonisation. A global standard creates a baseline, but other institutions immediately begin to sort operators according to how that baseline was administered and where. Insurers read flag choice as a signal. Charterers read port-state histories as a signal. Brokers read inspection cultures as a signal. Auditors and surveyors often tailor their own level of scepticism to what they know about the administrative environment surrounding the vessel. The result is not a breakdown of harmonisation. It is harmonisation filtered through reputation. A standardised regime still generates hierarchies of trust.

The same process affects exemptions and equivalent arrangements. A lawful exemption granted under one administration may be treated by a market as a carefully managed adaptation if the surrounding enforcement culture is regarded as technically serious. The identical exemption, granted elsewhere, may attract sharper insurer concern because the market has less confidence in the depth of review that produced it. The legal status of the exemption is unchanged. Its commercial meaning shifts. This is an uncomfortable fact for operators who prefer to think in binary terms - permitted or prohibited, compliant or non-compliant. Polar governance resists such neatness. It asks who approved, how carefully, in what administrative setting, and with what surrounding evidence of seriousness.

A second named example helps to clarify how this broader institutional memory develops. The *Crystal Serenity* transit through the Northwest

Passage in August 2016 was not merely a question of whether a large passenger vessel could complete a highly planned voyage. It was also a test of whether the supporting chain of documents, approvals, and contingency arrangements would be read by commercial actors as genuinely persuasive in a severe environment. The voyage drew extraordinary attention, and that attention itself mattered. High-visibility operations are often subjected to unusually thick layers of planning and review. Markets know this. They do not automatically generalise from them to more routine operations under lighter scrutiny. Uneven enforcement enters here as a problem of transferability: what was true under exceptional attention may not be true under ordinary administration.

One might object that harmonisation has nonetheless achieved a great deal, and the objection is fair. Without common polar standards, the existing variation would be wider, the room for weak operators greater, and the ability of insurers, charterers, and regulators to compare unlike vessels much poorer. A common code, shared technical language, and recognisable documentary expectations do reduce informational chaos. They make bad cases easier to spot and good cases easier to defend. They also permit cross-border markets to function with something more disciplined than rumour and local custom. That is no small achievement.

And yet this very success makes residual unevenness more rather than less important. Once commercial actors depend on harmonised standards as signals of competence, any variation in how those standards are enforced acquires greater significance. Operators do not merely carry their own records into the market; they carry the reputations of their flag, inspection history, administrative context, and route of compliance. A ship can meet the same formal code as another and still be priced or treated differently because the surrounding institutional chain inspires more or less confidence. Harmonisation creates comparability. It also sharpens the consequences of being compared.

The issue becomes more acute in cold-environment operations because the consequences of under-enforcement can be unusually expensive. A light-touch decision that lets a weak plan proceed may not fail immediately. It may only become visible after a casualty, delay, or operational near miss reveals that the documentary adequacy accepted on paper concealed poor real-world preparation. Markets know this. They therefore try to infer enforcement quality before loss occurs. They do so indirectly: through flag reputation, port-state histories, survey findings, patterns of deficiency, broker intelligence, and the tone of the operator's own file. Uneven enforcement thus enters underwriting as an uncertainty about uncertainty itself. That is one reason it is so heavily priced.

This gives standards a double life. Publicly, they are instruments of legal and technical order. Commercially, they are also reputational signals whose value depends on the credibility of the institutions applying them. A respected standard administered weakly can inspire less trust than a demanding operator's internal discipline backed by strong survey evidence. Conversely, rigorous public scrutiny can function as a kind of reputational capital that reduces informational asymmetry for insurers and charterers. The code is global. Confidence in its administration remains unevenly distributed.

The strategic result is not chaos, but layered governance. Operators do not move only within the formal space created by the Polar Code or similar standards. They move within an interpretive field shaped by flags, ports, markets, and the remembered character of institutions that sit around those standards. A vessel may be fully compliant on paper and still treated cautiously because the route to that paper was not trusted. Another may carry a more demanding administrative burden and benefit commercially because the burden reassures others that the standard meant something in practice. Unevenness does not destroy the regime. It changes what the regime is worth.

The quiet motif returns because the same page keeps landing differently. A manual, a certificate, an approval, an exemption, an inspection history - none speaks in a single voice once it travels across jurisdictions and markets. Each is translated by the institution receiving it. The operator who reads only the text misses half the story. The market reader watches the hands through which the text passed.

That leaves a harder question than simple compliance can answer. If global standards are meant to reduce uncertainty by harmonising expectations, what should an insurer, charterer, or regulator do when the rule looks familiar, but the enforcement culture behind it remains uncertain - and how much of Arctic access is really being decided not by the standard itself, but by whose version of seriousness the market has learned to trust?

Standards as signals to markets and regulators

In August 2016, the *Crystal Serenity* left Seward, Alaska, for its Northwest Passage transit under a level of scrutiny far beyond that of passenger curiosity or media fascination. Long before the ship moved through remote waters, insurers, charterers, regulators, technical reviewers, and a wider commercial audience had already begun reading the voyage through its documentation, planning discipline, and visible adherence to recognised standards. The question was not only whether the ship could make the passage. It was whether enough third parties could believe the operator's account of its own readiness. The certificate travels ahead.

That is the deeper commercial life of standards. They are often described as safety tools or regulatory requirements, and they are both. They are also signals. In markets where counterparties must make decisions under imperfect information, a respected standard does not merely organise conduct on board. It helps outsiders decide how much confidence to place in what they cannot directly observe. A charterer cannot inspect every system personally. An underwriter cannot watch every drill. A regulator cannot sit on the bridge for every difficult decision. Standards reduce that blindness by creating evidence that can travel across distance, institutions, and transactions. They do not eliminate uncertainty. They make it more legible.

This signalling function matters especially in polar operations because the underlying uncertainties are unusually severe and difficult to compare. Remote routes, sparse support, environmental sensitivity, and thin historical analogies make it harder for markets to rely on casual reputation or broad assurances. In easier trades, a respectable operator may benefit from familiarity alone. In polar service, familiarity helps less unless it is backed by documents, verifications, and planning that others recognise as serious. Standards answer that need by converting private claims into public signals. A company no longer says only, "trust us." It says, in effect, "here are the forms of proof that institutions already know how to read."

That is why adherence to respected standards reduces information asymmetry so powerfully. Information asymmetry is simply the condition in which the operator knows much more about the vessel, the crew, the maintenance culture, the route assumptions, and the true limits of preparation than the insurer, charterer, or regulator can know at the outset. Standards narrow that gap. They do so by requiring records of training, maintenance, operational planning, equipment readiness, risk assessment, and procedural discipline for review by people outside the company. The reduction is never perfect, but it is practical. A stronger file leads to a faster and often calmer screening process. A weaker one invites delay, extra conditions, and price.

Third-party verification gives those signals unusual strength. A company may write a convincing manual or present a careful submission, but self-description has obvious limits. Once an independent surveyor, classification society, auditor, flag administration, or other recognised body verifies elements of the company's claims, the information becomes more than self-report. It acquires reputational weight. This is why third-party verification often functions as a form of reputational capital. It can be accumulated, displayed, and spent in negotiations. An operator with a clean pattern of audit outcomes, credible class standing, closed recommendations, disciplined safety management records, and a reputation for taking standards seriously enters the market with an advantage no brochure can manufacture.

That advantage is visible in behaviour, not merely in status. Insurers may ask fewer speculative questions because the file already answers some of them. Charterers may spend less time worrying about baseline competence and more time discussing commercial particulars. Regulators may still inspect closely, but their starting assumption can be less defensive. Brokers can frame the account as a disciplined risk rather than as an uncertain one. None of this guarantees easy terms. It reduces friction. In specialised markets, reduced friction is valuable in itself.

A named example makes the point. When the *Venta Maersk* completed its 2018 trial passage through the Northern Sea Route, the voyage attracted interest not simply because a container ship had used the route, but because a major operator had done so in a way that markets could read as bounded and evidential. The significance lay less in spectacle than in legibility. An established company with recognisable technical discipline, documented planning, and institutional credibility provided a type of signal very different from that of an unknown entrant attempting the same route with thinner records and less trusted systems. Both might point to the same chart. Only one arrives with accumulated reputational capital strong enough to make the claim broadly intelligible.

This is one reason standards enable expansion. They make unfamiliar or severe operations comparable enough for outsiders to accept them under some conditions. Without standards, every Arctic proposal would look more singular, more opaque, and therefore more difficult to insure, finance, charter, or authorise. Standards create a common language through which novel activity can be made to resemble disciplined activity. They lower one barrier by reducing uncertainty about what counts as evidence of seriousness. In that sense, they do not merely constrain commercial ambition. They furnish the institutional bridge by which ambition becomes discussable at all.

The same process explains why regulators value standards not only as tools of formal compliance but as devices for sorting operators. A respected standard can help an administration decide where to focus limited attention. Operators with coherent records, credible manuals, disciplined training evidence, and strong third-party verification often look less likely to conceal basic disorder than those whose compliance appears thin, generic, or last-minute. Standards, therefore, help regulators triage uncertainty. They do not eliminate inspection. They help decide where inspection should bite hardest. This is another form of signalling, and it matters because administrative confidence, like insurance confidence, is scarce where conditions are severe.

And yet standards also constrain expansion, often through the very same mechanism. Once recognised standards become the language of entry, operators that cannot produce credible evidence find themselves exposed quickly. The market may not need to refuse them outright. It can price uncertainty more harshly, ask for more intrusive surveys, narrow cover, insist on tighter limitations, or simply conclude that the operation is too awkward to support on workable terms. The regulator may not prohibit the voyage in broad political language. It can require enough proof, adaptation, or procedural seriousness that casual or underprepared operators drift away. Standards, then, are not neutral doors. They are selective filters.

This selectivity is easy to misread as unfairness or bureaucratic excess, particularly from the perspective of newer entrants. An experienced operator with a long record of clean audits, well-regarded verification, and disciplined systems may appear to enjoy easier access, while a technically capable newcomer faces more suspicion. The appearance is not wholly false. Standards do reward accumulated proof, and that can reinforce existing hierarchies of trust. But the reward is not arbitrary. It reflects the institutional reality that severe environments punish weak information. When markets and regulators know less about an operator, they rely more heavily on the quality and credibility of the signals placed before them. A newcomer can still earn confidence. It must do so more explicitly.

A second named example shows the limits of the signal. After the *Costa Concordia* casualty off Giglio in January 2012, the maritime world was reminded with unusual force that formal systems, recognised standards, and visible compliance structures do not guarantee sound operational reality. A ship can belong to an orderly institutional world and still suffer disaster through failures of judgement, culture, emergency practice, or command. The relevance here is not passenger shipping alone. It is the broader truth that standards can be met formally while risk remains high in lived operation. A document can be correct. A drill can be recorded. A system can exist. The organisation may still behave badly when pressure arrives.

This is the central limit of standards as signals. They reduce information asymmetry, but they do not abolish it. They show that a company has done certain things, produced certain records, undergone certain reviews, or aligned itself with recognised expectations. They do not always show whether the bridge team will interpret deteriorating ice conservatively, whether the engineering culture treats anomalies early enough, whether senior management will support retreat over schedule, or whether the real emergency logic of the company survives once distance and cold stretch every response. Standards can therefore create false comfort if readers treat them as complete truth rather than as structured but partial evidence.

That is why the best insurers, charterers, and regulators read standards intelligently rather than reverently. They treat third-party verification as valuable because it narrows doubt, not because it ends doubt. They compare the standard with the operator's route, season, support context, and record of behaviour. They look for coherence: do the manuals match the trade, do the drills reflect the conditions, do the limits appear honest, do the survey responses suggest seriousness, does the file show a company that uses standards as discipline rather than decoration? In other words, they read the signal in context. Standards speak. Context tells them how loudly.

A credible limitation must be admitted from the other side as well. Some critics of standardisation overcorrect and treat standards as little more than bureaucratic theatre, useful mainly for appearances. That is too cynical. Without recognised standards and third-party verification, polar markets would be far more dependent on rumour, informal prestige, and local familiarity. The barriers to entry for competent but less connected operators would likely be higher, not lower, because outsiders would have fewer structured ways to judge them. Standards may be imperfect proxies, but they are often the best available common currency of credibility in difficult trades.

Still, their imperfection is precisely what makes them strategically interesting. They enable expansion by making trust portable. They constrain expansion by turning trust into something that must be earned through visible forms of discipline, not merely claimed. They reduce information asymmetry while creating a new competition over who can produce the most convincing evidence of competence. They protect markets and regulators from some kinds of blindness while exposing them to the danger of over-relying on formal compliance. This double character is not accidental. It is the essence of how private and public governance now work together in severe environments.

The strategic conclusion follows from that double character. Standards are not merely technical requirements bolted onto Arctic commerce after the interesting decisions have been made. They are part of the mechanism by which interesting decisions become possible or impossible. An operator with respected verification, coherent systems, and a credible record can use standards to widen access, lower friction, and make ambitious activity appear governable. Another operator may encounter the same standards as a narrowing force, finding that every unresolved recommendation, generic procedure, or weakly evidenced claim compounds into cost and distrust. The same regime opens and closes.

The quiet motif returns because the certificate still travels ahead, but never alone. It carries with it the reputation of the institution that issued it, the seriousness of the company that relies on it, and the judgment of the market that chooses how much weight to give it. A certificate can shorten the argument. It cannot guarantee the outcome. Arctic and polar commerce repeatedly turns on that distinction. The signal matters because no one can observe everything directly. The signal remains limited because harsh environments expose what paper could only ever suggest.

The question that remains is the one standards themselves cannot settle. If respected verification and formal compliance make an operator legible enough to enter the conversation, what should insurers, charterers, and regulators do when the documents are excellent but the operational reality still depends on forms of restraint, culture, and judgement that no certificate can fully certify before the ship sails?

Chapter 6

Compliance Documentation and Audit Trails

In March 1989, after the *Exxon Valdez* grounded in Alaska, one of the most enduring lessons was not only about navigation, fatigue, or environmental consequences. It was about records. After a serious casualty, institutions do not simply ask what happened. They ask what was written, what was approved, what was checked, what was overdue, what was missing, who knew, and whether the organisation's paperwork described a real operating discipline or merely an administrative costume. The folder opens slowly.

That is why documentation matters so much in Arctic operations. In easier trades, records can feel secondary to steel, weather, and judgement, as though the real seamanship happens on deck while the binders exist to satisfy offices ashore. Polar work strips away that illusion. A ship moving through cold, remote, and thinly supported waters must carry more than physical capability. It must carry proof: manuals that match the voyage, plans that fit the route, certificates that remain current, class records that hold together, survey reports that have been read rather than filed away, and a documentary trail strong enough to persuade sceptical readers that the operator knows what it is doing before anything goes wrong. The paper moves first.

This creates the chapter's central tension. Documentation is supposed to clarify reality, yet in severe environments it also helps create the reality under which a voyage becomes possible. A missing plan may delay cover. A thin maintenance trail may harden underwriting terms. An unresolved recommendation may alter a charterer's view of schedule reliability. A vague manual may make a regulator or auditor doubt whether the company's confidence has any operational substance behind it. The documents do not merely describe the voyage. They govern it.

That governing function matters because Arctic commerce is judged at a distance. Underwriters, charterers, auditors, flag administrations, class societies, and financiers rarely stand together in the same physical place to watch the vessel operate. They rely on documentary traces that can travel between institutions and survive disagreement later. Manuals, route plans, certificates, survey records, audit reports, non-conformity logs, maintenance histories, and training evidence form a practical stack through which multiple actors decide whether the operator is credible, whether the risk is bounded, and whether a later loss would reveal preparation or merely rhetoric. Documentation becomes a form of delegated sight.

The stakes are therefore larger than administrative neatness. Auditability creates accountability, and accountability changes behaviour before a casualty ever occurs. A company that knows its records will be examined by insurers, class, auditors, charterers, and perhaps later by claims handlers or courts has reason to close gaps earlier, explain deviations more carefully, and align practice with procedure more closely than it otherwise might. Arctic conditions intensify this discipline because remoteness, weather, cold, and limited support make retrospective reconstruction harder and more expensive. A well-kept trail can reduce doubt. A broken one invites it.

This is also why audits and inspections have such unusual commercial force in polar trades. They test whether the system lives outside the binder. A procedure may look coherent on paper; an audit asks whether people follow it, understand it, and update it when the operating context changes. An inspection asks whether the vessel's condition, equipment readiness, records, and onboard behaviour support the claims made ashore. In difficult environments, demonstrated competence becomes a tradable asset. Insurers read it as reduced uncertainty. Charterers read it as reduced disruption. Regulators read it as reduced dependence on optimistic self-description. Proof acquires market value.

Contract language then hardens that value into obligation. Warranties, conditions precedent, due diligence clauses, reporting duties, route restrictions, survey-related requirements, and documentary representations bind the operator to specific forms of conduct that can later be measured against the record. These clauses rarely sound dramatic. They are often technical, concise, and easy to underestimate. Yet they are where private governance bites. They determine whether a missing document is a minor annoyance or a material breach, whether a late update is a clerical lapse or a cover problem, whether improvisation remains tolerated or becomes commercially expensive. The contract turns the file into an enforcement mechanism.

The movement ahead follows that logic of hardening proof. It begins with the document stack itself, where the practical architecture of Arctic compliance becomes visible in the ordinary but consequential papers behind every serious voyage. It then shifts to audits and inspections, where institutions test whether the stack reflects real competence rather than tidy aspiration, before tightening around the contractual clauses that give documentation its sharpest edge by attaching operational consequences to what is recorded, omitted, or left unresolved. Across all three, the question remains the same: not whether documents exist, but what they do once other actors begin to rely on them.

The deeper significance is strategic. Arctic expansion is often narrated through routes, resources, vessels, and geopolitics. Yet many ventures advance or stall for quieter reasons: a missing operational plan, an unresolved survey item, a weak audit trail, an insurer's discomfort with incomplete records, a charterer's insistence that documentary proof reach beyond formal compliance. These are not side issues. They are the means by which institutions decide whether risk has been made legible enough to tolerate. A voyage may be technically possible and legally permitted, but if the folder opens to gaps, contradictions, or decorative paperwork, possibility shrinks very quickly.

That leaves a harder question than the language of compliance usually admits. When a vessel appears ready, which matters more: the strength of the ship, the confidence of the operator, or the quality of the documentary trail that lets strangers test both from a distance - and what happens when the weakest point in the Arctic venture is not the ice outside, but the missing page inside the file?

The document stack behind a voyage

In August 2016, the *Crystal Serenity* left Seward, Alaska, for its Northwest Passage transit carrying more than passengers, fuel, provisions, and reputation. It carried a dense paper life assembled long before the first line was cast off: certificates, plans, manuals, class records, reports, approvals, and the quieter written assurances without which a voyage of that kind would have struggled to exist on commercial terms at all. The public saw a ship entering remote waters. Insurers, charterers, regulators, and technical reviewers saw a file moving ahead of the hull. The file sailed first.

That is not a metaphor of convenience. In Arctic operations, the document stack is part of the vessel's operating equipment in every meaningful institutional sense. A ship may be strong, well crewed, and conservatively managed, yet still find its freedom narrowed if the documentary record does not make those qualities visible and auditable to outsiders. Manuals tell others how the company claims it will behave. Plans translate intention into sequence and limitation. Certificates establish formal standing. Class records trace technical legitimacy through time. Survey reports reveal what independent eyes have recently seen. Together they allow distant actors to decide whether the operator deserves trust before anything has gone wrong. Paper carries power.

The reason is simple, though its consequences are not. Arctic ventures are judged largely from ashore, and often by people who will never stand on the bridge, enter the engine room, or watch a cold-weather drill in person. Underwriters, brokers, P&I interests, charterers, financiers, auditors, flag officials, port inspectors, and counterparties all need a way to evaluate conduct they cannot directly observe. Documentation solves that problem imperfectly but indispensably. It turns a company's internal life into portable evidence. Without that portability, Arctic commerce would depend far more heavily on rumour, prestige, and local familiarity. With it, institutions can compare operators through records rather than through faith alone.

The stack itself is less glamorous than the ship it supports, which is why its importance is so often missed. Manuals sit near the centre because they state the system the company claims to operate: safety management, cold-environment procedures, contingency arrangements, reporting lines, maintenance logic, operational limits, and the decision thresholds meant to govern difficult moments. Plans then narrow those general claims into voyage-specific commitments. A route plan, an ice-informed operating plan, a communications plan, an emergency support concept, or a cargo-specific procedure does not merely fill a folder. It answers the practical question of how this vessel, on this service, in this season, intends to convert general readiness into actual conduct. Certificates and class records complete the formal picture by showing that the ship belongs within recognised legal and technical orders. Survey reports add friction to the entire structure by testing whether the paper resembles the vessel it purports to describe.

Each document has a separate role, yet the real force lies in their coherence. A manual that promises disciplined route thresholds means little if the voyage plan ignores them. A vessel's current certificates reassure less if class records reveal unresolved recommendations or if survey findings suggest maintenance drift. A risk assessment sounds serious until the emergency arrangements it assumes prove vague or unsupported. The document stack therefore operates as a single evidentiary ecology. One weak item can cast doubt backward and forward across the whole file. Institutions notice inconsistency quickly because inconsistency often signals that the operator's confidence exceeds its control.

This is why documentation functions not merely as record-keeping but as governance. Governance, in this setting, means the organised shaping of conduct through reviewable expectations and consequences. A company that knows its plans, records, and procedures will be read by outsiders writes and maintains them differently from a company that treats documents as decorative compliance. It closes recommendations faster. It explains deviations more clearly. It keeps class records current because stale records invite questions that spread into insurance terms or charter negotiations. It sharpens manuals because vague prose can become expensive when a market asks whether the organisation truly knows where its limits lie. Documents create auditability; auditability creates behavioural pressure.

That pressure matters especially in Arctic operations because retrospective reconstruction is difficult and often contentious. After an incident in remote cold waters, institutions do not simply ask what happened. They ask what the company had planned, what warnings were identified, which procedures were in force, whether thresholds were respected, what maintenance history surrounded the failure, who approved what, and whether the records align with the narrative offered after the fact. In more forgiving environments, a weak file may still be survivable. In the Arctic, the absence of a clear documentary trail can itself become part of the severity of the problem, not because paper floats better than steel, but because doubt multiplies when distance, delay, and sparse witnesses make facts harder to fix.

A named example helps show how much of Arctic legitimacy sits inside paperwork. The *Venta Maersk* transit through the Northern Sea Route in 2018 drew notice because it suggested that container movements through Arctic waters could be discussed in commercial rather than purely strategic or experimental terms. What gave the voyage wider significance, however, was not the charted route alone. It was the legibility of the operator. A company with established systems, known technical standing, disciplined documentation, and a risk submission others could actually read as bounded and coherent presented a very different institutional object from a newcomer making similar claims with thinner records. The ship and the route mattered. The file explained why anyone should treat either seriously.

This is also why a missing document can have consequences out of all proportion to its apparent modesty. Suppose an operator proposes a voyage in remote seasonal waters and can produce class standing, crew records, recent surveys, and broad cold-weather procedures, yet cannot provide a voyage-specific operational plan or a current supporting document clearly setting out route limits and contingencies. The absence may look narrow to the owner. To the insurer, it changes the character of the whole submission. Now the market cannot test how the general system is meant to operate in this specific case. Uncertainty that might have been priced conventionally becomes uncertainty about whether the operator has translated policy into practice at all. Cover may be delayed, narrowed, or quoted subject to further evidence. One missing plan can stall a voyage not because paper is fetishised, but because the absent document leaves too much of the intended conduct invisible.

That is how pricing penalties arise from documentary weakness. Markets do not always refuse deficient files outright. More often they express doubt through structure: higher premium, larger deductibles, tighter warranties, more intrusive survey requirements, route-specific conditions, narrower territorial wording, or shorter review cycles. The operator remains technically in the game, but at a cost that disciplines its behaviour and signals unease to counterparties. A charterer reading the insurance terms may infer weakness from the very conditions attached to cover. A financier may ask harder questions about operational control. Documentation therefore affects not only insurability in the narrow sense, but the wider commercial interpretation of the voyage.

The stack behind an Arctic voyage also carries institutional memory. Class records show whether recommendations recur. Survey reports show whether the same kinds of concerns keep returning. Maintenance and defect logs reveal whether the operator tends to repair early or defer awkward items until outside pressure rises. Audit trails show whether non-conformities were treated as serious signals or as paperwork nuisances. Training records indicate whether cold-weather competence is practised or merely claimed. These documents do not simply describe present condition. They allow outsiders to watch time at work inside the organisation. This temporal depth is one of the reasons documents command such authority in specialist markets. They show whether discipline is episodic or habitual.

A counter-example is worth admitting, because documents are not magical. Some operators write immaculate manuals, maintain beautiful files, and still run weaker ships than the paperwork suggests. The audit trail can be curated. Drill records can become ceremonial. Plans can be copied forward with only cosmetic revision. Maintenance logs can reflect a culture more concerned with evidentiary neatness than with technical honesty. Anyone who has spent time around compliance systems knows this danger well. To praise documentation too highly would be naive.

And yet the possibility of document theatre does not weaken the argument for the stack. It sharpens the need to read it properly. Serious underwriters, auditors, surveyors, and charterers do not rely on one document in isolation. They look for corroboration. Does the plan match the route and the season? Do the class records fit the claimed maintenance culture? Do the survey findings support the operator's account of itself? Do training records align with the complexity of the proposed trade? Does the company's response to prior recommendations suggest seriousness or defensiveness? A good stack is persuasive not because it is thick, but because its pieces reinforce one another under scrutiny.

This is where the notion of accountability becomes concrete. Accountability in Arctic commerce does not begin after an accident with lawyers and claims handlers. It begins when the operator is required to state, in advance and in writing, what systems it has, what limits it accepts, what support it assumes, what maintenance standards it keeps, and how it intends to manage a difficult voyage. Those written commitments become reference points against which later conduct is judged. The company is not merely asked to operate prudently. It is asked to leave traces of what prudence was supposed to mean before the event. Documentation therefore tightens the bond between preparation and responsibility.

The same logic explains why document requests often proliferate as Arctic exposure becomes more complex. More remoteness means more need to show contingency thinking. More environmental sensitivity means more need to show preventive discipline. More route novelty means more need to show why this plan is not just a generic template in polar dress. More passenger exposure, cargo sensitivity, or infrastructure dependence means more need to prove that someone has thought about the second and third consequences of failure, not merely the first. The stack thickens because the burden of explanation grows in proportion to the severity of uncertainty.

One can think of the document stack as the administrative hull of the voyage. The steel hull meets the ice. The administrative hull meets the institutions deciding whether the vessel may proceed on tolerable terms. If the first is weak, the ship is exposed physically. If the second is weak, the ship is exposed commercially and legally before departure and interpretively after any incident. Both forms of weakness matter, and in polar operations they increasingly interact. A technical concern with poor documentary support becomes a more troubling insurance concern. A well-maintained vessel with thin plans still looks risky. A capable crew without a convincing paper trail remains hard to price and harder to defend later.

The quiet motif returns because the file really does move ahead of the hull. It reaches the underwriter first, the charterer next, the auditor after that, perhaps the inspector later, and the claims handler if something goes badly wrong. Each reads the voyage through what the documents make visible and what they leave in shadow. Arctic operators succeed, in part, by understanding this early enough to build the documentary life of the voyage with the same seriousness they devote to steel, fuel, ice advice, and crew selection.

That leaves a revealing test at the edge of every proposed passage. When the vessel appears capable and the route looks open, what actually persuades the institutions around it to say yes: the strength of the ship, the confidence of the operator, or the integrity of the document stack that allows distant strangers to believe both before the water asks its own questions?

Audits, inspections, and evidence of competence

In January 2012, after the *Costa Concordia* grounded off Giglio, Italy, the maritime world did what it always does after a casualty large enough to strip away public illusions: it turned from the visible wreck to the less visible question of organisational truth. What had been claimed? What had been checked? What had been practised? Which procedures existed only in binders, and which had been made real in drills, reporting habits, and command culture before the ship ever entered danger? The answer mattered because a system on paper can fail twice: once when it is not followed, and again when everyone discovers too late that it was never truly believed. The clipboard remembers.

That memory gives audits and inspections their real force. They do not merely verify that documents exist. They test whether documents govern conduct. In ordinary maritime trades, weak systems can sometimes hide behind routine, repetition, and the forgiving rhythms of better-supported routes. Arctic operations do not offer the same mercy. Cold slows response. Remoteness lengthens the consequence. Sparse support makes small errors grow teeth. Under those conditions, the question is not whether a company has written down sensible procedures. It is whether people aboard and ashore have turned those procedures into reflex, habit, and disciplined restraint. Proof must move.

This is why audits and inspections are so much more than administrative ceremony in polar work. An audit asks whether the company can demonstrate that its safety management system lives in practice rather than resting as aspiration in controlled documents. An inspection asks whether the vessel, its records, its equipment, and its crew behaviour support the story the operator tells about itself. These are related but distinct forms of institutional scrutiny. The audit tends to read the organisation through procedure, responsibility, non-conformity handling, training records, and the internal logic of control. The inspection tends to read the system through condition, readiness, and observed conduct. Together they narrow the gap between claim and fact.

That gap matters commercially because Arctic operations magnify the value of demonstrated competence. Competence, in this context, is not a flattering adjective attached to a company profile. It appears in concrete things: drills run under realistic conditions, maintenance points closed before they become arguments, crew who can explain route limits without guessing, bridge teams who know when the procedure requires retreat rather than persistence, engineers who understand what cold does to systems that behave differently in benign waters, managers ashore who answer awkward questions with records instead of assurances. In harsher environments, institutions trust what they can examine. Competence becomes visible or it does not count for much.

A named example shows why this visibility matters. When the *Crystal Serenity* transited the Northwest Passage in August 2016, the public meaning of the voyage lay in access and spectacle. Its institutional meaning lay elsewhere. A large passenger vessel in remote waters created a setting in which audits, inspections, reviews, and preparedness evidence carried unusual weight. It was not enough that the operator could point to a compliant file. The surrounding chain of parties needed signs that the company's systems had been adapted to the realities of cold, evacuation complexity, communications strain, and delayed external support. In such a case, proof was not a bureaucratic afterthought. It was part of the voyage design.

This helps explain why Arctic operations place such a premium on demonstrated competence rather than declared competence. Any operator can state that crew are trained, that emergency procedures are understood, that maintenance is disciplined, that risk assessments are current, that route limits are respected. Audits and inspections ask a ruder question: show me. Show me the drill records and how they changed after weaknesses appeared. Show me the maintenance history and how minor anomalies were handled before they matured into larger concerns. Show me the training matrix and how it matches the actual voyage profile rather than an idealised one. Show me that the person answering knows the procedure as lived reality, not as a paragraph in a manual. The answer must be embodied.

The cold gives this demand its urgency. Human performance changes in low temperatures, under bulky gear, in darkness, on iced decks, with hands that lose dexterity and minds that must decide under greater physical strain. Machinery reliability shifts as seals, lubricants, heating arrangements, sensors, and exposed systems behave differently. Emergency response times lengthen because every movement takes longer and outside help sits farther away. These factors do not merely add up; they compound. A weak procedure plus delayed response plus fatigued crew plus awkward equipment access can turn what looked manageable in a temperate drill into something much more serious at sea. Auditors and inspectors know this. They therefore look for evidence that the company has internalised compounding risk rather than merely acknowledged it in generic language.

This is also why inspections often matter as much for what they reveal indirectly as for what they record directly. A surveyor or inspector may notice an item of equipment in questionable condition, but the larger significance may lie in what that condition says about maintenance culture. A crew member may answer one technical question vaguely, and the true issue may be whether training has been routinised rather than absorbed. A non-conformity log may show closure on paper, but the timing and quality of corrective action may reveal how seriously the organisation treats its own weak signals. In difficult trades, institutions read these details the way an experienced clinician reads symptoms: not as isolated curiosities, but as clues to the state of the whole body.

A second named example, though not Arctic in the narrow geographic sense, illustrates the broader institutional lesson. After the *Exxon Valdez* grounding in Alaska in March 1989, the maritime world learned again that competence cannot be inferred solely from the existence of formal systems. Investigations, claims, public scrutiny, and regulatory reaction all pushed attention towards how organisations supervise fatigue, navigation discipline, bridge practice, reporting culture, and managerial oversight. The relevance here is not simply historical. It is conceptual. Severe environments make the difference between nominal compliance and lived competence brutally expensive. Arctic operations inherit that lesson every time an auditor asks whether the procedure is practised, not merely approved.

Insurer confidence is shaped directly by these encounters. Underwriters do not read audit outcomes as abstract badges of virtue. They read them as evidence about whether the operator is likely to produce the kinds of avoidable surprises that turn routine cover into ugly claims. A clean audit trail, credible corrective action, coherent inspection history, and evidence that procedures are actually followed can soften suspicion in a setting where suspicion is otherwise cheap. An operator with strong evidence of competence may still pay more for Arctic exposure than for easier trade, but it often secures something just as valuable: better terms, broader confidence, fewer intrusive conditions, a willingness by markets to believe the rest of the file. Proof changes price.

The same is true for charterers, though the mechanism differs slightly. Charterers care about safety, but they also care about delay, reliability, cargo integrity, reputational exposure, and the possibility that a vessel's weak systems will turn operational friction into contractual damage. Audit outcomes and inspection histories therefore function as screens for commercial dependability. A charterer may not read every cold-weather procedure in detail, but it will care whether reputable audits support the operator's claims, whether inspection records reveal recurring weaknesses, and whether the vessel's documentary life suggests disciplined control rather than fragile performance. Evidence of competence becomes part of the freight conversation whether or not anyone says so explicitly.

This is where proof becomes an operational asset rather than a defensive archive. A company with strong audit outcomes, clean inspection responses, disciplined corrective-action records, and demonstrably relevant crew preparation can move faster through commercial scrutiny because it has already answered some of the questions others would otherwise need to ask at length. Brokers can place the risk more effectively. Insurers can narrow their doubts. Charterers can spend less time wondering whether the vessel will turn routine stress into delay. Regulators may still inspect rigorously, but their starting point becomes less guarded. Proof, then, is not only what protects the company after a casualty. It is part of what enables the voyage before one occurs.

Still, a limitation must be stated plainly. Audits and inspections can be gamed, softened, staged, or turned into rituals of presentation. Companies know when they are being watched. Records can be polished. Crew can be coached. Temporary tidiness can conceal chronic weakness. Some auditors are sharper than others. Some inspections are more probing than others. A strong paper outcome is therefore not a guarantee that the organisation beneath it is as competent as it appears. The clipboard remembers, but it can also be managed.

Yet this limitation only sharpens the value of serious scrutiny. Because audits and inspections can be performed badly, institutions that rely on them learn to read their texture rather than their headlines alone. They ask whether findings make sense in light of class history, survey outcomes, maintenance records, loss experience, and the overall coherence of the operator's story. They look at how the company handled previous non-conformities, how quickly it closed recommendations, whether the same weakness recurs in new language, whether drill and training records look lived or templated. In other words, they use audit and inspection evidence as part of a larger mosaic. Proof becomes more persuasive when its pieces fit.

This larger reading also explains why Arctic work makes demonstrated competence so commercially valuable. Where comparators are thinner and consequences broader, institutions are more reluctant to rely on instinct or reputation alone. They need transferable evidence. A strong audit culture can provide that. It shows not just that the operator obeyed a rule at one moment, but that the company has built routines capable of surviving recurring stress. Inspections add a second layer by checking whether those routines appear on the vessel itself. Together they convert competence from private self-belief into something others can price, approve, demand, or refuse.

The relationship between proof and operational freedom is therefore tighter than it first appears. An operator with weak evidence may still be technically permitted to proceed, but under conditions that narrow the voyage's commercial attractiveness: more surveys, tighter warranties, higher deductibles, more extensive charterparty protections, slower approvals, less room for improvisation. Another operator with stronger evidence can often secure a less punitive version of the same route or season. The sea has not become kinder for that operator. The institutions around the sea have become less uncertain. Proof has purchased room.

That room is not merely administrative. It alters conduct. When companies know that audit outcomes and inspection histories shape insurer appetite and charterer requirements, they begin to treat evidence production as part of operations rather than as something appended afterwards. Training becomes more deliberate because it must be shown and defended. Drills become more realistic because superficial ones will not withstand questioning. Maintenance records become more disciplined because weak records now carry market cost. Decision thresholds become clearer because vague discretion cannot easily be sold to distant counterparties. The audit trail does not just describe the organisation. It helps form it.

The quiet motif returns because the clipboard is more than a prop. It stands for the institutional demand that competence leave traces. Arctic operations magnify that demand because cold, distance, and limited support make invisible weakness disproportionately expensive. The company that understands this early treats audits and inspections as tools for discovering whether its self-image is true. The company that treats them as obstacles to be managed often learns, later and more painfully, that the real obstacle was not the auditor, the inspector, or the underwriter. It was the weakness that the questions were trying to uncover.

The unresolved question is not whether proof matters. It plainly does. The harder question is what counts as enough proof when the environment is severe, the consequences of error compound quickly, and the most important element of competence may still be the one thing audits and inspections can only infer indirectly: whether the organisation will remain disciplined when the cold slows every action and the easiest course is to pretend that the procedure is still working when it has already begun to fail.

Contract clauses that enforce compliance

In August 2016, when the *Crystal Serenity* prepared to transit the Northwest Passage from Seward, Alaska, the voyage depended on far more than the visible confidence of a large passenger ship entering remote waters. It depended on words buried in contracts: warranties about how the operation would be conducted, conditions tied to coverage and approvals, and undertakings that transformed broad promises of prudence into binding obligations. The itinerary looked adventurous. The language was strict. A route through ice is also a route through clauses.

This is one of the less theatrical truths of Arctic commerce. People tend to imagine compliance as something produced by rules, audits, class notations, and official permissions, as though contracts merely mop up the leftovers. In practice, contracts often do the sharpest governing work. They decide which precautions must be taken, which documents must exist, which disclosures must be made, which limits must be respected, and what happens if any of this fails. A ship may be technically capable and formally allowed to proceed. Contractual wording can still narrow, delay, or economically deform the voyage before the first line is cast off. The sentence bites.

That bite matters because contracts bind conduct in a way that broad standards alone often do not. A general duty to act prudently or maintain proper management leaves room for interpretation until something goes wrong. A warranty, a condition precedent, or a due diligence clause narrows that room in advance. It tells the operator that cover, payment, approval, or contractual performance depends on specified behaviour or on specified evidence of behaviour. The language may appear dry, but its practical effect is muscular. It takes what might otherwise remain an aspiration - sensible route planning, current documentation, competent crewing, timely disclosure, proper maintenance, compliance with operational limits - and turns it into a point on which money, liability, or access can swing.

A warranty is one of the clearest examples because it expresses obligation as continuing fact or required conduct. In marine and related commercial settings, a warranty can require that the vessel remain within a defined geographical or seasonal envelope, that a condition of class be maintained, that certain procedures or equipment remain in place, or that the ship not proceed under circumstances the underwriter or counterparty regards as intolerable. What matters here is not legal taxonomy in the abstract, but operational consequence. A warranty does not merely describe a preferred state of affairs. It establishes a behavioural line. Cross it, and the operator may find that what looked like routine freedom has become conditional or expensive very quickly.

Conditions precedent work with a different but equally forceful logic. They make certain steps necessary before a right arises, before cover attaches, or before performance is treated as contractually secure. In Arctic operations, this can matter enormously because the underlying trade is already burdened by thin margins of weather, support, and timing. If the condition requires, for example, that a survey recommendation be closed, that a plan be furnished, that a vessel obtain or maintain a specified technical status, or that route information be provided before movement into sensitive waters, then the absence of that step is not a clerical irritation. It becomes a threshold problem. The voyage may remain technically imaginable, but it is no longer commercially ready on the terms everyone assumed. The file is not complete. The rights do not ripen.

Due diligence clauses seem softer at first glance, but in polar trades they often perform some of the most consequential work. They are attractive because they recognise that not every future difficulty can be reduced to one perfect rule. Instead, they require the operator to demonstrate reasonable care, competent management, and serious efforts to prevent foreseeable harm. In less demanding settings, such clauses can leave meaningful room for judgment. In Arctic contexts, that room shrinks because the environment makes "reasonable" preparation denser and more specific. Due diligence comes to include route-specific planning, stronger maintenance discipline, clearer decision thresholds, better crew preparation, more conservative support assumptions, and more careful treatment of cold-weather constraints than generic shipping language might imply elsewhere. The clause may look open-textured. The environment fills it in.

This is why Arctic-specific clauses often tighten the room for improvisation. Improvisation is not always recklessness; seafaring has always required judgment under changing conditions. But harsh environments make later justification harder and retrospective scrutiny harsher. A clause requiring advance reporting of route changes, adherence to an operational manual, compliance with particular ice advice, closure of technical recommendations before entry into specified waters, or maintenance of certain crewing or equipment standards does not abolish seamanship. It tells the operator that the margin for ad hoc adjustment has already been priced and narrowed. To improvise outside that framework is to move from managed discretion into contractual exposure.

A named example helps make the point. When the *Venta Maersk* completed its trial Northern Sea Route voyage in 2018, much of the public attention centred on the route's commercial symbolism. The less visible truth was that a movement of this kind only becomes institutionally tolerable when the obligations surrounding it have been made legible to markets and counterparties. A ship may have the technical capability and operational planning to attempt such a voyage, yet the commercial chain still wants binding language around reporting, route discipline, support assumptions, liability allocation, and compliance with whatever standards, surveys, or approvals underpin the proposal. The contract becomes the instrument through which others decide whether the operator's account of discipline is merely persuasive or actually binding.

This is also how responsibility gets allocated across actors who would otherwise prefer to speak in the language of shared confidence. Owners, charterers, insurers, cargo interests, terminals, and service providers all benefit from presenting the voyage as an orderly undertaking. Once a clause assigns duties precisely, that comfort becomes more expensive to fake. If the owner warrants certain technical or operational conditions, the owner bears the burden of keeping them true. If the charterparty allocates responsibility for route information, ice advice, or delay consequences in a defined way, one side loses the luxury of saying later that everyone understood matters informally. If the insurer conditions cover on compliance with stated precautions, the insured can no longer rely on broad impressions of good faith alone. Contracts do not create all responsibility. They force it into clearer channels.

A clause can therefore turn a seemingly small act into a decisive commercial event. An overdue plan. An unresolved class recommendation. A failure to notify. A deviation from an agreed seasonal or geographical limit. A crewing arrangement thinner than represented. A maintenance point treated as minor because the ship seemed to be functioning well enough. In ordinary corporate language, these things can sound manageable. In contract language, they can alter whether cover responds, whether a fixture stands, whether an indemnity applies, or whether a counterparty can resist payment or shift blame. The operational significance lies not only in the clause itself, but in the way it transforms uncertainty into leverage.

A brief example illustrates how little is required for this leverage to become real. Imagine an operator seeking cover or contractual approval for an Arctic voyage where the file is broadly strong: current certificates, solid class standing, acceptable maintenance records, experienced bridge personnel, a credible route concept. Yet one voyage-specific operational plan or risk assessment required by the relevant wording has not been finalised or supplied. Nothing visible about the ship changes. No steel weakens. No weather worsens. And yet the absence may delay cover or trigger a conditional quotation because the contract has made that document a gateway rather than a courtesy. The missing page becomes an economic problem. That is what enforcement by clause looks like in practice.

Insurers rely on this kind of wording because it allows them to govern behaviour without having to supervise everything directly. They cannot stand on every bridge, inspect every chart table, or watch every drill. But they can require that specified facts remain true, that certain acts occur before liability attaches, and that the insured carry the cost of straying beyond agreed limits. This is not merely defensive drafting. It is a way of converting concerns about cold, remoteness, route novelty, support scarcity, and human fallibility into contractual mechanisms that discipline the trade. A policy is not only a promise to pay. It is also a behavioural instrument.

Charterparties and related operational contracts use similar tools for their own reasons. Charterers care about delay, cargo integrity, schedule reliability, off-hire exposure, and the possibility that a technically lawful voyage becomes a commercial mess when weather, ice, or administrative friction intervene. Clauses concerning permitted routes, ice conditions, notice obligations, due diligence, compliance with specific instructions, or the allocation of waiting time and diversion cost are therefore not procedural clutter. They are attempts to map uncertainty onto responsibility before the uncertainty becomes expensive. In Arctic trades, these clauses tend to become more exacting because the cost of loose allocation is so much higher once conditions deteriorate and external support is thin.

One can see why operators sometimes resent this. From their perspective, multiple overlapping clauses can make the voyage feel over-scripted. What class requires, insurance repeats. What the insurer asks, the charterer narrows. What the manual states, the terminal may supplement. The room for judgement seems to contract at every step. That perception is often accurate. It is also one of the ways private governance actually works. No single institution needs to forbid Arctic movement if several institutions, each pursuing its own cautious logic, bind the operator closely enough through contract that only the most documented, disciplined, and well-supported voyages remain attractive.

A second named example clarifies the broader logic from outside the Arctic itself. After the *Costa Concordia* casualty in January 2012, the commercial and legal afterlife of the disaster did not turn only on technical condition or command behaviour. It also turned on the ways contracts, procedures, and institutional obligations distributed responsibility for safety systems, passenger welfare, emergency conduct, and post-casualty consequences. The lesson for Arctic work is straightforward. Severe environments magnify the importance of binding language because the room for generous informal reconstruction after a loss is narrow. When consequences are large, parties read clauses hard.

Still, a limitation must be admitted. Contracts do not enforce themselves, and not every clause proves equally clear or equally effective. Overlapping wording can confuse as well as discipline. Some clauses are drafted broadly because parties cannot anticipate every operational variation. Others are negotiated under commercial pressure and later prove less elegant than anyone would like. Human judgment remains necessary in reading and applying them, especially when circumstances are unusual or when several documents appear to point in slightly different directions. It would be naive to treat contractual language as a perfect machine for controlling Arctic uncertainty.

Yet this limitation only strengthens the central point. Because clauses are imperfect, parties build more of them, read them more carefully, and fight more intensely over their meaning when exposure is severe. The existence of interpretation does not weaken contractual governance. It deepens it. Operators must think not only about what they intend to do, but about how that intention has been frozen into enforceable wording across policies, charterparties, service contracts, support agreements, and internal compliance commitments. The prudent operator learns to read across documents. The imprudent one reads each in isolation and discovers too late that the combined room for manoeuvre was far smaller than it appeared.

This is where contractual language becomes a map of operational freedom. A seasonal limitation in a policy may align with a route restriction in the operational manual and an ice clause in the charterparty. A due diligence obligation may be echoed by a warranty that effectively defines what diligence must look like in practice. A requirement to maintain class, provide notices, or close recommendations may appear in several places with slightly different consequences. The operator's real liberty lies not in any one clause, but in the narrow corridor left after all of them are laid over one another. In Arctic trades, that corridor can be surprisingly thin.

The strategic implication is broader than contract doctrine. These clauses do not merely allocate blame after the fact. They shape conduct before departure. They make some forms of improvisation too risky to contemplate. They reward companies that keep their records current, their manuals aligned with practice, their disclosures prompt, and their technical recommendations closed. They expose weaker operators not by denouncing them publicly, but by making uncertainty expensive and leaving less room to hide it behind broad declarations of experience or confidence. In that sense, contracts stand very close to insurers, class societies, and auditors as instruments of practical governance.

The quiet motif returns because the sentence really can bite. A single phrase - "subject to", "provided always that", "warranted", "condition precedent", "due diligence" - may look like ordinary drafting to a hurried reader. In Arctic work, it often decides what the voyage may become. The ship sails through weather and ice, but the operator sails through text as well. One kind of hazard is visible. The other is only obvious once something slips outside the contractual frame and the counterparty starts reading aloud.

The harder question, then, is not whether contracts matter. They plainly do, and in severe environments, they often matter before anyone fully notices. The harder question is what sort of operator can live inside them without mistaking bound discretion for free judgment - and how much Arctic access is really determined not by what the ship can physically endure, but by what the clauses surrounding it permit everyone else to insist upon.

Chapter 7

Flag State, Port State, and Control Points

In 1982, officials meeting in Paris agreed on the Paris Memorandum of Understanding on port state control and gave modern shipping one of its most consequential quiet instruments: a way for inspection findings to travel beyond the quay where they were first recorded. A deficiency was no longer only a local irritation. A detention was no longer only a temporary interruption. Port oversight began to harden into a system of signals that insurers, charterers, regulators, and shipowners could all read, compare, and remember. The stamp moved ashore.

That shift matters especially in Arctic and near-Arctic trade because harsh environments magnify the significance of every institutional checkpoint. A ship may be technically capable, formally compliant, and commercially ambitious, yet still find its prospects reshaped by the public authorities that certify it, inspect it, record its shortcomings, and circulate their judgments through wider maritime networks. The decisive barrier is often not ice alone. It is the pattern of trust and doubt created when official oversight meets private pricing.

The central tension lies here. Maritime law imagines a vessel as carrying the authority of its flag state, yet maritime commerce never stops there. The flag grants legal identity and formal oversight, but ports test what that identity means in practice, and markets ask whether the resulting record deserves confidence. A ship therefore moves through overlapping systems of control: one attached to registration and certification, another attached to arrival and inspection, and a wider one formed by insurers, charterers, and technical intermediaries who treat public findings as commercial intelligence. No single desk decides everything. Several desks narrow the margin.

That narrowing matters because flag state quality is never merely a constitutional curiosity. It becomes a risk indicator. A technically serious administration with credible oversight, consistent certification practice, and a reputation for taking difficult trades seriously can reassure markets before a voyage begins. A weaker or less trusted administrative setting may do the opposite, even when the vessel's formal papers are in order. Insurers and charterers read flags not only as symbols of nationality or legal attachment, but as shorthand for administrative capacity, seriousness, and the probable quality of the documentary and inspection trail behind the ship.

Port state control sharpens the picture because it turns oversight into encounter. Flags certify from the vessel's legal home. Ports test that confidence when the ship appears under another authority's eye. In or near Arctic trades, this matters intensely because minor deficiencies can carry larger implications than they might in easier waters. A repeated documentation lapse, a pattern of untidy maintenance, or a sequence of small operational shortcomings may be read not as isolated imperfections but as signs that the company's discipline thins under pressure. Enforcement data therefore acquires a second life. It ceases to be merely administrative record and becomes material for underwriters, brokers, charterers, and other readers deciding whether the operator is truly governable.

Inspection intensity itself then becomes part of the business environment. A stricter inspection culture may frustrate operators with delay, cost, and procedural burden, yet it can also offer a kind of harsh reassurance because expectations are clearer and the discipline applied to vessels is more predictable. A lighter-touch setting may feel commercially convenient while increasing uncertainty for markets that suspect weak scrutiny or uneven application. Safety is never the whole story. Capacity, regional politics, environmental sensitivity, and administrative style all shape how hard an inspection bites. Operators know this and seek not only compliant routes, but legible ones.

That is why information sharing matters so much. Port reports, class concerns, insurer questions, broker intelligence, charterer hesitations, and informal industry talk all move through the same channels with surprising speed, especially where Arctic voyages remain relatively few and highly visible. A vessel does not need a dramatic casualty to attract commercial consequence. A pattern of minor deficiencies, a difficult port interaction, or a reputation for variable documentation can spread quickly enough to alter renewal discussions, fixture opportunities, survey demands, or the willingness of counterparties to accept the account at all. In specialised markets, reputation can outrun formal process.

The movement ahead follows that chain of control from the vessel's legal attachment to the points where official scrutiny becomes market discipline. It begins with the flag administration and the practical limits of what a flag can genuinely guarantee, then shifts to ports as screening mechanisms whose inspection records feed directly into commercial judgment. From there the focus widens to the politics of inspection intensity, where enforcement style itself becomes a source of risk, before tightening around the pathways by which information circulates and reputations harden. Across all four, the same fact persists: public oversight and private governance do not compete neatly. They braid together.

The larger stake is strategic. Arctic expansion depends not only on steel, route planning, and insurance appetite, but on whether public control points generate confidence or unease as vessels move through them. A ship with a trusted flag and a clean inspection history can enter negotiations with a quieter file. A ship that accumulates small official doubts may find those doubts multiplied by private readers who never witnessed the original encounter but price its memory anyway. The ship crosses one frontier. The records cross many.

The difficult question, then, is not whether flag and port state institutions matter. They plainly do. The harder question is which matters more when the Arctic venture begins to look commercially fragile: the formal authority printed on the certificate, or the chain of inspections, deficiencies, and reputational signals that tells everyone else how much that certificate is really worth.

Flag state responsibilities and practical limits

In March 1989, after the *Exxon Valdez* grounded in Alaska, one of the questions that quickly surfaced beneath the spectacle of oil and coastline was a quieter one about governance: what exactly had the ship's flag state been expected to guarantee before the casualty, and what had everyone else merely assumed it would guarantee? That question has never lost its force. A flag is more than paint on the stern. It is the vessel's legal home, the source of core certification and oversight duties, and one of the first public signals that markets read when deciding how much confidence to place in what they have not yet seen for themselves. The flag speaks early.

That early signal matters because maritime commerce still depends on a basic fiction that must be made practical if it is to be useful: the idea that a vessel can carry one state's legal authority with it across the world. In ordinary explanation, the flag state certifies the ship, oversees its compliance with applicable standards, and bears responsibility for ensuring that the vessel remains within a recognised framework of safety and legality. In practice, especially in Arctic and near-Arctic trades, that framework is only as persuasive as the administrative capacity, technical seriousness, and enforcement culture behind it. The certificate is public. Confidence is comparative.

This is why flag state responsibility matters so much to commercial readers of polar risk. Insurers, charterers, class societies, auditors, and port authorities do not treat the flag merely as a constitutional formality. They read it as an indicator. They ask what kind of administration stands behind the papers, how consistently it supervises the ships on its register, how technically demanding it is likely to be, how it handles delegated authority, and whether its reputation suggests disciplined oversight or a thinner, more permissive culture. The flag, then, does not simply attach a vessel to law. It attaches the vessel to an administrative story that markets price.

The basic role of the flag administration is easy enough to state. It is responsible for registration, the issue or recognition of core certificates, the supervision of compliance with relevant international obligations, and the broader legal oversight of ships entitled to fly its flag. Much of this work is performed directly only in part. Modern flag administrations often rely on recognised organisations, especially classification societies, to conduct surveys and issue or support certificates on their behalf. Delegation is normal. But delegation does not erase responsibility. It changes the way responsibility is exercised. The flag state must still decide how it chooses recognised organisations, how closely it monitors them, how it responds to deficiencies, and how seriously it treats the quality of the ships and operators it accepts into its registry.

This is where practical limits begin to matter. Not all flag administrations possess the same technical depth, bureaucratic capacity, political priorities, or appetite for scrutiny. Some are better resourced, more selective, more experienced with severe-environment operations, or more willing to press operators hard before granting comfort. Others may be lawful, functional, and commercially efficient while still offering a lighter-touch experience that leaves more of the burden to class, insurers, and port states later in the vessel's life. Neither style exists in the abstract. Each creates a different compliance experience for the operator and a different confidence profile for outsiders.

Capacity is one source of variation. A flag administration with strong technical staffing, stable procedures, and credible supervisory habits can ask better questions, review difficult polar documentation more intelligently, and spot the difference between a vessel that is properly prepared and one that is merely well presented. A weaker administration may rely more heavily on formal sufficiency: the documents exist, the delegated survey was completed, the certificate can be issued. That may be perfectly lawful. It is not always equally reassuring. Markets notice whether an administration seems able to look behind the document or whether the document itself carries too much of the burden. Where the environment is harsh, that distinction becomes expensive.

Priorities matter just as much. Some flag administrations treat fleet quality and reputation as strategic assets. Others prioritise service speed, registry attractiveness, or administrative accessibility. These aims are not always incompatible, but they do produce different institutional cultures. An operator may find one flag demanding in ways that feel burdensome before sailing and valuable later when insurers and charterers read the file with greater ease. Another flag may feel smoother at the point of registration or certification yet leave more explanatory work to be done afterwards, because the market is less willing to infer seriousness from the papers alone. Ease at the administrative front end can produce friction later in pricing and negotiation.

A named example illustrates the broader principle, even though the lesson travels well beyond any one casualty. After the *Exxon Valdez* grounding in Alaska in March 1989, maritime institutions did not merely examine the actions taken on one bridge. They looked more closely at the surrounding chain of oversight, operator culture, and public responsibility. The relevance here is not that one flag state alone determined the event, but that severe losses cause markets to revisit what they had been willing to assume about certification, supervision, and administrative seriousness before the casualty occurred. Once a system has failed visibly, the flag behind it stops looking like a neutral legal fact and starts looking like a question mark that private actors must price.

This is why insurers and charterers often treat flag-related signals as risk indicators rather than as background information. An insurer does not usually ask only whether the certificate exists. It asks what kind of registry issued or recognised it, what inspection and deficiency patterns tend to follow that flag, how much independent comfort must be sought through extra survey or documentary support, and whether a harder pricing stance is needed because the public oversight signal feels thinner than it appears. A charterer behaves similarly, though with a different emphasis. It wants not only legal validity, but predictability: fewer surprises in port state encounters, fewer doubts about the credibility of certification, fewer reasons for cargo owners or terminals to become uneasy. The flag enters the commercial risk picture because it shapes the expected quality of the whole compliance environment.

One practical consequence is that a flag can alter the amount of supplementary proof an operator must produce. A vessel under a highly trusted administration may still face thorough scrutiny in Arctic service, but the starting point can be calmer. The papers invite fewer immediate suspicions. The same vessel under a less trusted or less technically respected flag may encounter requests for more detailed surveys, stronger documentary evidence, tighter warranties, or additional contractual safeguards before insurers or counterparties become comfortable. The ship itself has not changed. The burden of persuasion has. This is public administration converted into private pricing.

A second named example helps show how administrative reputation can shape interpretation in less catastrophic settings. When the *Crystal Serenity* prepared for its August 2016 Northwest Passage transit, the significance of its institutional profile lay not only in technical capability or route planning, but in the extent to which multiple actors could read the supporting chain of approvals, oversight, and documentation as credible. A high-visibility voyage of that kind does not allow public authority to remain abstract. It becomes part of the operator's market-facing identity. The flag administration's role in certification and oversight helps define whether the larger commercial and regulatory story looks disciplined enough to support such an operation without every counterparty having to start from distrust.

Still, a limitation deserves acknowledgement. It would be too simple to say that a highly reputed flag always produces excellent outcomes or that a more commercially accessible registry necessarily implies weak oversight. Good operators can exist under many flags, and poor operators can exploit respected systems if other controls fail. Port state control, class, audit culture, insurer scrutiny, and charterer discipline all create checks that may compensate for weaker administrative signals or expose stronger flags when individual vessels disappoint. The flag is influential. It is not destiny.

And yet this limitation only clarifies the larger point. Because the flag is not destiny, markets read it as one signal among several - but often an early and influential one. It shapes the baseline from which the rest of the file is interpreted. A trusted flag may help an operator secure a better hearing when other questions arise. A less trusted one may mean that every later imperfection is read more harshly because the original public signal carried less confidence to begin with. This is how public administration interacts with private pricing: not through direct command alone, but through reputation, administrative culture, and the costs imposed when others must compensate for uncertain oversight.

This interaction becomes particularly important in Arctic and polar-adjacent operations because the cost of being wrong about oversight quality is higher. If a vessel certified under a thinly trusted system enters remote waters where consequences escalate quickly, insurers and charterers cannot rely on fast correction after the fact. They must price the possibility that the papers overstate the underlying discipline of the operation. That is why they care about flags in a way that can seem almost political to outsiders. It is not politics in the narrow sense. It is institutional memory turned into risk selection.

The operator experiences this most clearly when formal legality and commercial confidence diverge. A ship may hold every necessary certificate and still find itself asked for extra surveys, more detailed route documentation, or tighter contractual obligations because the flag's reassuring power has not travelled far enough through the market. This can feel unfair, especially where the operator itself is serious and the vessel well managed. But from the market's perspective, the request reflects a simple calculation: if public oversight leaves doubt, private mechanisms must work harder. The certificate opens the door. The market decides how wide.

One can therefore use flag state responsibility as a lens on the broader structure of maritime governance. It shows how public authority does not vanish in a world dominated by insurers, class societies, and contracts. It changes form. Public administration establishes the legal identity and oversight baseline of the vessel. Private actors then interpret that baseline, extend it, distrust it, or price around it according to their own institutional purposes. The result is not a clean separation between state and market. It is a layered order in which the state's credibility becomes one of the raw materials from which private confidence is built.

The quiet motif returns because the certificate really does speak early. It tells the market where the ship belongs legally. It hints at how the vessel may have been supervised. It invites trust or caution before port state inspectors, surveyors, or underwriters have added their own voices. In polar trades, where administrative weakness can become commercially costly very quickly, that early voice matters more than many operators would prefer.

The unresolved question is not whether a flag administration has responsibilities. It plainly does. The harder question is what those responsibilities are worth once the vessel enters a market that prices not only the presence of public certificates, but the credibility of the state that issued them - and how much of Arctic access quietly turns on that difference.

Port state control as a screening mechanism

In 1982, the Paris Memorandum of Understanding on port state control was signed, and with that administrative step a decisive shift occurred in the way ships would be judged once they crossed into another state's harbour. A vessel could no longer rely only on the comfort of its flag papers and its owner's confidence. It would meet another authority's eyes. That encounter mattered because the port inspector was not simply checking boxes for local order. The inspector was testing whether the ship that had arrived under one jurisdiction's assurance could survive scrutiny under another's. The quay became a checkpoint.

That checkpoint matters with unusual force in Arctic and near-Arctic trade. A vessel operating around severe routes, remote support, and harsh weather does not carry only cargo or passengers into port. It carries the accumulated claims of its operator: that the manuals are lived, the maintenance disciplined, the class standing meaningful, the crew competent, the route limitations respected, and the paperwork equal to the conditions. Port state control turns those claims into something public and comparative. It asks, with bureaucratic calm and sometimes brutal practical effect, whether the vessel looks like the disciplined object its file says it is. The stamp can sting.

Port state control works as a screening mechanism because it does more than detect immediate danger. It sorts vessels into categories of confidence. A clean inspection tells insurers, charterers, brokers, and other ports that the ship has survived a public test under another administration's authority. A detention, a sequence of deficiencies, or even a pattern of small irregularities can do the opposite. It may say that the vessel is not merely unlucky or imperfect, but perhaps indicative of a wider organisational looseness. This is the key point. Enforcement data becomes meaningful not only when it stops a ship outright, but when it helps others infer whether the operator's internal culture is disciplined or thin.

The logic is especially sharp in polar contexts because minor shortcomings rarely remain minor for long once cold, distance, and sparse support are added. A missing or inconsistent document in a dense, forgiving trade may be irritating. In Arctic service, the same lapse can suggest that the operator is less capable of controlling its own systems than it claims. A maintenance issue that seems manageable near major repair infrastructure may look more serious when the vessel proposes movement through waters where technical failure could trigger delay, costly assistance, environmental harm, or liability escalation. Port state control therefore acts as a translator. It converts visible deficiencies into signals about what might happen later in less forgiving conditions.

This is why detention risk carries such disproportionate weight. A detention is, in the immediate sense, an enforcement action with obvious commercial consequences: delay, cost, reputational discomfort, possible fixture disruption. Yet its institutional afterlife often matters more than the event itself. Underwriters ask what it says about management. Charterers ask whether schedule reliability is now suspect. Brokers ask how to explain the matter at renewal or placement. Class societies and auditors may look more closely at the surrounding record. A single detention can trigger a chain of reinterpretation because it makes a public authority's doubt visible in a way that private suspicion alone never quite can. Once public doubt is recorded, markets do not forget quickly.

A named example shows the broader force of this mechanism, even beyond polar waters themselves. In March 1999, after the *Erika* broke up off the coast of France, the shipping world was reminded that visible deficiencies, oversight failures, and regulatory enforcement questions do not remain isolated inside one casualty. They travel outward into inspection culture, insurer appetite, regulatory reform, and market memory. The relevance here is not that the *Erika* was an Arctic case. It is that serious maritime losses train institutions to read port state information more aggressively. Once a casualty reveals that weak signals were missed or discounted, minor deficiencies elsewhere stop looking so minor. Arctic underwriting inherits that sharpened habit because the downside of underestimating weakness is even harder to contain in remote severe waters.

A pattern of minor deficiencies is often more commercially damaging than one dramatic but contained fault. One repeated paperwork lapse, one maintenance irregularity, one weak emergency record, one small operational issue - each may be corrected and explained. But when similar issues recur across inspections, ports, or periods, the pattern begins to suggest systemic weakness. This is the real screening function of port state control. It is not only looking for the catastrophic defect. It is watching whether a vessel and its operator display the kind of low-level disorder that, under harder conditions, might mature into something much larger. Markets read patterns the way experienced doctors read symptoms: not in isolation, but as signs of a deeper condition.

Imagine a vessel proposing trade in or near Arctic routes. Its file is respectable. Certificates are current. Class is maintained. The operator insists that the ship is fit for the intended service. Yet the port state record shows a string of apparently modest deficiencies over time - inconsistencies in documentation, overdue minor maintenance items, repeated observations on safety equipment housekeeping, occasional procedural lapses, no single one serious enough to dominate headlines. An insurer looking at this pattern does not merely count incidents. It asks whether the company repeatedly allows small controls to fray. If so, the vessel may still be insurable, but on harder terms, with more survey demands, more restrictive wording, or greater reluctance to support ambitious seasonal movement. Small defects become a character sketch.

This is one reason operators fear inspection histories even when they avoid headline detentions. Port state control produces records that move. They circulate through databases, broker conversations, underwriting discussions, chartering screens, and informal maritime talk. The information becomes market intelligence because it offers something rare: a publicly generated view of the vessel's condition and compliance culture under external scrutiny. In sectors where operators would otherwise present themselves through carefully managed documentation, this kind of externally generated record carries unusual weight. It is harder to curate. That makes it more trusted, though not always more nuanced.

A second named example shows how this logic operates in the age of Arctic commercial symbolism. When the *Venta Maersk* completed its Northern Sea Route trial voyage in 2018, the public narrative centred on route possibility and strategic implication. Commercial readers, however, would have understood that any attempt to normalise such activity depends not only on technical design or one successful passage, but on how vessels trading in those regions fare under the ordinary discipline of inspections. If a route is to become commercially routine, the ships using it must not merely survive the ice. They must survive the file. Port state control becomes part of the route's commercial biography, recording whether supposedly disciplined Arctic operations also look disciplined when they arrive for inspection under outside authority.

The role of port state control as a screening mechanism also depends on timing. Inspections at ports are often among the few moments when a ship entering or leaving severe service encounters a concentrated external test. In that sense, the port becomes a hinge between one operational environment and another. What the ship has done in transit is brought into contact with official scrutiny; what the port records will then shape the next round of insurance, chartering, or technical review. The inspection is therefore both backward-looking and forward-looking. It evaluates condition in the present while influencing what others think the vessel should be allowed to do next.

This makes port state control part of the business environment, not merely the legal environment. Operators planning Arctic or sub-Arctic trades do not simply ask whether they can comply with the relevant technical standards. They also ask how inspection risk will affect schedule reliability, insurance pricing, counterparty comfort, and the possibility that one deficiency will be interpreted as evidence of wider weakness. Ports with reputations for thorough but consistent enforcement may be inconvenient, yet they can offer a kind of institutional predictability. Ports or inspection cultures that appear erratic, heavily politicised, or uneven may create a different kind of risk altogether, because unpredictability itself must be priced into the operation.

Still, a limitation deserves careful notice. Port state control is not infallible, and deficiency histories can be over-read. Inspectors vary in style and emphasis. Minor findings can reflect temporary conditions, documentation irritants, or local inspection habits rather than deep operational disorder. A vessel may suffer a poor encounter and still be fundamentally well run. A lighter deficiency record does not always prove strong culture; sometimes it reflects luck, timing, or a less probing inspection environment. To treat every deficiency as a diagnosis of systemic weakness would be crude and occasionally unjust.

And yet the limitation does not weaken the central argument. It explains why market readers look for pattern, context, and recurrence rather than for one isolated mark. A serious underwriter or charterer asks not only what was found, but how often, where, how it was corrected, whether related issues recur, and what the operator's response reveals about management discipline. A ship that responds quickly, transparently, and durably to inspection findings can actually strengthen its standing over time because it demonstrates that external scrutiny produces internal learning. A ship that accumulates similar minor deficiencies despite repeated opportunity to correct them tells a harsher story. Port state control does not merely spot weakness. It also tests whether weakness is governable.

This is why enforcement data becomes so valuable as intelligence. It has a quality that self-reported documentation lacks: it reflects the meeting point between the vessel and an outside authority empowered to say no, delay, question, or record. In Arctic commerce, where consequence severity is high and signals are often thin, that kind of information is highly prized. It helps insurers refine pricing. It helps charterers screen reliability. It helps brokers anticipate objections. It helps ports and regulators compare ships not just by what their files promise, but by how they behave under scrutiny. The record acquires a second life far beyond the original inspection.

The strategic implication is broader than port administration alone. Arctic ventures are often narrated through route openings, vessel design, insurance appetite, and geopolitical ambition. Port state control reveals a quieter reality. Access is repeatedly filtered through ordinary public control points where weak discipline becomes visible and then travels outward into private judgement. A ship may be technically capable, legally documented, and commercially promising, yet a pattern of small enforcement problems can steadily harden market scepticism around it. That is not an accident of administration. It is one of the mechanisms through which maritime governance operates without grand announcement.

The quiet motif returns because the stamp does more than record a visit. It creates a signal that others read later, often more harshly than the operator expects. A deficiency noted on the quay may reappear as an underwriting question, a chartering hesitation, a survey requirement, or a tighter warranty months afterward. A detention may fade from operational memory long before it fades from market memory. The port inspector does not set the premium or write the charter party. The inspection nevertheless helps both.

The unresolved question, then, is not whether port state control can stop a bad ship. It plainly can and sometimes must. The harder question is what markets should do with the much more common case: the vessel that is not disastrously defective, yet leaves behind a trail of small public doubts - enough to sail, perhaps, but enough to make everyone else wonder whether the next Arctic voyage is being asked to carry more faith than the record deserves.

The politics of inspection intensity

On 1 January 2017, when the Polar Code entered into force through the IMO framework, it became easier to imagine that polar operations would now be governed by a clearer and more even set of standards. The text was global, the aims recognisable, the logic persuasive. Yet anyone who had spent time around ships, ports, and compliance regimes knew the harder truth already: a common rule does not guarantee a common encounter. The same vessel can meet one inspector's careful suspicion, another's routine confidence, and a third administration's strategic unease. The same form, different hands.

That difference matters because inspection intensity is never only a technical matter. It certainly has a safety dimension. Ports and authorities inspect vessels because ships fail, because paperwork can mislead, because poor maintenance and weak management reveal themselves imperfectly, and because severe environments punish relaxed assumptions. But inspection intensity also reflects capacity, institutional culture, policy priorities, local environmental concern, commercial posture, and the practical politics of how a jurisdiction chooses to signal seriousness. A hard inspection can say, "we take risk seriously." It can also say, "we have the staff, confidence, and incentive to ask more questions than others do." The clipboard is political.

This is not an accusation. It is a description of how administration works in the real world. No port state control regime applies itself. People do. Their habits, resources, supervisory expectations, legal culture, and local pressures shape how deeply the vessel is examined, how quickly minor deficiencies are treated as indicators of broader weakness, and how much room remains for the operator's own explanations. In Arctic and near-Arctic trades, those judgments gain unusual force because the cost of underestimating weakness is high, while the cost of over-inspecting can also be commercially significant. Inspection intensity therefore becomes part of the voyage before the ship arrives. It sits in route planning, schedule calculation, insurance conversations, and charter negotiations as a background variable that no prudent operator can ignore.

One reason these matters so much is that inspection intensity can reflect institutional capacity as clearly as institutional principle. A well-resourced administration with experienced inspectors, technical depth, and confidence in its own procedures can afford to inspect more searchingly and more consistently. It can treat small documentary gaps or maintenance irregularities not as isolated nuisances but as clues to the health of the whole operating system. A thinner administration may rely more heavily on visible formal sufficiency because it lacks the time, technical breadth, or institutional backing to push further. The result can be striking. Two ports may operate under similar international standards and yet produce very different compliance experiences because one has the administrative muscle to read beneath the surface and the other largely does not.

Policy priorities have a similar effect. A port authority or national administration may decide, explicitly or tacitly, that environmental sensitivity, public scrutiny, regional strategy, or recent incidents justify closer scrutiny of vessels trading in difficult waters. Another may give greater weight to traffic flow, commercial attractiveness, administrative speed, or the belief that existing technical and class systems should carry more of the compliance burden. Neither position needs to be lawless or irrational. Both sit comfortably within a range of lawful discretion. Yet they create different enforcement climates, and those climates become meaningful to markets because they shape delay risk, documentary burden, reputational exposure, and the probability that a minor issue will become a formal finding.

A named example helps expose the wider point. In 1982, the Paris Memorandum of Understanding on port state control established a more coordinated framework for inspections and information sharing across participating states. Its deeper significance lay not merely in the fact of coordination, but in the recognition that inspection could no longer remain a local administrative event if it was to discipline international shipping effectively. Once findings could circulate more easily, intensity in one port began to matter elsewhere. The relevant lesson for Arctic commerce is not that all inspections suddenly became uniform. It is the opposite. Coordination made unevenness more visible and therefore more consequential, because markets could now compare how regimes behaved and what those behaviours implied about future encounters.

This is where unpredictability begins to bite. Operators can live with strict regimes more easily than they can live with capricious ones. A port state known for careful, demanding, but consistent inspection creates burdens that can at least be planned around. Schedules can be adjusted, documentation sharpened, survey work completed in advance, and commercial terms negotiated with a realistic sense of likely friction. By contrast, an environment perceived as uneven, politically sensitive, or hard to read raises a different kind of operational risk. It is not only the risk of a deficiency or detention. It is the risk of surprise: a standard applied one way last season and another way this season, a minor issue treated informally in one call and formally in the next, a routine request suddenly expanded under the influence of heightened local concern or administrative mood. Uncertainty spreads fast.

That spread matters to insurers because unpredictability is expensive even when safety outcomes do not immediately deteriorate. Underwriters price not only the possibility of physical casualty, but the probability of disruption, delay, contractual friction, and administrative complications that can enlarge claims or distort the voyage's economics. An operator facing stable but strict inspection regimes may therefore appear less risky than one facing lighter-touch but erratic enforcement, because the first environment is easier to model and the second is harder to trust. This is a crucial point. Markets do not always reward leniency. They often reward legibility. A harder rule may be cheaper than an uncertain one once pricing begins.

Charterers make a similar calculation from a different angle. They care about whether the ship will be available when promised, whether cargo will move without ugly interruption, whether a detention or prolonged inspection will trigger off-hire, reputational embarrassment, or missed commercial windows, and whether a vessel trading through or near Arctic routes will repeatedly attract scrutiny that unsettles counterparties further down the chain. A stable inspection environment helps them estimate these risks. An unstable one forces them to build wider buffers, sharper clauses, or more sceptical assumptions into their contracts. Inspection intensity therefore becomes part of the business environment in the same practical sense as weather, port congestion, or fuel availability. It is not an afterthought attached to operations. It is one of the conditions of operation.

A brief contrast clarifies the point. Imagine two ports regularly encountered by vessels in cold-region trade. In the first, inspectors are known to be demanding, technically confident, and relatively consistent. They ask for the right records, test whether procedures are live rather than decorative, and treat recurring minor deficiencies as warnings of weak management. Operators may complain, but they know what a clean call requires. In the second, inspections are usually quick and sometimes light, but the tone changes sharply after public controversy, political pressure, or administrative turnover. Similar vessels are treated differently in close succession. Findings fluctuate in character. Markets begin to worry less about the burden of inspection than about the opacity of its triggers. The first environment is hard. The second is uncertain. For many commercial actors, uncertainty is the dearer of the two.

A second named example illustrates how quickly official intensity can become reputational signal. When the *Crystal Serenity* prepared for its August 2016 Northwest Passage transit, its visibility meant that no inspection, approval, or documentary weakness would remain quietly local for long. High-profile Arctic operations draw heightened attention not only because of risk, but because their symbolic weight is large. In such settings, inspection intensity often reflects more than routine administration. It can express environmental caution, political sensitivity, and the need of authorities to show that exceptional voyages will not be allowed to coast on prestige. That dynamic does not disappear when the vessel is less famous. It simply becomes more subtle. Markets still ask whether the port or inspection culture around a route is likely to behave as a stable technical system or as a stage on which broader concerns may suddenly become administratively real.

This does not mean operators always prefer the easiest ports or the least demanding inspection regimes. Serious operators often prefer stable seriousness to apparently convenient unpredictability. A demanding regime can function as a form of reputational support if the company knows it can satisfy the standard. A clean record in a hard-inspection environment travels well in insurance and chartering discussions because others infer that the vessel and operator have survived meaningful scrutiny. By contrast, a clean record accumulated in environments widely perceived as light-touch may carry less persuasive power, precisely because outsiders do not know how much the record really proves. Severity can therefore generate trust where softness generates doubt.

Still, a limitation deserves clear acknowledgment. It would be crude to treat all variation in inspection intensity as political distortion or hidden commercial signalling. Some of it reflects ordinary differences in risk profile, traffic mix, local conditions, and inspector judgment. Not every strict inspection culture is strategically motivated, and not every lighter-touch regime is lax in any meaningful sense. Good faith administrative variation exists, and shipping would become impossible if every difference in tone were read as coded politics. A serious account must leave room for that.

Yet the limitation does not disturb the larger argument. In practice, operators, insurers, brokers, and charterers cannot wait for perfect interpretive purity. They must decide how to read enforcement environments as they find them. They therefore watch patterns. Does a regime behave consistently over time? Do similar vessels receive roughly similar treatment? Are documentary expectations clear? Do minor deficiencies escalate unpredictably or according to a recognisable logic? Are detentions and findings explained in ways that fit a stable standard? Does the port's administrative posture appear to be drifting in response to external concerns beyond technical compliance alone? Markets answer these questions because they need to, and their answers feed directly into pricing and route choice.

The most important consequence is that inspection regimes stop being mere sites of legal compliance and become part of strategic planning. Operators think about where scrutiny is likely to be toughest, where it is likely to be most stable, and where unexpected administrative friction could destroy the economics of a carefully balanced Arctic or sub-Arctic operation. Brokers think about how a vessel's past encounters in certain ports will be read by underwriters. Charterers think about how much schedule slack or contractual protection is needed if a vessel will pass through unpredictable inspection environments. Public administration thus enters private calculation in a very practical way. The inspector is not outside the market. The inspector helps shape it.

This shaping effect is magnified by information sharing. Once a port's findings circulate, they stop belonging only to that port. A strict regime can thereby strengthen a vessel's market standing if the ship repeatedly emerges clean. An unpredictable or politically charged regime can unsettle the market even when the vessel survives the encounter, because others do not know whether the next call will produce the same result. Reputational cascades build from these patterns. A port becomes known as careful, erratic, permissive, severe, technically confident, politically nervous, or hard to read. Ships carry that knowledge with them. So do policies and charter clauses.

The quiet motif returns because the clipboard is never just a clipboard. It carries state authority, yes, but also local capacity, institutional mood, regional priorities, and the commercial afterlife of everything it records.

In Arctic-related trade, where windows are narrow and consequences disproportionate, that afterlife can matter more than the inspection itself. Operators do not only fear deficiencies. They fear environments in which the logic of deficiency is hard to predict and impossible to discount in advance.

The unresolved question, then, is not whether inspection intensity serves safety. Of course it does, or should. The harder question is what market actors are really pricing when they react to a port regime - the objective rigour of its safety culture, the unevenness of its administrative capacity, the force of local politics, or the uncomfortable fact that in polar commerce the costliest hazard may be not strict enforcement, but enforcement whose next move no one can confidently foresee.

Information sharing and reputational cascades

In August 2018, when the *Venta Maersk* completed its trial transit through the Northern Sea Route, the voyage did not end when the vessel reached St Petersburg. It began a second life in reports, calls, renewal discussions, broker notes, internal underwriting commentary, class conversations, and the unglamorous but potent movement of professional memory across the maritime world. A ship had crossed a difficult route. Soon, other things were crossing too: impressions of the operator's discipline, questions about repeatability, assumptions about route support, and the kind of half-spoken judgements that accumulate around any highly visible Arctic venture. The file moves faster still.

That speed matters because specialised markets do not wait for formal conclusions before they begin to form commercial opinions. Ports publish findings. Class records circulate within the institutions that maintain them. Insurers compare notes within their own files and across reinsurance relationships. Charterers ask brokers what they are hearing. Surveyors remember what they saw on sister ships or in earlier calls. None of this needs to amount to conspiracy or even to coordinated action. It is enough that different actors are reading overlapping signals from the same small set of events. In Arctic trades, where voyages are relatively few and attention disproportionately high, each signal travels further than it would in more routine shipping.

This is the core fact behind reputational cascades. Reputation in maritime commerce is often discussed as though it were a vague quality attached to companies by habit or prestige. In practice it is built from information flows. A vessel's deficiency history, a survey recommendation, a delayed correction, a route-specific concern raised in one market, a detention, a difficult port call, a clean audit, a persuasive response to an awkward query - each becomes material others may later use when deciding whether the operator belongs inside a zone of acceptable confidence. In ordinary trades, this process can be diffuse and forgiving. In Arctic operations, it is concentrated, because the market is narrower and the cost of underestimating weakness is higher.

The machinery of information sharing is partly formal. Port state control records, class notations, survey reports, audit outcomes, insurance submissions, loss notices, and certification histories all create documents that can be reviewed, compared, and interpreted by multiple institutions. A deficiency noted in port may reappear as a question at renewal. A class recommendation may prompt a charterer to seek clarification before confirming a fixture. A survey report may influence whether underwriters ask for an additional inspection before supporting a more ambitious route or season. Formal reporting systems matter because they generate stable points of reference. They are not gossip. They are traceable signals.

But formal systems do not exhaust the process. Much of maritime reputation also travels informally, especially in specialist polar and sub-polar work where a relatively small number of actors see the same names repeatedly. Brokers talk. Surveyors compare impressions. Underwriters remember awkward renewals. Chartering desks ask who has been reliable and who has needed excessive explanation. Technical managers hear which operators respond cleanly to recommendations and which behave as though every query were an insult. These informal signals are not always fair, and they are not always precise. Yet in a market where complete information is rarely available, they can carry serious commercial weight. The phone call matters.

This blend of formal and informal information has a particular force in Arctic ventures because of their visibility and low frequency. A vessel running a common route in a dense trade can disappear into the volume of ordinary movement. An Arctic transit, a polar support voyage, a specialised tanker movement, or a high-profile expedition voyage attracts scrutiny out of proportion to its numerical share of the world shipping market. That scrutiny is not only public. It is professional. People notice because the event may teach them something about route practicability, operator discipline, institutional seriousness, or the real meaning of standards under cold and remote conditions. One incident, therefore, becomes not merely an incident, but a reference point.

A named example shows how this works. When the *Crystal Serenity* transited the Northwest Passage in August 2016, the voyage instantly became more than a passenger itinerary. It became a test case for multiple audiences. Insurers watched how such a vessel could be planned for remote waters. Regulators and technical reviewers examined what level of preparation had been assembled. Charterers and operators in adjacent sectors drew their own lessons about what counted as credible Arctic discipline and how much support had to sit behind even a carefully bounded success. The significance of the voyage did not lie only in the passage itself. It lay in the information set it generated, and the way that information spread into later conversations far beyond cruise operations.

This is why reputation can turn quickly in specialised markets. It is not because people are fickle. It is because a single new fact can rearrange earlier uncertainty. Suppose an operator long regarded as competent accumulates a port-state record showing repeated minor documentary or maintenance deficiencies across a short period. No single finding is catastrophic. Together, they alter the story. What once looked like disciplined management now begins to look like slippage or complacency. Underwriters read the pattern against earlier confidence. Charterers begin to ask whether schedule reliability or route discipline deserves more scepticism. Surveyors look a little harder next time. Reputation shifts not because anyone issued a public denunciation, but because a fresh cluster of signals changes how the old file reads.

The opposite can happen too. An operator entering Arctic trade without deep prior standing may strengthen its reputation rapidly if the available evidence is unusually coherent. Clean inspection histories, well-handled audits, transparent responses to technical questions, credible route limitations, disciplined disclosure, and orderly closure of survey recommendations can build trust faster than broad branding or strategic rhetoric ever could. In this sense, information sharing can reward seriousness as well as punish weakness. The market is not only a gossip network. It is also a memory system through which evidence accumulates and begins to function as reputational capital.

That capital matters because insurers and charterers use it differently but convergently. Insurers ask whether the operator's information trail suggests fewer unpleasant surprises, better loss prevention, and a greater chance that any future claim will be documented and managed coherently. Charterers ask whether the same trail suggests reliability, lower disruption risk, and a reduced likelihood that small operational weaknesses will become off-hire, delay, or cargo trouble. The same port report, class note, audit history, or survey outcome can therefore travel into two distinct but related kinds of judgement. One concerns loss-bearing appetite. The other concerns commercial dependence. Reputation binds them together.

A brief example makes the mechanism plain. Imagine a vessel preparing for an Arctic season with current certificates, a plausible route plan, and technically acceptable class standing. The operator's submission appears competent. Then a broker mentions that recent port interactions revealed several minor procedural deficiencies, all corrected, none severe enough to detain the vessel. An underwriter does not ignore this because the deficiencies were small. The question changes. Is this random noise or a sign that the operator's internal controls are beginning to fray? A charterer hearing the same information asks a related question. If small things keep being missed, what happens when conditions deteriorate and small things matter more? The signal has become shared intelligence.

This is why governance in Arctic commerce is networked rather than siloed. Ports do not merely enforce. They generate records that insurers and charterers read. Class societies do not merely certify. Their findings, recommendations, and notations influence how public and private actors interpret the operator's discipline. Insurers do not merely price. Their terms and questions often reveal to charterers and others where confidence has softened. Auditors do not merely verify systems. Their conclusions help determine whether the organisation's claims about competence will be trusted at all. Each institution acts for its own reasons, but the effects overlap. The network governs through circulation.

A second named example shows how a casualty can accelerate this process dramatically. After the *Costa Concordia* grounding in January 2012, information did not move through a single official channel. It travelled through public investigations, insurance reflection, classification concern, operator benchmarking, passenger-sector alarm, training review, and countless quieter conversations inside maritime organisations. The relevance here is not that Arctic ventures resemble large cruise casualties in every respect. It is that visible maritime events can send corrective signals through many institutions at once, changing how later voyages are read even where no formal rule has yet changed. In Arctic trades, where the sample size is smaller and the margin for error thinner, that kind of cascade can be even more influential.

Still, a limitation must be faced honestly. Information sharing does not always produce wisdom. Informal signals can distort. A company may suffer reputational damage from an incident whose context was more benign or more quickly corrected than the market realises. One spectacular event can overshadow years of competent performance. Rumour can move faster than nuance. Formal reports can be read too aggressively, or port findings treated as though every minor deficiency were evidence of deep managerial weakness. Networked governance is powerful partly because it is efficient, but efficiency can come at the cost of overreaction.

And yet that limitation does not diminish the importance of the network. It clarifies why serious operators care so much about the quality of their information trail. They know that a weak explanation will travel badly, that delay in responding to a recommendation will be noticed, that defensiveness under scrutiny can damage confidence more than the original issue, and that in specialised Arctic markets silence often creates its own story. The prudent company therefore manages not only ships and routes, but the circulation of evidence about them. It closes loops. It answers quickly. It treats records as live signals rather than as archived residue. In such a setting, information discipline becomes part of seamanship by other means.

This is also why reputational cascades are often faster in severe-environment trades than in more ordinary shipping sectors. Arctic ventures are not only operationally difficult. They are symbolically dense. A single transit can be interpreted as proof of commercial opening. A single deficiency history can be read as proof that someone is overreaching. A single insurance restriction can be taken as a sign that the route remains more fragile than enthusiasts claim. Because the events are sparse, each one bears more argumentative weight. Markets form views quickly because they lack the comfort of large, repetitive data sets. Reputation fills part of that gap.

The practical consequence is that operators cannot afford to think of ports, class, insurers, auditors, and charterers as separate audiences. They are audiences in communication with one another, formally or informally, through documents, questions, records, memories, and comparisons. A clean audit may assist an insurance renewal. A poor port-state sequence may harden charterparty negotiations. A transparent response to a technical concern may improve how a later survey is read. The network does not have a single centre. That is what makes it strong. It governs through overlap.

The quiet motif returns because the file never sits still. It moves from desk to desk, but it also grows as it moves. A port report is read beside a class note; a class note beside an underwriting question; an underwriting question beside a charterer's hesitation; that hesitation beside a broker's recollection of how the last renewal felt. By the time the operator sees the final commercial effect, the original information may have changed meaning three times without ever becoming formally false. This is what a reputational cascade looks like in practice: not a dramatic denunciation, but a chain of small readings that eventually becomes a market fact.

The harder question, then, is not whether information sharing improves governance. It plainly can, and often does. The harder question is what sort of Arctic market is created when reputations can turn so quickly under the pressure of sparse but vivid evidence - and whether operators can ever truly control the meaning of their own record once it enters a network where every report, recommendation, and remembered hesitation may become somebody else's reason to price, delay, restrict, or walk away.

Chapter 8

Liability Regimes and Loss Allocation

In March 1989, when the *Exxon Valdez* grounded in Alaska, the disaster quickly became more than a story of navigation, fatigue, and pollution. It became a story about legal consequence: who would pay, on what basis, under which standard of responsibility, and how far the environment itself would enlarge the claims that followed. The visible oil slick mattered. So did the invisible architecture of liability already waiting beneath it. The bill had many authors.

That is the enduring significance of liability in Arctic commerce. A ship can survive a difficult passage and still leave behind a trail of legal exposure large enough to reshape the terms on which the next voyage is priced, planned, or abandoned. Harsh environments do not merely increase the chance that something costly may happen. They make it harder to determine exactly why it happened, who controlled the critical choices, what precautions were reasonable, and how much of the resulting burden should sit with owners, charterers, insurers, or public authorities. In easier trades, fault can look comparatively neat. In the Arctic, causation frays.

The central tension lies there. Liability law tries to sort responsibility through ideas that sound clean in theory - fault, strict liability, due care, causation, mitigation, indemnity. Arctic operations expose how untidy those ideas become when geography stretches time, evidence, and response. A machinery problem may also be a maintenance story, a crewing story, a route-decision story, and a support-failure story. A pollution event may be inseparable from weather, remoteness, and delayed intervention. A wreck may begin as a navigational incident and end as a months-long argument over salvage feasibility, public authority, and contractual allocation. The map turns into a ledger.

That matters commercially because liability expectations do not wait until after a casualty to shape behaviour. They influence design choices, route conservatism, response planning, charterparty drafting, insurance structure, and the level of evidence operators are expected to assemble before a voyage begins. A company that knows pollution claims could expand sharply in remote sensitive waters plans differently from one trading in more forgiving environments. An insurer that expects salvage or wreck removal to become ruinously complex in cold, distant locations prices accordingly. A charterer aware that routing advice or delay language may later determine indemnity fights harder over the wording at the outset. Liability is not the afterlife of Arctic trade. It is one of its organising pressures.

Environmental sensitivity gives that pressure a sharper edge. Pollution risk always matters in maritime law and insurance, but in Arctic settings it gathers extra force because response is harder, political attention more intense, and the line between operational failure and public controversy much thinner. The environment becomes not merely something to protect, but something that alters the whole legal and financial severity of a casualty. That is why response planning, evidentiary discipline, and careful documentation carry so much weight long before anyone speaks of fault. A weak plan can become a stronger claim. A stronger plan can become a better defence.

Geography exerts the same force through salvage and wreck. Moderate incidents in dense maritime regions may remain moderate because help arrives, heavy equipment exists nearby, and legal and operational channels are comparatively familiar. In or near Arctic waters, distance multiplies everything: delay, cost, uncertainty, public attention, and the practical difficulty of making obligations good. This means liability cannot be understood only as a matter of legal doctrine. It must be understood as doctrine meeting distance. What looks like a manageable casualty on paper may become a very different claims environment once the nearest answer lies far over the horizon.

The path ahead follows that enlargement of consequence from principle to practice. It begins with the basic logic of fault and strict liability, where the law's effort to allocate responsibility meets the evidentiary disorder of severe environments. It then turns to pollution, where environmental sensitivity becomes a driver of both compliance and price, before moving into salvage and wreck as the places where remoteness converts modest incidents into larger financial and legal events. From there the focus tightens around charterparties, indemnities, and the contractual distribution of operational control, and finally reaches the wider problem of legal uncertainty itself, where unclear jurisdiction, enforcement variability, and thin precedent become inputs into premium, cover, and caution.

The stakes are therefore wider than legal literacy. Liability regimes determine how losses are imagined before they occur. They shape which risks insurers will tolerate, which responsibilities charterers will try to shift, which documents operators must produce, and which forms of improvisation become too expensive to contemplate. A well-run Arctic trade is not simply one that avoids disaster. It is one that understands, in advance, where responsibility will likely be argued if the voyage deteriorates and how that argument will look once remoteness, environmental exposure, and fractured evidence enter the scene.

This is why markets dislike legal ambiguity even more than they dislike severe but legible risk. A known danger can be priced, bounded, and allocated. An unclear liability landscape - uncertain jurisdiction, variable enforcement, unstable precedent, or poorly aligned contracts - makes the cost of being wrong harder to estimate and therefore harder to insure on comfortable terms. Operators feel this as more than abstraction. It appears in tighter wording, more intrusive documentary demands, stronger emphasis on response planning, sharper operational limits, and less enthusiasm for ventures that depend on confident assumptions about how later disputes would be resolved.

The harder question, then, is not whether Arctic operations generate greater liability exposure. They plainly can. The harder question is what kind of operator, insurer, or charterer can live with that exposure intelligently: the one that treats loss allocation as a problem for lawyers after the event, or the one that understands from the start that every route choice, maintenance decision, emergency plan, and contractual phrase is already shaping the argument over who pays when the Arctic turns a manageable incident into a hard legal fact.

Fault, strict liability, and the logic of deterrence

In March 1989, the *Exxon Valdez* grounded in Alaska, and the immediate spectacle of spilled oil quickly gave way to another, quieter drama: the struggle to decide what kind of responsibility the law was about to impose and why. Some questions sounded familiar. Who made the critical decisions? Were those decisions careless? Could the damage have been avoided by better navigation, better management, better supervision? Other questions pressed from a different angle. Did it matter, in some parts of the liability picture, whether fault could be proved in the ordinary way at all? The answer mattered because the law was not only sorting blame after the event. It was teaching every later operator, insurer, and charterer what kinds of precaution the market and the courts would expect before the next voyage. The ledger was already open.

That is why liability in Arctic and near-Arctic operations cannot be understood as a dry legal afterthought. It is one of the forces that shapes behaviour in advance. When operators think about route choice, crewing, maintenance, emergency support, pollution response, or contractual allocation, they are not simply thinking about safety in the abstract. They are thinking, whether explicitly or not, about what kind of story they may later have to tell if something goes wrong. A system built around fault asks whether someone failed to take reasonable care. A system built around strict liability asks a harder and colder question: who should bear the cost even if proving personal blame is difficult, contested, or beside the point? Liability begins before loss.

The distinction between fault and strict liability can appear straightforward in textbooks and far messier in the Arctic. Fault-based responsibility depends, in broad terms, on showing that someone failed to meet a required standard of care. That can mean poor navigation, weak maintenance, careless planning, inadequate supervision, or any number of other departures from what the law, a contract, or a professional standard would regard as reasonable. Strict liability shifts the emphasis. Instead of asking first whether the actor behaved badly, it asks whether the nature of the activity, the sensitivity of the protected interest, or the policy of deterrence justifies imposing responsibility once the relevant harm occurs. The practical difference is profound. One system turns on proof of substandard behaviour. The other may turn on the fact of damage within a defined legal frame.

That distinction matters because each model drives prevention differently. Fault-based liability encourages operators to think in terms of defensibility. Can the route plan be explained? Can the maintenance record show that warnings were not ignored? Can the crew's qualifications and the master's decisions be justified against conditions actually encountered? Strict liability creates a different incentive. It tells operators that some harms are so serious, or so difficult to leave uncompensated, that the safer course is to avoid them or insure heavily against them rather than rely on later arguments about the quality of their conduct. In Arctic settings, where pollution, wreck, and response failures can become extraordinarily costly, the logic of strict liability often bites with unusual force. Deterrence is built into the bill.

The harsh environment complicates both models because it scrambles causation. A casualty in temperate, well-supported waters may still produce factual dispute, but the chain of events is often easier to reconstruct. In remote cold waters, the same chain can become murkier very quickly. Ice conditions shift. Weather interferes with observation. Communications degrade. Rescue and response take longer. Machinery problems that might have been minor elsewhere interact with fatigue, darkness, remoteness, and limited external assistance. By the time the facts are assembled, the event may no longer look like one simple mistake. It may look like a braided failure in which environmental severity, human judgement, technical weakness, and delayed intervention all contributed in overlapping ways. Proving fault under such conditions becomes harder, even where something clearly went wrong.

This evidentiary difficulty is one reason strict liability retains such attraction in environmentally exposed maritime settings. It reduces dependence on a complete and persuasive reconstruction of human error. If the law or a liability regime decides that certain harms should trigger responsibility regardless of whether fault can be shown in the ordinary way, victims, authorities, and insurers do not have to win the whole causal argument before costs begin to move. That serves compensation, but it also serves deterrence. Operators know that some categories of loss will attach financial consequence even where they believe their conduct was broadly careful. The rational response is to invest more heavily in prevention, documentation, and insurance design before the event rather than gamble on a favourable interpretation after it.

A named example makes the point. After the *Exxon Valdez* grounding, the dispute landscape did not revolve solely around whether one navigational or managerial failure could be isolated and blamed. The event also intensified the larger policy judgement that serious pollution in sensitive waters should not depend entirely on the elegance of a fault argument before legal and financial responsibility is engaged. The case became emblematic not simply because it was large, but because it exposed how inadequate a pure fault conversation can feel when environmental damage is extensive and public pressure is high. The lesson travelled well beyond Prince William Sound. Arctic operators learned that in some liability domains the safer assumption is that consequence, once triggered, will generate obligation whether or not the whole human story breaks neatly in their favour.

This does not make fault irrelevant. Quite the opposite. Fault continues to matter enormously because it shapes how operators are judged in negligence disputes, how insurers evaluate preventability, how charterers interpret contractual performance, and how courts or arbitrators assess whether the conduct in question was reasonable under the circumstances. It also matters because the presence or absence of fault can influence the reputational meaning of an incident. A company that can show conservative planning, credible limits, disciplined maintenance, and documented decision-making may still face liability under stricter regimes, but it stands in a better position when arguing over contributory causes, indemnity claims, operational allocation, or the fairness of particular sanctions. Fault is not everything. It is still a central language of commercial self-defence.

The Arctic sharpens that need for self-defence because reasonableness itself becomes harder to pin down. What is a prudent decision when ice information is incomplete, weather is closing, support is far away, and turning back imposes major commercial cost? What counts as adequate maintenance for systems that behave differently in sustained cold? What qualifies as competent voyage planning where conditions can deteriorate faster than updates travel? Liability regimes do not answer these questions in advance. They make them unavoidable later. That is why the operator's records matter so much. Logs, route assessments, drill histories, maintenance reports, communications records, survey findings, and documented thresholds for action all become part of the later inquiry into fault. Proof of care is built one entry at a time.

This is where deterrence stops sounding theoretical. A liability regime deters by changing what costs are likely to follow preventable failure and by shaping the burden of explanation after a casualty. If operators know that weak route planning, thin emergency arrangements, vague decision thresholds, or poor documentary discipline will leave them exposed not only to physical loss but to harsh legal interpretation, they have stronger reasons to invest in stronger systems before the voyage. Insurers reinforce this by reading liability exposure back into pricing. A risk that may produce expensive, causally messy, environmentally sensitive claims becomes a risk that attracts tighter wording, higher retentions, or narrower operational freedom. Liability doctrine and underwriting discipline begin to mirror one another.

A second named example shows the other side of the picture. When the *Costa Concordia* grounded off Giglio in January 2012, the public conversation naturally focused on command behaviour and passenger harm. But the event also demonstrated how fault analysis can widen rapidly once an apparently singular decision is placed inside a larger organisational frame. Questions emerged not only about the immediate navigation, but about training, emergency readiness, company culture, and whether the operator's systems had made bad judgement more likely or harder to correct. The relevance to Arctic trades is direct. Harsh environments do not merely create more excuses for failure. They create more pathways by which the inquiry into fault can spread from one moment to the structure surrounding it. A single error invites a systemic reading.

And yet strict liability has its own practical limits. It can compensate and deter, but it can also flatten morally relevant distinctions if used carelessly. An operator that has invested heavily in prevention, responded quickly, documented decisions carefully, and acted conservatively in difficult conditions may still face severe liability because certain harms trigger it almost automatically. That may be justified as policy, especially for pollution or other public harms, but it can also create resentment and the sense that careful conduct has been undervalued. Serious legal systems and serious insurers understand this tension. They may impose responsibility broadly while still caring, in adjacent disputes or pricing decisions, about whether the operator behaved with genuine discipline. Deterrence works best when it does not make prudence look pointless.

This is one reason insurance design in Arctic work is so attentive to the line between fault-sensitive and fault-insensitive exposure. Operators and markets know that some claims will turn heavily on contested behaviour, while others may attach by reason of the event itself or by the operation of statutes, conventions, or public powers that care more about consequence than about elegant proof of negligence. That knowledge affects how cover is structured, how P&I concerns are weighed, how exclusions are drafted, how support arrangements are reviewed, and how much documentary evidence is demanded before departure. Insurance is not merely paying for legal exposure. It is anticipating the kind of legal reasoning likely to follow the casualty.

The practical consequence is that legal concepts shape operational choices more directly than many non-lawyers realise. If fault is likely to be judged through the adequacy of planning, then route assessments, weather and ice advice, and abort criteria become more than navigational aids. They become future evidence. If strict liability looms over pollution or other public harms, then containment readiness, fuel management, machinery care, and environmental response planning take on a sharper commercial meaning. If causation is likely to be messy, then documenting the sequence of decisions, warnings, maintenance actions, and communications becomes part of risk control rather than mere record-keeping. Law moves quietly into daily practice.

A credible limitation should be admitted here. Operators do not always reason in explicitly legal terms before every difficult decision, nor should they. Seamanship cannot be reduced to a private seminar on liability doctrine. People act through training, culture, habit, and immediate operational judgement far more often than through fine-grained reflection on fault standards or strict liability policy. It would be artificial to suggest that masters or engineers routinely think in jurisprudential categories while ice closes around them.

Still, those categories shape the environment in which companies train, insure, document, and constrain those same actors. Senior management decides what thresholds must be written down. Insurers decide what behaviours need contractual support. Legal advisers and claims experience teach organisations where courts, arbitrators, regulators, and counterparties are likely to press hardest after an event. Over time, those lessons become embedded in manuals, training, route limitations, and emergency procedures. The crew may not be reciting legal theory, but it is often operating inside choices made under its shadow. Deterrence becomes organisational culture.

What emerges, then, is not a neat opposition between fault and strict liability, but a layered system in which both ideas govern the Arctic at once. Fault matters because the story of reasonable care still determines how conduct is judged, how disputes are argued, and how reputations survive. Strict liability matters because some harms are too severe, too public, or too difficult to leave hanging on contested blame alone. The combination produces a distinctive pressure. Operators must behave as though careful proof of prudence will matter greatly later, while also assuming that some categories of loss will generate serious financial consequence even if their own account of careful conduct is strong. That double pressure encourages prevention more forcefully than either model could alone.

The quiet motif returns because the ledger remains the best image of what liability does in Arctic commerce. Every plan, survey, log entry, maintenance decision, training record, and contractual clause writes something into it before the casualty. After the casualty, the law begins to read. Fault asks whether the entries show care or carelessness. Strict liability asks whether some costs belong on the operator's side of the page regardless. Insurers, charterers, and public authorities then translate that reading into premium, recovery, exclusion, indemnity, or future distrust. What looked like abstract doctrine becomes an accounting of choices made in cold conditions long before the bill arrived.

The question that remains is not whether fault or strict liability is the better concept in the abstract. The harder and more Arctic question is this: when remoteness, environmental exposure, and evidentiary uncertainty make every casualty harder to reconstruct, how much of responsible operation depends on being able to prove care later, and how much depends on acting as though proof will not be enough to protect you once the loss itself is on the table?

Pollution risk and environmental sensitivity

In March 1989, the *Exxon Valdez* grounded in Alaska, and the spill that followed altered more than public feeling or regulatory tempo. It changed the commercial imagination of pollution in cold waters. Oil on a shoreline is always costly, politically charged, and legally difficult. Oil in remote northern waters, where response is slower, logistics harsher, and ecological harm more symbolically potent, becomes something else again. The sea is not alone.

That difference still governs Arctic decision-making. Pollution liability looms larger in the far north not because the law suddenly becomes more philosophical there, but because the practical burden of prevention, response, proof, and compensation grows heavier as geography hardens. A release that might be grim but containable in a dense, temperate maritime corridor can become a sprawling legal and financial event in polar or near-polar waters. Distance slows equipment. Weather narrows windows. Ice complicates movement. Local communities and national authorities read the event through environmental sensitivity as well as through maritime fault. The same spill is not the same claim.

This is why pollution in the Arctic must be understood as a severity problem before it is understood as a volume problem. Commercial actors sometimes speak as though the central question were how much might be released. That matters, of course. But underwriters, P&I interests, regulators, and charterers worry just as much about where the release occurs, how quickly it can be addressed, what evidence can be assembled, how long the response may drag on, and how fiercely the event will be interpreted by public authorities and affected communities. A moderate release in a difficult place can become a larger financial fact than a bigger one in easier conditions. Geography changes meaning.

Environmental sensitivity sharpens that meaning because the Arctic is not treated as an ordinary maritime backdrop. It is a place where ecological concern is inseparable from politics, where response difficulty is obvious to outsiders, and where each incident is easily narrated as proof that commercial ambition has outrun stewardship. This gives pollution liability a wider radius. The event may trigger not only clean-up costs and third-party claims, but demands for stronger regulatory scrutiny, closer insurer questioning, harder renewal conversations, and reputational damage that migrates into later pricing. The environment becomes an accounting category.

That is the central argument here. In Arctic operations, environment ceases to be a side constraint and becomes a financial parameter. It influences insurer appetite, the depth of documentary scrutiny, the structure of coverage, the tone of charter negotiations, the plausibility of response plans, and the willingness of public authorities to accept broad operational assurances. A company proposing northern trade is not merely selling a voyage. It is asking markets to believe that any pollution event will be prevented if possible, controlled if not, documented coherently, and managed under conditions that make all of those tasks harder than usual. If that belief weakens, cost rises.

One can see this in how insurers read response planning. A pollution response plan is not valuable because it satisfies an administrative appetite for paperwork. It matters because it reveals whether the operator has understood that Arctic pollution is a chain problem rather than a single-event problem. What equipment is realistically available? How quickly can it arrive? What assumptions are being made about weather, daylight, ice movement, communications, local support, storage, crew endurance, and the legal authority of different responders? If those assumptions are vague, optimistic, or borrowed from easier waters, underwriters do not merely see a weak document. They see a likely claims amplifier.

A named example makes the point from outside the high Arctic but squarely within the logic that later governs it. The *Exxon Valdez* disaster in March 1989 became a defining lesson because it showed that pollution in northern waters cannot be priced or regulated as though the environment were merely scenery around the casualty. The spill's significance lay not only in the damage itself, but in the way difficult response conditions, environmental visibility, and legal and political consequences enlarged the event. For later Arctic operators and insurers, the lesson was blunt. A serious release in cold, exposed waters is never just a marine incident. It becomes a test of whether the operator had treated the environment as an operational variable before the casualty forced everyone else to do so.

This is one reason evidentiary demands become so much heavier in pollution-sensitive trades. After a collision or machinery incident, parties may already dispute timing, causation, and responsibility. Add a pollution component in remote waters, and the standard evidentiary difficulties multiply. Conditions may have prevented immediate observation. Response assets may have arrived in stages. Local authorities may have issued overlapping directions. Weather and ice may have altered the spread or the practicability of intervention. The legal argument is no longer simply whether pollution occurred, but whether response was timely, reasonable, proportionate, and adequately supported by prior planning. Documents that once looked routine now become decisive exhibits.

This evidentiary burden affects underwriting before any casualty takes place. Markets know that poorly documented decisions become expensive once pollution claims begin. They therefore ask more questions up front. They want clearer manuals, stronger route-specific planning, more exact statements of support arrangements, better records of drills, tighter maintenance evidence, and a more convincing account of what the operator will do when the first response assumption fails. The price of cover thus begins to reflect not only the possibility of a spill, but the quality of the record likely to surround it. Documentation becomes part of pollution control.

A brief example shows how response planning can reshape both compliance and pricing. Imagine two vessels proposing similar Arctic support voyages. Both have acceptable class standing, competent crews, and a plausible commercial purpose. The first operator presents a response plan that identifies realistic equipment access, clear chains of authority, communication routes, decision thresholds, and logistical constraints specific to the waters concerned. The second offers a generic plan with broad language about compliance, external support, and emergency action, but little evidence that the company has mapped actual response limitations in that environment. Regulators may allow both to continue through formal review, though with different questions. Insurers will rarely read them alike. The first file narrows uncertainty. The second broadens it. The difference becomes premium, wording, or reluctance.

This is where environmental sensitivity enters pricing most directly. Insurers do not merely ask how likely pollution is. They ask how politically visible, logistically difficult, legally expansive, and reputationally damaging a release would become in the operating area proposed. A vessel trading near infrastructure with ready support, clearer jurisdictional habits, and more developed response networks may still face substantial pollution exposure. A similar vessel in a remote Arctic setting faces a different severity horizon. The probable cost of the event includes not only containment and clean-up, but delay, specialist mobilisation, governmental intervention, possible criminal or administrative scrutiny, third-party claims, and the market memory that attaches to any operator linked to a northern pollution story. Environment enters the quotation as consequence density.

P&I clubs feel this sharply because pollution liability sits close to the core of what they are asked to mutualise. In Arctic contexts, the club's concern is not merely whether the member has complied with formal requirements. It is whether the operator's systems and behaviour make it less likely that the mutual pool will be exposed to a sprawling, hard-to-manage event. This is why clubs often react strongly to weak response planning, vague support assumptions, poor disclosure, or signs that the company has treated northern environmental sensitivity as a communications problem rather than an operational one. Mutuality makes prudence collective. One member's thin preparation can become everyone's financial burden.

Charterers, too, read environmental sensitivity through commercial risk. A cargo owner or chartering party may not speak in the language of ecological stewardship first, yet it will care deeply about the possibility that a pollution incident could halt a trade, damage counterparties, trigger public scrutiny, or embroil the shipment in prolonged disputes over delay, off-hire, indemnity, or force majeure. This is why chartering language in Arctic trades often sharpens around route choice, ice advice, operational limits, and compliance obligations. Pollution risk is not external to the freight relationship. It sits inside the question of whether the voyage remains commercially tolerable once environmental severity is recognised honestly.

A second named example shows how a vessel's planning can become central to how an otherwise impressive Arctic operation is interpreted. When the *Crystal Serenity* transited the Northwest Passage in August 2016, much public discussion focused on spectacle and symbolism. Commercial and regulatory readers would have paid equal attention to the density of planning surrounding the voyage, including the practical consequences of a pollution or emergency event in remote waters. The lesson was not that luxury cruising had made the Arctic ordinary. It was that high-visibility operations in sensitive waters attract heightened scrutiny precisely because the environment raises the cost of every weak assumption. Planning, in such cases, is not decorative reassurance. It is part of the legal and financial architecture of legitimacy.

Still, a limitation deserves clear acknowledgment. Environmental sensitivity can sometimes be invoked too broadly, as though every Arctic pollution scenario were equally catastrophic, equally unmanageable, or equally likely to trigger the same legal and political response. That would be imprecise. Routes differ. Seasons differ. Support capacities differ. Operator quality differs. Some northern trades are more mature, more infrastructurally supported, and more disciplined than others. It would be wrong to flatten all of them into one undifferentiated vision of looming disaster.

Yet this limitation strengthens rather than weakens the main point. Because conditions vary, markets and regulators ask for better evidence, not less. They want to know exactly what kind of environmental exposure this voyage presents, what response assumptions support the operator's confidence, and how much trust can be placed in those assumptions once the vessel moves beyond easy help. The more variable the setting, the more heavily the quality of the plan, the records, and the operator's prior conduct matter. Pollution risk is not priced through slogans. It is priced through the credibility of the file.

This is why environment becomes such a decisive financial parameter in Arctic expansion. It affects whether insurers will write the risk broadly or only under tight conditions. It affects how large deductibles become, how carefully exclusions are drafted, how hard P&I interests probe contingency planning, how much survey support is demanded, and whether charterers insist on sharper allocation of obligations around routeing, delay, and operational control. Environmental sensitivity does not sit outside commerce as an ethical commentary. It enters directly into cost structure and operational freedom.

The practical lesson is not simply that spills are bad, politically fraught, or expensive. Those things are true everywhere. The more useful lesson is that Arctic pollution liability forces commercial actors to price the interaction of law, geography, response difficulty, and public salience as one combined problem. A weak route decision can become a pollution event. A pollution event can become a claims cascade. A claims cascade can change renewal terms, counterparty confidence, and the next season's operating assumptions. Prevention, planning, and documentation therefore matter not because they are virtuous abstractions, but because they alter the financial shape of consequence before the casualty chooses its own scale.

The quiet motif returns because the sea is not alone. In Arctic pollution cases, the law, the weather, the shoreline, the local authority, the insurer, the surveyor, the charterer, and the public all arrive in the same claim eventually. The operator that grasps this early builds response planning as though it were part of the vessel's hull. The operator that does not may discover that the most expensive thing in the Arctic is not the fuel, the escort, or the survey requirement, but the moment when the environment ceases to be background and becomes the central measure of what the voyage was ever worth.

The unresolved question, then, is not whether environmental sensitivity increases Arctic pollution exposure. It plainly does. The harder question is what markets should demand before they believe an operator has really priced that sensitivity into its conduct rather than merely acknowledged it in its paperwork - and what happens when a voyage that looked commercially efficient on paper is judged later by the much harsher arithmetic of remote response, public scrutiny, and ecological consequence.

Salvage, wreck, and the costs of remoteness

In January 2012, the *Costa Concordia* lay stranded off Giglio, Italy, and the world watched a casualty become a long administrative and engineering campaign. The original grounding was dramatic enough. The real lesson for Arctic thinking arrived afterwards. A ship does not stop costing money when the immediate danger passes. It can begin costing more. When salvage, wreck removal, environmental protection, legal authority, public scrutiny, and technical uncertainty all gather around one damaged vessel, the event changes category. The ship is no longer only a casualty. It is a project.

Move that lesson north and the severity sharpens. In Arctic and near-Arctic waters, remoteness alters the financial meaning of damage before any legal argument is fully formed. A moderate grounding, machinery failure, collision, or loss of propulsion can become a much larger claims environment because assistance is farther away, heavy equipment scarcer, weather windows shorter, and every hour of delay more consequential. The issue is not only whether the vessel can be saved. It is whether the location turns salvage and wreck responsibilities into a second disaster made of time, logistics, and law. Distance adds weight.

That is why salvage and wreck removal matter so much to liability and insurance design. People often think first of the initiating event: a hull breach, a navigation mistake, a power failure, a ship on a lee shore. Yet underwriters, P&I clubs, public authorities, and experienced operators know that the more revealing question comes next. What will it take to stabilise the vessel, protect life, prevent pollution, move the ship if possible, and remove it if necessary under the conditions actually present? In Arctic settings, that question can dominate the whole financial picture. Geography becomes an invoice.

Salvage, in broad terms, concerns the effort to save maritime property from peril and to prevent a worsening of the casualty. Wreck removal concerns the duties and pressures that arise when a vessel, or part of it, must be removed because it poses danger, obstruction, or unacceptable ongoing risk. These categories overlap in practice, especially in harsh environments. A ship may move from salvage attempt to wreck problem gradually, with legal and financial consequences expanding as hope narrows. The important point is not doctrinal neatness. It is operational escalation. A vessel that might have been recoverable under easier conditions can become a semi-permanent liability when distance, weather, and political urgency strip away time.

This is where remoteness does its most expensive work. It multiplies mobilisation cost. It slows expert attendance. It complicates towage. It stretches crew endurance. It forces decision-makers to work with thinner information for longer. It reduces the margin for waiting, yet often makes waiting unavoidable. It increases the chance that temporary measures become prolonged ones. A casualty that might have been resolved with manageable effort in a dense maritime region can, in remote cold waters, turn into a layered campaign involving emergency support, specialist contractors, pollution precautions, public authority oversight, and weeks or months of logistical sequencing. The event has not only become costlier. It has become harder to bound.

A named example shows why this matters conceptually even outside the Arctic itself. The *Costa Concordia* salvage and removal effort after January 2012 made plain that once a large casualty enters the domain of stabilisation, salvage planning, environmental protection, and public expectation, the distinction between "accident cost" and "after-accident cost" becomes increasingly artificial. The relevance to Arctic trade lies not in copying the facts of Giglio, but in recognising the severity logic. If a casualty in relatively accessible waters can evolve into a vast technical and financial undertaking, the same progression in remote cold regions can become even harder to price, manage, and conclude. The wreck remains.

This is one reason insurers and P&I clubs scrutinise contingency arrangements with such intensity. They are not indulging an appetite for theoretical preparedness. They are trying to understand what happens when the vessel no longer enjoys the comfort of ordinary infrastructure. What towage assumptions are realistic? What heavy equipment could be mobilised, from where, and with what delay? What support ports or sheltered locations exist, if any? What specialist salvage resources are plausibly available? How would the operator and local authorities coordinate if the casualty drifted from salvageable difficulty into pollution threat or wreck status? These questions matter because, in the Arctic, the answer is often not that help is unavailable, but that help is slower, thinner, and more expensive than early optimism prefers to admit.

Contingency planning therefore becomes a form of claims forecasting. A company that has identified realistic support limitations, escalation routes, communications channels, and decision thresholds offers markets something precious: evidence that it has thought beyond the initiating event to the ugly middle period when the casualty is not yet solved but already costing heavily. A weaker company tends to stop planning too soon. It thinks about the incident itself, not the weeks that may follow. Insurers notice this difference because the weeks that follow are often where severity truly blooms. The first response is only the beginning.

A brief example makes the point in practical terms. Imagine two vessels trading in cold, remote waters with otherwise similar technical credentials. One operator can show how emergency towage would be pursued, what contractors have at least been identified, what pollution containment assumptions are realistic, and where the practical limits of local support begin. The other offers broad reassurance that all necessary arrangements would be made if required. Both may be legally permitted to operate. They are not equally insurable. The first narrows uncertainty around the cost of escalation. The second asks the market to finance improvisation. That difference appears in premium, deductibles, conditions, or simple reluctance to offer comfortable terms.

The role of wreck removal obligations sharpens the same logic. A damaged or stranded vessel does not become less politically sensitive as time passes. In many cases it becomes more so. Public authorities worry about obstruction, continuing pollution risk, navigational hazard, and the reputational cost of allowing a visibly compromised wreck to remain. In Arctic and sub-Arctic settings, those concerns can be intensified by environmental sensitivity and by the fear that a partially contained problem may deteriorate through weather, ice movement, or seasonal change before full removal becomes possible. Wreck liability is therefore not merely a legal tail to a maritime incident. It is often a central reason why moderate casualties become large claims.

This is also why P&I clubs read remoteness through the lens of severity rather than frequency alone. A casualty may be unlikely, or at least not readily comparable with dense-route incidents elsewhere. But if it occurs, the mutual exposure may become unusually broad: pollution liabilities, wreck responsibilities, third-party costs, public authority demands, possible crew or passenger claims, and the prolonged expense of managing a casualty far from easy resolution. Mutual insurance disciplines this exposure by asking hard questions in advance. What is the operator assuming about external help? What evidence supports those assumptions? How will the company respond when the salvage problem becomes a legal problem and the legal problem becomes a political one?

A second named example shows how quickly a northern casualty can exceed its immediate physical description. The *Exxon Valdez* grounding in March 1989 remains emblematic not only because of pollution, but because it demonstrated how a maritime event in sensitive northern waters can produce a long afterlife of response cost, public intervention, legal consequence, and widened severity assumptions for later operators. The relevance here is not to collapse salvage, pollution, and liability into one category, but to recognise that remote environmental casualties resist neat compartmentalisation. Once the ship is in trouble, the cost structure broadens. Later markets remember that broadening when they price the next voyage.

Remoteness also changes negotiation dynamics during the casualty itself. Salvage decisions are rarely made in perfect calm with complete information. They are made under pressure, with uncertain weather, difficult access, limited windows, and the knowledge that delay can destroy options. In easy waters, this pressure may still be substantial. In Arctic contexts, it can become acute enough that every hour seems to carry both financial and legal consequence. Operators, salvors, authorities, and insurers then enter a common arena where logistical reality and liability exposure shape one another continuously. The geography is no longer background. It is a bargaining force.

This helps explain why moderate incidents can turn into major claims without any dramatic second accident. The vessel does not need to break apart spectacularly for severity to rise. It may simply remain hard to reach, hard to stabilise, hard to move, hard to protect from worsening conditions, or hard to remove within a politically tolerable timeframe. Each of those complications adds contractors, specialist equipment, delay, oversight, and legal uncertainty. Each enlarges the claims environment. The event grows by persistence. Arctic severity is often cumulative in precisely this way.

A credible limitation should be admitted. Not every remote casualty becomes a monster claim, and not every Arctic operation stands one bad moment away from unmanageable salvage complexity. Routes differ. Support networks differ. Vessel types differ. Some operators build genuinely serious contingency systems and choose service profiles that reduce the likelihood that a casualty will tip into prolonged wreck or salvage exposure. It would be melodramatic to suggest that remoteness always defeats control.

And yet that limitation strengthens rather than weakens the core argument. Because the outcomes vary so sharply, markets demand evidence that the operator understands where its own operation sits on that spectrum. The question is not whether every casualty will become disastrous. It is whether the company has realistic enough planning to prevent a difficult casualty from becoming expensive by ignorance. Insurers and P&I clubs do not ask for contingency detail because they expect failure as normal. They ask because the penalty for thin thinking in remote regions is unusually severe. A good plan does not abolish geography. It makes geography less financially surprising.

This is why salvage realities and wreck obligations reshape operational choices before any incident occurs. They influence route conservatism, escort decisions, seasonal windows, maintenance discipline, machinery redundancy, communications support, and the willingness to retreat when conditions narrow. A master deciding whether to continue in worsening conditions is not only weighing immediate seamanship. The organisation behind that decision should also be weighing the possibility that a manageable difficulty could, in that location, become a salvage or wreck crisis the balance sheet and insurers would remember for years. Liability here is not the legal tail of operations. It is one of their steering forces.

Charterers feel the same pressure from a different angle. A trade that looks attractive in freight terms can become much less attractive if a moderate casualty would likely produce a long salvage interruption, a politically sensitive wreck issue, or a prolonged dispute over who controlled the routeing and who pays for delay. This is one reason Arctic chartering structures tend to press harder on operational allocation, ice advice, and delay consequences. Geography is telling the contract what to fear. The farther the help, the tighter the language often becomes.

The strategic takeaway is therefore plain and unforgiving. Geography changes the liability calculus. It changes it not by rewriting legal doctrine from first principles, but by altering the practical cost of making obligations good once the vessel is in trouble. Salvage, wreck, and response are not secondary matters that begin after the "real" casualty. They are often the real casualty in financial terms. The hull breach or grounding starts the story. Distance, weather, and sparse support determine its commercial length and legal density.

The quiet motif returns because the wreck remains - not always physically on the seabed or shoreline, but in the file, in the renewal discussion, in the underwriting memory, in the charterer's hesitation, in the next season's route restrictions, and in the sharper questions asked of every operator who claims that a northern voyage can be controlled cheaply enough. A company can survive one casualty and still discover that the most durable damage was the market's revised understanding of what remoteness does to severity.

The harder question, then, is not whether salvage and wreck removal are expensive in remote waters. They plainly are. The harder question is what kind of operator is truly prepared for that fact: the one that treats contingency arrangements as reassuring annexes to the voyage, or the one that understands that in the Arctic a moderate incident may already contain, within the first bad hour, the outline of a much larger legal and financial campaign.

Charterparties, indemnities, and operational control

In August 2018, when the *Venta Maersk* completed its trial voyage through the Northern Sea Route, the public discussion turned quickly to distance saved, strategic symbolism, and the old dream of an Arctic shortcut made commercially plausible. The quieter and more decisive question sat elsewhere. Who, exactly, controlled the critical choices if conditions changed, ice advice shifted, delays mounted, or the route became less manageable than anticipated? A voyage is never only a movement through water. It is also a movement through allocated responsibility. The clause steers too.

That is why charterparties matter so much in Arctic trades. They do not merely record a commercial bargain between owner and charterer. They distribute operational control, economic exposure, and the legal burden of explaining decisions later if the voyage sours into dispute. In ordinary trades, these allocations can already be intricate. In polar and near-polar work they become sharper because ice, weather, remoteness, response limits, and schedule fragility make it harder to treat operational decisions as casual matters of shipboard judgement alone. The environment forces the contract to say who carries which risk, and on what terms.

At a basic level, chartering structures divide functions that commercial outsiders often collapse into one. Owners provide the ship and, depending on the form of charter, may retain varying degrees of control over navigation, crewing, technical management, and maintenance. Charterers provide employment, cargo opportunity, scheduling pressure, route preferences, and the commercial purpose to which the vessel is put. Even before the Arctic enters the picture, this means that the person profiting most directly from a voyage is not always the person controlling every operational choice that may later matter in liability. Arctic conditions make that split far more consequential. Once ice advice, route alteration, waiting time, abort thresholds, and support assumptions begin to shape whether the voyage remains prudent, the allocation of decision-making stops being theoretical. It becomes the anatomy of later blame.

This is why allocation language deserves to be read as a map rather than as legal ornament. A charterparty tells the parties, in advance, where command is expected to lie, where information duties sit, who bears the cost of delay under defined circumstances, what happens when the route becomes unsafe or commercially unattractive, and how far one party may rely on the other's representations about conditions or instructions. It does not remove the need for seamanship or judgment. It tells the parties whose judgment counts for what and who must pay when judgments collide. In Arctic trades, where outcomes can swing quickly with weather, ice, or support constraints, those lines become especially valuable because memory after a casualty is always tempted to blur them.

Ice advice is one of the clearest points at which this map becomes practical. A charterer may push for a schedule, a loading sequence, or a routeing pattern that makes economic sense only if conditions remain within certain assumptions. The owner, through the master and technical management, may retain responsibility for navigation and safety decisions while still operating inside commercial pressure created by the charter. If the agreement does not state with enough clarity how ice information is to be obtained, weighed, communicated, and acted upon, later disputes can become ugly very quickly. Was the master free to reject the route? Was the charterer entitled to insist on a timetable that narrowed the margin for waiting? Who bore the risk that available ice advice was incomplete, late, or commercially inconvenient? In Arctic service, those are not academic questions. They are latent claims.

Routeing intensifies the same difficulty. In easier trades, the distinction between commercial instruction and navigational control may remain relatively stable. In the Arctic, the line can wobble. A charterer may not direct the helm, but it may structure the voyage around assumptions that exert strong indirect pressure on route choices. An owner may insist that navigational control remains entirely onboard while still accepting contractual incentives that make conservative delay expensive. A master may technically retain discretion and yet know that every hour of waiting in ice-sensitive waters alters the freight economics of the whole fixture. The contract cannot solve this pressure entirely, but it can reveal whether the parties have recognised it honestly or preferred to bury it under broad language about lawful orders and prudent navigation.

A named example helps clarify why Arctic routeing attracts this tighter scrutiny. When the *Crystal Serenity* transited the Northwest Passage in August 2016, the voyage's public image rested on rarity and spectacle. Its institutional significance lay in the extent to which major decisions had to be bounded rather than romanticised. Whatever the detailed contractual arrangements behind such an operation, a voyage of that kind could not sensibly proceed on the basis of soft understandings about who would decide what if conditions tightened, support assumptions weakened, or the itinerary began to conflict with safety logic. The broader lesson travels well beyond cruise operations. The more severe and visible the trade, the less tolerable it becomes to leave routeing and delay consequences in vague commercial shadow.

Delays are especially revealing because they turn time into liability. In Arctic operations, delay is rarely just lost efficiency. It can mean missed seasonal windows, worsening ice, crew fatigue, increased fuel use, altered support availability, rising exposure to port state or inspection trouble, and a narrowing of exit options. Charterparties therefore often work very hard in polar trades to say whether waiting time, diversion, rerouting, or weather-related interruption falls financially on owner, charterer, or some mixture of both. This is not simply a matter of fairness. It is a way of deciding who will feel the pain of caution most immediately. If one side bears too little of that pain, it may press more aggressively for persistence when prudence suggests restraint. Allocation language can therefore affect operational temperament long before a dispute arises.

Indemnities sit at the sharp end of this structure because they are promises about who will hold whom harmless if specific categories of cost or liability materialise. In Arctic commerce, indemnity language often attracts special attention not because parties are unusually litigious, but because the environment makes knock-on consequences so much harder to contain. A routing decision can produce delay, which can trigger off-hire arguments, cargo deterioration concerns, support-contract costs, pollution-response exposure, or even salvage consequences if conditions worsen. The parties, therefore, try to decide in advance how far responsibility follows control, instruction, or benefit. Indemnities are not merely legal shields. They are forecasts of where the parties believe later pressure will land.

This forecasting function is one reason insurers and P&I clubs read chartering structures so closely. They do not ask only whether the ship is technically fit or the route superficially plausible. They ask how operational control has been distributed and whether the contract aligns commercial incentives with prudent conduct. A poorly aligned charter can unsettle insurers even where the vessel itself looks strong. If the wording leaves too much ambiguity around ice advice, waiting time, route deviation, emergency support assumptions, or compliance with technical limitations, the insurer sees not merely a contractual quirk but a possible amplifier of future claims. Legal uncertainty and operational uncertainty begin to merge. The policy cannot ignore the charterparty because the charterparty may shape the casualty.

A second named example from outside the Arctic proper helps show why allocation language acquires such force after visible casualties. Following the *Costa Concordia* grounding in January 2012, questions of direct command failure were obvious, but so too were the broader institutional questions about how responsibilities had been framed, supervised, and distributed within the operator's system. The Arctic lesson is not that charterparties resemble passenger-command structures in simple form. It is that when serious events occur, legal and commercial readers rarely stop at the immediate mistake. They ask how the surrounding structure encouraged, constrained, or failed to discipline the choice that proved costly. Allocation language matters because it tells later readers whether the parties had thought clearly about where control truly lived.

A difficulty must be acknowledged. Contracts cannot perfectly map dynamic reality. Arctic conditions change faster than clauses can. Ice moves, weather closes, communications falter, local advice evolves, and operational judgment remains essential in ways no drafting exercise can entirely replace. It would therefore be wrong to suggest that tighter allocation language eliminates ambiguity or removes the need for trust between parties. Even the best charterparty will eventually meet conditions more complicated than its own foresight.

And yet this limitation only strengthens the case for careful allocation. Because reality outruns drafting, the contract must at least clarify the principles by which later decisions and losses will be read. If the vessel must choose between commercial schedule and conservative navigation, which side of the bargain will the law and the market later regard as primary? If ice advice proves inadequate, who was supposed to seek, verify, or act upon better information? If delay expands into a larger casualty or pollution event, who benefits from saying the critical choice belonged to the other side? The contract cannot answer every factual question, but it can stop the argument from beginning in total fog.

This is why Arctic trades often tighten allocation around ice advice, routeing, and delays more than ordinary fixtures do. Those are the areas where commercial desire and operational restraint are most likely to rub against one another under conditions of severe consequence. Broad clauses that work tolerably well elsewhere may become too loose once the cost of misalignment rises. The parties are not merely being cautious lawyers. They are trying to prevent the worst version of hindsight, the one in which both owner and charterer insist that the other effectively controlled the decisive choice while the vessel itself carried the consequences in real time. Clearer language does not abolish hindsight. It makes it harder to rewrite.

There is also a broader strategic point. Charterparties reveal that Arctic governance is not housed in public regulation alone, nor in class, nor in insurance, nor in operational manuals. It is distributed across private instruments that quietly decide who can demand what from whom when conditions deteriorate. A charterer may never touch the rudder and still shape the risk profoundly through scheduling pressure and route expectations. An owner may proclaim navigational autonomy while accepting commercial structures that make retreat increasingly expensive. The contract becomes the place where these tensions are either recognised and bounded or left to explode later in dispute. It is governance by allocation.

One should not romanticise this process. Sometimes the language is clearer on paper than in practice. Sometimes parties sign because the market is moving quickly and trust their future selves to sort out what present caution has not resolved. Sometimes bargaining power produces wording that reflects leverage more than principled risk distribution. These imperfections are real. But they do not make the charterparty peripheral. They make it more revealing. A contract drafted under pressure still shows where the pressure was.

The quiet motif returns because the map remains the right image. Owners, charterers, insurers, and sometimes public authorities all look at the same voyage and ask where responsibility lies if the route narrows, the ice shifts, the advice conflicts, or the delay becomes ruinous. The charterparty draws those lines before the weather tests them. If the lines are blurred, everyone later tries to redraw them in self-protective ways. If they are clearer, the voyage may still suffer, but the argument begins from a more disciplined place.

The unresolved question, then, is not whether Arctic contracts should allocate responsibility carefully. They plainly must. The harder question is whether the allocation in any given fixture truly follows operational control as it will exist at the decisive moment, or merely reflects what each party hopes to say afterwards when the ice, the delay, and the bill have made the map look far more important than it did on signing day.

Legal uncertainty as a pricing input

In September 2013, after the *Arctic Sunrise* was seized by Russian authorities following a Greenpeace protest in the Pechora Sea, the incident quickly became more than a confrontation between a state and a campaigning organisation. It became a harsh reminder that maritime ventures in sensitive northern waters do not move only through weather, ice, and engineering. They move through legal reach, enforcement mood, and the practical question of what happens when the jurisdictional ground shifts beneath the ship. The chart ended at law.

That matters because markets can live with many kinds of danger so long as those dangers are legible. A known ice season, a known support gap, a known technical limitation, even a known severity profile can usually be priced, documented, and bounded. Legal uncertainty is harder. When insurers cannot tell with confidence which authority will act, how aggressively it will act, what liability basis may be asserted, how a court or tribunal may later read the event, or how fast an operator can secure procedural clarity, the problem is not only that risk increases. It becomes difficult to describe what the risk actually is. Ambiguity is expensive.

This is the central mechanism by which law becomes cost in Arctic operations. Jurisdictional reach, enforcement practice, precedent, and administrative style are not academic abstractions sitting outside commercial life. They alter whether cover is broad or narrow, whether premiums harden, whether deductibles rise, whether voyage-specific conditions appear, whether underwriters demand more surveys, and whether operators are pushed towards more conservative routes and tighter operating thresholds. Markets dislike uncertainty more than known danger because known danger at least permits an argument about probability and severity. Legal uncertainty can destabilise both at once.

Jurisdictional uncertainty is one of the clearest drivers. Arctic and near-Arctic activity often unfolds in waters or coastal zones where multiple legal logics sit close together: flag-state authority, coastal-state powers, port-state control, environmental legislation, contractual forums, and the practical influence of public authorities acting under political pressure after a visible incident. None of this needs to produce formal chaos to unsettle insurers. It is enough that the line between ordinary marine regulation and exceptional governmental intervention feels difficult to predict. Underwriters then ask not merely what the vessel may face at sea, but what claims environment may emerge afterwards if the event is interpreted through a broader public or strategic lens.

Enforcement practice matters just as much as formal jurisdiction. Two places may operate under recognisably similar legal frameworks and still produce different commercial reactions because one is known for stable, technically reasoned administration while another is associated with abrupt escalation, uneven interpretation, or a readiness to turn legal discretion into operational pressure. The formal rule may look familiar. The lived consequence may not. Markets react to that lived consequence because it affects claim duration, legal spend, detention possibility, documentary burden, and the probability that a moderate casualty will become a prolonged argument about authority as well as fault.

Precedent has a peculiar role here because Arctic operations often remain too sparse or too distinctive to generate the kind of settled, repetitive legal comfort that insurers prefer. In dense maritime trades, claims handlers and underwriters can often look to a deeper stock of disputes, settlements, and judicial or arbitral treatment to infer how similar cases are likely to unfold. In harsher northern environments, every event can feel more singular. The facts vary. The politics vary. The response capacity varies. The environmental framing varies. Thin precedent does not mean total ignorance, but it does mean that later legal treatment is harder to bound. The empty shelf matters.

A named example helps clarify the commercial meaning of this uncertainty. The *Arctic Sunrise* episode in 2013 did not involve an ordinary marine casualty, yet it demonstrated with unusual force that vessels operating in politically and environmentally charged northern settings can enter legal terrain far less predictable than standard underwriting templates prefer. A state action, a disputed basis of authority, a prolonged detention, and an international legal dispute together showed that the cost of uncertainty is not confined to physical damage or pollution alone. The incident revealed how quickly the question "what law applies and how?" can become a central commercial problem in its own right.

This is why markets often treat ambiguity as a severity multiplier. A collision, machinery incident, or pollution event in a legally stable environment may still be costly, but the range of plausible legal outcomes is easier to estimate. A similar initiating event in a setting where enforcement practice is uncertain, public authority intervention less predictable, or precedent thin can expand into a much wider spread of possible outcomes. Claims may take longer to resolve. Defence and response costs may increase. Cover interpretation may become more contested. Contractual indemnities may be tested under stresses the parties did not model cleanly. The legal tail lengthens.

Underwriters respond to this in familiar but significant ways. They may raise premium because the uncertainty cannot be comfortably carried at ordinary price. They may increase deductibles to push more of the ambiguous risk back onto the insured. They may narrow cover, carve out particular liabilities, or add warranties and conditions requiring stricter compliance with routeing, reporting, or technical limits. They may ask for more detailed submissions, clearer contingency plans, stronger evidence of local legal and response understanding, or a more conservative operating concept altogether. The policy begins to reflect not only where the ship will go, but what the law might do there.

This is where stronger documentation becomes indispensable. If markets know that a later dispute may turn on who knew what, when decisions were made, what information was available, what thresholds were set, what support assumptions were relied upon, and whether the operator behaved conservatively in the face of uncertainty, then the quality of the record becomes part of the risk itself. Documentation is no longer only proof of compliance. It is part of the operator's defence against legal ambiguity. Good logs, clear route assessments, coherent manuals, prompt reporting, and disciplined records of maintenance and decision-making help narrow the space in which later authorities or counterparties can imagine recklessness, concealment, or casual disregard.

Conservative operating limits emerge from the same logic. Operators sometimes speak as though legal uncertainty were something to be handled by lawyers after the fact. Insurers rarely accept that comfort. They prefer the uncertainty to be managed operationally where possible. That means tighter route boundaries, clearer abort criteria, stronger weather and ice thresholds, more cautious assumptions about support, and greater reluctance to proceed in marginal conditions where a later authority might argue that the operator pressed on imprudently. Law thus reaches backwards into navigation and management. It changes conduct before any dispute begins.

A second named example shows how visible casualties can harden this tendency even where the legal issues are more conventionally maritime. After the *Exxon Valdez* grounding in March 1989, the legal and political afterlife of the spill extended well beyond immediate clean-up. The event reinforced a wider lesson for markets: environmentally sensitive northern incidents can produce legal consequences more expansive, more politically freighted, and less easily bounded than older underwriting habits had assumed. The significance here is not only historical. It is structural. Once a market has watched one northern casualty acquire a wider and longer legal life than expected, it becomes more cautious about any later operation that might enter similarly uncertain territory.

A credible limitation should be admitted. Legal uncertainty is not the same thing as legal lawlessness, and markets can sometimes overstate ambiguity where the real position is manageable with proper preparation and experience. Arctic trades are not inherently beyond legal understanding. Some routes, authorities, and claims environments are more stable than outsiders imagine. Skilled operators, specialist counsel, seasoned brokers, and informed insurers can often reduce uncertainty substantially through planning, local knowledge, and disciplined documentation. Not every northern legal question deserves panic pricing.

And yet this limitation only sharpens the main point. Because some uncertainty can be reduced and some cannot, the market begins by asking how much of it the operator has already done serious work to narrow. Has the company identified the relevant public authorities and likely interventions? Has it aligned its contracts with realistic legal exposure? Has it thought about evidence preservation, reporting obligations, pollution response, and the possibility of overlapping or competing demands after an incident? Has it chosen routes and seasons that reduce avoidable ambiguity rather than maximise headline efficiency? Where the answers are weak, premiums rise not because insurers love caution for its own sake, but because the operator is asking them to finance avoidable uncertainty.

This is why markets often seem more tolerant of severe but familiar risk than of less severe but murky risk. A difficult ice passage with strong records, clear support assumptions, settled contractual language, and a legally legible environment may be commercially preferable to an easier physical voyage whose aftermath could enter a fog of disputed authority, unstable enforcement, or uncertain precedent. Physical difficulty and legal uncertainty are not perfectly correlated. Sometimes the calmer sea carries the darker file. Underwriters know this. So do the best operators.

The practical result is a visible chain from law to cost. Jurisdictional ambiguity or erratic enforcement increases underwriter discomfort. Underwriter discomfort appears as higher premiums, larger retentions, narrower cover, and heavier documentary demands. Those terms influence charter negotiations, route choice, maintenance timing, crew selection, and the decision to proceed at all. The operator that hoped law would remain background discovers that it has become a design input. The voyage is still possible. The legal shadow is priced into it.

One should also notice how this affects reputation. A company repeatedly trading through uncertain legal environments with disciplined documentation and conservative operating habits may gradually build enough trust to soften some market unease. Another operator may deepen insurer concern if it appears casual about reporting, vague in its route logic, or overly reliant on broad assurances that any dispute would surely resolve in its favour. Legal uncertainty does not fall equally on all participants. It weighs more heavily on those whose records and judgment give others less reason to trust them when the line between caution and overreach later becomes contested.

The quiet motif returns because the empty shelf remains instructive. Where precedent is thin, where enforcement practice feels unstable, or where public authority may stretch further than the operator hoped, insurers are not only pricing what has happened before. They are pricing the lack of settled guidance about what will happen next. That absence produces caution, and caution is translated into the familiar language of premium, deductible, exclusion, survey, and warranty. The law becomes visible in the quote.

The harder question, then, is not whether legal uncertainty costs money. It plainly does. The harder question is how much of that cost reflects the genuine difficulty of Arctic jurisdiction and enforcement, and how much reflects an operator's failure to reduce ambiguity where it could have been reduced by stronger documentation, clearer contracts, and more conservative limits before the first incident made uncertainty impossible to treat as merely theoretical.

Chapter 9

P&I Clubs and Reinsurance Structures

In March 1989, when the *Exxon Valdez* grounded in Alaska, the immediate picture was local and physical: oil, shoreline, weather, response, outrage. The financial picture was neither local nor simple. Third-party liabilities did not stop at the owner's balance sheet, nor even at one insurer's desk. They moved through clubs, pools, reinsurers, correspondents, claims handlers, and the wider architecture of shared maritime risk. The spill spread in water. So did the liability.

That wider architecture matters because maritime liability is not financed in the same way as ordinary property damage. A ship may be one hull in one place, but the claims that follow collision, pollution, personal injury, cargo loss, wreck removal, or governmental intervention can become too large, too varied, and too legally untidy to sit comfortably inside a narrow bilateral insurance relationship. P&I clubs arose to solve that problem by mutualising third-party exposure among members who are, in effect, insuring one another against certain classes of maritime consequence. The arrangement sounds technical. It is also moral. Shared liability creates shared discipline.

The tension begins there. Mutual insurance promises collective security, yet it also gives private institutions a direct interest in policing the conduct of their own members. A club that pays claims from a common pool cannot remain indifferent to weak maintenance, thin documentation, vague route discipline, poor reporting, or adventurous conduct in severe environments. Prudence stops being a private virtue. It becomes a burden carried by others if one member behaves badly. That is why clubs matter so much in Arctic trades. They do not merely reimburse loss after the fact. They help decide what kinds of risk-taking the mutual body is willing to tolerate in advance.

This pressure becomes sharper once reinsurance enters the picture. Clubs do not simply absorb every large exposure themselves. Risk is spread upward and outward through pooling arrangements and reinsurance structures that connect local voyages to global capital. That connection is one of the least visible but most consequential facts in Arctic expansion. A shipowner planning a northern operation may think chiefly about vessel capability, route timing, ice advice, and compliance obligations. Far away, reinsurers may be asking a different question: how much correlated Arctic liability does the market really want to carry, on what terms, and after which recent incidents has that appetite hardened or thinned? Local access is often shaped by remote caution.

That matters because capital dislikes surprise, and it dislikes legally messy surprise most of all. P&I structures exist to absorb complicated third-party liabilities, but they also exist to preserve the conditions under which those liabilities remain bearable. Once a high-profile casualty reveals that pollution, wreck, passenger exposure, environmental intervention, or long-tail claims in cold waters may be broader or more politically charged than previously assumed, the consequence does not remain confined to the original ship. Terms can tighten across a class of voyages. Exclusions appear. Sublimits harden. Calls rise. Documentation demands thicken. A single event can alter the willingness of global reinsurance capital to stand behind later Arctic ambition.

Claims handling is the place where this caution becomes concrete. After an incident, clubs and their representatives do not simply write cheques. They test facts, examine conditions, reconstruct decisions, compare documents, assess compliance, and decide what the case teaches about the member and the trade. In harsh northern settings, that work has unusual importance because poor records, weak reporting, and vague contingency planning can make liability disputes expand rapidly. Claims files are not only instruments of settlement. They are workshops in future governance. What is learned there often returns later as revised requirements, stricter questions, or altered underwriting tone.

This is why the chapter's movement matters as a chain rather than as a set of separate topics. It begins inside the mutual logic of P&I, where collective insurance becomes collective discipline, then widens into pooling and reinsurance, where the price of Arctic liability is partly determined far beyond the voyage itself. From there it enters claims handling, where facts are tested and the next generation of caution is quietly assembled out of the last incident's paperwork, arguments, and losses. The route through the chapter follows the route by which liability moves from one ship to many desks.

The larger stake is strategic. Arctic commerce is often narrated through ships, routes, resources, and states. Yet many of its real boundaries are drawn by institutions that sit in the background until a serious third-party claim forces them into view. A club's willingness to require additional controls, a reinsurer's discomfort with clustered northern exposure, a claims team's memory of one badly documented casualty, or a pooled market's reluctance to subsidise uncertainty can all shape who gets access and on what terms. Mutual insurance is not merely a funding mechanism. It is a private order of discipline held together by shared exposure and professional memory.

That makes the most important question both simple and difficult. When an Arctic voyage asks a club, a pool, and the reinsurance market behind them to carry the consequences of collision, pollution, injury, wreck, or state intervention, what exactly are they being asked to trust: the ship, the operator, the documents, the route, or the hope that this time the shared fund will not be taught another expensive lesson about how far north confidence can safely travel?

Mutual insurance and collective discipline

In March 1989, when the *Exxon Valdez* grounded in Alaska, the financial consequences did not remain inside the familiar boundaries of hull damage or cargo loss. They widened into pollution liabilities, governmental claims, third-party losses, and the kind of long legal afterlife that ordinary marine insurance was never designed to absorb neatly. That is the world in which protection and indemnity clubs matter most. They exist because some maritime liabilities are too sprawling, too politically charged, and too difficult to price as one-off bilateral bargains between a shipowner and a commercial insurer. The pool matters.

That pool is not simply a financial convenience. It is a social arrangement with teeth. A P&I club is a mutual institution whose members are, in substance, insuring one another against certain classes of third-party exposure. When one member's casualty produces a large pollution claim, passenger liability, wreck removal burden, or collision-related loss, the cost does not vanish into abstract capital. It travels through a shared structure funded and sustained by the membership as a whole. This changes the moral weather of insurance. A member's imprudence is not merely its private mistake. It can become everyone else's bill.

That is why mutual insurance creates discipline in a way ordinary transactional cover often cannot. In a conventional insurance relationship, the insurer's interest in prevention is real but external. It sits across the table from the insured and prices, excludes, or conditions risk accordingly. In a mutual structure, the logic runs deeper. The member belongs to a community of exposure. Clubs therefore carry not only an underwriting interest in prudent conduct, but an institutional obligation to protect the common fund from behaviour that shifts excessive risk onto fellow members. Mutuality makes caution collective.

The practical consequence is that P&I clubs care intensely about third-party liabilities precisely because third-party liabilities are the kinds of losses that can escape neat containment. Pollution is one obvious example, but the same logic reaches personal injury, cargo-related claims, wreck removal, governmental intervention, and the many hybrid disputes in which environmental sensitivity, public authority, and contractual blame collide. These are not losses that can be understood solely by looking at the ship's physical damage. They require a wider view of legal consequence, public reaction, and post-casualty management. Clubs specialise in that wider view because mutual insurance was built for it.

A named example helps explain the force of this arrangement. After the *Exxon Valdez* casualty in March 1989, the wider maritime market was reminded that a single northern pollution event could produce a liability field extending far beyond immediate clean-up: public claims, reputational damage, prolonged legal contest, and a broad reassessment of what prudent tanker operation should mean in sensitive waters. The lesson for mutual insurance was especially sharp. A claim of that nature does not affect one insured in isolation. It affects how the whole mutual system thinks about exposure, member discipline, documentation, and the kinds of operations that may need tighter control before cover is offered on comfortable terms. One loss can teach the whole club.

This teaching function is central. P&I clubs do not only reimburse members after the fact. They study how claims arise, what documentation fails, where route discipline breaks down, how government authorities intervene, and which operational assumptions prove too optimistic under pressure. From those lessons come recommendations, conditions, circulars, special requirements, and a more exacting view of what a prudent member should do next time. The mutual structure therefore turns claims experience into behavioural regulation. A club that ignored lessons from one member's casualty would be asking the rest of the membership to subsidise forgetfulness. Mutuality cannot afford that luxury.

This is why clubs can require specific risk controls without behaving as though they were maritime regulators in the public-law sense. Their authority comes from membership and cover, not sovereignty. But that authority is still substantial. A club may insist on stronger documentation, more credible response planning, additional surveys, tighter route information, clearer pollution precautions, or more conservative operating assumptions before it is willing to carry a member's Arctic exposure on acceptable terms. It does so not merely to look serious. It does so because the club's promise to one member depends on the collective willingness of all members to stand behind the fund. If the fund is endangered by weak controls, prudence becomes a condition of solidarity.

Arctic operations sharpen this logic because severity is harder to bound there. A moderate incident in a well-supported region may remain moderate. The same incident in remote cold waters can escalate through delayed response, environmental sensitivity, political scrutiny, and the practical difficulty of making legal and operational obligations good. Clubs know this. They therefore read Arctic proposals through a heightened lens of collective exposure. They want to know not only whether the ship is technically capable, but whether the operator's plans, records, support arrangements, route limits, and reporting culture are strong enough that the common fund is not being asked to absorb avoidable uncertainty. The farther north the risk, the more mutual discipline tends to tighten.

This is also why clubs often seem preoccupied with matters that owners might initially treat as operational detail. A vague contingency plan, an unresolved survey recommendation, a weak pollution response concept, a thin crewing profile for severe conditions, a pattern of small port deficiencies, or a habit of late reporting can all signal something larger: that the member may not be controlling its liabilities as tightly as the mutual structure requires. The club does not need to prove that such weaknesses will cause the next casualty. It needs only to recognise that if they do, the cost will not fall on the careless member alone. The shared ledger makes little things matter.

Peer pressure is therefore built into the system, even when it is expressed through formal processes rather than through direct member confrontation. Clubs are run through governance structures, committees, technical reviews, underwriting practice, and claims experience, all of which are shaped by the reality that members do not wish to subsidise behaviour they regard as unnecessarily hazardous. That pressure may show itself in the hardening of terms for certain trades, in demands for better evidence, in reluctance to extend cover for ambitious polar operations without clearer safeguards, or in a generally more sceptical posture towards members whose records suggest weak discipline. The pressure may feel institutional rather than personal. It is peer pressure all the same.

A second named example shows the same dynamic from a different angle. When the *Costa Concordia* grounded in January 2012, the casualty exposed not only direct liabilities but the wider vulnerability of systems that had looked orderly enough before the event. For mutual insurers, the lesson was not confined to passenger ships. It was broader and more unsettling. Large third-party claims often reveal organisational weaknesses that routine underwriting had failed to price adequately or that documentation had masked. Clubs do not easily forget such lessons. They return later as sharper expectations about drills, reporting, command culture, contingency planning, and the credibility of the member's own account of its operations. Mutual memory is conservative for a reason.

Still, a limitation should be faced plainly. Mutual insurance is not a morally pure community of prudent shipowners all rowing in disciplined harmony. Clubs compete for members, face commercial pressures, and must work within a world where members differ in quality, bargaining power, fleet profile, and political importance. Some risks will be tolerated because the commercial relationship matters. Some controls may be applied unevenly or softened in practice. Mutuality does not abolish business incentives. It refracts them through a shared structure.

And yet this limitation only clarifies the main point. Because clubs are both mutual and commercial, their discipline is not sentimental. It is practical. They do not demand controls because they enjoy bureaucracy. They demand them because the economics of shared liability punish indifference. A member with weak documentation, poor route discipline, or inadequate response planning is not simply a weak account. It is a potential burden on the community of insureds. Clubs may express this in careful wording, technical correspondence, or additional requirements rather than in moral rebuke, but the underlying logic remains collective. Cover depends on conduct.

This is why P&I clubs sit so close to the centre of Arctic governance. They transform shared financial exposure into incentives for preventive discipline. They connect documentation quality to member credibility. They treat response planning, reporting, surveys, pollution precautions, and route conservatism not as private preferences but as matters of common concern. They also remind operators that third-party liabilities are not only priced externally by insurers and reinsurers. They are judged internally by institutions whose members have reason to care how one another behave. Mutual insurance is therefore not passive protection. It is an organised expectation of prudence.

One can see the effect in how operators adapt. A member that understands the club's logic tends to build better records, respond faster to technical concerns, disclose awkward facts earlier, and take Arctic operating limits more seriously because it knows the mutual system reads such behaviour as proof that shared exposure is being handled responsibly. Another member may comply formally while resenting the discipline as overreach, only to discover after a claim or a difficult renewal that clubs are patient but not forgetful. The mutual structure may look soft compared with direct state command. In practice it can be more persistent because it acts through continuing membership, repeated renewals, and the long memory of claims.

The quiet motif returns because the pool is never neutral. It gathers money, yes, but also lessons, frustrations, demands, and comparisons between members who may never meet and yet remain financially entangled. A poor casualty response, a thin Arctic submission, or a badly documented pollution incident enters that common water and changes how later risks are read. The club's caution is therefore not an abstract institutional mood. It is the accumulated self-protection of a collective that knows one ship's failure can ripple through everyone else's cover.

The harder question, then, is not whether P&I clubs insure third-party liabilities. They plainly do. The harder question is what kind of operator truly belongs inside a mutual system built on collective discipline: the one that treats cover as a shield after the event, or the one that understands from the start that in Arctic trade the club is also asking, before it shares the pool, whether your conduct is good enough for everyone else to live with.

Pooling, reinsurance, and capacity limits

In March 1989, when the *Exxon Valdez* grounded in Alaska, the spill did not merely test a shipowner, a coastline, or a legal system. It tested the architecture of global risk-bearing. The liabilities that followed were too large, too politically charged, and too legally untidy to sit comfortably within one neat layer of cover. They moved outward: through mutual arrangements, into shared pools, and on into reinsurance markets far removed from Prince William Sound. The casualty happened locally. The capital did not.

That outward movement is essential to understanding Arctic access. A vessel entering cold, remote, environmentally sensitive waters may look like a local operational proposition, but the money standing behind its third-party liabilities is usually dispersed across institutional layers. Clubs mutualise. Pools spread. Reinsurers absorb. Each layer narrows the amount any one actor must carry alone, but each layer also introduces a fresh source of caution. A northern voyage therefore does not ask only whether the ship is fit, the operator disciplined, or the route seasonally plausible. It asks whether distant capital believes the resulting liabilities remain tolerable when viewed as part of a larger book of exposure. The answer is not written on the chart.

Pooling is the first part of this story because mutual systems cannot leave every large claim at the level of the individual member or club. If one member's pollution event, wreck removal liability, or passenger-related catastrophe were to sit almost entirely inside one institution, the promise of mutual insurance would become fragile very quickly. Pooling spreads that burden across a wider collective. This is not generosity in the sentimental sense. It is engineering for financial resilience. A wider pool can absorb unusual losses more steadily than a narrow one. Yet spreading the burden also spreads vigilance. Once the cost of a casualty is shared more broadly, so is the interest in preventing the next one. A member's Arctic ambition becomes a question for many balance sheets.

Reinsurance extends that logic even further. Beyond the mutual and pooled levels sits a market for larger, less frequent, and potentially more catastrophic exposures. Reinsurers do not care very much for romance about northern opening or strategic passage. They care about severity, correlation, uncertainty, and the possibility that a single difficult event may reveal a wider mispricing across a class of risks. This makes Arctic exposure peculiarly sensitive to appetite shifts. Physical remoteness is only half the challenge. Financial remoteness matters too. A reinsurer in one market can harden its view after a northern casualty, and the result may be felt by an operator planning a very different voyage months later in another region altogether.

This is why Arctic exposures can strain appetite even when actual traffic volumes remain modest relative to denser maritime trades. The issue is not simply how many ships are moving north. It is how large and awkward the liabilities may become if something goes badly wrong. Pollution in remote waters, prolonged wreck removal, governmental intervention, passenger evacuation, environmental claims, and long legal afterlives all produce a severity profile that makes capital uneasy. Reinsurers tend to dislike risks that are sparse in frequency, hard to compare, legally messy, and capable of producing public pressure out of proportion to their numerical occurrence. Arctic operations combine all four often enough to leave a mark.

That mark appears in ordinary commercial language before most outsiders notice it. Capacity constraints do not usually announce themselves with a grand refusal. They surface as exclusions, sublimits, tighter conditions, higher retentions, reduced lines, more searching documentation requests, or higher calls within mutual structures. A shipowner may still hear "yes" to a proposal. What changes is the quality of that yes. The broader protection hoped for may no longer be available. A specific peril may be carved back. A class of voyage may remain covered but under a narrower and more conditional understanding. Capacity does not need to disappear to constrain access. It need only become more selective.

A named example shows how one incident can reshape an entire conversation. After the *Exxon Valdez* casualty in March 1989, markets did not merely absorb one large northern pollution loss and move on. The event altered the way many institutions thought about environmental severity, public authority response, legal sprawl, and the practical difficulty of managing third-party liabilities in sensitive cold waters. The significance was not limited to one tanker, one owner, or one location. A single highly visible casualty forced pooled and reinsurance capital to ask whether older assumptions about northern exposure had been too comfortable. Once that question is asked seriously, it rarely remains confined to the original file. It migrates into later terms for adjacent voyages and similar classes of operation.

This is one reason high-profile incidents matter so much in Arctic trades. The market for such exposure is not infinitely deep, and the events themselves are often too sparse to be absorbed as mere background noise. One publicised casualty can become an organising memory. Underwriters and reinsurers begin to compare new submissions against it. Clubs become more cautious about what they ask the wider capital structure to support. Operators with no connection to the original incident find themselves answering sharper questions about route limitations, response plans, pollution precautions, passenger management, or wreck contingencies because a previous event taught the market that optimism had been underpriced. Memory becomes a market condition.

A brief example makes the mechanism plain. Imagine a class of Arctic support voyages that has been commercially acceptable, if not warmly embraced, under moderately tight but workable terms. Then a single well-publicised casualty in broadly comparable waters reveals that the liabilities associated with delayed response, public intervention, and environmental management are much wider than many had assumed. No formal ban follows. No treaty suddenly closes the route. Yet at renewal or placement, operators discover that sublimits have appeared, exclusions are proposed for certain costly elements of exposure, and club or reinsurance appetite has thinned enough that higher calls or tougher terms are discussed. The voyage remains possible. The structure carrying it has changed.

This is why global capital structures shape local access so powerfully. A shipowner deciding whether to attempt a northern voyage may think in practical operational categories: ice information, support availability, crewing, class, timing, fuel, route constraints. All of these matter. But above them sits a less visible question: what does the global risk-bearing chain currently believe about this class of exposure? If the answer has hardened, the local voyage can become uneconomic even if nothing about the ship or the route has worsened physically. A change in reinsurance appetite on one desk can travel down through pooling decisions and club caution until it becomes a narrower policy, a bigger bill, or a lost fixture far away. The voyage meets global capital whether it realises it or not.

Clubs themselves respond to this pressure because they cannot ignore the terms on which reinsurance is available. Mutuality gives them a collective logic, but it does not free them from dependence on wider capital. If reinsurers become more cautious about certain northern liabilities, clubs must either absorb more risk internally, charge more for doing so, narrow what they are prepared to support, or insist on stronger controls to make the exposure more attractive. That is why operators sometimes experience clubs as suddenly more exacting after a major external event. The club may not have changed its philosophy overnight. The capital behind its promise may have changed the price of confidence.

This helps explain why capacity limits often feel indirect and yet bite hard. The operator is seldom told that the market has philosophically rejected Arctic ambition. Instead, the message arrives through fragments: a lower line than expected, a request for more information before terms can be considered, a pollution-related constraint, more restrictive conditions around routeing or timing, a reluctance to support passenger carriage, a sharper focus on contingency arrangements, or a reminder that certain liabilities may sit awkwardly with the available structure. Each fragment can be managed. Together they redraw access. Markets govern through calibration more often than through prohibition.

A second named example clarifies the broader pattern from a different kind of casualty. After the *Costa Concordia* grounding in January 2012, the maritime liability community was reminded that high-profile third-party losses can reshape attitudes far beyond the immediate class of vessel involved. Passenger exposure, evacuation difficulty, wreck removal cost, reputational severity, and long claims tails all became more vivid in the financial imagination. The relevance to Arctic trades is not that cruise casualties and polar support voyages are identical. It is that a single complex event can tighten the terms on which capital stands behind whole categories of maritime liability. The market learns across classes when severity feels underappreciated.

A limitation should be admitted. Capacity constraint is not always a simple expression of fear, nor is it always permanent. Reinsurance appetite can soften again. Better data, stronger operator discipline, improved documentation, more credible contingency planning, or a clearer distinction between one problematic class of voyage and another can restore some market confidence. Arctic exposure is not doomed to remain financially suspect in one fixed way. Capital moves. Memory also fades, though slowly.

And yet this limitation does not weaken the central point. Because capacity is mobile and conditional, operators must treat it as part of the strategic environment rather than as background insurance plumbing. The quality of the submission, the seriousness of the route concept, the coherence of the pollution and salvage planning, the record of previous compliance, the visibility of the trade, and the market's recent claims experience all affect how much capacity will be made available and on what terms. Capital is not abstract. It reacts to evidence, memory, and uncertainty. Arctic access depends on that reaction more than many route planners like to admit.

This is where exclusions and sublimits become especially revealing. They are not merely hostile drafting habits. They show what the wider structure is unwilling to carry comfortably in full. A pollution element may be narrowed because remote environmental severity worries reinsurers. A wreck-related exposure may be capped or scrutinised more closely because recent experience has shown how quickly such liabilities expand. Passenger or delay-related elements may harden because evacuation or prolonged interruption in cold regions looks too volatile. Read carefully, the shape of the cover reveals the shape of global discomfort.

Higher calls within mutual structures tell a related story. Members are being reminded that shared exposure has a price, and that price may rise not because their own conduct has worsened, but because the collective burden of certain liabilities has changed. This can feel unfair from the operator's point of view. Yet from the club's perspective it reflects the exact logic of mutuality: if the common fund is asked to stand behind more expensive or less predictable northern risk, members must either accept stronger discipline, narrower support, or a higher cost of participation. The pool demands realism.

The deeper lesson is that local access to Arctic routes is never purely local. It depends on a staircase of confidence reaching from the ship and operator through the club, across the pool, into the reinsurance market, and back down again in the form of conditions, price, and available capacity. Every step matters. A technically capable vessel with a disciplined operator may still find the staircase narrowing because the upper levels have become uneasy about what one more northern claim could mean for the whole structure. Geography and capital meet in the quotation.

The quiet motif returns because the pool is wider than it looks. A casualty in one place ripples outward, and later voyages in other places feel the water move. Arctic commerce often imagines itself in terms of local mastery: good ice advice, strong steel, experienced crew, sound planning. All of that remains essential. None of it prevents a loss from being judged by a global market that has learned, sometimes painfully, to ask how many more such surprises it wishes to mutualise and reinsure on tolerable terms.

The unresolved question, then, is not whether pooling and reinsurance make Arctic liability financially possible. They plainly do. The harder question is what happens when the global capital structure that makes local access possible decides that one more northern surprise is too many - and starts saying so not with a dramatic refusal, but with the colder language of exclusions, sublimits, and a thinner willingness to stand behind the voyage at any price.

Claims handling as governance

In March 1989, after the *Exxon Valdez* grounded in Alaska, the legal and financial aftermath did not begin with payment. It began with reconstruction. What happened first? What did the bridge know, and when? What had been reported, maintained, planned, or deferred before the casualty? Which obligations had been triggered, and which precautions had existed more convincingly on paper than in practice? The claim opened as an argument about facts. It became an argument about systems. The file did not merely record the incident. It started to govern the meaning of the incident.

That is why claims handling matters so much in Arctic and near-Arctic trades. It is often imagined as the administrative phase that follows the real drama, a slow professional clean-up once steel has buckled, oil has spread, or schedules have collapsed. In truth, claims handling is one of the places where maritime governance becomes most visible. It tests facts, enforces conditions, measures the gap between what was promised and what was done, and quietly writes the rules that future operators will later experience as new expectations. The claim does not end the voyage. It rewrites the next one.

This is especially true where P&I clubs, mutual structures, and reinsurers are involved, because claims are never only about one insured's loss. They are also about what the incident reveals regarding the discipline of the member, the quality of the documentation, the reliability of route and response planning, and the degree to which the wider pool has been asked to absorb avoidable uncertainty. A claims file is therefore not neutral terrain. It is a site of institutional learning and institutional self-protection. The clubs and markets involved do not merely ask what they owe. They ask what they have just been taught.

The first lesson usually concerns facts. Claims processes begin by narrowing the story from competing narratives into evidence that can survive scrutiny. Logs, route plans, maintenance histories, survey records, weather and ice information, communications, drill records, photographs, class status, notices, and contract terms all begin to matter at once. In easier trades, the factual picture may still be disputed, but the surrounding conditions are often more forgiving: more witnesses, more infrastructure, faster access, cleaner chains of contemporaneous information. Arctic casualties rarely offer that luxury. Delayed response, harsh weather, sparse support, fragmented communication, and the sheer distance between the event and outside oversight make factual reconstruction harder. Claims handling becomes, in part, a struggle against disappearance.

That struggle is why documentation quality so often determines dispute trajectories. A strong record does not guarantee a favourable outcome, but it gives the operator and its insurers or clubs a coherent basis from which to explain decisions, demonstrate compliance, and resist exaggerated or poorly founded allegations. A weak record does the opposite. Missing logs, vague route assessments, thin maintenance histories, incomplete drill evidence, patchy reporting, or contradictory communications invite suspicion even before any formal accusation is fully developed. The document gap becomes a liability multiplier because it widens the room in which others can infer carelessness, concealment, or indifference. Silence acquires cost.

A named example from outside the Arctic proper shows the institutional mechanism clearly. After the *Costa Concordia* grounding in January 2012, the claims and legal aftermath did not turn only on the visible fact of the casualty. It turned on the quality of records, the integrity of procedures, the timeline of decisions, the adequacy of emergency conduct, and the wider organisational story those materials revealed. The relevance to Arctic trade is not that every polar casualty resembles a cruise disaster. It is that claims handling in severe-environment cases quickly moves beyond the single event into a broader inquiry about whether the operator's systems were real, timely, and defensible. The file becomes a test of truthfulness under pressure.

This explains why claims processes enforce conditions as well as interpret losses. Policies, club rules, warranties, reporting duties, and contractual obligations do not remain dormant once a casualty begins. Claims handlers and correspondents examine whether notices were given on time, whether surveys had been completed, whether operational limits were respected, whether response planning matched what had been declared, whether class-related conditions were current, and whether the insured or member had complied with specific requirements that shaped the availability or scope of cover. These are not merely technical exercises. They determine whether shared capital is being asked to respond to a managed risk or to a venture that drifted beyond the conditions on which support had originally been offered.

In Arctic settings, this enforcement function becomes sharper because the margin for improvisation is smaller and the cost of retrospective generosity is larger. A route deviation that might appear minor elsewhere may look far more serious if it entered heavier ice, delayed response, or complicated environmental management. A late notice to the club or insurer may seem more damaging where public authority intervention began quickly and evidence needed to be preserved under difficult conditions. A weak pollution response record may take on new significance where containment and clean-up were slowed by remoteness. Claims handlers know this. They read compliance failures not only as breaches or omissions, but as clues to whether the operator's control of the voyage had already begun to thin before the casualty made that weakness public.

A second named example shows how this logic can spread through the market after a visible northern event. Following the *Exxon Valdez* disaster in March 1989, claims handling did not merely settle one enormous pollution case. It generated a body of institutional memory about environmental response, evidentiary burden, public authority intervention, documentation weakness, and the severity that can attach to a casualty in cold, politically sensitive waters. Markets learned from that claims experience. Clubs learned. Operators learned. Later requirements around planning, documentation, pollution preparedness, and route discipline did not appear out of nowhere. They grew from the file. Claims handling became a source of future governance.

That is the deeper point. Claims do not simply produce settlements. They produce lessons. Those lessons may be formalised in revised underwriting questions, sharper club circulars, tighter survey expectations, more intrusive documentary demands, narrower route limits, or stronger contractual clauses. Sometimes the change is explicit: a new requirement, a clearer notice obligation, a revised expectation about response planning. Sometimes it is atmospheric: underwriters ask harder questions, charterers treat certain gaps less generously, surveyors interpret similar facts more conservatively, clubs become slower to accept broad assurances unsupported by records. In either form, governance is operating after the incident. The claim is a regulatory workshop by other means.

This is one reason disputes about causation matter beyond the money immediately at stake. In harsh environments, causes rarely line up neatly. Ice, weather, fatigue, machinery, support limitations, route pressure, communication delay, and public authority response may all contribute to the eventual shape of the claim. A good claims process does not merely identify one fault and stop. It examines how the incident escalated and what parts of that escalation were foreseeable, documented, and controlled. That broader inquiry can change future underwriting even when the formal legal outcome remains limited. An operator may win a narrow argument and still lose trust, because the claims file revealed operational habits the market now dislikes. Victory can be expensive.

A limitation should be stated plainly. Claims handling is not a perfectly wise process. It can become defensive, overly legalistic, or distorted by hindsight. A badly documented but genuinely careful operator may suffer because the record is poor. A well-documented but weaker organisation may appear more credible than it deserves. Clubs and insurers, like other institutions, can overlearn from exceptional cases and impose burdens that do not always distinguish cleanly between one troubling incident and a whole class of operations. A claim is a powerful teacher, but not an infallible one.

Yet this limitation only makes disciplined claims handling more important. Because the process is interpretive, documentation quality, speed of response, internal coherence, and candour under pressure matter enormously. A member or insured that reports promptly, preserves evidence, aligns its account with contemporaneous records, explains gaps honestly, and shows that its procedures were lived rather than ornamental stands a much better chance of steering the dispute onto manageable ground. A party that delays, improvises narratives, or discovers too late that key documents are missing gives others room to construct a harsher version of events. Claims handling therefore rewards not only prevention, but evidentiary maturity.

This is why operators who treat claims as something for lawyers and adjusters to solve after the event usually misunderstand the system. The dispute trajectory is often determined long before external counsel becomes dominant. It is shaped by the quality of the route assessment, the maintenance trail, the clarity of reporting lines, the seriousness of drills, the discipline of communications, the completeness of notices, and the consistency with which the company has aligned paperwork with actual practice. In Arctic trades, where the evidentiary environment is harsher, these things are not supporting materials. They are part of the claims outcome itself.

The clubs and insurers know this, and they price accordingly. An operator with a strong record of documentation, timely reporting, transparent cooperation, and disciplined post-incident conduct may still face liability, but it is often seen as more governable. A company whose claims history reveals confusion, thin records, disputed compliance, or recurring documentary weakness becomes more expensive even if its incidents were not the largest. The market is not only pricing casualties. It is pricing how the operator behaves when the casualty enters the claims system. Claims handling thus reaches forward into future underwriting stances as much as it reaches backward into one event.

The quiet motif returns because the file remains central. Before the casualty, it is a record of preparation. During the casualty, it becomes a record of response. After the casualty, it becomes a record of truth, memory, and institutional consequence. One missing report, one vague plan, one late notice, one unresolved recommendation may not decide every dispute. But each can shift the tone of the claim and, through that shift, the future conditions under which similar voyages are allowed to feel commercially routine. The file learns, and the market listens.

The harder question, then, is not whether claims handling belongs to governance. It plainly does. The harder question is what kind of Arctic operator can survive not only the casualty itself, but the searching reconstruction that follows - and whether the next tightening of terms, the next club requirement, or the next underwriter's scepticism is already being written today in the quality of the records that will one day have to carry the whole weight of the story.

Chapter 10

Claims, Disputes, and Precedent Effects

In March 1989, when the *Exxon Valdez* grounded in Alaska, the incident did not enter the legal and insurance world as a fixed set of facts. It entered as a struggle over sequence, cause, responsibility, and meaning. Logs were read against memory, technical reports against witness statements, public outrage against formal doctrine. The casualty itself was only the beginning. What followed was a contest over narrative.

That is the first hard truth about Arctic claims. Loss does not arrive in the market as raw reality. It is translated. Someone writes the incident report. Someone explains the route decision, the machinery condition, the weather, the ice, the communications, and the warnings that were heeded or missed. Experts then turn physical traces into opinions. Lawyers and claims handlers sort those opinions into arguments that can support payment, resist payment, widen liability, or narrow it. By the time a dispute matures, the event at sea has already become something else: a file thick with interpretation. The folder grows teeth.

This matters because Arctic conditions make reconstruction unusually difficult. Distance delays attendance. Weather interferes with observation. Ice alters physical evidence. Machinery can fail for several reasons at once. Human decisions made under fatigue, limited information, or severe environmental pressure look different in hindsight than they looked on the bridge. A moderate factual uncertainty in easier waters can become a serious dispute in the far north because the evidentiary margin is thinner and the financial stakes larger. The same casualty may support more than one plausible story, and each story points liability in a different direction.

The central tension lies there. Claims systems promise resolution through evidence, expertise, and procedure, yet many of the most consequential Arctic outcomes do not produce clean public rules. Some disputes are arbitrated. Some settle confidentially. Some vanish into adjusted figures, guarded correspondence, and professional memory. That means the market learns constantly, but not always openly. Underwriters, clubs, brokers, surveyors, and charterers absorb lessons from claims even when formal precedent remains thin or invisible. Hidden outcomes still govern.

That hidden governance matters because it shapes both trust and price. When markets cannot rely on a rich public body of decisions, they lean harder on documentation quality, disclosure discipline, technical experts, and rumours about how similar disputes have ended. Opacity does not calm risk. It tends to harden it. A known adverse rule can be priced. A half-known settlement, a whispered expert disagreement, or a quietly abandoned recovery action produces a different and colder response: more caution, more paperwork, more restrictive terms, and less willingness to assume that the next case will resolve benignly. Uncertainty survives inside memory.

This is also why subrogation and pursuit decisions belong inside the same conversation. After a loss, the question is not only what happened, but who is worth pursuing, on what evidence, and at what commercial cost. In Arctic trades, multiple parties may have influenced routeing, technical readiness, loading, timing, or support assumptions. Yet remoteness, sparse records, and overlapping control can make recovery difficult even where fault seems broadly shared. Choices about whether to pursue another party, therefore, reveal more than legal doctrine. They reveal incentives, relationships, evidentiary confidence, and the practical limits of post-loss accountability.

The chapter's movement follows that pressure from fact-making to market memory. It begins where every serious dispute begins, with the conversion of incident into claim narrative, then enters the technical battlefield where experts fight over causation and often prolong uncertainty rather than dissolving it. From there, it passes into arbitration, litigation, and settlement, where many outcomes shape behaviour without ever becoming clear public precedent, before tightening around subrogation and the pursuit of responsibility across fragmented operational control. It ends where all significant claims eventually arrive: in the learning loop by which repeated losses become new conditions, and in the disclosure and reputational habits that determine how long a market remembers.

The stakes are larger than dispute resolution. Claims are one of the main ways a market writes policy without calling it policy. A cluster of similar failures can produce new warranties, new survey expectations, tighter deductibles, or requirements that begin as advice and harden into obligation. An operator that treats a claim as an isolated historical inconvenience misunderstands the mechanism. Claims are archives of embarrassment, but they are also engines of rule-making. The next season's caution often begins in the last season's correspondence.

That leaves a harder question than any incident report can answer cleanly. When the Arctic casualty enters the claims system, what carries more force in the end: the physical event itself, the quality of the evidence preserved around it, or the market memory that will outlast both and quietly decide what future operators must now prove before anyone agrees to trust their version of the risk?

From incident report to claim narrative

In March 1989, the *Exxon Valdez* grounded in Alaska, and the casualty entered public memory as an environmental disaster of unusual scale and consequence. Yet for insurers, lawyers, clubs, and claims handlers, the event did not arrive as a finished truth. It arrived as fragments: bridge records, timings, weather observations, crew recollections, technical assumptions, gaps in communication, and the later work of experts trying to fix sequence and responsibility onto a moving chain of decisions. The spill was real enough. Its legal meaning had to be assembled.

That act of assembly lies at the heart of every serious marine claim, and it becomes particularly fraught in Arctic and near-Arctic operations. An incident at sea is not the same thing as the claim narrative that later governs payment, liability, recovery, or settlement. Between the two lies a long process of translation. Logs are read for timing and omission. Witness statements are tested for consistency and perspective. Expert reports convert ice, machinery, routeing, weather, fatigue, and vessel condition into explanations that lawyers and insurers can use. What looks like one event on the water becomes several competing versions on paper. The record starts to steer.

This distinction matters because claims are rarely decided by brute fact alone. They are decided by facts arranged into a persuasive sequence. A good claim narrative does not simply say that something happened; it shows why it happened, who controlled the relevant choices, what was known at the time, what standards or limits applied, and whether later losses flowed naturally from the original event or from some avoidable failure in response. In Arctic trades, this work is harder because the environment destroys neatness. Ice changes position. Weather closes in. Communications falter. External assistance arrives slowly. Physical evidence may degrade before it is fully examined. By the time the incident is being narrated ashore, certainty has already been eroded by distance and delay.

That erosion makes the first documents disproportionately important. The initial incident report is often treated by non-specialists as a neutral account, a kind of administrative starting pistol before the real legal and technical debate begins. In practice, it is already part of the struggle over meaning. The language chosen, the facts emphasised, the sequence implied, the omissions left unfilled, and the confidence with which uncertain conditions are described can all shape what follows. If the report frames the event as a sudden encounter with unforeseeable ice movement, later arguments about prudent routeing begin from one place. If it frames the same event as a foreseeable consequence of pressing on under narrowing margins, the later legal terrain changes at once. The first telling matters.

Logs occupy a similar position. They can appear dry and technical, but in dispute they become narrative anchors. They establish time, location, course changes, communications, equipment status, weather observations, warnings received, and the operator's own contemporaneous account of what seemed important. In Arctic cases, this contemporaneity becomes precious because later recollection is so vulnerable to hindsight. A master who justified a route change at the time by reference to available information may look reckless later if the log is vague, sparse, or inconsistent with other records. A careful operator, by contrast, may survive a harsher retrospective reading because the log shows that the decision was taken within a documented frame of prudence rather than out of casual optimism. The line on the page can carry extraordinary weight.

Witness statements complicate the picture rather than simplifying it. Maritime casualties usually produce multiple human perspectives even in benign settings. In Arctic conditions, the gap between perspectives may widen because visibility is poorer, events unfold under greater stress, and different parts of the ship experience the incident differently. Bridge officers may describe one set of pressures, engineers another, deck crew another again. Fatigue, cold, stress, and limited situational awareness influence how events are seen and later remembered. Claims handlers therefore do not read witness statements as transparent truth. They read them as positioned accounts, shaped by role, perception, and the natural desire to explain one's own conduct in the best possible light. Human memory is evidence, but unstable evidence.

This is where expert reports enter, not to end disagreement, but to reorganise it. Experts translate the physical and operational traces of the incident into disciplined interpretation. They assess ice damage, machinery failure, hull response, routing decisions, visibility, communications reliability, bridge resource management, and the feasibility of alternative actions. Their authority matters because most legal and claims actors cannot themselves decide whether the pattern of damage suggests prior weakness, whether a machinery failure began before the incident became visible, or whether the route selected fell within a prudent operational envelope under the conditions then known. Expert opinion fills that gap. It also creates a new battleground, because experts often disagree not about the raw data alone, but about what that data means.

A named example makes this painfully clear. After the *Exxon Valdez* casualty, the later struggle was not confined to proving that a grounding had occurred. The harder questions concerned how the event should be understood: what sequence of human and organisational decisions mattered most, what warnings and conditions were significant, what legal responsibilities attached to whom, and how subsequent losses should be allocated across operators, insurers, and the wider liability system. The broader lesson for Arctic claims is direct. A serious incident does not move in a straight line from event to payment. It moves through narrative construction, and that narrative will shape both legal outcome and market memory long after the physical traces have faded.

Arctic conditions intensify the role of contested interpretation because causation is often layered rather than singular. A route decision may have been defensible in broad terms yet still have interacted badly with deteriorating weather, incomplete ice information, or a minor technical weakness that would not have mattered elsewhere. A machinery issue may have been manageable in ordinary service and decisive only because remoteness lengthened response time. A response that appears slow in hindsight may have reflected genuine physical and communications constraints at the time. This multiplicity invites argument. One side frames the event as an unfortunate convergence of harsh conditions. Another frames it as the predictable result of pushing into uncertainty without adequate margin. Both use the same underlying incident. They tell different stories.

That difference in story matters because liability allocation follows narrative structure. If the claim narrative places the decisive weight on unforeseeable environmental movement, the owner's and insurer's position may harden around fortuity and limited preventability. If the same narrative places weight on navigational choice, weak route discipline, or disregard of available warnings, then fault and contractual breach become more plausible and settlement leverage changes. If the story broadens to include charterer pressure, poor ice advice, or deficient documentation, new parties may enter the frame. Claims are not allocated by physics alone. They are allocated by the legal meaning imposed on physics through narrative.

A brief example shows how route decisions become central in hindsight. Imagine a vessel proceeding through a marginal northern corridor after receiving advice suggesting deteriorating ice conditions later in the day. The master adjusts course slightly but continues, judging that the ship's capability and the available window remain sufficient. Hours later, damage occurs. The incident report may initially describe an encounter with unexpectedly difficult ice. Later, logs show earlier hesitation, witness statements reveal disagreement on the bridge, and experts suggest that the chosen route left too little room to retreat once conditions tightened. What was first narrated as environmental misfortune becomes, through accumulation of evidence, a dispute about judgment. The route becomes the claim.

This is why settlement dynamics are so sensitive to documentation quality. A party with coherent logs, disciplined reports, preserved communications, technically plausible expert support, and witness accounts that align within normal human limits can often move a dispute towards narrower argument and earlier resolution. A party with patchy records, retrospective correction, or unexplained gaps hands leverage to the other side. The dispute broadens. Causation becomes more contestable. Compliance issues creep in. Insurers ask harder questions about cover and disclosure. Third parties become less willing to compromise because uncertainty now works in their favour. Weak records do not merely weaken legal defence. They lengthen the life of the dispute.

A second named example shows the broader pattern from a different sort of casualty. After the *Costa Concordia* grounding in January 2012, the later legal and insurance struggles were not governed only by the visible fact of the casualty. They were shaped by the narratives built from witness evidence, voyage records, command decisions, company procedures, and competing technical explanations of what should have happened and why it did not. The relevance to Arctic claims lies not in the vessel type but in the institutional mechanism. Once an incident enters serious dispute, the quality of the story becomes almost as important as the severity of the loss itself. A casualty with a strong narrative may settle faster than a smaller event whose documentary foundation is fractured.

A limitation should be admitted. Narrative is powerful, but it is not infinitely elastic. Some events carry physical traces so strong, or documentary clarity so compelling, that the range of plausible interpretation narrows quickly. Courts, tribunals, clubs, and insurers are not merely audiences for literary persuasion. They test stories against hard materials. Overstating the plasticity of claims narrative would be a mistake.

And yet that limitation only sharpens the practical lesson. Because hard materials matter, the party that preserves, organises, and explains them best usually enters the dispute on better ground. In Arctic settings, where the environment itself conspires against clean reconstruction, that advantage becomes more valuable. It is not enough to have been prudent; prudence must have left traces. It is not enough that conditions were difficult; the difficulty must be shown in records and expert support rather than asserted later as a generic excuse. It is not enough that a route decision seemed reasonable at the time; the basis for that reasonableness must survive translation into a claims file months later.

This is one reason claims handlers and underwriters read incident files not merely to settle the present matter, but to assess the operator's broader competence. A company whose narrative is coherent because its records are coherent appears governable. A company whose narrative changes with each new document, witness statement, or expert intervention appears riskier even if the original casualty was not the largest in the market. The claims process thus produces a reputational surplus or deficit that outlives the case. Narrative becomes commercial memory.

The quiet motif returns because the record starts to steer. It steers liability allocation, because the better-told and better-supported narrative attracts stronger legal leverage. It steers settlement dynamics, because uncertainty changes who fears delay and who profits from it. It steers future underwriting, because the claims file teaches clubs and insurers what kinds of operators document reality clearly enough to be trusted when conditions turn ugly. The sea writes the incident; the file determines much of what the incident becomes.

The harder question, then, is not whether Arctic claims are shaped by narrative. They plainly are. The harder question is what kind of operator understands this early enough to act on it - not by manipulating the story after the event, but by creating, before anything goes wrong, the logs, reports, witness discipline, and technical trace that will later decide whether the Arctic casualty is remembered as misfortune, misjudgment, or something far more expensive in between.

The role of experts and technical causation

In January 2012, after the *Costa Concordia* grounded off Giglio, Italy, the visible facts seemed brutally plain: a large passenger ship, a failed voyage, a wreck that became a public humiliation as much as a maritime casualty. Yet the dispute that followed did not turn on visibility alone. It turned on explanation. What exactly had failed first? Which human decisions mattered most? How did bridge practice, vessel response, company culture, equipment readiness, and emergency conduct interact? The wreck was obvious. Causation was not.

That distinction is even sharper in Arctic and near-Arctic claims. A damaged hull, a disabled engine, a delayed response, or a vessel beset by ice may look like a single incident when viewed from the outside. Inside the claims process, it quickly becomes a contest over technical sequence. Did the ice create damage that no prudent operator could have avoided, or did the vessel enter conditions outside its real operating margin? Did machinery fail because of latent weakness, maintenance deficiency, crew handling, temperature effects, or some combination of all four? Did human judgement break down because conditions were genuinely extraordinary, or because the operator had normalised risk until the environment exposed the weakness? Experts step into that uncertainty because someone has to translate physical traces into legally usable meaning. The fracture line matters.

Technical expertise matters in maritime disputes because most serious claims hinge on questions that neither lawyers nor claims handlers can answer by instinct alone. A bent propeller, fractured plating, damaged rudder stock, degraded seal, failed lubrication system, fatigued crew response, or disputed route decision may all carry possible explanations. A naval architect reads structure differently from a marine engineer. An ice navigator reads track choices differently from a general casualty analyst. A human-factors specialist reads decision pressure differently from a master with decades of conventional sea time. None of these perspectives is decorative. They form the machinery by which an event is turned into an argument about responsibility. Causation must be built.

This is why expert evidence often begins with apparently modest questions. What pattern of scoring or indentation does the hull show? Does that pattern fit one severe ice contact or repeated exposure beyond the vessel's intended conditions? Did the machinery failure originate before the vessel entered difficulty, or did environmental strain turn a manageable weakness into a disabling event? Were alarms, records, and maintenance logs consistent with the operator's later explanation? Was the crew responding to rapidly changing conditions with appropriate caution, or merely carrying forward a course of action that had ceased to be prudent? Each question sounds narrow. Together they define the claim.

Ice damage is one of the clearest examples of why technical causation becomes contested so easily. Arctic ice is not a single hazard with a single forensic signature. Damage may result from heavy pressure, repeated minor contact, impact with harder, older ice, poor speed control, routeing decisions that left too little room to manoeuvre, or a vessel whose real condition did not match its documentary strength. The claimant, the club, the hull underwriter, the charterer, and any third party may all prefer different stories. A shipowner may emphasise the unpredictability of local conditions. Another party may argue that the damage pattern shows a voyage pressed too far into known or foreseeable severity. The expert does not merely identify damage. The expert gives the damage a narrative direction.

Machinery failure works in much the same way. A shaft line does not simply fail; it fails within a history of loading, temperature, maintenance, vibration, design assumptions, operational stress, and human response. In severe cold, this history may be harder to reconstruct because low temperatures can alter system performance, emergency workarounds may have been attempted under pressure, and external support may have arrived too late to preserve the cleanest forensic picture. Expert engineers are therefore asked to decide not just what broke, but when the failure truly began and what other conditions turned technical weakness into casualty. The answer matters enormously. If the failure began as deferred maintenance, the liability story points one way. If it arose from conditions no prudent preparation could fully absorb, it points another.

Human factors complicate both ice and machinery cases because the bridge and engine room never operate as pure technical theatres. People read instruments, interpret advice, manage fatigue, communicate under stress, and decide whether to slow down, alter course, continue, or retreat. In Arctic trades, those judgments are strained by imperfect information, darkness, weather, cold, and the knowledge that delay can have commercial as well as operational cost. Human-factors experts do not arrive to moralise. They examine how attention, stress, workload, training, authority gradients, and procedural design shaped what people actually did. That work can be uncomfortable because it often shows that the line between individual error and organisational weakness is thinner than a party would like. The voice on the bridge is never only one voice.

A named example helps to show how this broadens the dispute. After the *Costa Concordia* casualty in January 2012, the legal and insurance struggle did not depend only on proving that a grounding had occurred. It required experts to explain command decisions, vessel track, emergency timing, systems performance, evacuation behaviour, and the relationship between visible human failure and wider organisational design. The relevance to Arctic claims is direct. Even where the casualty type differs, the process is similar: experts do not simply describe damage or error. They decide how far outward the circle of causation expands. That expansion often determines who must pay.

This is why expert disagreement can prolong disputes so severely. In public imagination, technical expertise is often treated as a solvent that dissolves uncertainty. In claims reality, it frequently sharpens it. One expert may see damage consistent with unforeseeable ice pressure. Another sees cumulative overexposure to known conditions. One engineer may locate the root cause in prior maintenance weakness. Another emphasises abnormal environmental stress. One human-factors specialist may argue that the master's decision was understandable within the information then available. Another may say the system had already created conditions in which a prudent master should have withdrawn earlier. Once competing expert frameworks emerge, the dispute becomes more than evidentiary. It becomes methodological.

Methodological disagreement is expensive because it lengthens the life of the claim. More inspections may be needed. More records are demanded. Parties seek further testing, further modelling, further interviews, and more extensive critique of each other's technical assumptions. Costs rise not only through legal fees, but through delay, uncertainty, operational distraction, and the simple fact that a file in dispute remains a live financial problem for everyone carrying it. The Arctic amplifies this because expert reconstruction often begins from thinner or more degraded evidence than anyone would prefer. When the physical record is compromised by remoteness or late access, interpretation gains power. So does disagreement.

A second named example shows how one highly visible incident can alter later technical reading well beyond its own facts. After the *Exxon Valdez* grounding in March 1989, the wider maritime world did not merely learn a lesson about a single navigational failure. It learned that in sensitive northern waters, technical explanations would be read through environmental consequence, public pressure, and the broader question of whether the operator's systems deserved trust at all. Later experts, underwriters, and regulators approaching northern casualties did not begin from innocence. They began from a history in which small interpretive choices could have enormous legal and financial consequences. Once an earlier event has taught that lesson, later technical findings enter a market already primed to ask harder questions.

This is where causation becomes a governance battleground. The stakes are not limited to the immediate dispute. Once a technical explanation gains institutional acceptance, even informally, it can shape future survey focus, underwriting questions, club requirements, and operating assumptions. If a cluster of claims suggests that certain hull areas repeatedly suffer damage under specific ice profiles, surveyors begin looking harder there. If machinery casualties in cold conditions repeatedly reveal common weaknesses in heating, lubrication, or monitoring practice, insurers and clubs begin asking for clearer evidence that operators have adapted. If human-factors analysis repeatedly shows route decisions being distorted by schedule pressure or poor escalation culture, manuals, audits, and charter language often tighten around those points. Technical causation leaks outward.

That leakage matters because many operators still imagine claims as backward-looking events. In fact, the technical findings inside one dispute often become the raw material of later rule-like expectations. At first the lesson may appear as advice: a stronger recommendation, a request for more specific planning, a survey note about areas needing closer attention, a club circular hinting at concern. Later it hardens. What began as wise practice becomes expected practice. What was once a persuasive extra becomes the thing whose absence now triggers premium increase, additional survey, or tougher conditions. Experts do not make policy in the legislative sense. Their causal stories often become policy in the market sense.

Still, a limitation must be admitted. Experts are not neutral machines delivering pure truth from damaged steel and tired witness accounts. They work within instructions, available evidence, professional cultures, and the strategic needs of the parties who retain them. Good experts may disagree honestly. Poor experts may overstate certainty. Some fields, especially those involving human factors and harsh environmental judgement, leave more room for interpretation than any party would like. Treating expertise as infallible would be naive.

Yet this limitation does not diminish its governing power. It explains why the most important disputes are often won not by the party with the most dramatic rhetoric, but by the party whose technical explanation is best aligned with the documents, the physical evidence, the operating context, and the institutional expectations of those deciding the claim. Expertise persuades when it joins the record rather than floating above it. An operator with coherent logs, disciplined reporting, preserved evidence, clear route assessments, and credible maintenance history gives its experts something solid to work from. An operator with patchy documentation invites the opposite. In the Arctic, where environment already thins certainty, the quality of the record can determine whether expertise clarifies or merely multiplies doubt.

This is also why technical experts matter before the casualty, though their names may not yet appear. The questions they will later ask shape how prudent operators prepare. Which systems are most likely to come under forensic scrutiny? Which decisions need clearer documentation? Which kinds of ice exposure, maintenance shortcut, or route compromise are hardest to defend later? Claims history teaches markets which technical arguments recur. From there come stronger surveys, adjusted manuals, more specific training, and narrower operating thresholds. In that sense, the expert is present in every serious Arctic file long before the casualty arrives, as an imagined future reader of what the company is doing now.

The quiet motif returns because the fracture line is more than physical. It runs through metal, yes, but also through memory, method, and institutional trust. One side sees unavoidable ice damage. Another sees overconfident routeing. One sees a cold-stressed system. Another sees neglected maintenance meeting cold at last. One sees a hard decision made under pressure. Another sees the predictable end of a culture that had stopped listening to its own limits. Expert evidence gives each fracture a language. The market then decides which languages it wishes to hear again.

The harder question, then, is not whether experts help explain Arctic casualties. They plainly do. The harder question is what happens when their explanations begin to shape not just one dispute, but the ordinary assumptions of surveyors, clubs, underwriters, and charterers - and whether operators recognise soon enough that the next governing rule may arrive first not as law, but as a technical opinion nobody in the market is willing to ignore.

Arbitration, litigation, and confidential settlements

In January 2012, after the *Costa Concordia* grounded off Giglio, Italy, the world saw a casualty in bright public light. What it saw less clearly was the second life of the dispute once the cameras moved on: the choice of forum, the handling of claims, the strategic pressure to settle some matters quietly and contest others hard, and the slow conversion of visible catastrophe into partial rulings, negotiated outcomes, and fragments of knowledge that not every outsider would ever read in full. A wreck is public. Resolution often is not.

That contrast matters deeply in maritime disputes, and it matters even more in Arctic and near-Arctic trades. An incident may be spectacularly visible while its legal consequences remain partly hidden inside arbitration, settlement agreements, club correspondence, insurer files, expert exchanges, and commercially cautious compromise. The result is a peculiar legal atmosphere. People in the market know that outcomes exist, that money changed hands, that arguments were won or lost, that certain explanations persuaded and others failed. Yet the wider market may not receive a full public account of what exactly happened in legal terms. The door closes softly.

Marine disputes move through several institutional routes, each with its own tempo and consequences. Litigation in court offers the possibility of public judgment, formal reasoning, and, at least sometimes, an accessible precedent that others can read and apply later. Arbitration offers privacy, procedural flexibility, specialist decision-makers, and a mode of resolution often preferred by commercial actors who do not wish to conduct operational autopsies in open court. Confidential settlements sit somewhere else again. They can end disputes before a full judgment or award ever emerges, preserving relationships, reducing cost, and limiting reputational damage, while also keeping much of the underlying reasoning from wider view. None of these routes is inherently suspect. Each solves one problem and creates another.

The problem created by opacity is not ignorance in the simple sense. Maritime markets are rarely wholly ignorant. They hear things. Brokers hear which arguments failed to move a tribunal. Clubs learn which evidentiary weaknesses made a case expensive. Underwriters remember which type of routeing dispute settled on painful terms. Surveyors and lawyers carry impressions from one matter into the next. The difficulty is that such knowledge often arrives unevenly. It circulates through professional memory and private networks rather than through a stable public record. That changes how risk is priced. Markets become cautious not because they know nothing, but because they know something incomplete.

This is why confidentiality can preserve uncertainty even while resolving the immediate dispute. A settlement may end the argument between the parties and still leave the wider market unsure which technical explanation prevailed, which contractual weakness proved decisive, how close the losing side came to success, or whether the payment reflected legal merit, evidentiary anxiety, commercial fatigue, or reputational calculation. In public litigation, even a flawed judgment can at least be studied. In private resolution, the market is left to infer. Inference is expensive. It tends to generate conservative pricing rather than confident distinction.

A named example helps clarify the broader institutional logic. The *Exxon Valdez* disaster in March 1989 produced extensive public litigation and legal attention, making it one of the comparatively rare northern casualties whose consequences entered a wider public archive. That very visibility illustrates the contrast. When a case is litigated openly and followed closely, markets can at least anchor some of their later caution to visible judicial reasoning, public evidence, and a documented chain of argument. Even then, uncertainty remains. Where disputes are resolved through private mechanisms or fragmented settlements, much less of that reasoning becomes widely available. The market then learns through echoes rather than through text.

This difference matters because Arctic claims are often too sparse and too operationally distinctive to generate a deep, tidy body of public precedent. Many incidents are resolved in ways that leave only partial traces. A charterparty dispute may settle after expert exchange. A club matter may conclude through negotiated contribution. A pollution-related claim may be resolved with confidentiality provisions that prevent broad discussion of the crucial reasoning. A technical dispute over ice damage may never reach a public award. To the outsider, nothing much seems to have happened. To the market, something certainly has. Terms change. Questions sharpen. A quiet case leaves a loud memory.

Arbitration occupies a particularly important position in this landscape because it offers something commercial parties value intensely: a degree of privacy combined with specialist attention. For maritime actors, that can be attractive for obvious reasons. Technical disputes may be better understood by arbitrators familiar with shipping practice than by general courts. Sensitive documents may be handled with less public exposure. The parties may preserve more control over timing and structure. Yet the very strengths of arbitration from the parties' perspective can produce wider uncertainty from the market's perspective. If the reasoning behind an important outcome remains largely unavailable, later actors must price the possibility that similar facts may be treated harshly without ever being able to read the full path that led there.

Litigation, by contrast, can create clearer public markers, but not always at the speed or cost commercial actors desire. Court proceedings may expose internal records, operational weaknesses, or uncomfortable facts more fully than the parties would prefer. They may also generate judgments that are valuable precisely because they are public, reasoned, and citable. That openness can reduce uncertainty for the wider market even while increasing pain for the immediate parties. A public loss may therefore have one peculiar virtue: it teaches clearly. Private resolution may spare the parties some damage while teaching everyone else less explicitly and, in some respects, more nervously.

A brief example shows how opacity affects behaviour. Imagine an Arctic machinery casualty leading to disputed claims about whether damage arose from ordinary wear, maintenance failure, or ice-related stress beyond the vessel's contemplated envelope. The matter is referred to arbitration. Experts disagree sharply. Documents are exchanged. The parties eventually settle before a final published award. What does the market learn? It learns that the issue was serious enough to resist easy adjustment. It may hear that documentation weaknesses hurt one side, or that expert opinion divided badly, or that the settlement figure surprised those close to it. But it does not learn, with confidence, which factual and legal analysis truly drove the outcome. The next operator with similar exposure will likely face harder questions and not necessarily because the market has mastered the issue. The market has not mastered it. It has become wary of it.

This is how hidden outcomes still shape behaviour through rumour and risk perception. Rumour is too dismissive a word if it suggests idle invention. What actually circulates is often half-verified professional knowledge: enough to influence judgment, not enough to anchor it securely. A broker knows that a certain kind of routeing dispute recently ended badly. A club knows that weak logs created leverage in a technical causation fight.

An underwriter has heard that a confidential settlement on a northern pollution matter was more painful than expected. A charterer senses that certain contractual formulations now attract more resistance than before. None of these fragments amounts to binding precedent. Together they alter conduct.

This is why markets so often react conservatively to opacity. They cannot safely distinguish between a one-off ugly compromise and a deeper pattern if the outcomes remain largely hidden. The prudent commercial response is therefore to tighten terms, demand more documentation, narrow assumptions, ask for more surveys, press for clearer route limitations, and resist generous readings of ambiguous facts or clauses. Confidentiality solves one problem - the immediate dispute - while spreading another problem outward: a diffuse uncertainty that no public decision has fully disciplined. Hidden law becomes visible caution.

A second named example shows the same institutional truth from a different angle. After the *Costa Concordia* casualty in 2012, certain aspects of the aftermath were highly public, but many practical disputes within the broader claims ecosystem did not produce a fully transparent market record. The wider lesson for Arctic disputes is straightforward. Even where one event is famous, many of the most commercially instructive outcomes still emerge through partial visibility. The market may know enough to grow stricter without knowing enough to become truly precise. That gap between awareness and clarity is one of the defining conditions of marine risk pricing.

A limitation deserves clear acknowledgement. Confidential settlements and private arbitration are not necessarily enemies of good governance. They can reduce delay, control cost, protect commercially sensitive information, preserve working relationships, and allow technical disputes to be resolved by people with appropriate expertise rather than performed for public effect. In many cases they are practical, rational, and fair. It would be childish to imagine that every valuable lesson must be taught in open court.

And yet this limitation only sharpens the central point. Because private resolution is often sensible for the parties, the wider market cannot count on public precedent to clarify recurring northern risks. That means behaviour is shaped by shadows as well as by rules. Operators face questions sharpened by cases they cannot fully read. Underwriters price concerns that were strengthened by outcomes they cannot cleanly cite. Clubs and charterers adjust language in response to disputes whose decisive reasoning remains partly hidden. Governance continues, but it continues through a mixed medium of formal law, private memory, and professional caution.

This mixed medium makes disclosure and internal record-keeping even more important. Where public precedent is thin, the best defence against market anxiety is often not argument alone but a file strong enough to reduce the room in which hidden outcomes can be imagined against you. Good logs, coherent route assessments, clear notices, disciplined survey responses, and honest reporting do more than support one future dispute. They help resist the market tendency to assume the worst where it cannot see clearly. Opacity raises the default level of suspicion. Strong records lower it only partly, but often meaningfully.

The quiet motif returns because the door closes softly, but not silently. What happens behind it does not stay there in any pure sense. It leaks into renewal conversations, club attitudes, broker warnings, survey focus, and the tone with which similar Arctic proposals are later received. The absence of a public ruling does not mean the absence of market effect. On the contrary, it often means the effect will be diffused, harder to contest, and more deeply embedded in collective caution.

The harder question, then, is not whether arbitration, litigation, or settlement resolve disputes. They plainly do, each in their own way. The harder question is what kind of Arctic market is produced when too many decisive outcomes remain only partly visible - and whether operators can ever truly know how much of the price they are paying reflects the law itself, and how much reflects the lingering power of closed files and half-seen defeats.

Subrogation and pursuit of responsibility

In March 1989, after the *Exxon Valdez* grounded in Alaska, the question was never only who would pay first. It was also who, later, might be pursued for what had been paid. That second question is less theatrical than the casualty itself, but often more revealing. Once an insurer or club has met a loss, the file does not automatically close. It may turn outward, towards others whose conduct, decisions, or contractual role arguably helped produce the event. The bill starts walking.

That outward movement is the practical heart of subrogation. In plain terms, it means that once an insurer has paid an insured loss, it may step into the insured's position and pursue recovery from another party that is said to bear responsibility. The doctrine sounds technical because the word is technical. The logic is simple. The person or institution that paid does not always intend to be the one left carrying the final cost if someone else was legally or contractually at fault. In maritime trade, where owners, charterers, managers, pilots, contractors, terminals, and public actors may all influence the same voyage, this matters enormously. A casualty rarely belongs to one pair of hands.

Subrogation becomes especially important in Arctic and near-Arctic operations because operational control is often distributed in ways that look manageable before a loss and deeply contested after one. A charterer may shape scheduling pressure and route preference while insisting that navigation remained with the owner and master. A technical manager may have supervised maintenance while distance and weather later obscure what that supervision meant in practice. Ice advice may have come from one source, commercial urgency from another, and the final decision to continue from the bridge. Once a claim has been paid, the paying party asks a cold question: who else should now be carrying part of this burden? The answer is rarely obvious.

This is why subrogation is not merely a procedural afterthought to claims handling. It is one of the main ways the market tests its own story about responsibility. If an insurer or club believes that another party's conduct materially contributed to the loss, pursuit is a means of converting that belief into recovery. If recovery appears weak, uncertain, too expensive, or too commercially damaging, the absence of pursuit tells its own story. Post-loss strategy therefore becomes a map of incentives. It shows who looks blameworthy, who looks solvent, who matters too much to alienate, and where the evidence is strong enough to survive scrutiny rather than merely to support grumbling.

A named example illustrates the broader point. After the *Costa Concordia* grounding in January 2012, the public focus naturally settled on immediate responsibility and visible failure. Yet the wider legal and insurance environment around a casualty of that scale inevitably raised the further question of what claims could or should be pushed onwards once initial liabilities had been met. The relevance here is not to compress every party into one simple chain of blame. It is to show how major maritime losses force the institutions paying first to think hard about who else in the surrounding web of control, service, advice, or management can realistically be pursued. The first payment is often only the beginning of allocation.

The complexity of that allocation grows in Arctic cases because evidence degrades faster and control fragments more easily. A routeing decision that looks central afterwards may have been shaped by incomplete ice information, uncertain communications, commercial pressure, delayed support assumptions, and the physical difficulty of obtaining a clearer picture in real time. The shipowner, insurer, or club considering pursuit must therefore ask not only whether another party arguably contributed, but whether the evidence can carry that argument far enough to justify the cost and risk of subrogation. A plausible grievance is not the same thing as a recoverable case. In remote waters, that distinction can be decisive.

This is where legal prospects and commercial relationships begin to pull against each other. In theory, subrogation follows liability. In practice, it also follows value, leverage, and future business. A club or insurer may have a colourable claim against a charterer, contractor, tug provider, adviser, or technical service company and still hesitate if the recovery path is weak, the evidentiary record thin, the likely defendant poorly capitalised, or the commercial relationship strategically important. Conversely, a pursuit that looks modest in legal principle may become attractive if the target is clearly responsible, well insured, and central enough that allowing the loss to remain unrecovered would signal institutional softness. Subrogation is law under commercial pressure.

This is why the doctrine matters so much when multiple parties share operational control. Maritime casualties often invite the comforting illusion that one decisive act caused everything. Subrogation tends to destroy that illusion. It forces the paying party to examine the chain more closely. Who selected the service profile? Who controlled the maintenance regime? Who gave or failed to give route advice? Who was obliged to disclose conditions or limitations? Who benefited commercially from pressing on? Who had authority to stop? Who had the documents? Once those questions are asked seriously, a casualty begins to look less like one actor's misfortune and more like a contested field of contribution. The claim widens.

A brief example makes this clearer. Imagine a vessel taking a northern route under commercial pressure to meet a seasonal window. The charterer encouraged schedule discipline. The operator relied on external ice information that later proved incomplete. The vessel suffered damage, and the insurer or club responded to immediate liabilities. Subrogation then forces a different inquiry. Was the charterer's pressure merely part of ordinary commercial life, or did it materially narrow safe options? Was the information provider contractually responsible for the quality of route advice? Did the owner fail to preserve a genuinely independent navigational margin? Each possible path of recovery depends on evidence, contract language, and the paying institution's appetite for a second fight. The post-loss strategy becomes a continuation of the original governance struggle.

Arctic remoteness complicates that struggle at every stage. Physical evidence may be harder to preserve. Witnesses may be dispersed by the time detailed interviews occur. Logs and digital records may be incomplete or ambiguous because communications were poor and attention was absorbed by immediate survival or response. External experts may reach the vessel late, by which time ice conditions or damage patterns have already changed. Local authorities may have intervened in ways that disrupted clean evidence collection. Even where the paying party strongly suspects another actor's share of responsibility, the practical foundation for recovery may be thin. Remoteness does not simply enlarge the original loss. It narrows the clarity available afterwards.

That narrowing has financial consequences because subrogation is itself an investment decision. Clubs and insurers do not pursue simply because blame is imaginable. They pursue where the likely recovery justifies the time, expert cost, legal spend, documentary burden, and relationship risk involved. In Arctic matters, this calculation can become particularly severe. A case may be morally satisfying and strategically foolish. Another may be legally uncertain but worth pressing because the amount at stake is large and the target significant. A third may be quietly abandoned because the evidence has been weakened by the very remoteness that enlarged the original claim. The doctrine remains the same. The economics change.

A second named example helps bring out the larger institutional lesson. After the *Exxon Valdez* disaster in March 1989, the world learned to think of northern maritime losses as events with unusually long legal afterlives. The direct relevance to subrogation lies in that duration. Large, environmentally sensitive, politically visible losses encourage wider scrutiny of who should bear final responsibility, yet they also produce such complex layers of causation and response that recovery actions may become more difficult rather than easier to prosecute cleanly. A major casualty does not guarantee clean opportunities for pursuit. It often guarantees the opposite: more parties, more evidence, more pressure, and more reasons for legal and commercial strategies to diverge.

This is one reason subrogation reveals the real structure of incentives better than public rhetoric often does. Before a loss, all parties may speak the language of shared safety, cooperation, and prudent operation. After a loss, pursuit decisions expose who trusts whom, whose records are strong, which contracts actually allocated responsibility meaningfully, and how much appetite exists for turning a commercial partner into an adversary. A party that loudly insists it did nothing wrong but settles quietly under recovery pressure has revealed something. A paying institution that complains about another actor's role yet declines pursuit has also revealed something. Incentives leave fingerprints.

A limitation should be acknowledged plainly. Not every failure to pursue reflects weakness, compromise, or hidden doubt. Sometimes the best commercial and legal decision is genuinely to stop. The evidence may be too thin, the costs too high, the target too marginal, or the causal chain too uncertain to justify a second dispute. Subrogation is not a moral duty to punish every contributor. It is a practical tool for rational recovery. Treating every non-pursuit as capitulation would be simplistic.

And yet this limitation only sharpens the core argument. Because pursuit decisions are selective, they are also informative. They show which losses markets think are legally clean enough to chase, which relationships are too important to rupture, which kinds of evidence survive Arctic conditions well enough to support recovery, and where contracts did or did not map responsibility effectively. Over time these patterns shape behaviour. Operators draft more carefully. Clubs ask harder questions. Insurers demand better records. Charterers resist or refine allocation language. The possibility of later pursuit disciplines the structure of the voyage long before a casualty makes it relevant.

This is why subrogation belongs inside a chapter about claims, disputes, and precedent effects rather than inside a technical appendix on recovery rights. It is part of how losses are turned into lessons. A failed pursuit can teach markets that evidence in remote Arctic events will often be too weak unless records improve. A successful one can make charterers, service providers, or technical managers much more careful about how their responsibilities are documented and performed. Recommendations turn into clauses. Clauses turn into scrutiny. Recovery strategy becomes part of policy formation by experience rather than decree.

The quiet motif returns because the bill keeps moving. It begins with the casualty, then passes to the insurer or club, then seeks another set of hands to hold it. Sometimes it stops quickly. Sometimes it travels for years through correspondence, experts, contracts, and negotiations. In Arctic trade, its path is shaped as much by evidence and relationships as by abstract legal entitlement. The party that pays first is not always the party that pays last, but neither is the eventual resting place determined by doctrine alone. It is determined by what can be proved, what is worth proving, and what the market decides it can afford to contest.

The harder question, then, is not whether subrogation exists to shift losses towards the responsible party. It plainly does. The harder question is who, in a fragmented Arctic operation, can still be shown to be meaningfully responsible once distance has thinned the evidence, contracts have blurred control, and the commercial value of preserving certain relationships begins to compete with the legal logic of pursuit.

Learning loops: how claims change future terms

In March 1989, after the *Exxon Valdez* grounded in Alaska, the immediate legal and environmental consequences were obvious enough. Less obvious, but ultimately just as important, was the institutional afterlife of the loss. The casualty did not end when claims began to be paid. It entered underwriting files, club discussions, technical reviews, survey priorities, and the long internal memory of markets that rarely forget an expensive lesson. A spill became a rule before anyone called it one.

That is how learning loops work in marine insurance and liability practice, and the Arctic sharpens them. Claims are not merely events to be adjusted and closed. They are raw material for future caution. When insurers, clubs, reinsurers, surveyors, and charterers see similar losses recur across voyages, vessel types, routes, or operating patterns, they do not treat those losses as isolated bad luck for very long. They begin to ask whether the market has been tolerating a weakness that should now be priced harder, controlled more explicitly, or removed from the category of acceptable discretion altogether. The file starts teaching.

This matters because insurance is often described as though it were reactive: a mechanism that absorbs loss after the fact and only then retreats into accounting. In reality, serious claims generate institutional memory that quickly becomes operational pressure. A cluster of machinery failures in cold conditions may lead to more intrusive survey questions, stronger maintenance expectations, narrower cover, or equipment-related requirements that would once have been left to owner judgment. A sequence of routeing disputes may harden into stricter warranties or reporting duties. A pattern of pollution-response weakness may produce higher deductibles, tighter conditions, or demands for more credible contingency planning. The claim does not simply end with settlement. It changes what must be true next time.

This is why claims history often functions as a form of policy-making. No legislature needs to meet. No public regulation need be promulgated. Markets can still change the effective rules of access by adjusting the terms on which cover will be offered. If repeated losses suggest that a certain practice, omission, or design feature is too dangerous to leave within the wide field of operator choice, insurers respond in the language they control: exclusions, deductibles, recommendations, survey expectations, equipment conditions, navigation limits, and the quiet but powerful shift from optional prudence to expected prudence. Policy emerges from recurrence.

A named example makes this logic plain. After the *Exxon Valdez* casualty, marine liability and pollution markets did not merely absorb one spectacular northern loss and continue as before. The broader institutional effect was to alter how sensitive-water exposure, response readiness, and the severity of northern pollution claims were imagined. Even where no single new universal rule immediately settled every question, the market's internal threshold for acceptable uncertainty changed. Operators proposing similar exposure later faced a harder climate of inquiry. What had once looked arguable now looked under-controlled. That is how a claim becomes a policy signal.

The mechanism begins with pattern recognition. One claim can alarm. Several similar claims create structure. Underwriters and clubs pay close attention to repetition because repetition suggests that the underlying cause is not random misfortune but a recurring weakness in vessels, documentation, equipment, procedures, or operating culture. The recurrence need not be identical in every detail. It is enough that the family resemblance becomes clear. A valve fails in cold conditions on one vessel, heating systems underperform on another, sensors behave erratically on a third, and response logs show the same delay in recognising what the technical symptoms meant. Soon the market is no longer looking at three separate claims. It is looking at a category.

Once a category forms, financial terms begin to shift. Higher deductibles are among the simplest tools because they force the insured to carry more of the immediate cost, thereby reducing small-claim frequency and making the operator internalise more of the risk the market now distrusts. New warranties go further by converting what had been a desirable practice into a continuing contractual condition. If a certain class of routeing, reporting, equipment maintenance, or technical readiness is now seen as essential, the market can say so in the policy. The owner is no longer merely encouraged to behave prudently. The owner is required to.

Mandatory equipment upgrades emerge through the same logic, though often more slowly and with more institutional diplomacy. A market rarely begins with absolute compulsion unless the losses are glaring, politically charged, or clearly connected to one remediable deficiency. More commonly, the new expectation appears first as a recommendation, guidance note, survey observation, club circular, or underwriting preference. The language is soft. The memory behind it is not. If claims continue, or if the initial recommendation proves widely ignored, the same measure returns with sharper consequences. What was once "recommended" becomes "expected". What was once "expected" becomes a condition of cover, a survey prerequisite, or the sort of omission that produces higher terms so punitive that the requirement has effectively become mandatory.

A brief example shows how this hardening works. Imagine a series of Arctic and sub-Arctic machinery casualties in which emergency heating arrangements do not fail completely, but perform weakly enough under prolonged cold stress to worsen otherwise manageable incidents. The first market reaction may be modest: underwriters ask more questions, clubs circulate a cautionary note, surveyors begin paying closer attention, and operators with stronger arrangements find the renewal conversation easier. After several more losses, the same issue may appear in policy discussions as a recommended upgrade or as something owners are told prudent practice should now include. If the pattern persists, insurers stop speaking in the language of prudent preference and start using the language of terms. The equipment has not changed its physical nature. Its institutional status has.

This gradual hardening is especially important in Arctic operations because the environment magnifies the cost of being wrong about whether a precaution is truly optional. A tolerable technical compromise in temperate service may become an expensive lesson in northern waters where response is slower, conditions harsher, and the room for improvisation much thinner. Markets understand this. They therefore respond to clustered northern losses more quickly and sometimes more sternly than they might in easier trades. The logic is not melodrama. It is severity management. If a weakness repeatedly proves more consequential in remote cold regions, the market becomes less willing to leave it to operator taste.

A second named example from outside the polar sphere helps illuminate the wider mechanism. After the *Costa Concordia* casualty in January 2012, insurers, clubs, operators, and technical reviewers across passenger and other shipping sectors did not treat the event solely as a one-off command disaster. They read it for systems lessons: emergency preparedness, documentation, bridge resource management, evacuation logic, and the degree to which formal procedures matched live practice. The Arctic relevance lies not in copying the facts of a cruise casualty onto northern cargo or support operations. It lies in seeing how claims teach later markets to distrust broad assurances and to demand more concrete controls. A large loss alters the vocabulary of reasonableness.

This is also why learning loops often produce changes before public law does, or in places where public law remains comparatively silent. Insurers and clubs do not need to wait for legislatures, conventions, or regulators if the claims experience already tells them that a weakness is too expensive to leave untreated. They can change cover language at renewal. They can insist on surveys. They can ask for equipment upgrades, stronger documentation, narrower route limits, and more explicit reporting duties. The speed of this private response is one reason markets exercise such quiet regulatory force. They are not merely pricing what happened. They are trying to stop it from happening again at mutual or reinsured expense.

Claims history also changes survey focus in practical ways. Surveyors rarely arrive after a cluster of losses with a blank mind. They know what the market has recently been taught to fear. They look harder at the component, process, or omission that has featured in recent files. They ask sharper questions. They are less easily reassured by generic answers. The vessel owner may experience this as increased fussiness or moving goalposts. More often it is the visible sign that claims have shifted the centre of technical suspicion. The survey is where market memory walks aboard.

A limitation should be acknowledged plainly. Learning loops can overcorrect. A few vivid cases may harden into market-wide caution even where the real problem was narrower than later terms imply. Underwriters and clubs can mistake clustered visibility for universal relevance. Operators with strong systems may end up paying for the failures of weaker peers. Requirements born from genuine claims experience can become clumsy if they are applied too broadly or without sufficient attention to distinctions between vessel types, seasons, routes, and operating models. Private policy-making is often nimble. It is not always subtle.

And yet this limitation does not diminish the central point. It clarifies why claims history matters so much. Because markets respond through pattern, not through moral contemplation, even imperfect pattern recognition can change the cost and structure of Arctic access. Owners and charterers who treat claims as closed files misunderstand the process. Each claim remains alive as a precedent in the informal sense, shaping what later submissions must prove, what later surveys must show, and what later policies will quietly assume about acceptable conduct. The insurer's question at renewal is often the afterlife of someone else's casualty.

This is why claims loops reward organisations that learn early rather than late. A company that sees a recommendation hardening through the market and acts before it becomes compulsory may preserve better terms and stronger credibility. Another may wait until the same point appears as a warranty, a deductible increase, or a survey condition that is harder to negotiate around. Markets rarely say, in dramatic language, "this is now the rule because too many claims taught us to fear the alternative". They seldom need to. The pricing says it. The wording says it. The survey says it. That is enough.

The quiet motif returns because the file keeps teaching long after the cheque is paid. One casualty becomes a recommendation. Repetition turns recommendation into expectation. Persistence turns expectation into obligation. Somewhere along that sequence, a company realises that what used to feel like discretionary operating judgement has been recast by the market as a condition of trust. The Arctic sharpens this progression because losses there so often teach harsh lessons about delay, remoteness, and the cost of underpreparedness. Claims history becomes a form of governance without ceremony.

The harder question, then, is not whether claims change future terms. They plainly do. The harder question is how soon an operator can recognise that a suggestion in today's renewal meeting may be the first quiet form of tomorrow's mandatory requirement - and whether the real dividing line in Arctic commerce lies between those who treat claims history as someone else's bad luck and those who understand it as the earliest draft of the next rule they will be required to live under.

Reputation, disclosure, and market memory

In March 1989, after the *Exxon Valdez* grounded in Alaska, the legal and environmental consequences were severe enough to command public attention for years. Yet one of the most durable effects took shape in quieter rooms: renewal meetings, underwriting reviews, club discussions, broker conversations, and the long private memory of a market deciding what the casualty had revealed about trust. The oil did not need to remain visible for the operator's reputation to remain altered. The file stayed open.

That is the deeper meaning of disclosure in specialised maritime insurance and liability markets. Disclosure is not merely the formal act of answering questions honestly when cover is sought or renewed. It is the practice through which an operator tells the market what kind of risk-bearing partner it intends to be. In Arctic and near-Arctic trades, where the sample of comparable voyages is thinner and the consequences of error can be broader, this practice takes on unusual importance. The market is often deciding not only whether the ship is acceptable, but whether the operator's account of itself deserves belief. Trust leaves a paper trail.

This is why incomplete disclosure can be punished so sharply. The problem is not limited to the hidden fact itself, though that may matter greatly. The larger problem is that incomplete disclosure poisons the market's confidence in everything else surrounding it. If an operator omitted a prior technical difficulty, softened the seriousness of a routeing problem, delayed notification of a material incident, or failed to present a meaningful change in trading pattern, underwriters and clubs do not simply adjust one part of the file. They begin to ask what other parts were described with similar optimism. A missing page can stain the whole folder.

That reaction is especially severe in Arctic contexts because the market already works under thinner information and a harsher severity horizon. In a dense conventional trade, a vessel or operator may be buffered by broader data, more frequent comparators, and a larger stock of known experience. In a specialised Arctic operation, each disclosed or undisclosed fact carries more weight because there are fewer comfortable generalisations available to soften it. A prior machinery scare in cold conditions, an awkward port-state interaction, a disputed survey recommendation, or a route deviation that once seemed minor may become highly material once the market realises that the operator withheld or minimised it. Thin information makes omission feel larger.

This is how reputational signals acquire financial force. Reputation in maritime insurance is not a vague aura attached to a company name. It is built from visible behaviour: how the operator reports bad news, how early it discloses emerging concerns, whether it distinguishes clearly between resolved issues and continuing vulnerabilities, how candidly it handles awkward claims history, and whether its documents become more informative under pressure or more evasive. Underwriters and clubs watch these behaviours closely because they know that the worst casualties are often preceded by smaller moments in which the truth was softened, delayed, or framed too hopefully. Reputation is therefore not separate from disclosure. It is disclosure remembered over time.

A named example makes the mechanism easier to see. After the *Exxon Valdez* casualty, the market did not merely price pollution exposure more harshly. It learned to watch operators' candour about northern risk, preparedness, and control more closely. The significance of the event lay not only in the loss itself, but in the way it sharpened institutional suspicion around what operators claimed to know, what they failed to anticipate, and how honestly they later represented the chain of events. In that sense, one casualty altered not just liability expectations but the market's appetite for optimistic storytelling. The lesson was reputational before it was actuarial.

Renewal negotiations are where these lessons become most concrete. By the time a vessel or operator returns to the market for continued cover, the underwriter is not meeting a blank risk. It is meeting a remembered one. Previous claims, survey issues, reporting style, document quality, and even the tone of earlier exchanges all shape the atmosphere of the renewal. A company with strong technical records but a habit of late or partial disclosure may find that markets focus less on its machinery than on its candour. Another with an awkward claims history but a reputation for brutal honesty and orderly documentation may secure a more patient hearing. What is being priced is not only the hazard of the voyage. It is the credibility of the narrator.

This is why incomplete disclosure can draw such disproportionate consequences. The market often reacts more severely to concealment or serious omission than to the underlying operational weakness that should have been disclosed. A known problem can be debated, surveyed, priced, limited, or excluded. An unknown problem that should have been known to the market generates a different kind of alarm. It suggests that the operator may treat the duty of fair presentation as negotiable, and once that suspicion takes hold, later reassurance becomes much harder to sell.

The issue is no longer simply whether the ship is risky. It is whether the operator is governable.

A brief example makes the point. Imagine an operator seeking renewal after a season of otherwise successful northern trading. The file looks broadly sound. Then it emerges that an earlier machinery anomaly in cold conditions, though apparently resolved, had not been fully disclosed when renewal materials were first submitted. The underwriter's response is unlikely to focus only on whether the anomaly itself would have changed the original terms. The deeper question becomes why the operator chose not to raise it clearly and early. Premium may rise. Terms may narrow. Survey demands may harden. The market is disciplining not only the incident, but the withholding of it.

Market memory is what gives this discipline its longevity. Formal investigations may close. Public attention may move on. Claims may settle, sometimes confidentially. Yet the market remembers through renewal files, broker notes, internal commentary, club experience, and the simple persistence of professional conversation in a specialised field where the same names recur. Memory does not need to be perfectly documented to be effective. It can survive in tone, in the next round of questions, in the hesitation before a quotation is offered, in the insistence on an additional survey, or in the quiet instruction that a certain operator's submissions should be read with more care than before. The stapled corner remains.

A second named example shows how this memory can outlast formal process. After the *Costa Concordia* grounding in January 2012, public inquiries and legal proceedings occupied much of the visible aftermath. But inside the insurance and maritime liability world, memory outlived the formal stages. Operators, clubs, brokers, surveyors, and underwriters did not simply wait for final public closure before adjusting their judgement. They absorbed what the event suggested about command culture, emergency credibility, documentary integrity, and institutional trust. Arctic markets behave the same way, often more intensely, because their worlds are smaller and the consequences of misplaced confidence can be more severe.

Still, a limitation must be admitted. Market memory is not perfectly fair. It can overstate the importance of one ugly event, understate quiet improvement, or preserve suspicion longer than the evidence strictly justifies. A company may reform materially while still paying for an earlier reputation. Another may benefit from the market's fading attention longer than it deserves. Memory is efficient, but not always balanced. In specialised Arctic trades, where stories travel quickly, and data remains comparatively sparse, this imbalance can become particularly stark.

And yet that limitation only reinforces the practical reality. Because reputation is partly social and partly documentary, operators cannot rely on formal closure alone to restore trust. A settled claim, a completed investigation, or a technically resolved deficiency does not by itself erase market unease. Trust returns only if later disclosure is fuller, documentation cleaner, and communication steadier than before. The market wants evidence that the operator has learned to tell the truth in a way that allows others to price it. Silence, vagueness, or defensive disclosure after a reputational bruise merely confirms the bruise.

This is why trust is priced with such realism in Arctic contexts. The environment already presents uncertainty around routeing, weather, ice, response, causation, and legal aftermath. Markets do not want to add uncertainty about the operator's candour to that list. If they must, they charge for it. They charge through harder renewals, tighter warranties, broader reporting obligations, narrower cover, more intrusive surveys, and a generally lower tolerance for arguments that facts were immaterial or misunderstood. Reputation here is not an abstract moral category. It is a cost input.

One can see the whole mechanism as a loop. Disclosure shapes reputation. Reputation shapes the reading of later disclosure. Claims and incidents feed market memory. Market memory alters the next renewal conversation. That altered conversation changes the terms on which the next voyage is possible. A company with disciplined disclosure habits can therefore turn trust into an operational asset. A company with weak or selective disclosure habits turns trust into a recurring tax. The difference becomes visible not in slogans about transparency, but in the policy wording and the price.

The quiet motif returns because the stapled corner still catches the eye. Somewhere in the file lies the earlier omission, the awkward survey issue, the delayed notice, the claim that settled without full public explanation, the broker's careful note that the operator was less than forthcoming at first. It may no longer dominate the conversation, but it shapes its temperature. Arctic insurance markets, being small, technical, and severity-conscious, do not require a dramatic blacklist to make this work. They need only memory.

The harder question, then, is not whether disclosure matters. It plainly does. The harder question is how much trust an operator can lose through one serious omission in a specialised Arctic context - and whether the real price of incomplete disclosure is ever confined to the fact withheld, or whether it is more accurately measured by the years of cautious reading that follow every time the market opens the file again.

Chapter 11

Premium Shocks and Market Withdrawal

What changes faster in an Arctic venture: the ice, or the price of believing the ice can be managed? The question sounds rhetorical until a voyage that looked commercially disciplined one quarter begins to look marginal the next, not because the ship has aged overnight or the route has moved on the chart, but because the market's willingness to carry the risk has shifted. A project can remain technically possible and still become financially implausible with startling speed. The quote moves first.

That speed is one of the defining facts of northern insurance markets. In dense, familiar trades, repricing can still be severe, but it often arrives through deeper pools of capacity, longer institutional memory, and broader habits of comparison. Arctic exposure sits on thinner foundations. Capacity is narrower. Correlated loss fears are stronger. A public incident travels quickly through a relatively small circle of underwriters, brokers, clubs, surveyors, and charterers. The result is a market that can harden with unnerving abruptness. What looked like a manageable premium yesterday can become a warning signal today and a practical barrier tomorrow.

The deeper issue is that premium shocks are rarely about premium alone. They are arguments about meaning. Has the underlying risk truly changed, or has the market's interpretation of that risk changed faster than the operational reality on the water? A casualty, a reinsurance shift, a new exclusion, a cluster of near-similar losses, or a fresh concern about correlated exposure can all produce repricing. Some of these changes reflect harder facts. Others reflect a hardening of sentiment under conditions where sentiment itself has financial force. In Arctic trades, the distinction matters because operators often misread a change in mood as a change in physics, or the reverse. The invoice can lie about its cause.

That is the chapter's central tension. Insurance markets present themselves as measuring devices, yet they are also social systems of memory, fear, comparison, and institutional self-protection. They price losses, but they also price uncertainty about losses, uncertainty about responses, and uncertainty about what other capital providers are about to do. When that layered uncertainty gathers around Arctic activity, the market may not withdraw in one dramatic act. It may instead narrow cover, enlarge deductibles, harden exclusions, or make delay and disruption so expensive that a formally insurable venture no longer works as a business. Retreat often arrives disguised as conditional acceptance.

This matters because Arctic expansion rarely fails at the point of pure feasibility. Steel can be strong enough. Crew can be competent enough. Routes can be seasonally open enough. The real failure often occurs where insurability, schedule reliability, and contractual tolerance stop overlapping. If delay becomes too expensive, if exclusions shift too much operational cost back onto owners or charterers, if narrow cover leaves too many losses sitting naked on the balance sheet, the venture stalls without any public prohibition. Market withdrawal can therefore be partial, quiet, and devastatingly effective. Access closes softly.

It also matters because the responses to repricing are never merely tactical. Operators do not answer hardened markets with courage alone. They answer with paperwork, route discipline, redundancy, partnerships, slower promises, and institutional redesign. Those responses may begin as coping strategies, but under pressure they become the next layer of governance. What starts as one company's attempt to remain insurable can become a wider market expectation about what a serious Arctic operator now looks like. A hedge becomes the norm. A norm becomes a requirement. Pressure writes rules.

The movement ahead follows that pressure from cause to consequence. It begins with the forces that make premiums jump so abruptly in thin, reputation-sensitive markets, then turns to the quieter tools by which insurers restrict access without abandoning it outright. From there, the focus tightens around time itself, where delay, inspection friction, and limited repair options become priced hazards rather than operational irritants, before widening again to the institutional adaptations through which operators try to remain viable and, in doing so, help create the next generation of market discipline.

The stake is not simply whether Arctic insurance is expensive. Everyone in this field already assumes difficulty carries a price. The harder issue is how to read the moment when a market is signalling more than the cost. A sharp repricing may mean the risk has worsened, that memory has hardened, that reinsurance capital has thinned, that correlated exposure suddenly looks uglier, or that the market has lost patience with operators who still talk about possibility when the underwriter is thinking about accumulation and exit. Misreading that signal can produce the classic pattern of stop-start northern expansion: bursts of confidence followed by years of caution that participants later describe as surprising only because they ignored the warning already embedded in the terms.

So the real question is not whether Arctic ventures can survive one more premium increase. It is whether the people behind them can recognise when the market is no longer merely charging more for the same proposition, but quietly redefining what kind of proposition it is prepared to recognise as governable at all.

What causes sudden repricing

In March 1989, when the *Exxon Valdez* grounded in Alaska, the immediate damage was visible enough. Less visible, but no less important, was the speed with which the loss altered the market's imagination of northern liability. One casualty did not simply produce one bill. It changed how underwriters, clubs, reinsurers, and charterers thought about pollution severity, response difficulty, legal sprawl, and the true cost of being wrong in cold remote waters. The water moved. So did the premium.

That movement matters because premium shocks in Arctic trades rarely arrive as tidy mathematical adjustments to a stable reality. They arrive as judgments under pressure. A market that tolerated one set of assumptions last season may abruptly reject them after a loss, a near miss, a new exclusion, a harder reinsurance stance, or a widening fear that several risks once treated as separate are in fact linked. The operator sees a sharper price or narrower terms. The deeper question is why the market's confidence changed so fast. Price is the surface. Appetite is the structure beneath.

The first driver is always loss experience, but loss experience does not act alone. One serious casualty can force a market to reconsider how severe a northern incident truly is once pollution response, wreck obligations, state intervention, delay, and reputational fallout are taken seriously. A series of smaller incidents can do something similar by revealing a pattern the market had preferred to describe as coincidence. The crucial point is that claims do not merely deplete capital. They alter interpretation. When a market learns that a class of Arctic voyages can produce broader or messier liabilities than previously assumed, repricing becomes more than an accounting exercise. It becomes a correction in belief.

That correction is often sharper in Arctic insurance because capacity is thin. Thin capacity does not simply mean fewer willing participants. It means fewer buffers against collective alarm. In deeper markets, one underwriter's retreat may be absorbed by others with different views, broader books, or more tolerance for temporary volatility. In Arctic trades, the circle is smaller and the room for disagreement narrower. If several participants grow uneasy at once, the effect is felt quickly. A hardening that might look gradual elsewhere can feel like a trapdoor here. There are fewer desks to say yes.

Loss events therefore act as catalysts rather than as isolated causes. A pollution casualty in cold waters may trigger concern not only about pollution, but about salvage duration, public authority intervention, documentary adequacy, and the broader competence of operators who once looked merely ambitious. A routeing dispute may begin as a technical matter and end as a wider reappraisal of whether masters, charterers, and advisers are sharing control in ways the market has underpriced. One event teaches several lessons at once. The premium changes because the market has learned to fear more than the original incident seemed to contain.

A second driver lies in exclusions, especially new ones or newly sharpened ones. Markets do not always respond to growing discomfort by openly withdrawing. More often they redraw the perimeter of what they are prepared to carry. An exclusion is not only a legal device. It is a message about what the market now regards as too uncertain, too severe, too correlated, or too politically exposed to remain inside ordinary terms. When exclusions harden after a casualty or cluster of losses, premium may rise even for cover that remains nominally available, because the exclusion has changed the whole balance of what the policy is now worth. The insured item survives. The insurable proposition changes.

This is why operators sometimes misread premium shock. They assume the market has become irrationally nervous when, in fact, the market has also changed the underlying product. A higher premium attached to narrower cover is not simply a more expensive version of the same bargain. It is a different bargain. If the market has stripped out some of the exposures that once made the voyage commercially tolerable, the premium increase may understate the true hardening. Repricing is therefore often structural before it is arithmetic. The language of the terms matters as much as the number in the quotation.

Reinsurance tightening forms a third and often decisive cause. Arctic exposures do not sit quietly at the primary level. They travel upward into broader structures of risk-bearing, where reinsurers ask harsher questions about severity, accumulation, and legal unpredictability. A primary underwriter may like the operator, trust the vessel, and admire the route discipline, yet still harden terms because the capital supporting the book has become more reluctant. This is one of the least visible but most consequential forces in Arctic repricing. The ship meets weather. The premium meets global capital. The two encounters are not equally dramatic, but they are equally real.

A named example helps fix the point. After the *Exxon Valdez* disaster in March 1989, the market did not merely price one notorious tanker loss. It re-evaluated northern pollution exposure more broadly. The incident's significance lay not only in the immediate claims burden, but in the way it altered how insurers and reinsurers imagined the severity of environmentally sensitive cold-water casualties. Later Arctic operations were not charged only for their own qualities. They were charged for what the market had learned, or believed it had learned, from a highly visible prior event. One loss rewrote a category.

A fourth driver is changing perceptions of correlated risk. Correlation is one of those words that can sound abstract until it reaches underwriting. In Arctic trades it means the fear that what appeared to be separate exposures may in fact fail together. Several vessels may depend on the same short seasonal window, the same thin support infrastructure, the same inspection bottlenecks, the same limited repair options, or the same assumptions about ice information and route access. A market that once saw isolated voyages can suddenly start seeing a portfolio problem. When that happens, premium hardening may reflect not the worsening of one ship's individual risk, but a new fear that several losses or disruptions could cluster in one geography or one season.

This matters because correlated risk is often discovered psychologically before it is proved statistically. A high-profile casualty, a series of delays, or a single season of strained support capacity can make underwriters and reinsurers see connections they had previously discounted. Sometimes this is rational learning. Sometimes it is collective overreaction. Often it is both. The distinction between risk change and sentiment change is therefore crucial. Risk change means the underlying conditions have genuinely worsened or been newly understood. Sentiment change means the market's emotional and institutional tolerance has altered faster than the physical operating reality. Premium shocks often contain both elements, but they do not contain them in equal proportions.

Arctic markets are particularly prone to this mixture because reputations travel fast. In specialised trades, information circulates quickly through brokers, clubs, surveyors, claims handlers, and underwriters. A weak file, a messy casualty response, a surprising survey finding, or a contentious renewal does not remain private in any pure sense. Even where details stay confidential, impressions spread. One operator's trouble can make the whole class of voyage look less governable. A market with thin capacity and strong memory does not need perfect information to become more expensive. It needs only enough shared unease to shorten patience. Reputation becomes an accelerant.

A second named example shows how a seemingly modest event can ripple through perception. When the *Venta Maersk* completed its Northern Sea Route transit in 2018, the voyage was widely read as proof of possibility. Possibility, however, cuts two ways. What one season presents as feasible, another may reprice as more tightly bounded once markets ask whether repeatability, support conditions, and correlated exposure have been too lightly assumed. The lesson is not that success triggers panic, but that visibility itself invites recalculation. Every notable Arctic voyage teaches markets something. The premium reflects not only the ice encountered, but the interpretation left behind.

A credible limitation should be admitted. Not every premium shock reflects deep structural change. Markets can overreact. A vivid casualty may harden sentiment beyond what the underlying facts justify. Reinsurers may retreat from a class of exposure for reasons only partly connected to Arctic specifics. An exclusion may be introduced more as a symbolic reassurance to nervous capital than as a precise response to demonstrated loss drivers. It would be wrong to imagine that every repricing is a perfect expression of objective risk. Insurance markets are disciplined institutions, but they are still human institutions.

And yet this limitation only sharpens the practical lesson. Because repricing blends fact and feeling, operators need to read market moves with unusual care. A premium rise after a casualty may reflect newly recognised severity. A sudden hardening after a season of noisy discussion may reflect sentiment outrunning evidence. A narrower line may reflect reinsurance discomfort rather than primary underwriting distrust. A fresh exclusion may signal fear of accumulation more than fear of one vessel's poor conduct. Distinguishing these motives matters because each demands a different response. Some call for technical adaptation. Others call for better evidence, slower ambition, or simply the patience to understand what the market is really punishing.

This is why premium shocks are so central to the stop-start rhythm of Arctic expansion. Ventures do not stall only because ice is thicker, ships weaker, or regulations harsher. They stall because the market that once tolerated a level of uncertainty abruptly decides that the same uncertainty now deserves a much higher price, a smaller line, or a harder boundary around what it will carry. Operators then pull back, redesign, partner, document more heavily, or wait for appetite to return. Expansion resumes later under new terms, until another cluster of events re-teaches the market to fear a different part of the exposure. The cycle is not random. It is memory acting through price.

The quiet motif returns because the quote moves first. Before public commentary catches up, before industry optimism or gloom finds its language, the terms often already reveal the shift. A modest premium increase may hide a deeper reclassification. A severe increase may be less ominous than a subtle narrowing of scope. A refusal may matter less than a grudging yes wrapped in conditions that make the voyage economically frail. The market seldom announces its mood plainly. It writes that mood into price and wording.

The harder question, then, is not whether Arctic premiums can jump suddenly. They plainly can. The harder question is how to tell when the jump reflects a real change in the underlying loss environment and when it reflects a thinner, faster, more reputation-driven market convincing itself that the safest way to handle uncertainty is to make access expensive enough that only the most disciplined operators remain.

Exclusions, sublimits, and narrowing cover

In March 1989, after the *Exxon Valdez* grounded in Alaska, the market did not respond only by asking whether northern pollution risk should cost more. It also began asking a quieter and more decisive question: which parts of that risk should remain inside ordinary cover at all. That distinction matters. A premium increase is visible. A shrinking promise is subtler. A voyage may still be described as insured while the most dangerous edges of its exposure have already been cut away. The policy can say yes while meaning not much.

That is the practical significance of exclusions and sublimits in Arctic insurance. Markets do not always withdraw dramatically from difficult trades. More often they remain present while narrowing what they are willing to bear. An exclusion removes a category of loss or a defined circumstance from the promise of indemnity. A sublimit keeps the category inside the policy but caps the insurer's exposure below the broader limit that might otherwise have applied. Both are techniques of selective retreat. They allow insurers to stay in the room, preserve commercial relationships, and avoid the appearance of exit while materially altering who carries the risk once the voyage begins to go wrong. Cover thins.

This is why operators can be insured and still operationally constrained in ways outsiders rarely see. A vessel may have hull cover, liability support, and all the outward signs of insurability, yet find that the most commercially threatening parts of Arctic exposure now sit partly or wholly back on its own balance sheet. A route may remain open, but only if the owner is willing to absorb more delay cost, more pollution-adjacent expense, more wreck-related uncertainty, or more consequential equipment failure than before. Charterers, financiers, and counterparties often detect this before the public does because they read the terms rather than the headlines. The certificate remains. The freedom contracts.

The logic behind narrowing cover is straightforward. Insurers use exclusions and sublimits when they believe a class of exposure has become too severe, too uncertain, too correlated, or too politically sensitive to bear on broad terms. Arctic trades invite this response because many of their most expensive consequences do not behave like routine marine losses. Pollution response can be slow and public. Wreck removal can become logistically punishing. Delay can spiral into contractual and operational distress. Support infrastructure may be sparse, inspections unpredictable, and evidence harder to preserve. Rather than abandon the trade entirely, insurers often separate the parts they still find tolerable from the parts they would rather push back onto the insured. The structure changes before the voyage does.

This selective retreat is one of the main reasons stop-start Arctic expansion can look so puzzling from the outside. Observers ask why a route or project appears commercially alive one season and strangely fragile the next, even though no new public prohibition has been announced. The answer often sits in the wording. A market may not need to refuse a voyage if it can make key elements of that voyage economically brittle. Narrower pollution cover, a sublimit on some costly consequence of delay or recovery, tighter geographic language, exclusions tied to specified conditions, or a more aggressive treatment of ice-related damage can all leave the operator nominally insured and practically more exposed than the business model assumed. Restriction arrives without declaration.

A named example helps fix the broader point. After the *Exxon Valdez* casualty in March 1989, the market did not merely harden in the abstract around northern environmental exposure. It also learned to distinguish more sharply between the losses it was willing to mutualise or insure in broad form and the losses it wanted more carefully bounded. The enduring lesson was that a severe northern casualty can expand in ways that make standard promises look too generous in hindsight. Once that lesson enters market memory, exclusions and sublimits become attractive because they reduce the chance that one visible event will again teach the same costly truth. The next policy remembers the last spill.

This is where the operational meaning of narrowing cover becomes concrete. Suppose a vessel trades in or near Arctic waters under a policy that still responds to major marine perils in general but now contains an exclusion or a tight sublimit directed at a category of expense associated with remote, difficult incidents. The owner remains insured in the broad sense. Yet the economics of the voyage change immediately. The operator may need to provision more internal contingency funds, renegotiate charter terms, narrow the route, slow the schedule, or insist on support arrangements that were previously optional. The policy has not banned the venture. It has changed what prudence now costs.

A brief example shows how costs shift. Imagine a northern cargo voyage with cover that remains broad for ordinary physical loss but excludes, or sharply limits, a class of consequential expense tied to delay following an ice-related incident or to certain environmental management costs that may arise before a full casualty develops. The owner is still insured for part of the event, but not for the part that may make the voyage commercially unbearable. Those uncovered or partly covered costs do not disappear. They move. They may land on the owner, be pushed contractually towards the charterer, or become the subject of tense renegotiation once everyone realises that the voyage's real vulnerability was sitting outside the policy all along. One sentence in the wording can change the commercial map.

This is why exclusions and sublimits matter so much to chartering structures. Charterers often care less about the poetry of insurance than about who will ultimately absorb disruption, waiting time, rerouting, emergency service expense, cargo deterioration, or the widening circle of costs that can follow a northern incident. When insurers narrow cover, these burdens do not vanish. They are redistributed through charterparties, indemnities, side letters, operational demands, and pricing adjustments. The operator who thought itself adequately insured may discover that counterparties now insist on more conservative routeing, tighter scheduling assumptions, or more protective clauses because the policy has shifted too much uncertainty back into the commercial chain. Insurance wording leaks into freight negotiations.

A second named example illustrates the same institutional logic from another angle. After the *Costa Concordia* grounding in January 2012, maritime markets far beyond passenger shipping were reminded that large, visible claims can change not only premium but the architecture of willingness behind cover. The relevance to Arctic trades is not that cruise casualties and northern cargo or support voyages are identical. It is that a single complex event can teach insurers to stay present while narrowing scope. Markets do not always say, "we are leaving". More often they say, "we are still here, but not for that part". The distinction is commercially enormous.

This is also why the phrase "insured" needs handling with care in severe-environment trades. Insurance is not a binary condition. It is a layered arrangement whose practical value depends on what remains inside it once pressure begins. A broad policy with harsh sublimits can be less useful than a seemingly narrower policy aligned carefully with the operator's real points of vulnerability. An exclusion can matter more than a premium increase if it lands on the very category of loss that most threatens schedule reliability, charter performance, environmental response, or survival of the voyage's economics. Markets know this. Sophisticated operators know it too. The less sophisticated learn it in the claim.

A limitation should be admitted. Exclusions and sublimits are not always hidden acts of bad faith or cynical retreat. They can reflect legitimate attempts to distinguish between exposures a market understands and exposures it cannot responsibly absorb on ordinary terms. In some cases they provide a way for insurance to remain available at all where a full exit might otherwise have occurred. A market that narrows cover may still be offering a better outcome than a market that disappears entirely. That is an important truth, especially in Arctic trades where severity can genuinely exceed comfortable modelling.

And yet this limitation only sharpens the main argument. Because narrowing can be rational and still constraining, operators must read it as governance rather than as mere drafting detail. The insurer is telling them which uncertainties now belong more squarely to the operator, which contingencies require stronger contractual planning, and which parts of the voyage are no longer treated as acceptable within shared risk-bearing arrangements. Exclusions and sublimits therefore do more than limit recovery. They shape behaviour. They encourage conservative routing, heavier documentation, stronger technical preparation, more selective partnerships, and tougher internal discipline precisely because the policy has signalled that the old margin of insured improvisation is gone.

This is one reason access can be restricted without any public announcement. No state needs to close the route. No insurer needs to issue a theatrical market bulletin. No port needs to refuse entry. It is enough that cover remains nominally available while the meaningful burdens of delay, environmental management, remote recovery, or specified casualty consequences shift back onto those planning the voyage. Projects then stall quietly. Charterers hesitate. Financiers ask harder questions. Operators recalculate and postpone. Outsiders see no formal ban and assume the route remains open. Insiders read the wording and know it has narrowed.

The quiet motif returns because the policy can say yes while meaning not much. It can continue to reassure casual readers while warning careful ones that the cost of being wrong has migrated back to the shipowner or the commercial chain around it. This is how insurance markets often govern Arctic expansion most effectively: not by leaving, but by remaining on terms that make only the best prepared, best documented, and most conservatively structured ventures truly viable. Narrowing cover is often more powerful than refusal because it preserves deniability while changing conduct.

The harder question, then, is not whether insurers sometimes stay in the market while shrinking what they will carry. They plainly do. The harder question is how many Arctic ventures that appear insured in formal terms are already being governed by exclusions and sublimits strong enough to decide, long before any casualty occurs, which operators can really afford to proceed and which are only one uncovered cost away from discovering that access had already been quietly withdrawn.

The economics of delay and disruption

In August 2018, when the *Venta Maersk* completed its trial voyage through the Northern Sea Route, public attention gathered around distance, symbolism, and the old question of whether Arctic shipping had at last become commercially normal. But a harder commercial question always sits beneath such moments: not whether a voyage can be completed once, but whether it can be completed on time often enough, and on terms predictable enough, to survive insurance scrutiny, charter commitments, and the ordinary penalties of business life. Feasibility is one thing. Reliability is another.

That distinction is where many Arctic ventures begin to weaken. A ship may be technically capable of a route, suitably classed, competently crewed, and legally permitted to proceed. None of that guarantees that the voyage can absorb delay without becoming financially distorted. Ice conditions shift. Weather closes. Inspections take longer than hoped. Repairs require parts or facilities that are farther away than in conventional trades. Insurance terms may continue to support the venture in broad outline while quietly transferring more delay-related pain back to the operator or the charter chain. In this environment, time stops behaving like a neutral backdrop. It becomes a hazard with a price.

This is the central point. Arctic projects often fail not because the sea proves physically impassable, but because the economics of disruption become too difficult to carry. A delay of modest length in a dense, well-supported trade can remain just that: a commercial nuisance. A similar delay in a northern context may push the vessel into heavier ice, narrower weather windows, tighter seasonal margins, sharper port-state scrutiny, crew fatigue, missed laycans, or expensive waiting for specialist repair or escort support. By the time the delay ends, the original problem may no longer matter most. The cost of lost predictability does.

Insurance terms play a direct role in this transformation because they shape how much of the disruption sits with the market and how much is driven back onto the operator. A policy may still respond to certain classes of physical loss while leaving consequential delay, schedule disruption, or some categories of associated expense either only partly covered or not covered at all. The owner remains insured in a formal sense, yet the voyage becomes commercially brittle because the temporal consequences of difficulty are not shared as broadly as the operator assumed. This is why discussions of Arctic insurability that focus only on casualty response often miss the more decisive point. The venture may survive the incident and fail on the timetable.

A named example helps show why this matters commercially rather than symbolically. The *Venta Maersk* voyage in August 2018 was widely read as evidence that Arctic routeing could have a place in global trade. But the real institutional question such a voyage raises is not whether one passage is possible under managed conditions. It is whether delay can be made tolerable often enough that insurers, charterers, and cargo interests continue to treat the route as dependable rather than merely dramatic. A successful passage proves capability. It does not, by itself, prove schedule discipline under the full range of conditions that matter to contracts and cover. One voyage may arrive. A trade needs regularity.

This is why schedule reliability sits so close to insurance economics. Charterparties, financing assumptions, cargo commitments, and operational planning all depend on some tolerable expectation of timing. Where that expectation weakens, the voyage accumulates financial stress in several directions at once. Charterers may press harder for protective clauses. Off-hire risk becomes more salient. Cargo deterioration or missed onward commitments may move from abstract concern to likely cost. Owners may need to hold larger operational cushions or accept narrower trading windows. Underwriters, observing the same vulnerability, may ask whether the risk of prolonged disruption has been underpriced even where pure casualty risk appears manageable. Time begins to look like exposure rather than inconvenience.

The connection between delay and cover is therefore much tighter than many operators like to admit. An underwriter pricing a northern venture is not only asking whether the ship may be damaged. It is asking what follows if the voyage is slowed, held, inspected, diverted, or pushed into waiting for assistance or repair under conditions where alternatives are sparse. If the policy structure does not spread enough of that burden, or if the burden is structurally difficult to quantify, the market often responds by narrowing terms, hardening deductibles, or asking for stronger operational margins. It is trying to price time lost under circumstances where time itself can trigger a much wider circle of cost.

Inspection regimes amplify this problem in ways that are often underappreciated. A strict but stable inspection environment can be burdensome without necessarily being fatal to commercial planning. Operators can build in margin, prepare documents more rigorously, and treat the expected delay as part of the voyage design. But Arctic and sub-Arctic operations may also encounter inspection cultures whose timing, intensity, or practical effect interacts badly with seasonal pressure and route fragility. A vessel delayed for what looks, on paper, like an ordinary official reason may find that the delay pushes it into materially different ice conditions, a missed support slot, or a narrower repair window. The inspection does not merely cost hours. It rearranges the risk field.

This is one reason seemingly minor deficiencies matter so much in northern trades. In a forgiving commercial environment, a documentation issue or modest technical observation may be irritating but containable. In Arctic contexts, the same matter can trigger delay at exactly the wrong moment, forcing new route choices or exposing the vessel to conditions that were not contemplated when the voyage began. Insurers and charterers know this. They read inspection risk not just as a compliance question but as a possible accelerator of disruption. A ship that attracts scrutiny is not only more likely to be delayed. It is more likely to have that delay converted into broader operational cost by the environment surrounding it.

Limited repair options magnify the same logic. In conventional trades, a mechanical irregularity that cannot be resolved at once may still be manageable because alternative ports, specialist technicians, spare parts, and repair yards exist within a relatively dense network. In northern operations, the same defect may require a diversion of much greater commercial significance. The cost does not lie only in the repair invoice. It lies in extra steaming, lost position, rescheduled cargo operations, altered seasonal timing, charterparty strain, crewing consequences, and the possibility that a manageable technical matter now becomes the event that destroys the voyage's economic rationale. Distance lengthens the bill.

A brief example illustrates how quickly this can happen. Imagine a vessel on a carefully timed northern service suffers a machinery issue that does not disable the ship but requires attention beyond what onboard resources can prudently provide. The insurer may still respond to the direct technical element under agreed terms. Yet if the nearest suitable repair option lies far outside the intended corridor, the resulting delay may produce off-hire, cargo complications, missed windows, or secondary operational penalties for which the cover is partial, contested, or absent. The ship is not lost. The venture may be. A modest technical event becomes a commercial turning point because time, not steel, carries the greater severity.

This is why Arctic operators who succeed tend to treat redundancy and margin not as heroic virtues but as institutional necessities. Additional documentation, stronger maintenance discipline, conservative routeing, partnerships for support, spare-parts planning, and tighter thresholds for aborting or waiting are all responses to the market's understanding that delay is not neutral. They are attempts to reduce the chance that a single interruption cascades into a wider claims and contractual problem. Where they become common enough, they cease to look optional. Markets begin to treat them as baseline signs of seriousness. Coping becomes governance.

A second named example from outside the Arctic proper makes the broader lesson clearer. After the *Costa Concordia* grounding in January 2012, one of the most visible features of the aftermath was how a casualty's cost expanded through time as much as through physical damage. Salvage, disruption, legal process, reputational harm, and prolonged uncertainty all enlarged the event beyond its initiating moment. The relevance to northern trade is not the similarity of casualty type. It is the reminder that maritime losses often become expensive through duration and sequence, not simply through impact. The Arctic turns that reminder into an operating principle.

A limitation should be admitted. Not every delay destroys a voyage, and not every northern trade is equally vulnerable to schedule disturbance. Some operations are built with enough margin, technical support, and contractual flexibility that they can absorb interruption better than outsiders assume. It would be melodramatic to suggest that Arctic commerce lives one late inspection or one awkward repair away from collapse in every case. Serious operators can and do manage disruption with discipline.

And yet this limitation sharpens the main argument rather than weakening it. Because some operators cope well and others do not, markets look closely at whether the venture has been structured to survive time loss rather than merely to survive contact with ice. Underwriters ask how delays are likely to propagate through contracts and logistics. Charterers ask whether schedule promises are backed by enough margin to remain credible once inspection, weather, repair, and route variation begin to interact. The issue is not whether delay can happen. It is whether the operator has designed the trade so that delay does not instantly become a claim on everyone else's patience and capital.

This is why predictability sits at the core of Arctic economics. A route may be physically feasible and still commercially inferior if too many of its profits depend on everything happening on time. Insurance terms expose that dependency because they force the operator to confront which parts of delay are shared, which are excluded, and which will return through charterparty consequences or internal balance-sheet stress. The voyage is not judged only on whether it can be completed. It is judged on whether it can be completed within a range of temporal uncertainty that the surrounding institutions still recognise as tolerable.

The quiet motif returns because time has become a priced hazard. It appears in premiums, deductibles, sublimits, off-hire risk, harder charter language, survey expectations, route conservatism, and the subtle market preference for operators who seem able to absorb interruption without making it everyone else's emergency. The shipowner who sees only weather or only technical capability misses the more comprehensive truth. The real vulnerability may lie in the interaction between one lost day and all the costs that gather behind it.

The harder question, then, is not whether Arctic voyages can be made to work when conditions cooperate. They often can. The harder question is whether they have been built to survive the more ordinary and more decisive reality that in northern trade the voyage seldom fails because the ship cannot move at all; it fails because too many people priced it as though time would remain cheap once the first delay began to spread.

Coping strategies that reshape governance

In August 2018, when the *Venta Maersk* completed its trial passage through the Northern Sea Route, the most interesting question was never simply whether one container vessel could make one northern voyage. The harder question was what kind of institutional scaffolding had to sit behind that voyage before markets, counterparties, and regulators would treat it as more than a stunt. The ship moved through ice, but it also moved through underwriting scrutiny, technical review, route discipline, and a thick web of expectations about what a credible operator now had to show. The checklist grows.

That growth matters because Arctic coping strategies are often misunderstood as feats of nerve or engineering daring. In practice, they are usually less romantic and more revealing. Operators respond to market hardening not by becoming heroes, but by becoming administrators of uncertainty. They document more, route more conservatively, build partnerships, invest in redundancy, and slow down the claims they make about what their vessels can do. These responses do not merely help them survive a difficult insurance cycle. They gradually redefine what the market comes to regard as ordinary prudence. Adaptation becomes governance.

This is the central point. Under pressure, coping strategies do not remain private workarounds for long. They acquire institutional significance because insurers, clubs, reinsurers, charterers, surveyors, and port authorities begin to treat them as evidence of seriousness. An operator that once documented a route in unusually careful detail to reassure a nervous underwriter may discover, a few renewals later, that this level of detail is now treated as the expected baseline. A company that invested in redundancy to preserve commercial freedom may find that markets have quietly recast redundancy as a sign of basic competence. What begins as adaptation ends as norm. The market learns from survival.

Enhanced documentation is the clearest example because it is usually the first response to distrust. When premiums harden, exclusions appear, and Arctic exposure is read through a lens of severity and thin capacity, operators quickly realise that broad assurances no longer carry enough weight. They respond by thickening the file: more detailed route plans, clearer operational limits, stronger evidence of crew preparation, tighter maintenance records, more explicit contingency arrangements, more disciplined reporting lines, and more careful preservation of the reasoning behind difficult decisions. This is not mere paperwork inflation. It is an attempt to make risk legible enough that others can tolerate it. The thicker file buys room.

A named example helps illuminate the point. The *Crystal Serenity* transit through the Northwest Passage in August 2016 mattered not only because a large passenger vessel moved through a high-profile Arctic route, but because the operation rested on a level of planning, support logic, and institutional preparation that made the voyage readable to outsiders. That readability was part of the voyage itself. The broader lesson is that when markets distrust generic confidence, operators answer with documentation dense enough to make the undertaking appear governable. Once a voyage of that kind becomes the reference point in professional memory, later operators are judged against the discipline it displayed whether they like it or not.

Conservative routing follows naturally from the same pressure. If the market has become less willing to subsidise optimistic timing, marginal ice margins, aggressive seasonal ambition, or route choices dependent on everything going right, operators begin to price caution into the plan.

They leave wider margins. They choose slower or less exposed passages. They wait more readily. They avoid the narrow window that would look commercially brilliant if it worked and institutionally foolish if it did not. This response can appear to be simple prudence, and in one sense it is. But it is also a market-shaped behaviour. The operator is reacting to the knowledge that insurers and counterparties now read routeing decisions as evidence about the whole culture of the enterprise. The route speaks.

Partnerships form another important strategy, especially where thin capacity and sparse support make solo competence harder to persuade. Operators in Arctic trades often seek credibility through relationships: with more experienced partners, with specialised service providers, with better-established technical managers, with escort or ice-advice arrangements, or with local infrastructure and response networks that make the venture look less improvisational. These partnerships matter because they spread more than operational burden. They spread confidence. A market uncertain about one operator's standalone capability may become more comfortable if the risk is embedded in a web of recognised competence. Trust is borrowed before it is earned outright.

Investment in redundancy works in a similarly revealing way. Extra systems, spare capacity, duplicated functions, thicker maintenance margins, stronger communications arrangements, and more resilient support concepts all cost money and often look inefficient when measured against ordinary shipping logic. Yet in Arctic insurance terms they are frequently cheaper than uncertainty. Redundancy reduces the chance that one technical problem becomes a commercial crisis. More importantly, it signals a certain institutional philosophy: the operator is not planning on thin tolerance and fast recovery, but on slower, more robust control under adverse conditions. Markets like that signal because it aligns with their own fear of cascading failure in remote environments.

This is why these coping strategies should not be romanticised as the triumph of individual excellence. They are institutional adaptations to a system that has become more demanding. An operator does not usually choose exhaustive documentation, conservative routeing, costly redundancy, or carefully staged partnerships because it enjoys administrative burden or slower apparent efficiency. It chooses them because the alternative has become less insurable, less financeable, or less charterable. The pressure comes from outside as much as from inside. Governance evolves when repeated market pressure changes what counts as normal effort.

A second named example shows how this evolution can travel across sectors. After the *Exxon Valdez* casualty in March 1989, markets did not only become more cautious about one class of pollution exposure. They became more attentive to preparedness, response logic, evidentiary quality, and the operator's ability to show that environmental severity had been taken seriously before the casualty occurred. That broader lesson did not remain confined to one file. It changed what later operators in sensitive waters had to demonstrate in order to look credible. A claim had become a standard without ever being announced as one.

This is how new norms are enforced. No single institution needs to declare them formally at first. Underwriters ask harder questions. Clubs require stronger submissions. Surveyors focus on newly sensitive points. Charterers ask for clearer route limits and more protective clauses. Port and flag interactions are read through a tighter lens. A coping strategy that once gave one operator an advantage becomes, through repetition, the thing whose absence now causes doubt. This process is often incremental, which is why it can be overlooked. The change does not come only through public rule-making. It comes through converging expectations that make deviation more expensive year by year.

One can see this clearly in the movement from recommendation to requirement. A market concerned about northern delay risk may initially encourage stronger contingency planning, better communications back-up, or more explicit support arrangements. Operators who adopt the recommendation gain slightly easier renewals or fewer awkward questions. If subsequent losses confirm that the concern was justified, the same recommendation begins to lose its softness. It appears in survey expectations, policy conditions, or club requirements. Before long, the operator who does not comply is no longer simply adventurous. It is non-standard in a way that has become commercially penalised. The suggestion hardens.

Still, a limitation should be acknowledged. Not every coping strategy deserves to become a universal norm, and markets can overlearn from the practices of the best-resourced operators. A large or well-capitalised company may be able to sustain levels of redundancy, documentation, and partnership-building that smaller but otherwise competent operators cannot match without severe economic strain. When markets convert such strategies too quickly into baseline expectations, they can inadvertently narrow access in ways that favour scale over merit. Governance under pressure is not always fair. It can become conservative in both senses of the word.

And yet this limitation does not weaken the argument. It clarifies what is at stake when coping strategies reshape governance. The issue is not merely whether operators can adapt. It is which adaptations become legible enough to satisfy the market, and which then harden into norms that others must emulate or be priced out. Arctic governance does not evolve only through better rules or worse accidents. It evolves through competitive imitation under conditions of financial pressure. The operator that survives one hard market cycle often helps define the behavioural template of the next.

This makes the Arctic commercial order more dynamic than it first appears. Markets do not simply impose discipline from above while operators obey from below. Operators respond creatively, but their creativity is filtered through what insurers, clubs, and counterparties choose to recognise as credible. Some responses become temporary tactics. Others become the new grammar of insurable conduct. The line between the two is usually visible only in retrospect, when the strategy that once marked a sophisticated outlier has become the thing every renewal file is expected to show.

The quiet motif returns because the checklist keeps growing. What began as one operator's extra route note, added back-up arrangement, partnership, or redundant system to calm a nervous market later reappears as an ordinary question in another file. The market remembers what worked, or what appeared to work, and turns memory into expectation. In that sense, Arctic governance evolves less like a revolution and more like sediment: one hard season, one difficult renewal, one painful claim, one successful adaptation laid down on top of another until the whole operating surface has changed.

The harder question, then, is not whether operators can cope with pressure. Many can, at least for a time. The harder question is which coping strategies are quietly becoming the next mandatory signs of seriousness - and whether the Arctic market is still rewarding adaptation, or has already begun converting yesterday's survival tactics into today's minimum conditions for entry.

Chapter 12

Ports, Terminals, and Infrastructure Risk

In August 2016, when the *Crystal Serenity* departed Seward, Alaska, for its Northwest Passage transit, the public eye fixed on the ship, the route, and the spectacle of a large passenger vessel moving through waters long imagined as distant and difficult. But the more revealing question sat onshore. What kind of port access, tug support, medical reach, repair capacity, communications discipline, and emergency response credibility had to exist before such a voyage could be treated as commercially governable rather than merely technically possible? The hull carried the passengers. The shore carried the argument.

That is the enduring blind spot in many accounts of Arctic expansion. They describe ships as though ships were self-sufficient units of risk, little floating worlds whose design, class, and crewing tell the essential story. Yet severe maritime environments punish that illusion quickly. A vessel does not trade alone. It trades inside a chain of berths, terminals, pilots, tugs, medical arrangements, repair options, fuel interfaces, cargo-handling rules, weather windows, and response capacities that may be thin, distant, seasonal, or politically fragile. Once those shore-side limits are admitted, access stops looking like a question of vessel capability alone. It starts to look like a systems problem.

That shift matters because infrastructure changes the meaning of every incident. A technical fault near dense support may remain a manageable interruption. The same fault in a region with sparse repair options, long mobilisation times, limited medical support, and narrow terminal capacity can turn into a materially different insurance and contractual event. Markets know this even when public discussion does not. Underwriters often care as much about where a ship can go for help, what standards a terminal will impose, and how credible a response plan appears in local conditions as they do about the vessel's formal design strength. The pier is part of the risk.

The central tension lies there. Arctic expansion is often sold through images of movement and access, yet the true constraint frequently sits still. It lives in the tug not available, the berth that cannot accommodate delay, the terminal checklist that quietly exceeds baseline law, the repair yard too far away, the medevac assumption that looks plausible in a presentation and thin in bad weather. Infrastructure is not the background to maritime access. It is the hidden governor of it. Where shore-side capacity is narrow, ships are judged more harshly because there is less room for failure, improvisation, or administrative optimism.

This matters now and later because infrastructure multiplies risk in ways markets price without always announcing them plainly. A project may appear insurable on paper until the underwriter asks what happens after the first injury, the first machinery fault, the first delayed berthing window, or the first pollution scare that requires more than a generic plan and a hopeful timeline. A terminal may appear to be a passive point of transfer until its indemnities, inspections, operating rules, and document demands make clear that it is also allocating risk and filtering entry. A response plan may look like a compliance annex until a lender, club, or insurer starts reading it as evidence of whether the whole venture is financeable. Preparedness becomes commercial speech.

The stakes are therefore larger than port convenience. Shore-side weakness does not merely add cost. It changes bargaining power. It strengthens the hand of terminals, service providers, and insurers who can insist on conditions others must accept if the trade is to proceed at all. It also changes who can compete. Large operators with deeper partnerships, stronger documentation, and the ability to invest in support arrangements may convert infrastructure scarcity into advantage, while smaller entrants find that the route is physically open but institutionally closed. What looks like remote geography becomes market structure.

From that pressure comes a particular path of inquiry. The analysis begins where every northern voyage eventually lands, in the hard fact that limited infrastructure can enlarge any casualty or interruption into something categorically more expensive and more difficult to control. It then moves into the terminal and port interface, where private owners and operators use checklists, entry rules, inspections, and indemnities to shape conduct long before public law says very much. From there it reaches emergency response planning, where the question is no longer whether a plan exists, but whether the plan describes real capability under local conditions rather than a paper exercise designed to reassure distant readers.

What makes this chapter difficult is that infrastructure risk seldom arrives with a dramatic announcement. It appears as a longer wait for tug availability, a more demanding terminal questionnaire, a financing delay tied to weak emergency assumptions, a stricter insurance clause around response capability, a repair option too distant to preserve schedule credibility, or a medical contingency that suddenly looks central once people ask who can actually get there in time. Each piece seems manageable. Together they define whether the Arctic venture belongs to the category of disciplined expansion or to the category of thinly supported ambition. The quay decides quietly.

So the real question is not whether a ship can enter Arctic waters with the right class, crew, and confidence. The harder question is what sort of shore-side world has to exist before everyone else - terminal, port, insurer, financier, charterer, club, and state authority - believes that if the voyage stops being routine, it will still remain governable rather than merely stranded between the map and the nearest credible help.

Arctic infrastructure as a risk multiplier

In August 2016, the *Crystal Serenity* departed Seward, Alaska, for its Northwest Passage transit and drew the kind of attention that usually gathers around ships rather than around the quieter systems that make ships survivable. Yet the deeper commercial question was never only whether a large vessel could move through Arctic waters. It was whether enough shore-side support existed, or could be credibly assembled, to keep a manageable problem from turning into a ruinous one. A ship can carry steel, fuel, and expertise. It cannot carry its own port.

That is the first hard truth about Arctic infrastructure. The danger does not lie only in cold, ice, or distance taken separately. It lies in what those conditions do when ports are sparse, tugs are few, repair yards are distant, medevac options are thin, and weather or communications can delay help precisely when help matters most. A machinery fault near dense coastal infrastructure may remain an inconvenience. The same fault in the Arctic can become a salvage concern, a pollution concern, a liability concern, and a schedule-destroying commercial event before anyone has finished naming the original problem. The pier may be far away. Its absence still governs.

This is why infrastructure gaps influence underwriting as much as vessel design. Shipowners often prefer to talk about hull strength, ice class, propulsion redundancy, or crew competence because those are qualities attached to the vessel and therefore easier to present as matters of internal control. Underwriters care about all of these, but they ask a ruder question as well: what happens after the first failure, injury, grounding, delay, or contamination scare? If the nearest realistic assistance is far off, if the berth that can accept the ship is limited, if the tug that can intervene is not immediately available, or if specialist repair capacity lies several decisions away, then even a well-designed vessel sits inside a harsher severity profile. Infrastructure makes the same ship look different.

The concept here is not complicated, though its consequences are. Infrastructure acts as a risk multiplier because it determines how fast an incident can be stabilised, how many options remain open once conditions deteriorate, and how expensive the interval becomes between problem recognition and meaningful intervention. In ordinary maritime settings, a failure can often be managed through access to towage, spare parts, pilots, sheltered waiting areas, yard availability, medical evacuation, and nearby regulatory or technical support. In Arctic settings, each of those assumptions may weaken at once. The gap between a problem and a solution lengthens. So does the bill.

A named example clarifies the institutional point. The *Crystal Serenity* voyage in August 2016 attracted attention because it made visible how much of Arctic viability depends on support planning beyond the vessel itself. The public image was one of polar passage. The underwriting and operational reality rested on a more prosaic question: how much external capacity had to stand behind that passage before the vessel could be treated as governable in the event of illness, technical malfunction, delay, or worse? The lesson reaches well beyond cruise operations. A ship may be extraordinary. The system around it still decides whether extraordinary can be treated as commercially acceptable rather than merely brave.

Ports are the most obvious component of this system because they anchor every other logistical promise. A port in the Arctic is not only a place to berth. It is an emergency option, a point of refuge, a transfer node, a repair possibility, a customs and inspection site, a medical access point, and a symbol of whether the region can absorb maritime trouble without immediately escalating it. Where ports are few, shallow, seasonally constrained, or technically limited, the consequence is not simply less convenience. It is less room for error. Underwriters notice this because the number of usable harbours often matters more to severity than the nominal openness of the route itself.

Tugs reveal the same logic in a sharper form. In benign discussions of trade corridors, tug availability sounds like a secondary port-services issue. In real casualties it becomes one of the clearest dividing lines between controllable disruption and cascading loss. A tug is not merely a support craft. It is often the first external instrument by which a drifting, disabled, or awkwardly positioned ship can be kept from turning a technical setback into a grounding, collision, pollution event, or wreck problem. Where tug support is thin, distant, weather-limited, or committed elsewhere, the underwriting meaning of even a modest propulsion problem changes immediately. The ship's problem becomes the market's problem faster.

Repair yards matter just as much because the difference between a delay and a claims event often depends on whether technical defects can be addressed within a commercially survivable radius. A minor machinery failure does not stay minor if the nearest yard capable of dealing with it lies far outside the intended trade pattern, or if specialist parts and technicians require long mobilisation into a narrowing seasonal window. In such circumstances, the cost of repair is rarely the decisive number. The real severity lies in the chain surrounding it: diversion, off-hire, cargo complications, inspection exposure, knock-on weather risk, altered crew schedules, and the possibility that the vessel returns too late for the remaining season to justify the original economics. A remote yard changes the meaning of the wrench.

Medical support is often treated as a humanitarian issue rather than a core underwriting variable, which is a serious mistake. In Arctic operations, limited medevac reach or delayed clinical access can enlarge ordinary onboard incidents into legal, reputational, and insurance events of a different order. A serious illness, injury, or exposure that might be handled rapidly in a dense coastal environment may in the far north trigger difficult decisions about evacuation timing, diversion, communications, weather tolerance, and the interaction between commercial schedule and duty of care. Passenger operations make this especially obvious, but cargo and support voyages are not exempt. Human vulnerability does not disappear because the cargo is industrial. The clinic may be farther away than the chart admits.

This is why expansion must be understood as a system, not a ship. Vessel design remains crucial, but design is only one side of the severity equation. A stronger hull, better heating, or more disciplined crew cannot abolish the underwriting significance of sparse ports, thin towage, distant repair, and delayed medical response. Indeed, better ship design can paradoxically make infrastructure gaps more visible, because the shipowner begins to assume that enhanced vessel capability has solved a problem that the market knows remains only partly addressed. The vessel can survive more. The region may still not support that survival economically.

A second named example shows how a casualty can alter the market's view of supporting infrastructure long after the specific event is over. After the *Exxon Valdez* grounding in March 1989, the lesson absorbed by markets was not confined to pollution and navigation. It also concerned response capacity, logistical reach, and the practical difficulty of managing major incidents in northern environments where infrastructure is limited and consequence spreads quickly. That lesson has never wholly left the file. Each later Arctic proposal is judged, in part, against remembered failures of support as much as against remembered failures of ship handling.

This is one reason infrastructure gaps influence underwriting almost as much as vessel design. Underwriters do not simply ask whether the ship can withstand expected ice. They ask whether the surrounding system can withstand the ship's failure to do so. They compare the quality of emergency options, the density of operational fallback points, the credibility of shelter and assistance assumptions, and the likelihood that a manageable incident will remain manageable once geography begins to act against time. A technically impressive vessel proposed for a thinly supported corridor may be treated as a harder risk than a more modest vessel operating within a thicker infrastructure envelope. The market insures systems, not fantasies.

Still, a limitation should be acknowledged. Sparse infrastructure does not automatically make every Arctic voyage commercially irrational or uninsurable. Some operators compensate through careful route selection, stronger partnerships, escort arrangements, enhanced onboard capability, stricter abort criteria, and detailed contingency planning that materially narrows the danger created by shore-side weakness. Infrastructure gaps are not destiny. They are a severity driver whose force depends partly on how honestly the operator has incorporated them into the voyage concept.

And yet that concession reinforces the broader argument. Because infrastructure weakness can sometimes be compensated for and sometimes cannot, it becomes one of the main sites at which the market distinguishes between disciplined operations and wishful ones. A proposal that treats sparse support as a manageable inconvenience invites suspicion. A proposal that builds the lack of support into routeing, schedule, equipment, staffing, and response logic appears more governable. The difference is not moral.

It is institutional. One operator is asking the market to believe in a resilient system. The other is asking it to ignore a brittle one.

This is where infrastructure risk begins to shape access itself. A route may be legally open and seasonally passable, yet functionally restricted because the supporting chain behind it is too thin to satisfy insurers, clubs, charterers, or financiers on workable terms. No public closure is required. The port limitations, towage gaps, repair distances, and medical uncertainties do the work quietly by increasing severity and reducing tolerance for disruption. Expansion then slows, not because the ship cannot move, but because the system around the ship cannot absorb interruption cheaply enough. The absence of infrastructure becomes a form of governance.

The quiet motif returns because the ship cannot carry its own port. It cannot carry its own tug fleet, repair yard, hospital, or all-weather refuge either. It carries only a promise that those things exist in adequate reach, or that their absence has been compensated for credibly enough that the voyage remains governable. Markets spend much of their time deciding whether that promise is serious. In Arctic trades, that decision often matters more than public debate about whether the route is open.

The harder question, then, is not whether vessels can be designed for Arctic conditions. They can, and increasingly are. The harder question is what degree of shore-side weakness a market is still willing to tolerate once it asks what happens after the first injury, the first mechanical failure, or the first forced diversion - and whether many ventures celebrated as maritime breakthroughs are, in truth, only as viable as the distant port, tug, yard, or medevac option they hope never to need.

Terminal requirements and contractual interfaces

In August 2016, when the *Crystal Serenity* prepared to transit the Northwest Passage from Seward, Alaska, the voyage depended on much more than the ship's own technical readiness and the formal permissions attached to it. It depended on whether the shore-side institutions receiving, servicing, and protecting the operation regarded the vessel as acceptable on their own terms. That distinction matters. A ship may satisfy baseline law and still find that the terminal, the port operator, or the infrastructure owner has written a harder version of access into checklists, operating rules, and indemnity language. The gate is private too.

This is one of the least appreciated realities of Arctic maritime commerce. We are taught to think of regulation as something issued by states, enforced by public authorities, and recorded in legislation, codes, and official certificates. All of that matters. Yet in difficult environments, terminals and port operators often exercise a quieter authority that can feel just as decisive. They decide what documentation must be supplied before arrival, what inspections will be conducted before berthing, what tug or escort conditions will apply, what transfer operations are acceptable in given weather or ice conditions, and what liabilities must be assumed by the vessel, owner, or charterer as the price of using the facility. The clipboard belongs to the infrastructure owner as well.

This private authority grows stronger where infrastructure is scarce, specialised, or expensive to interrupt. A terminal handling fuel, minerals, project cargo, or strategically important supply in a northern setting is rarely interested in relying solely on the minimum legal baseline if the commercial consequences of an accident are severe. It may impose pre-arrival vetting, bespoke operating procedures, additional mooring expectations, tighter pollution safeguards, mandatory communications routines, proof of insurance in forms more exacting than statute requires, or indemnities that shift certain categories of loss sharply back towards the visiting vessel. These conditions are not merely housekeeping. They are instruments for allocating risk before the first line is made fast.

That is why terminals can act as de facto regulators. They do not pass public law, and they do not need to. Their leverage comes from operational necessity. If the cargo, the route, or the project depends on access to a specific berth or specialised facility, the terminal's rules can become more consequential than the general law for the operator standing at its gate. This is especially true in Arctic trades, where alternative terminals may be limited, weather windows narrow, and infrastructure substitution impractical. A vessel that cannot satisfy the terminal's private requirements may be legally entitled to sail and commercially unable to perform. Access is filtered through contract.

The mechanism usually begins with entry requirements. Before the ship comes close enough to matter physically, it is often required to matter administratively. Terminal operators may ask for detailed particulars on class, ice capability, cargo-handling arrangements, pollution equipment, mooring configuration, crew competence, communications systems, emergency procedures, prior inspection outcomes, and insurance support. Some of these requirements mirror statutory expectations. Others go further. They are designed not to honour regulatory sufficiency, but to protect the facility's own appetite for interruption, contamination, damage, public scrutiny, or expensive uncertainty. In that sense, the terminal is not asking, "is this ship lawful?" It is asking, "is this ship acceptable to us?"

A named example helps clarify the broader institutional point. The *Crystal Serenity* voyage in August 2016 mattered because it made visible how much of Arctic legitimacy rests not simply on navigation through remote waters, but on the willingness of shore-side actors to treat the operation as disciplined enough to receive, support, and absorb if something goes wrong. The lesson travels well beyond cruise operations. High-profile northern voyages force terminals, ports, and service providers to ask whether their own facilities, staff, liabilities, and reputations can tolerate the vessel's risks on terms the vessel may not have expected. A berth is never just concrete and bollards. It is a contract with nerves.

Inspections are where this private authority becomes tangible. A port state inspector tests public compliance. A terminal inspection often tests operational confidence. The terminal wants to know whether the vessel's procedures, equipment, crew behaviour, and documentary discipline are good enough not merely to satisfy a regulation, but to protect the terminal's own infrastructure, schedule, reputation, and insurance position. That difference is subtle and crucial. Public law may ask whether the ship is fit to trade. The terminal may ask whether the ship is fit to trade here, under these facility-specific conditions, with these local sensitivities, at this moment in the season. The answer can be yes in the first sense and no in the second.

This is why a terminal checklist can exceed baseline statutory requirements without any drama. Imagine a vessel arriving with valid certificates, current class, and all necessary legal permissions for the service in question. The terminal may still require more: tighter communications routines during approach, additional tug availability, stricter weather hold points, proof of specific spill-response arrangements, documented crew familiarity with berth procedures, or an indemnity structure that covers categories of facility damage or business interruption not explicitly addressed by public regulation. Nothing in this sequence implies that the ship is unlawful. It implies that the infrastructure owner is pricing and governing risks the public framework leaves more open. The law says enough. The terminal says not enough for us.

That difference matters enormously for risk allocation. Contractual interfaces between ship and terminal are where broad liability concepts are turned into live obligations. The terminal's operating rules, berth regulations, side letters, indemnity provisions, notification duties, and incident-reporting expectations shape who will bear cost if the cargo operation is delayed, if shore equipment is damaged, if pollution control becomes necessary, if access channels are obstructed, or if weather and ice disrupt the planned sequence. These clauses do not merely tidy up legal uncertainty. They structure the commercial life of the voyage. An owner or charterer may think it has priced the marine risk, only to discover that the shore-side contract has redistributed a critical slice of that risk into a more expensive place.

A brief example makes the point more sharply. Suppose a northern terminal requires a vessel to accept an operational checklist that includes specific tug arrangements, tighter pre-transfer inspection routines, and an indemnity for defined categories of delay or facility impact arising from a vessel-side deficiency, even where public rules would have stopped at more general safety compliance. The owner may comply because the terminal is commercially indispensable. If an incident later occurs, the operator discovers that the most costly parts of the problem sit not only within marine insurance questions, but within the agreed shore-side allocation. The checklist becomes a liability map. What looked like access paperwork becomes a claims document.

Insurance markets understand this perfectly, which is why they read terminal interfaces with such care. Underwriters do not assess the vessel in isolation. They ask how the terminal's requirements alter the vessel's real risk profile and whether the contractual allocation pushes too much exposure back onto the insured. A terminal with disciplined procedures, credible emergency arrangements, and clear operating thresholds can actually reassure a market because it narrows uncertainty and demonstrates that the shore side is actively managing risk. Another terminal may unsettle insurers if its contractual language is expansive, its expectations hard to satisfy in practice, or its operational rigidity likely to amplify delay and claims friction. The facility's rules become part of the underwriting story.

A second named example shows how broad this lesson is in maritime practice. After the *Exxon Valdez* disaster in March 1989, the market learned not only to fear pollution and navigational error more sharply in northern waters, but to examine much more closely how shore-side systems, response capacity, and facility-level risk allocation would behave after a serious incident. The relevance here is not to suggest that every terminal rewrote itself overnight. It is to show that highly visible losses teach infrastructure owners to protect themselves more assertively and teach markets to expect that assertiveness as part of serious northern operations. The port remembers too.

Still, a limitation deserves acknowledgement. Terminal requirements are not always wise merely because they are strict, and private operators can impose burdens that reflect institutional anxiety, bargaining power, or reputational self-protection as much as clear-eyed risk management. A facility may overreach. A checklist may become bloated. An indemnity may shift exposure in ways that feel commercially one-sided. It would be naive to treat every terminal rule as technically immaculate. Private governance, like public governance, can be clumsy, conservative, or self-interested.

And yet this limitation only reinforces the main argument. Because terminals possess real leverage, even imperfect private rules shape conduct. Owners adapt vessel procedures. Charterers renegotiate obligations. Insurers revise assumptions. Surveyors ask different questions. Masters enter berth approaches knowing that facility rules may be stricter than the generic legal environment suggested. Over time, these adaptations can become normalised. What began as one terminal's precaution can, through repetition, come to define what the market regards as prudent behaviour near a whole class of Arctic facilities. The private condition hardens into a wider norm.

This is how infrastructure owners shape governance without making speeches about governance. They write rules into access conditions, write liabilities into indemnities, write expectations into checklists, and then rely on the fact that operators cannot always choose another berth. The result is a layered order in which public law provides the floor while terminals quietly adjust the ceiling of acceptable risk. In northern trades, where infrastructure is often scarce and consequences severe, that ceiling may matter more in practice than many formal statutes.

The quiet motif returns because the gate is private too. The vessel approaches carrying certificates, plans, cover, and commercial urgency. The terminal receives all of that and then asks its own question: will we allow our berth, equipment, staff, and schedule to be exposed to this ship on anything less than our preferred terms? When the answer is no, the route does not close on the chart. It closes at the interface.

The harder question, then, is not whether terminals and port operators impose conditions beyond baseline law. They plainly do. The harder question is how much of Arctic access is really being decided not by what states formally permit, but by what infrastructure owners are willing to accept contractually once they ask who will actually pay when a legally sufficient ship turns out to be commercially and operationally too costly to welcome.

Emergency response planning and credible capability

In March 1989, after the *Exxon Valdez* grounded in Alaska, one of the most enduring lessons was not simply that northern waters punish mistakes. It was that response capacity cannot be assumed into existence once the casualty has already begun. Plans that sound reassuring in offices far from the scene can collapse quickly against weather, distance, darkness, logistics, and the blunt question of who can actually arrive, with what equipment, and on whose authority. The map is not the plan.

That distinction is central to Arctic maritime risk. Emergency response planning is often treated as a compliance exercise, an annex to the main commercial undertaking, a document that proves seriousness without necessarily determining the fate of the venture itself. In remote environments, that view becomes untenable. A response plan is not only a safety tool. It is evidence. It shows regulators, terminals, financiers, insurers, and clubs whether the operator has translated general caution into a plausible operational sequence for a place where help is slow, options are thin, and a small failure can enlarge before the second phone call is finished. The binder must travel.

This is why emergency response planning occupies an unusual position in Arctic commerce. It sits at the junction of law, insurance, infrastructure, finance, and seamanship. Public authorities want it because casualties in remote settings can quickly exceed local tolerance. Insurers want it because the severity of claims depends not only on the initiating event but on the speed, coherence, and credibility of the response that follows. Terminals and lenders want it because a project without believable contingency arrangements may be technically legal and still commercially indefensible. Preparedness, in this setting, is not an ethical flourish. It is a condition of access.

The quality that matters most is credibility. A response plan does not become credible merely because it is detailed, professionally formatted, or aligned in broad terms with general regulatory language. It becomes credible when its assumptions survive contact with actual Arctic conditions. Who is expected to respond? From where? By what means? In what weather? With what delay? Under whose command? With what communication pathway? What happens if the first response asset is unavailable, the port of refuge is inaccessible, the medevac weather minima are not met, or the spill-response equipment takes longer to mobilise than the standard scenario prefers to admit? The plan must answer not only the first question, but the second and third questions that follow once the first answer goes wrong.

A named example helps illuminate the standard by which such plans are really judged. When the *Crystal Serenity* prepared for its August 2016 Northwest Passage transit, the public meaning of the voyage lay in spectacle and symbolic access. Its institutional meaning lay elsewhere. A vessel of that profile could not be treated as commercially or politically tolerable in remote waters unless the supporting emergency logic looked thick enough to withstand scrutiny from insurers, authorities, and service providers. The lesson extends far beyond passenger operations. High-profile Arctic activity forces the market to ask whether the response plan is written for the route on the page or for the conditions on the ground. Only one of those is insurable.

This is why generic templates fail so badly in northern settings. A template may satisfy an administrative appetite for structure, but it usually carries assumptions imported from denser maritime regions: readily available tugs, predictable communications, nearby repair, quick casualty attendance, easy access to specialist contractors, stable weather windows, and medical evacuation within broadly familiar timeframes. Arctic operations punish these assumptions. When a plan quietly borrows infrastructure density from another geography, it is not merely weak. It is misleading. Underwriters and experienced reviewers recognise that very quickly. They are not only asking whether a plan exists. They are asking whether the plan belongs to the place it claims to describe.

This matters because the consequences of an implausible plan are rarely confined to safety review. Insurance markets read response planning as a proxy for organisational seriousness. A company that can specify realistic response assets, fallback options, command structures, communications protocols, logistical limits, and environmental contingencies appears more governable than one offering broad statements about compliance and cooperation. The difference shows up in terms. Better plans may support broader appetite, less punitive conditions, or a more patient reading of the rest of the file. Thin plans do the opposite. They invite exclusions, tighter wording, heavier survey demands, or simple reluctance. A weak response concept can harden a market before any ice has even been encountered.

The same is true for finance. Lenders and project backers may not discuss response plans with the same technical granularity as clubs or specialist underwriters, but they understand one central fact: where emergency capability is not credible, the downside of a project becomes harder to model, harder to cap, and harder to defend to committees or co-investors. This is especially true where terminals, energy installations, high-consequence cargoes, or politically sensitive routes are involved. A project with an elegant revenue story and a soft emergency backstop often discovers that the capital stack cares more about the second document than the first. Finance distrusts improvisation.

A brief example makes the mechanism plain. Imagine two operators proposing similar northern services. Both have competent vessels, current certificates, and plausible commercial rationale. The first submits a response plan that identifies specific support pathways, likely delays, command responsibilities, communications vulnerabilities, and what happens if primary assistance cannot arrive as hoped. The second submits a general manual promising prompt response, coordination with authorities, and use of suitable contractors, but without demonstrating that these assumptions have been tested against local infrastructure and seasonal reality. Both plans may look respectable in outline. Only one reduces uncertainty enough to change terms materially. The other tells the market that if trouble comes, the real plan will have to be invented under stress.

This is why response capability so often determines whether a project is financeable or insurable on workable terms rather than merely whether it is formally permitted. Formal permission may require the existence of a plan. Workable insurance and finance require belief in it. This difference is crucial. A project may satisfy baseline legal expectations and still fail commercially because the institutions carrying its downside do not trust the response architecture enough to price it comfortably. The operator then experiences a familiar but poorly understood frustration: no one has said no, yet the venture no longer works. Preparedness was the hidden variable all along.

A second named example shows how the market learns from visible northern failure. After the *Exxon Valdez* casualty in March 1989, the lesson absorbed by insurers, authorities, and infrastructure owners was not only about navigation or pollution. It was also about the gap between nominal response arrangements and the real difficulty of acting quickly and effectively in sensitive northern waters. That lesson has lingered. Every later Arctic proposal is judged against the institutional memory that once a casualty begins, weak assumptions about mobilisation, command, and support can become part of the claim itself. Response planning is therefore never assessed in innocence. It is read against remembered failure.

Still, a limitation deserves open acknowledgement. No response plan can abolish Arctic uncertainty. Weather can make good assets unusable. Communications can break. Multiple failures can arrive at once. Human judgment under stress can still degrade even inside a well-constructed system. It would be naive to suggest that better planning guarantees tidy outcomes in remote conditions. Maritime emergencies do not respect paper confidence.

And yet this limitation makes credible planning more, not less, important. Because uncertainty remains, institutions want to know whether the operator has at least identified where the uncertainty truly sits and how it intends to live with it. A plan that openly recognises weak points, fallback options, likely delays, and operational limits can inspire more confidence than a smoother document that quietly assumes frictionless rescue and coordination. In severe environments, realism often reads as competence. Fantasy reads as risk.

This is also why emergency response planning reshapes behaviour before any emergency occurs. Once operators realise that preparedness is being priced, they begin to invest differently. They strengthen documentation. They build partnerships. They secure support arrangements. They rehearse communication chains. They narrow routes and seasons. They align the plan with the charterparty, the insurance submission, the terminal interface, and the actual availability of people and equipment. Over time these adjustments cease to look like voluntary prudence. They become part of what the market recognises as normal Arctic discipline. The plan stops being a document and becomes an operating posture.

The quiet motif returns because the binder really must travel. It has to travel from ship to insurer, from project sponsor to lender, from terminal to club, from exercise room to casualty scene. If its assumptions cannot make that journey intact, then the underlying venture is being built on borrowed confidence. Markets have become increasingly unwilling to subsidise that kind of borrowing in northern operations. They price preparedness because they know the absence of it is what turns a difficult incident into an unaffordable one.

The harder question, then, is not whether Arctic projects need emergency response plans. Plainly they do. The harder question is what sort of plan deserves to count as capability rather than theatre - and whether the operators seeking northern access are building documents that would still make sense when the weather closes, the first contact fails, and everyone discovers that the real test of preparedness was never whether the plan looked complete, but whether anyone believed it could actually work.

Chapter 13

Community Impacts and Social Licence Risks

When an Arctic project clears its permits, satisfies its class requirements, secures cover, and signs its contracts, what exactly has it won? It has won legality, perhaps. It has not necessarily won acceptance. A vessel may be entitled to sail and still enter a zone of distrust dense enough to alter charter decisions, harden underwriting questions, unsettle financiers, and trigger political or administrative attention that no one priced cleanly at the start. The papers may be complete. The argument may only be beginning.

That gap between permission and acceptance matters more in the Arctic than many operators first admit. Remote maritime activity is rarely judged only by its compliance with formal rules. It is watched by communities who live with the consequences of disruption, by scientific bodies concerned with fragile systems and uncertain baselines, by civil society groups skilled at turning technical disputes into public controversy, and by a broader field of observers who treat northern operations as tests of institutional seriousness rather than as ordinary commercial events. The project reaches the water. The file reaches the public.

The central tension lies there. Commercial actors often prefer a world in which risk is bounded by contract, certificate, and premium. Social licence resists that neatness. It introduces forms of scrutiny that are not always reducible to breach, liability, or direct loss, yet can still migrate into all three. A community challenge may slow a schedule. A scientific concern may sharpen monitoring obligations. A public campaign may change how an insurer thinks about administrative burden, brand exposure, or the cost of standing behind a controversial operation. Legitimacy, in this sense, is not soft reputation work hovering outside the real business. It is a practical variable in whether the business can proceed on tolerable terms.

That is why this chapter belongs inside a book about insurance, classification, and law rather than at its moral edge. Social licence risk changes the economics of Arctic activity because it widens the field of actors whose judgement can affect insurability, contract stability, and operating freedom. The hull may be sound. The route may be seasonally open. Yet if communities distrust the process, if scientific uncertainty remains poorly evidenced, or if activism turns the project into a reputational test for insurers and terminals, the commercial consequences can become as real as any machinery defect. Trust becomes a cost-bearing condition.

The stakes run in two directions at once. In the near term, weak legitimacy can convert into friction: slower approvals, tighter contractual protections, more demanding evidence requests, cautious counterparties, and a growing tendency for every operational problem to be read through a wider story about whether the project should have been attempted as structured. Over time, the effect is deeper. Repeated disputes teach markets what kinds of consultation, monitoring, disclosure, and community interface they now regard as signs of competent risk control. What once looked like optional engagement can harden into a baseline expectation for serious operators. Social pressure enters governance not only through protest, but through routine commercial memory.

This is also why the Arctic punishes simplistic ideas about stakeholder management. The issue is not merely public relations. It is whether operators understand that people outside the contract can still influence the contract's life. Communities can shape the pace and tone of projects long before any formal conflict becomes visible in court. Scientific bodies can alter the evidentiary environment in which incidents are later judged. Civil society can make controversy itself part of the underwriting problem. Under these conditions, social licence is not a decorative layer added after technical planning. It is one of the ways technical planning is tested for seriousness.

The movement ahead follows that widening of the risk map. It begins where many commercial files remain too narrow, in the recognition that scrutiny from communities, researchers, and campaigners can change the practical insurability of an operation even when formal permission exists. It then tightens around process, where consultation and consent questions reshape schedules, routes, and contingency logic, before turning to monitoring as both an operational discipline and an evidentiary reserve for the disputes that may come later. From there the focus reaches the sharper edge where activism meets underwriting and public controversy becomes a private-market concern.

A useful way to see the whole field is through the notebook. Some operators arrive with a notebook full of contracts, certificates, and technical assurances and assume the rest will follow. Others understand that the notebook must also contain local knowledge, a record of engagement, a defensible baseline for environmental change, and an account of why the project deserves confidence from those who did not sign the fixture or the policy. The first notebook may be formally complete. The second is more likely to survive contact with the Arctic's political and social reality. Markets increasingly know the difference.

The harder question, then, is not whether a lawful Arctic venture can still attract opposition, scrutiny, or reputational pressure. Plainly it can. The harder question is what sort of operator recognises early enough that legitimacy is being priced alongside ice, weather, and machinery - and that a project's real vulnerability may lie not in the strength of the hull, but in the weakness of the story it can tell when communities, scientists, insurers, and campaigners all begin asking whether this operation deserves to continue on the terms it first demanded.

Stakeholders beyond the contract

In September 2013, when Greenpeace's *Arctic Sunrise* was seized by Russian authorities after a protest in the Pechora Sea, the episode exposed a fact the Arctic has a habit of teaching more quickly than easier waters do: a vessel may be lawfully present and still become the centre of a political, reputational, and commercial storm large enough to alter how markets read the entire operation. The dispute was not a routine casualty. It did not need to be. It showed that Arctic activity is judged by more audiences than the signed counterparties to a voyage or project. The hull was in the water. The argument was everywhere.

That is the starting point for understanding stakeholders beyond the contract. Arctic operations do not unfold inside a closed legal box containing only owner, charterer, insurer, terminal, and state authority. They unfold under the gaze of communities who live with the consequences of disruption, scientific bodies that shape the language of environmental plausibility, and civil society actors skilled at converting local concern into wider scrutiny. These audiences may not hold the policy, sign the charterparty, or operate the berth. They still matter because they can change the practical conditions under which those formal relationships continue. The file has more readers than the operator expects.

This matters because legality and legitimacy are not the same achievement. A company may obtain permits, comply with class and insurance requirements, and still fail to persuade others that the venture deserves confidence on the ground. In Arctic settings that gap is unusually consequential. Local communities may judge the project through hunting patterns, shoreline use, emergency burden, cumulative industrial pressure, or memories of previous promises. Scientific institutions may focus on uncertain baselines, seasonal sensitivity, or the weakness of data used to support confident safety claims. Civil society organisations may ask whether the project represents disciplined operation or an attempt to normalise commercial reach ahead of adequate safeguards. None of these judgements is identical to formal law. All of them can become commercially real.

That commercial reality often arrives indirectly. A reputational problem rarely appears first as a neat legal prohibition. More often it enters through cancellations, delayed approvals, harder terminal requirements, more cautious charterers, more intrusive insurance questions, nervous financiers, or political actors suddenly less willing to defend administrative discretion. This is the key conversion the Arctic performs so effectively: social doubt becomes contractual risk. A counterpart looking at public controversy may not say, "we oppose this venture morally". It may say, "we require stronger indemnities, more evidence, narrower route limits, better contingency planning, or a right to walk away if scrutiny intensifies". The vocabulary stays commercial. The pressure did not begin there.

A named example helps clarify how this works beyond one dramatic protest event. The *Arctic Sunrise* episode in September 2013 was not a standard shipping dispute, but it demonstrated that Arctic operations can become vessels for broader arguments about legitimacy, governance, and acceptable risk. The market learned something uncomfortable from that visibility. Administrative burden, public attention, and political escalation do not need a hull casualty to grow expensive. Once an operation becomes controversial enough, insurers, service providers, terminals, and commercial partners begin to ask what else might now accompany the project besides its formal loss profile. Controversy itself becomes a factor in the risk selection process.

This is why communities matter even when they hold no formal veto within the contract structure. They influence the surrounding field in which contracts are interpreted and renewed. A vessel serving a northern project may enter waters used, watched, and understood by people whose knowledge of conditions is practical rather than actuarial. If those communities conclude that the operator is dismissive, extractive, opaque, or overconfident, the damage is not confined to public feeling. Distrust alters the ease with which schedules are maintained, consultations proceed, local support is mobilised, incidents are interpreted, and future permissions are defended. Underwriters and charterers know this. They do not need to endorse every community claim to understand that conflict increases unpredictability, and unpredictability carries a price.

Scientific bodies perform a different but related role. They may not speak in the language of fixture performance or policy wording, yet they shape the evidentiary climate in which Arctic projects justify themselves. Scientific uncertainty about species movement, spill behaviour, seasonal sensitivity, ice conditions, or baseline environmental data does not remain in journals and advisory reports once controversy grows. It enters hearings, public submissions, monitoring expectations, emergency planning reviews, and the narratives used by activists, communities, and political decision-makers. Markets care because scientific criticism can undermine the confidence with which operators present their risk models and response assumptions. If a project's technical case begins to look thinner under scientific scrutiny, its insurability can weaken even before any incident occurs.

Civil society actors then amplify these pressures by making them legible to broader publics and more expensive for brands and institutions to ignore. Activism does not have to stop a vessel physically to change the economics around it. It can increase administrative friction, sharpen media attention, widen the reputational exposure of insurers and counterparties, and make routine decisions feel politically charged. In Arctic projects, where visibility is often high and symbolism thick, this amplification can be especially powerful. A company may have expected to debate operational details with regulators and underwriters. Instead it finds itself drawn into a larger argument about whether the venture should exist in its proposed form at all. Once that shift occurs, risk expands beyond hull and machinery into governance burden, controversy cost, and institutional patience.

A second named example shows the same logic in a different register. After the *Exxon Valdez* disaster in March 1989, the event's significance did not remain confined to pollution law and tanker operations. It also shaped public and community memory about northern industrial activity more broadly. That memory matters because later projects are never received into a vacuum. They arrive in places where previous losses, previous assurances, and previous failures have already influenced what communities, scientists, and activists are willing to believe. Market actors absorb this too. A technically sound project proposed in a context of inherited distrust is not being underwritten against technical data alone. It is being underwritten against memory.

This is one reason legitimacy affects insurability more deeply than many operators assume. Insurers are not public-relations consultants, but neither are they indifferent to the wider conditions under which a claim may become politically costly or administratively burdensome. A project facing sustained community opposition, scientific criticism, or activist attention may still be insurable, yet often on terms that reflect the extra friction surrounding it. That friction can appear as narrower cover, higher retentions, stricter reporting obligations, greater concern with emergency planning, or a more conservative reading of route and schedule risk. The underwriter is not pricing sentiment as such. The underwriter is pricing what sentiment can do to the surrounding system of permission, response, and dispute.

Still, a limitation should be stated clearly. Not every criticism from outside the contract is well founded, and not every public campaign reflects superior judgement about operational reality. Communities are not monolithic. Scientific views may differ in emphasis and confidence. Activist narratives can simplify. Operators sometimes face scrutiny that is strategically selective, politically motivated, or only loosely connected to the actual structure of the project. It would be naive to romanticise every external stakeholder as automatically wiser than the institutions financing or operating the venture.

Yet that limitation does not weaken the central point. It strengthens it. Because external scrutiny is varied, sometimes fragmented, and often emotionally charged, it becomes even more important as a source of commercial uncertainty. Markets do not need every criticism to be correct in order to become more cautious. They need only recognise that criticism can trigger delay, harder conditions, reputational exposure, and administrative burden. Legitimacy risk is powerful precisely because it does not depend on unanimous public judgement or formal legal victory. It depends on the practical difficulty of carrying on commercial activity while doubt accumulates around it.

This is why the Arctic risk map must widen. Hull, machinery, class, ice capability, ports, and insurance remain indispensable. But they do not exhaust the conditions under which a project becomes durable. A venture that treats communities as background, science as a hurdle, and civil society as a communications nuisance may still secure its contracts and discover too late that those excluded audiences have altered the value of the contracts it celebrated. The route is the same. The operating climate has changed. Social licence, then, is not a sentimental add-on to hard commerce. It is one of the ways hard commerce decides whether to stay.

The quiet motif returns because the file has more readers than the operator expects. The insurer reads it for severity. The charterer reads it for reliability. The community reads it for consequence. The scientist reads it for evidentiary honesty. The activist reads it for inconsistency and vulnerability. The political system reads it for defensibility. Arctic operations survive more easily when those readings do not diverge too violently. When they do, the contract itself starts to wobble.

The harder question, then, is not whether Arctic ventures face scrutiny from people outside the formal bargain. Plainly they do. The harder question is how long an operator can treat that scrutiny as peripheral before it discovers that the real determinant of insurability was never only whether the ship could physically perform, but whether enough influential observers believed the project had earned the right to keep asking others to carry its risk.

Consultation, consent, and operational constraints

In August 2016, when the *Crystal Serenity* prepared to transit the Northwest Passage from Seward, Alaska, the voyage depended on much more than charts, class, and insurance. It depended on whether the operator could make its planning legible to people whose concerns did not begin and end with maritime legality. Remote shipping in the Arctic is rarely judged only by whether the ship may go. It is judged by whether the process leading to the voyage has earned enough confidence that others believe the operator knows where caution truly lies. Process failure travels fast north.

That is the practical meaning of consultation in Arctic operations. It is often misunderstood as a procedural courtesy attached to a project already designed elsewhere, a conversation that may improve public tone but does not materially alter the operational core. In reality, consultation can change schedules, routes, reporting routines, contingency assumptions, and the very definition of what counts as prudent planning. Where communities, local organisations, and other affected actors possess detailed knowledge of seasonal use, ice behaviour, shore access, wildlife movement, emergency limitations, or cumulative industrial pressure, the process is not merely reputational theatre. It becomes part of the operating environment itself.

This matters because consent, or the absence of it, rarely appears first as a single dramatic veto. More often it alters the conditions under which a project remains commercially manageable. A consultation process that has been rushed, defensive, or obviously performative may produce delay, harder scrutiny, narrower tolerance for disruption, and a tendency for each later problem to be read as proof that the original process was weak. A process treated seriously can do the opposite. It can reduce ambiguity, improve route choices, sharpen contingency planning, and lower the risk that local concern hardens into conflict at exactly the moment the operator needs cooperation, flexibility, or benefit of the doubt. Engagement changes the temperature of operations.

The key point is that consultation quality influences conflict risk because it influences what sort of uncertainty survives into the project. A shipping plan prepared entirely from distant technical assumptions may look coherent on paper while leaving unanswered questions about local traffic patterns, seasonal sensitivities, informal landing use, communications blind spots, or realistic emergency support. Consultation, at its best, is not a moral accessory to this uncertainty. It is one of the ways uncertainty is reduced before it becomes expensive. At its worst, it does the reverse: it leaves the operator with formal permission and a residue of distrust large enough to destabilise the project later. The meeting room reaches the chart table.

A named example shows why this is so. The *Crystal Serenity* transit mattered not only because a large passenger vessel moved through a high-profile Arctic route, but because such a voyage could not credibly be planned as if local conditions were exhausted by navigational data alone. In operations of that visibility, route choices, contingency assumptions, and emergency reasoning are judged partly by whether they appear to have engaged seriously with the realities of the places traversed. The broader lesson is not confined to cruise shipping. Highly visible Arctic voyages teach markets that confidence in process and confidence in operations are rarely separable for long.

A second example makes the same point from a different direction. Baffinland's proposed shipping expansion associated with the Mary River project in Nunavut became, in 2021, a debate not simply about industrial ambition but about whether community concerns in and around Pond Inlet had been taken seriously enough in designing marine operations. What matters here is not the legal detail of that dispute, but its practical lesson. Shipping plans, frequencies, timings, and supporting assumptions did not remain purely internal operational questions once local use, local knowledge, and local concern entered the frame with force. Consultation became an operational variable. The route was no longer just a line of efficiency. It was a line of contest.

This is why local knowledge deserves attention not as folklore appended to technical planning, but as a genuine source of risk intelligence. People who live with Arctic waters often understand practical features that are difficult to capture fully in standard project files: where seasonal use concentrates, when conditions become less predictable than historical summaries imply, which stretches of coast carry more consequence in an emergency, where communications may fail in inconvenient ways, or how vessel timing may intersect with activities not visible in a generic risk matrix. A consultation process that allows this knowledge to modify scheduling, routing, reporting, or standby logic can produce a safer operation in the most practical sense: it reduces the range of things the operator has not yet imagined.

A brief example shows how that reduction works. Imagine a vessel service planned around an apparently efficient corridor and timetable. Community input then reveals that the proposed period overlaps with a locally important seasonal use pattern or that a fallback anchorage assumed by the operator is less realistic than the planners believed under certain conditions. Nothing in that revelation requires romantic language about traditional wisdom defeating science. It simply means the original plan contained an uncertainty that local experience could narrow. A revised route, an adjusted timing window, or a different standby assumption may cost convenience. It can also reduce the chance that an ordinary disruption becomes a conflict-laden incident. Knowledge changes exposure.

This is one reason consultation can function as a risk-control measure. Insurers, charterers, and financiers may not use the language of community relations first, but they care deeply about the consequences of unresolved conflict. A project facing sustained local distrust is more likely to encounter public challenge, political pressure, reputational strain, delay, and a harsher reading of later mishaps. A project whose process has produced credible engagement and visibly altered planning where appropriate often appears more governable, even when the underlying physical risks remain substantial. The difference is not sentimental. It affects insurability, scheduling confidence, and the willingness of other institutions to stand behind the venture when conditions tighten.

Still, a limitation must be admitted. Consultation is not a magical solvent. Communities are not monolithic, and local views may conflict. Some engagements are burdened by historical distrust too deep to be repaired within one project cycle. Operators may encounter demands that are commercially or operationally hard to reconcile with one another. There are also situations in which consultation is performed carefully and conflict still arrives. It would be naive to present process quality as a guarantee of social peace or underwriting comfort.

And yet that limitation only clarifies the value of the process. Because perfect agreement is rare, what matters is whether the operator has reduced avoidable conflict and avoidable uncertainty. A well-run consultation process does not eliminate disagreement; it often makes disagreement more legible, better bounded, and less likely to erupt as surprise. That matters enormously in Arctic trades, where surprise is expensive. Markets can often live with known friction more easily than with unresolved doubt that may later convert into delay, protest, tightened conditions, or emergency-response weakness. Process, then, is not mainly about consensus. It is about governing uncertainty before uncertainty governs the voyage.

This is also why consultation reshapes contingency planning rather than sitting beside it. Once operators begin to understand that engagement affects the credibility of emergency assumptions, route logic, and local support expectations, consultation stops being a public-affairs exercise and becomes part of the operational file. Meeting records, route revisions, response adjustments, seasonal limitations, and communications protocols all start to reflect what the process has disclosed. Over time, these adjustments can harden into market expectations. What began as one operator's prudence becomes another operator's baseline requirement. Engagement becomes a quiet source of governance.

The image that best captures this is the margin on a chart. The original route may look neat, direct, and technically defensible. Consultation writes in the margins: not here at this time, not this fallback point, not this assumption about access, not this sequence without a stronger response arrangement. Those markings can look inconvenient to a planner seeking efficiency. They may also be the difference between a project that merely passes legal review and one that remains commercially and socially survivable when the first disruption arrives. A chart without margins is usually a chart that has not been read against the place itself.

The harder question, then, is not whether consultation can slow a project or complicate a timetable. Plainly it can. The harder question is whether operators and markets have learned to treat that complication as wasted time, or as one of the few practical ways to turn local scrutiny into better routing, better contingency logic, and a lower chance that the next Arctic incident will become expensive not only because of what happened on the water, but because of what the process failed to hear beforehand.

Environmental monitoring and evidentiary expectations

In March 1989, after the *Exxon Valdez* grounded in Alaska, one of the most enduring difficulties was not simply the scale of the visible damage. It was the struggle over what could be known with confidence about conditions before the spill, the spread afterwards, and the extent to which later claims about environmental effect rested on measured change rather than on assumption, memory, or political urgency. The oil was obvious. The baseline was not.

That distinction matters acutely in Arctic operations because remote environments punish evidentiary weakness. A casualty in a heavily studied, densely trafficked, and regularly sampled region may still generate fierce dispute, but the argument usually begins from a thicker body of prior information. In the Arctic, operators often work in places where baseline data are thinner, seasonal variability sharper, and the practical burden of collecting reliable observations much heavier. When something goes wrong, parties do not only argue about what happened. They argue about what was already true before the event and what can properly be attributed to it afterwards. The notebook matters.

This is why environmental monitoring deserves to be treated as more than a scientific courtesy or a regulatory afterthought. Monitoring commitments become part of compliance narratives because they show whether an operator took the evidentiary burden of working in a fragile and contested setting seriously before trouble arrived. A project with coherent baseline sampling, ongoing observation, and credible methods can tell a different story about its own discipline than one that relied on generic assumptions and retrospective reconstruction. Underwriters, regulators, communities, and counterparties read that difference closely. The existence of evidence is not the whole argument, but it changes the tone of every later argument.

The central point is simple and often resisted: evidence is a form of resilience. Operators tend to see monitoring first as cost, delay, and administrative drag. In one sense it is all three. Sampling programmes, reporting obligations, seasonal surveys, data management, expert review, and public-facing disclosure all impose burden before any revenue or operational emergency compels them. Yet in Arctic settings that upfront burden frequently buys something more valuable than tidy compliance. It buys a narrower field of dispute. If an incident occurs, better baseline data can reduce the space in which exaggerated, opportunistic, or simply confused claims expand. The record holds.

A named example helps clarify the stakes. After the *Exxon Valdez* spill, the force of subsequent legal and political argument did not arise only from the disaster itself. It also arose from the challenge of describing environmental consequences with the precision that a courtroom, an insurer, or a serious public inquiry would eventually demand. The relevance here is not that every Arctic project faces catastrophe on that scale. It is that highly visible northern incidents quickly expose the weakness of thin baseline knowledge. Once that weakness has been exposed in one generation of cases, later operators are judged more harshly if they seem content to enter sensitive environments with less evidence than the seriousness of the setting requires.

Monitoring also matters because it changes what compliance means in practice. A licence, approval, or operating permission may appear to rest on formal adherence to technical and procedural conditions. Over time, however, many projects discover that their monitoring record becomes one of the most important pieces of their compliance identity. Did the operator gather the data it promised? Did it keep the methods consistent enough that later comparison is meaningful? Did it report adverse or ambiguous findings promptly, or only the information that supported its preferred narrative? Did it respond to anomalous results with investigation and adjustment, or with defensive minimisation? In Arctic contexts, where public trust is often fragile and institutional memory long, these questions are not secondary. They shape whether compliance is understood as real or merely documentary.

This is one reason monitoring commitments can migrate from the environmental side of a project into its insurance life. Underwriters are not environmental tribunals, but they care deeply about the conditions under which disputes grow or narrow after an incident. An operator that can show robust baseline work and credible follow-up monitoring appears more governable because it has already reduced one major source of post-loss uncertainty. A company with thin or generic environmental evidence may face a harsher reading not only from communities or regulators, but from the insurance market itself. The insurer sees a higher chance that any future incident will produce a sprawling factual contest about causation, extent, and pre-existing conditions. That contest is expensive even before liability is decided.

A brief example makes this plain. Imagine two operators proposing similar northern projects. Both meet the basic legal threshold. Both offer response plans and technical assurances. The first has invested in site-specific monitoring sufficient to describe ordinary seasonal variation and to identify which changes would genuinely look abnormal if an incident occurred. The second relies largely on general regional information, public datasets of mixed relevance, and a promise to monitor more closely once operations begin. On paper, the difference may look like the difference between expensive diligence and pragmatic efficiency. In a claims setting, it becomes something else entirely. The first operator can defend a narrative with evidence. The second must begin by arguing about the absence of evidence itself.

This is why better baseline data can reduce argument after an incident even if it raises burden before one. The reduction does not lie in abolishing disagreement. Disputes will still arise over methods, interpretation, significance, and causation. The reduction lies in changing the quality of those disputes. When parties share a thicker factual record, they are more likely to argue over degree than over existence, over attribution than over raw possibility. That may sound like a modest gain. In insurance, liability, and public controversy, it is a major one. Broad uncertainty is where severity grows.

A second named example shows how the same logic can work outside the context of a single shipping casualty. In the controversy around Baffinland's proposed shipping expansion associated with the Mary River project in Nunavut, the practical force of monitoring and baseline evidence lay not only in scientific interest, but in whether the project could defend its own claims about impact, adaptation, and uncertainty against sceptical scrutiny. The point here is not to settle that debate. It is to show that in Arctic operations, environmental evidence quickly becomes part of the commercial architecture. Weak data do not remain a scientific problem. They become a financing, reputational, and insurability problem as well.

This evidentiary role becomes even sharper once a claim is made. Claims defensibility depends not only on whether the operator complied formally, but on whether it can demonstrate, with contemporaneous and credible records, what conditions were before the incident, what changed afterwards, and what chain of causation is realistically sustainable. Without that foundation, every party with an interest in widening the loss field gains more room to manoeuvre. Regulators may press broader interpretations. Communities may distrust narrow ones. Opponents may suggest that absence of evidence reflects absence of care. Insurers and clubs, meanwhile, face a file whose factual instability may lengthen adjustment, increase legal spend, complicate recovery action, and harden the market's later view of similar projects. A poor monitoring record therefore damages the present case and the next renewal simultaneously.

Still, a limitation deserves frank acknowledgement. Monitoring is not neutral magic. Data can be partial, methods contested, seasons atypical, and interpretation politically loaded. Better evidence does not guarantee consensus, nor does a large monitoring programme necessarily mean that the operator is wiser or more honest. In some cases, more data can generate more arguments because it creates more points of methodological or interpretive attack. It would be naive to suggest that monitoring dissolves conflict.

And yet that limitation only strengthens the broader argument. Because data can be contested, the quality, continuity, and transparency of the monitoring effort matter even more. Serious operators do not monitor because they expect everyone to agree with them afterwards. They monitor because without a credible evidentiary base, disagreement becomes structurally unbounded. The dispute then expands beyond the facts of the incident into a more corrosive question: whether the operator ever took the burden of proof seriously enough to deserve confidence in the first place. In Arctic settings, that is often the more dangerous accusation.

This is why environmental monitoring has become part of the compliance narrative rather than an attachment to it. It shows whether the operator understands that social licence, claims management, and insurance confidence all depend on something sturdier than assertion. A company that monitors well signals that it expects to be judged later and wants that judgment to rest on more than rhetoric. A company that treats monitoring as a reluctant box-ticking exercise signals the opposite. Markets notice the difference. So do communities, scientists, and tribunals.

The image that best captures the issue is the notebook. Before operations begin, it looks like burden: field notes, sampling records, seasonal observations, chain-of-custody discipline, reports no one outside the project team seems eager to read. After an incident, it becomes shelter. It does not stop the storm, but it gives the operator somewhere firmer to stand while others widen claims, question assumptions, and test the truth of what had once been promised in easy language. Where the notebook is thin, the argument spreads. Where it is thick and credible, the argument may still be fierce, but it becomes harder to invent.

The harder question, then, is not whether environmental monitoring costs money, time, and managerial patience. Plainly it does. The harder question is whether Arctic operators truly understand that the cost of not knowing - or not being able to prove what they knew before the incident - is usually much higher once insurers, communities, regulators, and claimants all begin asking the same unforgiving question: compared with what, exactly, did the damage occur?

When activism meets underwriting

In September 2013, the *Arctic Sunrise* was seized by Russian authorities after a Greenpeace protest in the Pechora Sea, and a lesson that underwriters already knew in fragments became impossible to ignore in public: an Arctic operation does not need to suffer a conventional marine casualty before it becomes harder to insure. A campaign, an arrest, a government response, a surge of scrutiny, and the sudden transformation of a technical project into a symbolic contest can all alter market appetite. The hull may be untouched. The file may already be burning.

That is the starting point for understanding how activism meets underwriting. Insurance markets are often described as if they respond only to expected physical loss, measurable liability, and the familiar arithmetic of claims. They do respond to those things. But underwriters also read controversy, administrative burden, and reputational exposure as part of the total cost of carrying a risk. In Arctic contexts, where projects are highly visible, politically charged, and easily narrativised as tests of institutional seriousness, this wider reading becomes especially important. A campaign can change the meaning of a voyage long before it changes the law.

The point is not that underwriters secretly moonlight as political theorists. The point is that controversy has practical consequences which markets must carry. Public campaigns can generate pressure on terminals, financiers, charterers, and public authorities. They can sharpen disclosure burdens, increase the chance of regulatory intervention, lengthen claims handling, complicate renewals, damage brands, and push insurers into a posture where even technically manageable risks begin to look administratively exhausting. In that sense, activism enters underwriting not as abstract ideology but as operational friction. The poster reaches the policy.

This matters because Arctic insurance sits inside a relatively thin and reputation-sensitive market. Capacity is not infinite. Institutional memory is long. High-visibility events travel quickly through brokers, clubs, reinsurers, and underwriters who may never have to agree politically in order to share one commercial judgement: this risk now comes with more trouble attached to it than the underlying engineering alone would suggest. A public campaign does not need to persuade every actor that the project is unsound. It needs only to raise the expected burden of standing behind it. Once that burden rises, terms harden.

A named example shows how quickly this can happen. The *Arctic Sunrise* affair in September 2013 was not a standard marine loss, yet it demonstrated that Arctic operations can become lightning rods for arguments about sovereignty, environmental legitimacy, protest rights, and the acceptable boundaries of industrial presence. The market lesson was not confined to one vessel or one episode. Insurers and related institutions were reminded that a controversial northern operation may require them to manage not only claims risk, but attention risk: more scrutiny, more internal review, more public explanation, more compliance checking, more sensitivity around brand association, and more concern that one file will become an emblem. That kind of burden is difficult to model and easy to resent.

This is where reputational tolerance enters the picture. Every insurer has some capacity to carry reputational exposure, just as it has some capacity to carry financial exposure. The two are related but not identical. A technically sound project may become unattractive if the insurer expects it to trigger repeated questions from stakeholders, board-level discomfort, unfavourable press attention, activist targeting, or pressure from investors and counterparties who would rather not be linked to the controversy. In Arctic settings, these effects are magnified because the projects often carry symbolic weight beyond their immediate economics. A vessel or installation can become shorthand for a larger argument about climate, extraction, local rights, or corporate seriousness. Once that happens, underwriting is no longer only about the expected loss event. It is also about whether the insurer wants to be in the photograph.

This does not mean every campaign produces hard market retreat. Underwriters are perfectly capable of distinguishing noise from structural pressure. Yet the distinction is not always stable, and that instability matters. A protest that appears theatrical at first may reveal genuine gaps in consultation, monitoring, emergency planning, or political support. A campaign that seems legally irrelevant may nonetheless raise the prospect of stricter permit conditions, harder contract negotiations, or administrative delay. A public incident may prompt reinsurers to ask broader questions about cluster risk, governance quality, or how much explanation the primary market is likely to owe its own stakeholders if the project remains on risk. Sentiment can become structure with surprising speed.

A brief example makes the commercial pathway clearer. Imagine a northern project with technically adequate vessels, current permits, and reasonable insurance terms. A public campaign then draws sustained attention to the route, the communities affected, and the operator's emergency assumptions. No law changes overnight. No court halts the project. Yet terminals begin asking harder questions, charterers seek more protective clauses, financiers want reassurance, and the insurer starts to worry that any later delay, spill scare, or administrative misstep will be interpreted through the controversy already attached to the venture. At renewal, the underwriter may not say, "we are reacting to activism". It may ask for more documentation, narrower cover, stronger exclusions, or a higher price for the same nominal risk. Politics has entered the market through governance burden.

This is one reason sudden tightening after public events can feel mysterious to operators who think only in casualty terms. They ask what loss event has occurred to justify the change. The market may answer, in effect, that the risk now includes a wider field of plausible difficulty. If a project has become controversial, the underwriter may expect more reporting complexity, more intense oversight, more sensitivity in claims handling, more reputational downside from association, and more uncertainty about how calmly institutions will behave if something small goes wrong later. None of these elements may sit comfortably inside a conventional actuarial box. All of them are commercially real.

A second named example helps place this in a broader pattern. After the *Exxon Valdez* disaster in March 1989, the market did not simply reprice pollution and tanker exposure in northern waters. It also absorbed a lesson about public memory and symbolic consequence. Once a visible Arctic or near-Arctic event becomes shorthand for institutional failure, later projects are judged against that memory whether or not their own technical circumstances are better. Activism works on this same terrain. It seeks to make one operation stand for more than itself. When it succeeds, underwriters are pushed to price not only the physical risk, but the possibility that the insured venture has become a reputational proxy for a larger political argument.

Still, a limitation deserves acknowledgment. Not every activist campaign reveals a hidden underwriting truth, and not every high-profile incident should lead insurers to treat controversy itself as evidence of unsound operations. Public campaigns can simplify, select facts strategically, or impose symbolic meanings that exceed the actual structure of the risk. An insurer that reacts too mechanically may end up mistaking noise for genuine exposure and penalising disciplined operators for the visibility of the sector rather than for the weakness of the file. Markets can overreact. They sometimes do.

And yet this limitation sharpens rather than weakens the central argument. Because the line between noise and structural pressure is hard to fix in advance, controversy increases uncertainty. Underwriters do not need to agree with every activist claim in order to become more cautious. They need only recognise that activism can trigger wider scrutiny, raise the administrative cost of carrying the risk, and narrow the room for forgiving interpretation if something goes wrong later. The result is that even where physical risk remains broadly stable, reputational tolerance may fall. Once that happens, pricing and wording begin to move.

This is why activism matters to underwriting most powerfully when it intersects with existing institutional doubts. A campaign is far more likely to bite where consultation has been thin, monitoring weak, emergency assumptions generic, or community opposition already sharp. Under those conditions, activism does not invent the market's anxiety. It concentrates it. It gives outside shape to worries the file already contained in quieter language. The underwriter then reacts not merely to the campaign, but to the way the campaign exposes that the project's governance may be thinner than its formal legality suggested. Public pressure becomes evidentiary pressure.

The broader consequence is that Arctic projects cannot treat public controversy as something external to insurability. If a venture becomes hard to defend in reputational terms, the insurer may remain on risk only at a higher price, under narrower cover, or with a lower appetite for discretion once claims, delays, or ambiguities arise. The project is still technically insurable. It is no longer insurable on the same social terms.

That difference can decide whether a venture remains commercially viable or becomes one more example of Arctic expansion slowed not by ice or steel, but by the cost of being too publicly difficult to carry.

The image that best captures this is the photograph. Some risks arrive as files. Others arrive as files with cameras pointed at them. Underwriters understand that difference instinctively. A controversial Arctic operation is not just a technical proposition sitting quietly in a portfolio. It is a proposition that may require explanation to boards, investors, journalists, civil society, or internal governance committees if the next event goes badly or merely noisily. The extra burden may never appear in the policy heading. It is still being priced.

The harder question, then, is not whether activism can unsettle Arctic insurance markets. Plainly it can. The harder question is how much controversy a market is willing to absorb before it concludes that the expected loss is no longer the whole story - and that the real danger of standing behind a project lies in the possibility that the next public event, however small in physical terms, will demand a level of institutional defence that the insurer no longer wishes to provide.

Chapter 14

Geopolitics, Sanctions, and Security Externalities

What happens when a vessel is technically seaworthy, commercially wanted, and physically capable of the route, yet the voyage still begins to fail before it leaves the dock? The answer often lies in a category of risk that does not announce itself with ice on the bow or damage in the engine room. It appears in a sanction screen that takes longer than expected, in a policy clause that now carries a sharper edge, in a financing committee made uneasy by the strategic profile of an asset, or in an insurer's sudden reluctance to explain why ordinary cover no longer feels ordinary. The cargo may be routine. The context is not.

This is the harder commercial truth about Arctic expansion. Projects in the far north do not move only through geography and engineering. They move through a political atmosphere dense with state rivalry, legal sensitivity, reputational caution, and the persistent possibility that a transaction which looked merely commercial yesterday may be read as strategically significant tomorrow. Arctic operations often inherit these pressures even when the operator has no geopolitical ambition of its own. A resupply voyage, a terminal service agreement, a financing structure, or an insurance renewal can all become sites where broader tension enters through procedure rather than proclamation. The map is no longer the whole story.

That matters because geopolitics rarely arrives in commercial life as a dramatic banner. More often it enters quietly, through the wording of exclusions, the scope of cancellation rights, the appetite for disclosure, the intensity of counterparty screening, and the growing discomfort attached to assets that seem capable of serving more than one purpose. The result is a market in which legality, insurability, and strategic perception begin to lean on one another. A project may remain lawful and still become awkward to support. It may remain technically unchanged and still attract a harsher reading because the world around it has changed the meaning of ordinary transactions.

The central tension lies there. Commercial actors prefer to separate routine logistics from high politics, yet the Arctic resists that separation. Shipping lanes, port interfaces, data flows, infrastructure partnerships, and insurance structures all sit close to issues of state concern, sanctions risk, contested attribution, and suspicion about dual use. Once that proximity sharpens, the market begins to behave differently. Underwriters do not only ask what may be lost physically. They ask what may become difficult to defend institutionally, what may attract administrative burden, and what may place private firms uncomfortably near public disputes they never intended to arbitrate. A policy can become a weather vane.

The stakes are practical rather than theatrical. Political risk inside insurance wordings can alter whether a vessel remains covered through a period of tension or whether an operator suddenly discovers that cancellation language, exclusions, or heightened disclosure demands have narrowed the space for routine trade. Sanctions compliance can slow deals, complicate payments, and make ordinary documentation feel insufficient because the cost of error now includes penalties, reputational injury, and the possibility of being seen as careless around sensitive counterparties. Security incidents with uncertain attribution can make claims handling and route planning more conservative because ambiguity is hard to insure gracefully. None of this requires open conflict to matter. Friction is enough.

The longer consequence is even more important. Once strategic sensitivity enters the underwriting and financing imagination, the market begins to teach itself new habits. Assets near certain routes or facilities acquire a different profile. Partnerships that once looked commercially rational attract sharper scrutiny. A project labelled strategic, fairly or unfairly, may find its timeline altered by questions that have little to do with its engineering merit and much to do with how others fear it may be perceived. In that environment, insurers and other private actors can begin to function as practical limits on Arctic activity, not because they wish to make foreign policy, but because they are managing capacity, reputation, and uncertainty under pressure.

That is the path of inquiry ahead. The pressure first appears in the fine structure of commercial wordings, where political uncertainty is absorbed into exclusions, cancellation mechanisms, and disclosure logic that can quietly reshape the meaning of cover. It then enters sanctions compliance, where legality itself begins to act as an operational drag on timing and documentation. From there, the focus shifts to incidents whose attribution remains uncertain, making evidence, routing, and claims treatment more cautious than the physical event alone would justify. It then widens again to the problem of strategic infrastructure and dual-use perception, before returning to the market itself and the uncomfortable possibility that private insurance decisions can end up constraining Arctic development in ways no state clearly ordered and no single actor fully controls.

A useful image here is the customs desk. A voyage arrives thinking of itself as cargo, tonnage, route, and timetable. The desk asks another set of questions. Who is involved? What else could this asset be for? What legal regime now shadows this transaction? What if the incident cannot be clearly attributed? What if support itself becomes controversial? The Arctic has increasingly acquired that desk-like quality. Transactions are inspected not only for efficiency and safety, but for the strategic signals they may carry, intentionally or otherwise.

The harder question, then, is not whether geopolitics can intrude on Arctic commerce. Plainly it can. The harder question is how to recognise the moment when it has already ceased to be an external backdrop and has begun to reorganise the commercial file itself, so that what looks like ordinary insurance, routine screening, or prudent caution is in fact the private market's way of deciding how close it is still willing to stand to a region where law, strategy, and logistics no longer keep politely separate from one another.

Political risk inside commercial wordings

In September 2013, the *Arctic Sunrise* was seized by Russian authorities after a Greenpeace protest in the Pechora Sea, and one lesson moved quickly through the insurance and shipping world: a vessel can remain physically intact while its commercial risk profile changes abruptly because politics has entered the file. No hull breach is required. No cargo loss is necessary. A voyage that looked routine in technical terms can become harder to insure, harder to finance, and harder to defend simply because the political environment around it has shifted. The policy starts to speak differently.

That shift rarely arrives with theatrical clarity. Political uncertainty does not usually announce itself in the language of grand strategy when it enters marine insurance. It appears in narrower ways: an exclusion with sharper geographic or causal edges, a cancellation clause that now feels less theoretical, a request for fuller disclosure about counterparties, routes, cargoes, ownership links, communications arrangements, or state-facing permits. The wording remains commercial. The pressure beneath it is not purely commercial at all. In Arctic trades, where sovereignty questions, sanctions sensitivity, strategic rivalry, and heightened state attention sit close to ordinary logistics, this pressure can change the shape of cover long before it changes the ship.

That is why policy structure deserves to be read as geopolitical signal rather than as mere technical drafting. Insurers do not need to issue political statements in order to register political concern. They can register it through form. A policy that once treated a northern route as an ordinary trading extension may later surround it with more conditional language, broader rights to review or cancel, or more intrusive informational demands. The operator may still be offered cover, but the cover now carries evidence that the market sees the surrounding environment as less stable, less interpretable, or less defensible than before. Politics has entered the contract through caution.

Exclusions are the clearest example because they allow insurers to remain in the market while quietly redefining what they are willing to carry. A political or quasi-political exclusion does not always name a grand theory of conflict. It may instead carve out losses arising from state action, seizure, detention, sanctions-related breach, hostile or ambiguous interference, or circumstances that sit uncomfortably between conventional marine peril and public power. The key point is not doctrinal precision. It is behavioural consequence. Once such wording sharpens, operators understand that certain outcomes previously imagined as extraordinary background risk now sit closer to the centre of the underwriting imagination. The map changes in the margins first.

Cancellation clauses work in a related but subtler way. They remind all parties that the insurer's willingness to remain bound may depend on a changing political environment rather than on vessel condition alone. In easier markets, cancellation rights can feel remote, a standard contractual contingency rarely expected to matter during ordinary trading. In Arctic settings marked by strategic sensitivity, that same clause becomes a practical device for managing a world in which sanctions, diplomatic deterioration, administrative pressure, or changing risk perceptions can move faster than annual renewal cycles. The insurer is not saying the voyage is prohibited. It is saying the commitment to support the voyage may itself be conditional on events beyond the operator's direct control. Time becomes political.

Heightened disclosure demands complete the picture because they shift the burden of legibility onto the insured. Once political uncertainty rises, underwriters want to know more and know it sooner. They ask about ownership chains, chartering structures, cargo end use, ports of call, transhipment arrangements, service providers, affiliations, routing logic, and the identity of counterparties whose names might once have passed with little comment. The request for detail is not administrative fussiness. It reflects a fear that a routine logistics chain may conceal political exposure that only becomes visible after a public event, a compliance inquiry, or a dispute over attribution. Better disclosure is the market's attempt to avoid being surprised by the political life of commerce.

A named example helps clarify how this works beyond a single protest incident. After Russia's annexation of Crimea in 2014, marine and trade-related insurance markets across various sectors faced a changed environment in which sanction sensitivity, territorial dispute, and state action began to reshape how certain voyages, counterparties, and regions were read. The Arctic lesson is not that every northern transaction became suddenly comparable to a sanctions flashpoint. It is that once the political environment hardens, commercial wordings begin to absorb that hardening quickly. Operators may still be moving ordinary goods. The market is already asking whether the route, the counterparty chain, or the legal exposure can still be treated as ordinary.

This matters because Arctic geopolitics affects even routine logistics. Fuel deliveries, research support, mining-related shipments, terminal services, equipment transfers, and seasonal resupply may all appear operationally banal in isolation. Yet in politically attentive regions, the question is never only what the ship is doing. It is also where, for whom, through which institutional chain, under what legal climate, and with what possibility that a later development will recast today's neutral service as tomorrow's problematic transaction. The same voyage can therefore be read through two lenses at once: logistical in the operator's office, geopolitical in the underwriter's file.

This dual reading has practical consequences for pricing and access. A risk may harden not because expected physical loss has worsened, but because the administrative and reputational cost of carrying the risk has increased. If the insurer expects more internal review, more board-level attention, more screening work, more document verification, or a higher chance that a claim will be complicated by state action or politically charged dispute, the premium may rise or the wording may narrow even if the vessel's technical characteristics remain unchanged. Political uncertainty behaves like a severity multiplier because it enlarges the number of ways a routine problem can become difficult to resolve. Ambiguity fattens the claim.

A brief example makes the mechanism concrete. Imagine an operator conducting a northern support voyage that would once have attracted standard scrutiny. The vessel is sound, the route familiar, and the cargo commercially unremarkable. Then the political context surrounding one coastal area, one ownership connection, or one service provider becomes more sensitive. At renewal or placement, the operator is asked for fuller beneficial ownership information, more exact route declarations, clearer statements about end users and service chains, and acceptance of tighter rights for the insurer to review or withdraw if the environment shifts. Nothing in the ship's steel has changed. Yet the operator is now carrying a form of political volatility inside what still outwardly looks like routine marine cover.

This is why common institutional mechanisms matter more than grand jurisdictional arguments for the commercial reader. One need not settle every disputed question of public law to see how politics enters insurance. The mechanisms are enough. Exclusions narrow the field of protection. Cancellation clauses shorten the insurer's horizon of commitment. Disclosure demands widen the operator's duty to explain itself. Together, they produce a structure in which the policy becomes an instrument for managing geopolitical unease without needing to declare a geopolitical doctrine. The market does not have to name the storm to reef the sail.

Still, a limitation should be faced directly. Not every sharpening of wording reflects a deep or coherent geopolitical judgement. Sometimes markets overreact. Sometimes they import broader political anxiety into transactions whose actual exposure is more modest than the wording suggests. At other times the new clause is partly symbolic, a way of signalling prudence to reinsurers, compliance teams, or internal governance committees rather than a measured response to the precise facts of the trade. It would be naive to imagine that every exclusion or disclosure request is perfectly calibrated to the real political risk on the water.

And yet this limitation strengthens rather than weakens the central point. Because markets are uncertain, they protect themselves through form. The policy wording becomes a place where uncertainty is translated into manageable structure. Even if the calibration is imperfect, the effect on operators is real. They must document more, disclose more, route more carefully, and recognise that a once-routine northern movement may now be treated as a higher-order institutional question. Geopolitics is therefore not only a matter for diplomats and ministries. It becomes operational through the documents required to move cargo and sustain cover.

This dynamic also explains why policy language can move ahead of visible political events. Underwriters often respond not only to what has happened, but to what they fear may become harder to interpret if something happens later. A seizure, detention, sanctions inquiry, administrative intervention, or disputed incident in a politically tense northern setting may produce claims problems far larger than the underlying physical event would justify. The insurer therefore writes defensively before the incident occurs. To the operator, the new language may feel premature or excessive. To the market, it is an attempt to avoid discovering too late that an apparently ordinary Arctic trade had already become politically brittle.

The image that best captures the process is the change of font in a contract. The voyage description remains. The insured value remains. The route may remain. Yet somewhere in the clauses the lettering grows denser, more conditional, more alert to interruption by forces not visible in the engine room or on the chart. That shift is easy to dismiss as paperwork. It is nothing of the kind. It is the commercial trace of a political reading.

The harder question, then, is not whether Arctic geopolitics can affect marine insurance. Plainly it can. The harder question is how early an operator can recognise that the politics have already entered the file - not through a public announcement or a state warning, but through the quiet rearrangement of exclusions, cancellation rights, and disclosure duties that tell the careful reader the market no longer regards routine logistics in that region as quite routine at all.

Sanctions compliance as operational friction

In 2014, after Russia's annexation of Crimea, sanctions risk stopped looking like a specialist legal concern that could be managed somewhere far from the moving parts of ordinary commerce. It became a daily operational problem for banks, insurers, commodity traders, shipowners, brokers, and service providers trying to decide whether a transaction that looked commercially routine might carry hidden legal exposure. In Arctic logistics, where routes, assets, counterparties, and state interests often sit unusually close together, that lesson has remained sharp. The cargo may be ordinary. The paperwork is not.

That is the starting point for understanding sanctions compliance as operational friction. Sanctions do not only prohibit. They slow, complicate, and unsettle. A voyage may remain physically feasible, commercially desirable, and technically insurable, yet become harder to execute because every stage of the transaction now requires more proof, more screening, more internal sign-off, and more caution about who ultimately benefits, controls, or touches the deal. The ship can move faster than the file. In sensitive northern contexts, that mismatch matters because timing, weather windows, berth availability, and seasonal limits often punish delay more severely than in easier trades.

This is why legality becomes an operational constraint rather than a background condition. In ordinary commercial imagination, legality is often treated as a threshold question: either the transaction is lawful or it is not. Sanctions compliance in practice rarely feels so clean. Institutions must test beneficial ownership, contractual chains, payment routes, service providers, ports, cargo use, and links that may be formal, indirect, or politically sensitive. Each question can generate requests for documents, clarifications, certifications, and further review. Even where the final answer is yes, the process of getting to yes can alter schedules, pricing, and counterparties' appetite for involvement. Law enters the voyage as drag.

The most obvious form of drag is documentary burden. Once sanctions sensitivity rises, routine commercial materials stop being enough. A counterparty's name is no longer treated as a neutral commercial fact but as the beginning of an inquiry. Who owns the entity? Through what chain? Has the ownership changed recently? Who finances the operation? Which banks will touch the payment? What flags, ports, agents, charterers, or subcontractors sit downstream from the deal? Arctic operations often draw harder scrutiny because infrastructure is thin, ownership structures can be layered, state links may be closer, and the strategic meaning of apparently ordinary services may be less easy to dismiss. The request for more paper is therefore not clerical excess. It is a form of institutional self-defence.

This matters because compliance risk can be priced much like physical risk when the penalties and reputational stakes are high. An insurer, financier, or service provider does not need to expect a fine with actuarial precision to behave cautiously. It is enough that a misstep could produce legal exposure, public criticism, internal governance trouble, or regulatory attention severe enough to outweigh the revenue from the transaction. In that setting, sanctions compliance begins to resemble a peril category of its own. It may not puncture a hull, but it can still delay a voyage, collapse a payment chain, trigger policy review, exclude a counterparty, or make a commercially viable project too awkward to carry on workable terms. The screen becomes part of the risk model.

A named example helps illuminate the wider mechanism. After the Crimea-related sanctions environment hardened in 2014, maritime and trade institutions did not merely update legal memos. They changed workflows. Counterparties connected, directly or indirectly, to politically sensitive jurisdictions or ownership chains began to attract sharper review. Transactions that might once have cleared with ordinary due diligence now required additional certifications, legal review, and internal escalation. The Arctic relevance is plain. In regions where state presence, strategic infrastructure, and politically sensitive actors often overlap with routine logistics, compliance scrutiny does not remain a one-off legal hurdle. It becomes part of the cadence of operations.

This cadence affects insurance directly. Insurers are not simply asking whether a loss might occur at sea. They are asking whether the risk can be bound inside a transaction they are comfortable touching at all. A technically strong Arctic operator may still find that cover is slower to place or narrower than expected because sanctions-sensitive links in the wider transaction chain have made the file harder to clear. Enhanced disclosure clauses, rights to cancel or review, stronger warranties about compliance, or demands for updated counterparty information may all appear. The policy is still marine insurance. It now carries a compliance pulse.

A brief example shows how counterparties may be screened more intensely in sensitive regions. Imagine a vessel performing a seemingly routine support service in northern waters. The owner is sound, the vessel classed, the route operationally familiar. Yet one service provider in the chain has ownership links that require closer examination, one port call raises questions about downstream exposure, and one payment route brings an additional bank into the review. None of these issues necessarily bars the voyage. Taken together, they slow approvals, delay contract finalisation, and make insurers or financiers ask for fuller assurances before they commit. By the time the file clears, the transaction has already absorbed cost, uncertainty, and lost time. Physical risk has not changed. Operational risk has.

This is one reason sanctions compliance is so often underestimated by technically minded operators. They assume that if they have no intention of evasion and no obvious prohibited conduct in mind, the compliance burden should remain modest. That is not how institutions exposed to sanctions risk usually behave. They do not only price intent. They price uncertainty, complexity, and the consequences of being wrong. Where the ownership picture is opaque, the strategic context tense, or the transaction chain long, caution expands even in the absence of any proven breach. The cost arises from the need to prove cleanliness, not merely from the danger of deliberate contamination.

A second named example helps show how this becomes a wider market habit rather than a narrow legal response. After the *Arctic Sunrise* affair in September 2013, insurers and related market actors were reminded that politically sensitive Arctic operations can become administratively and reputationally difficult even without conventional marine loss. The relevance here is not that sanctions and protest are identical. It is that both teach institutions to distrust simplicity in the Arctic file. Once an operation becomes entangled with wider political meaning, screening intensifies, tolerance falls, and administrative burden becomes part of the underwriting and financing calculation. The legal question and the reputational question begin to travel together.

Still, a limitation deserves acknowledgement. Compliance review is not always a sign that a transaction is inherently improper or that the operator is facing extraordinary danger. Many files clear after careful screening. Some institutions over-screen or repeat work inefficiently. In certain cases the burden reflects internal caution rather than genuine proximity to prohibited conduct. It would be a mistake to treat every additional request for documentation as evidence that the underlying operation is strategically suspect. Sometimes the drag is the price of institutional nervousness rather than of material legal hazard.

And yet that limitation reinforces the central point. Because sanctions risk is judged through institutional caution as much as through bright-line prohibition, the burden of proving acceptability becomes part of the operating environment. A transaction can be lawful and still commercially weakened by the time and cost required to show that it is lawful. In Arctic settings, where delays propagate easily into missed windows, strained counterparties, and harder insurance placement, this burden matters more than it might elsewhere. The friction is cumulative. One extra review can become one missed berth, one delayed premium confirmation, one revised charter timetable, or one underwriter now reading the whole venture as more brittle than before.

This is also why compliance risk can harden market structure over time. Institutions learn which regions, counterparties, service chains, and asset types repeatedly generate difficult screening exercises. They then respond by asking for more up front, narrowing appetite, or preferring operators whose ownership and contractual arrangements are easier to read. Complexity itself becomes a quasi-peril. Projects with cleaner structures, stronger disclosure habits, and more transparent chains enjoy smoother passage through the legal machinery around them. Others discover that the compliance burden, though not formally prohibitive, effectively taxes them out of flexibility. Governance emerges through repetition.

The image that best captures the process is the checkpoint. The vessel may be ready to sail, the cargo ready to move, the crew ready to work. Yet the transaction pauses at successive desks where people who will never see the ice ask whether the names, links, banks, ports, documents, and contractual routes ahead can still be defended if questioned later. Most Arctic operators think first about moving through physical chokepoints. Increasingly, they must also move through legal ones. Those chokepoints are slower, quieter, and often just as decisive.

The harder question, then, is not whether sanctions compliance can complicate Arctic operations. Plainly it can. The harder question is how much of the real cost of a northern venture now lies not in the ship's exposure to weather or ice, but in the accumulation of legal frictions that arise when every counterparty, payment path, and supporting service must be made legible enough for institutions to believe that routine logistics in a strategically sensitive region are still routine after all.

Security incidents and contested attribution

In September 2022, the Nord Stream pipeline explosions in the Baltic Sea made one fact impossible to ignore: a major infrastructure incident can transform global debate before anyone can say with confidence who caused it. Evidence may be incomplete, contradictory, politically filtered, or simply inaccessible at the moment when markets are already being asked to decide what the event means. The blast comes first. Attribution lags.

That sequence matters profoundly in Arctic commerce. In remote and strategically sensitive regions, a security incident with unclear attribution does not behave like an ordinary marine casualty. It produces not only physical uncertainty, but interpretive uncertainty. Was the event accidental, negligent, malicious, state-linked, activist, criminal, technical, environmental, or some unstable mixture of several possibilities? Each answer points towards a different claims pathway, a different evidentiary burden, and a different underwriting memory. Until the answer stabilises, institutions price the fog.

This is why contested attribution creates a distinctive form of risk. Most marine losses already involve disputes about sequence, causation, and responsibility. Arctic and near-Arctic security incidents add a further layer because the uncertainty often concerns not merely how the incident happened, but what category of event it belongs to at all. A machinery failure may be a machinery failure. A communications outage, a suspicious collision, unexplained damage, interference with navigation systems, or an abrupt disruption to strategically located infrastructure may sit in a much more unstable frame. The event itself may be measurable. Its meaning may remain highly contested. The signal breaks twice.

Claims handling becomes immediately more difficult under those conditions because insurance is structured around distinctions that attribution can unsettle. Different wordings may respond differently to accident, negligence, malicious conduct, hostile acts, state action, or politically charged interference. If the facts do not clearly support one classification, the claim does not move smoothly through the ordinary logic of adjustment. It stalls in argument. Experts are retained. Evidence is preserved and re-read. Insurers, clubs, reinsurers, and counterparties become more cautious because the financial implications of the label may exceed the direct physical loss. A dispute about what happened becomes a dispute about which legal and contractual universe governs what happened.

A named example helps illuminate the mechanism. The Nord Stream explosions in September 2022 were not an Arctic shipping casualty, yet they offered a stark demonstration of what contested attribution does to commercial and political reasoning. Even before public certainty was available, states, markets, commentators, and institutional actors began to interpret the event through competing narratives. The relevance to Arctic trade is direct. In a strategically charged northern setting, a serious incident can trigger claims and underwriting reactions long before attribution becomes stable, precisely because waiting for complete certainty is often not how commercial systems operate under stress. They react while the evidentiary ground is still shifting.

This unsettles evidence collection as well as claims classification. Arctic and sub-Arctic conditions are rarely kind to forensic clarity. Distance delays attendance. Weather interferes with inspection. Ice, currents, darkness, and limited infrastructure complicate preservation. State authorities may control access or shape the timing and terms under which evidence is gathered. Operators may have only partial records from the moment of disruption, especially where communications were degraded or the incident affected systems needed for detailed logging. By the time experts begin their work, the physical scene may already be altered. Contested attribution thrives in exactly this environment because uncertainty is not only political. It is material.

That material uncertainty explains why underwriters often respond conservatively even before a case is resolved. They do not need to know the final truth to understand that ambiguity itself is expensive. A claim with unclear attribution may trigger prolonged adjustment, harder internal review, greater reinsurer concern, more complicated policy interpretation, and a higher chance that similar incidents will later be read through the most troubling available scenario rather than the most benign one. This is the commercial logic of caution. If an underwriter cannot distinguish cleanly between accident and interference, or between technical failure and hostile action, it may widen exclusions, ask for more disclosure, reduce appetite, or price the route as though uncertainty itself were a peril. Doubt carries its own premium.

A second named example shows the same pattern in a more directly Arctic political register. The *Arctic Sunrise* seizure in September 2013 was not a classic attribution dispute about physical sabotage or unexplained damage, but it demonstrated how quickly a northern incident can be absorbed into competing political narratives that complicate the commercial reading of events. The lesson for insurers and operators was not that all controversial incidents are alike. It was that once a project or voyage enters a contested geopolitical frame, the ordinary separation between operational fact and political meaning becomes harder to maintain. Markets remember that difficulty and respond by narrowing tolerance for ambiguity later.

This is one reason operators may be required to adopt additional reporting and routing measures even when no specific incident has yet occurred on their own file. Markets and counterparties seek to reduce ambiguity before it matures into a claim. They ask for more precise route declarations, faster incident notification, stronger communications discipline, fuller preservation of navigational and technical data, clearer protocols for suspicious events, and more explicit authority chains for escalation. These measures can look burdensome or even paranoid from the bridge. From the insurer's perspective, they are attempts to prevent the next uncertain event from becoming evidentially unmanageable. Reporting becomes a defensive architecture.

Routing measures follow the same logic. In politically sensitive or strategically exposed northern waters, a route is never only a path of navigational convenience. It is also a path of interpretive exposure. Certain corridors, proximate assets, or operational behaviours may attract more suspicion or make later explanation harder if an incident occurs. Underwriters and charterers therefore become more interested in why a route was chosen, what alternatives were considered, what intelligence or advisories were available, and whether the operator maintained enough margin to show that prudence rather than opportunism guided the choice. A route defended poorly after an ambiguous incident becomes an underwriting problem for the whole class of voyage.

A brief example makes the connection plain. Imagine a support vessel transiting a northern corridor near sensitive infrastructure when it suffers a sudden systems disruption followed by minor physical damage of uncertain origin. The direct repair cost may be modest. The claims environment is not. If records are thin, reporting is delayed, routing logic is weakly documented, and communications are patchy, the event may produce a dispute far larger than the steel would suggest. Was the cause internal, environmental, accidental external contact, interference, or something else? Until that question is narrowed credibly, insurers, clubs, and counterparties will treat not only the vessel but the operational pattern itself with greater suspicion. The uncertainty spreads beyond the hull.

Still, a limitation deserves honest acknowledgement. Not every ambiguous incident justifies maximum geopolitical alarm, and markets can overreact to uncertainty by importing strategic fear into events that later turn out to have ordinary technical explanations. Ambiguity is not proof of hostile action. In some cases the most conservative institutional response may later look excessive once better evidence emerges. This matters, because overreaction can distort access and penalise operators whose real failing was simply to be unlucky in a sensitive place.

And yet this limitation strengthens rather than weakens the central point. Because the truth may emerge slowly, the cost of ambiguity is often paid before the truth arrives. Operators, insurers, and counterparties cannot suspend commercial life indefinitely while attribution matures. They act under uncertainty, and the tendency under such conditions is to protect against the more troubling plausible interpretations. That means tougher reporting obligations, stricter routing expectations, harder renewals, and a more conservative reading of neighbouring risks. Even if the final explanation later softens, the market memory of uncertainty may outlast the resolution of the specific case. The file keeps its stain.

This is why contested attribution belongs in a discussion of governance rather than in a narrow catalogue of security threats. The problem is not simply that bad actors may exist or that sabotage is conceivable. The problem is that commercial systems must operate while the identity, motive, and category of the event remain unsettled. That unsettledness changes how policies are drafted, how claims are handled, how projects are screened, and how later incidents are interpreted. Security enters commerce not only through violence, but through the difficulty of classifying disruption with confidence. The uncertain incident governs more than the proved one.

The image that best captures the issue is the broken signal. Something happened. The operator knows that much. The insurer knows that much. The market knows that much. What nobody knows quickly enough is what kind of event it was, who stood behind it if anyone did, and which clauses, obligations, and assumptions now govern the aftermath. In ordinary trades that delay is troublesome. In Arctic contexts, where strategic sensitivity already thickens the atmosphere, it can become the most expensive part of the event. Ambiguity fills the gap between fact and payment.

The harder question, then, is not whether security incidents in sensitive regions can be difficult to attribute. Plainly they can. The harder question is how much operational freedom remains once insurers and counterparties begin to assume that the next unexplained disruption will be judged not by what is eventually proved, but by what could plausibly be feared in the days and weeks when decisions about claims, routes, and future appetite must still be made without certainty.

Strategic infrastructure and dual-use concerns

In August 2022, the United States blocked the proposed sale of the Jektafjardur landholding in Iceland to a Chinese investor, and the public explanation quickly moved beyond ordinary property or tourism logic into a broader argument about location, sensitivity, and strategic implication. The land itself did not change overnight. What changed was the meaning attached to it. That shift is central to Arctic commerce. An asset can remain technically civilian, commercially plausible, and legally intelligible, yet become harder to finance, insure, or partner around once others begin to read it as relevant to security, influence, or future state use. The label arrives first.

That is the difficulty of dual-use concern in the Arctic. Ports, airstrips, communications systems, data platforms, energy support facilities, subsea infrastructure, logistics hubs, and even apparently mundane service assets often occupy two categories at once. They have an obvious commercial purpose and a possible strategic significance that may be vague, contested, or only partly formed. In easier regions this ambiguity may remain background noise. In the Arctic, where distance, sparse infrastructure, state presence, and military sensitivity sit unusually close together, the same ambiguity can migrate quickly into approvals, insurance, partnership decisions, and political scrutiny. A pier may be a pier. It may also be something else.

This is why perception matters as much as fact. A project does not need to be secretly military, covertly intelligence-linked, or deliberately geopolitical to attract strategic treatment. It is enough that decision-makers, insurers, compliance teams, financiers, or public authorities believe the asset could alter access, surveillance, logistics, communications, or influence in ways they do not wish to ignore. Once that belief takes hold, the commercial file changes. Additional questions appear. Counterparties grow cautious. Timelines lengthen. Cover becomes narrower or more conditional. The operator may protest, sometimes correctly, that the asset has a straightforward commercial rationale. The market may answer that straightforward rationales do not settle strategic reading. The fence goes up.

The institutional mechanism is usually quieter than outright prohibition. Strategic sensitivity often expresses itself through review rather than rejection, hesitation rather than formal refusal, and conditionality rather than public closure. Approvals slow as agencies or counterparties ask for more information about ownership, access rights, data handling, end use, long-term control, service arrangements, and the practical consequences of the asset's location. Insurers may seek fuller disclosure or introduce wording designed to reduce exposure to state action, sanctions risk, or politically charged disruption. Financiers may request stronger governance assurances or become uneasy about exit risk. Potential partners may simply decide the transaction now involves too much explanation. Feasibility has not disappeared. Friction has grown teeth.

A named example helps clarify the broader pattern. The blocked Icelandic land transaction in 2022 mattered because it showed how quickly a northern asset can be read through strategic geography rather than through ordinary commercial use alone. The lesson is not confined to land. In Arctic settings, the location and function of infrastructure can invite a reading that exceeds the operator's stated purpose. Ports can be seen as logistics nodes for more than cargo. Communications facilities can be read as information assets. Airstrips and service depots can appear relevant to mobility and access beyond civilian supply. Once an asset is placed in that strategic frame, every commercial discussion around it acquires extra weight.

This matters for insurance because underwriters do not only price physical hazards. They price interruption, political reaction, reputational burden, and the widening circle of uncertainty that follows once an asset becomes strategically controversial. A port support facility near a sensitive route, a terminal adjacent to nationally important infrastructure, a communications installation embedded in a sparse northern network, or a partnership tied to state-adjacent actors may all begin to look different once they are labelled strategic. The direct physical risk may remain manageable. The risk of delay, cancellation, state intervention, sanctions scrutiny, or claims entanglement grows harder to bound. Underwriters do not need a formal military designation to become cautious. They need only a plausible path by which the asset's meaning could shift under pressure.

A brief example shows how this works in practice. Imagine a commercially sensible proposal to upgrade a remote Arctic port so that it can support larger seasonal traffic, project cargo, and emergency refuge functions. On paper, the benefits are clear. The same upgrade also increases the port's logistical utility for other actors and future uses not central to the immediate project file. A lender asks whether ownership and access controls are stable. A public authority asks whether the facility could alter regional dependence patterns. An insurer asks whether any later disruption, protest, seizure, or state-imposed restriction would now have a strategic dimension that ordinary marine terms do not carry gracefully. The concrete has not changed. The risk treatment has.

Dual-use concern also complicates partnerships. Commercial Arctic projects often rely on consortia, service agreements, joint ventures, and infrastructure sharing because the region is too sparse and expensive for every operator to build everything alone. That commercial logic can sit uneasily beside security perception. A partner whose capital, technology, logistics, or data systems would ordinarily look attractive may trigger sharper review if its state links, jurisdictional ties, or perceived strategic affiliations make other participants uncomfortable. The project then slows not because the partnership is commercially unsound, but because others fear what the partnership could be taken to mean. This is one of the quiet ways strategic competition enters local feasibility. The signature becomes a signal.

A second named example illustrates how the Arctic repeatedly attracts this kind of reading. The proposal by a Chinese investor to acquire land at Grimsstadir a Fjollum in Iceland, which drew sustained public and official concern in the earlier 2010s, became notable not because the formal project description settled every question, but because many observers judged location and context to matter as much as the stated use. The relevance here is not to litigate that case. It is to show that strategic concern in the Arctic often arises where commercial explanation and geopolitical suspicion overlap without fully resolving one another. That overlap is precisely what insurers and counterparties dislike, because it makes future treatment of the asset harder to predict.

Still, a limitation should be acknowledged. Not every asset described as dual-use genuinely deserves heightened alarm, and strategic labelling can become a blunt instrument for blocking ordinary commercial development, excluding certain investors, or importing rivalry into projects whose practical significance is modest. Perception can exaggerate. Some assets are simply commercial, even if they sit in a region where imagination runs ahead of evidence. It would be careless to pretend that every strategic concern is equally grounded or equally honest.

And yet this limitation strengthens the central point rather than weakening it. Because perception is uneven, political, and often preventative, operators cannot assume that technical innocence will protect them from strategic treatment. The market reacts to plausible future complications, not only to proved present intention. If an asset might attract state review, reputational discomfort, or awkward questions about control and access, insurers and partners may already start adjusting terms. They do not need definitive proof of strategic misuse. They need only enough uncertainty that being wrong would be costly. Under such conditions, perception itself becomes an underwriting factor.

This is why strategic labelling changes risk treatment even when nothing visible happens to the asset. Premiums may harden. Cover may narrow.

Cancellation rights may feel less remote. Governance expectations around ownership, reporting, cyber controls, physical access, and emergency cooperation may thicken. Partners may ask for stronger contractual exits or more intrusive compliance assurances. The operator experiences all of this as friction. In truth it is the market's way of saying that the asset no longer sits inside a purely commercial category. A different file is being built around the same project.

The broader significance is that local Arctic feasibility can no longer be read only from engineering need, cargo demand, or vessel compatibility. A commercially rational facility may still struggle because broader strategic competition has altered how that facility is classified by people who control approvals, capital, cover, or public legitimacy. The project can remain technically elegant and institutionally awkward. That awkwardness is often decisive. Arctic commerce does not fail only on the ice. It can fail in the committee room where somebody says the asset may be more important than its sponsors admit, and nobody in the market feels relaxed enough to test that proposition cheaply.

The image that best captures the issue is the label on the folder. Yesterday it read port upgrade, terminal support, logistics hub, communications enhancement. Today another word has been pencilled in at the corner: strategic. Nothing physical has changed in the folder's contents. Yet every reader now turns the pages more slowly, asks different questions, and imagines different futures if the project proceeds. That is what dual-use concern does in practice. It alters the institutional pace around an asset before it alters the asset itself.

The harder question, then, is not whether certain Arctic infrastructure projects can be perceived as strategically sensitive. Plainly they can. The harder question is how a commercial actor is supposed to proceed once that perception has attached itself to the file - and whether the real dividing line in Arctic development now lies not between sound and unsound projects, but between those assets that can still be read as merely useful and those whose usefulness has become too entangled with strategic imagination for markets to treat them as ordinary any longer.

Insurers as inadvertent foreign policy actors

In 2014, after Russia's annexation of Crimea, a great many commercial decisions began to change without waiting for a formal public theory of Arctic order. Policies tightened. Counterparties were screened more carefully. Certain routes, relationships, and assets became harder to support, not always because states had issued perfectly comprehensive instructions, but because insurers, banks, brokers, and compliance teams no longer wished to stand as close to the uncertainty as they had before. The state moved. The market moved too.

That sequence matters because insurers do not need to intend foreign policy in order to help shape its practical effects. They do not command fleets, negotiate treaties, or issue sanctions lists. Yet they decide what sorts of ventures can obtain cover on workable terms, what exclusions now sit inside routine wordings, how much capacity remains available for certain regions or counterparties, and how much reputational strain they are willing to tolerate before a technically lawful project begins to look institutionally unattractive. In Arctic commerce, where insurability is often a precondition of movement rather than a decorative afterthought, those private decisions can alter what expansion is possible in practice. The pen can close routes.

This is the right place for caution. It would be easy, and wrong, to claim that insurers secretly run foreign policy by other means. They do not. States retain coercive power, diplomatic authority, and formal control over sanctions, territorial claims, and public regulation. But it would be equally wrong to treat insurers as neutral mirrors reflecting state decisions without adding anything of their own. Markets interpret, amplify, soften, fragment, and sometimes outpace official policy through ordinary institutional mechanisms: limited capacity, narrower cover, tighter exclusions, higher disclosure burdens, and a declining willingness to attach corporate names to politically awkward files. The result is not private sovereignty. It is something subtler and often more consequential for operators: de facto constraint.

The first mechanism is capacity. Insurance capacity is not an abstract ocean waiting to absorb whatever lawful trade presents itself. It is a finite and selective willingness to carry risk. In Arctic contexts, that willingness is already shaped by remoteness, sparse infrastructure, and thin claims comparators. Once geopolitical sensitivity is added, the available capacity can contract further, sometimes quickly. An insurer may remain legally free to support a venture and still decide that its capital is better used elsewhere, its internal governance no longer likes the exposure, or its reinsurers have become too uneasy about the surrounding politics. The operator sees a commercial problem. In effect, a private institution has helped set the outer boundary of feasible activity.

A named example helps fix the point. After the Crimea-related sanctions environment hardened in 2014, the practical effect on trade and insurance was not limited to direct state commands. Commercial institutions recalibrated their own tolerance. Some exposures became difficult to place not because every aspect of the transaction had been specifically prohibited, but because market actors no longer wished to spend scarce capacity on risks that now carried heightened compliance complexity, reputational tension, or the possibility of being recast by later political events. The Arctic lesson is plain. Where routes, ports, services, and assets sit close to strategic dispute, market withdrawal or thinning can exceed the precision of formal policy. Capacity turns caution into geography.

Exclusions are the second mechanism, and they often matter even more than open refusal. An insurer that stays nominally in the market can still reshape Arctic activity by carving out losses linked to state action, politically sensitive disruption, sanctions exposure, or contested events whose classification has become too awkward to carry broadly. Exclusions do not need to name grand strategy to have strategic effect. They reduce the willingness of private capital to stand behind certain forms of movement, infrastructure use, or commercial partnership. A voyage remains possible in law and brittle in practice. In that sense, exclusions can align with state intentions, exceed them, or sit somewhere beside them, because they are drafted to protect the insurer's position rather than to execute a public doctrine faithfully.

Reputational thresholds form the third mechanism. Insurers live inside systems of board oversight, investor scrutiny, public branding, regulatory expectation, and market comparison. A project can therefore become difficult to support even when legal analysis remains inconclusive or permissive. If a northern asset, route, or partnership begins to look strategically controversial, publicly indefensible, or administratively exhausting, the insurer may step back simply because the institutional cost of saying yes has risen too far. This is not foreign policy in any formal sense. Yet the effect can resemble it. A project loses cover, a partnership stalls, a terminal upgrade becomes harder to finance, or an operator discovers that lawful does not mean supportable. Reputation becomes a shadow regulator.

This is why private governance can both align with and depart from state intentions. Sometimes insurers tighten when states tighten, and the relationship looks straightforward. At other times markets go further, not because they are trying to punish more broadly, but because they fear ambiguity, compliance burden, and reputational spillover more than the state does. A government may leave room for lawful trade to continue under careful conditions, while insurers decide that the remaining room is too narrow or too costly to occupy confidently. The reverse can also occur. States may use strong political language while some market actors continue to support carefully structured activity that remains legal and commercially manageable. The important point is not perfect correlation. It is the existence of independent private filtering.

A second named example shows how this filtering can appear in a strategically sensitive setting without any neat public doctrine behind it. The blocked Icelandic land transaction in 2022 demonstrated how rapidly an Arctic asset can move from commercial category to strategic category in the minds of decision-makers. The insurer or financier observing such episodes does not need to adopt an official geopolitical stance to react. It needs only to recognise that similar assets may now attract more scrutiny, more delay, more controversy, or more chance of intervention than before. A private decision to narrow appetite after such a signal may not replicate state policy exactly. It still reshapes the field in which Arctic development proceeds.

Still, a limitation deserves emphasis. Insurers are not all-powerful. They depend on law, respond unevenly, compete with one another, and often act with imperfect information. Different markets may read the same exposure differently. Capacity can return. Wordings can soften. Political anxieties can prove temporary or exaggerated. It would be overstated to imagine a coherent private bloc deciding Arctic futures in concert. What exists instead is more fragmented and, in some ways, more realistic: a series of decisions by institutions trying to protect themselves under uncertainty, whose cumulative effect may resemble strategic governance without ever being centrally designed.

That fragmentation is precisely why the model must stay sober. Private insurers do not need to coordinate in order to create meaningful external constraint. They need only to share certain incentives. If capacity is limited, if exclusions become more common, if reputational thresholds harden, and if reinsurers or compliance departments begin to ask sharper questions about Arctic exposure, the cumulative outcome may be a significant narrowing of what is commercially feasible. No one institution has made foreign policy. Yet Arctic operators may find themselves governed by a web of private refusals, conditions, and silences that state officials neither fully intended nor fully control.

This matters for the book's larger argument because it shows how non-state power works most effectively when it presents itself as ordinary prudence. A policy clause looks technical. A reduced line looks commercial. A decision not to quote looks internal. Together these choices can influence which projects proceed, which routes remain viable, which partnerships are acceptable, and which kinds of infrastructure become too awkward to support. The result is not dramatic. It is often more powerful because it is dispersed, deniable, and embedded in familiar procedures. The market becomes a channel through which geopolitics acquires operational bite.

The image that best captures this is the empty chair at a negotiation table. The state is present in the background through law, sanctions, and strategic posture. The insurer is present in the foreground through capacity, wording, and appetite. Neither wholly controls the other. Yet if the insurer decides not to sit down, or sits down only on terms that make the project commercially fragile, the practical effect on Arctic expansion may be immediate. The absence speaks.

The harder question, then, is not whether insurers sometimes influence Arctic outcomes beyond the narrow payment of claims. Plainly they do. The harder question is how far a region can be reshaped by private institutions acting from caution rather than command - and whether the most consequential constraints on Arctic development may increasingly emerge not from a single state's explicit prohibition, but from the quieter point at which enough insurers decide that standing behind a lawful venture now asks them to absorb more political, reputational, and strategic ambiguity than they are willing to carry.

Chapter 15

Scenarios for Arctic Access and Governance

What would actually make the Arctic easier to insure: thinner ice, or thicker institutions? The question matters because the seductive answer is usually the wrong one. It is tempting to imagine that better ships, better sensors, and better models will do the decisive work. They matter. But the deeper obstacle has never been technology alone. The harder problem lies in whether incidents are reported honestly, whether responsibilities are allocated clearly, whether ports and response systems can absorb disruption, whether enforcement behaves predictably, and whether documents can be trusted to mean the same thing across markets, flags, and claims. Steel helps. So does paper.

That is the paradox at the end of this book. The Arctic is often narrated as a frontier of movement, yet its commercial future may depend less on motion than on routine. Better access will not come only from bold design or seasonal opportunity. It will come from the slow and unglamorous work of making risk more legible to institutions that hate surprise. When underwriters, clubs, charterers, regulators, financiers, and communities can compare operators with greater confidence, argue less wildly after incidents, and rely on a thicker infrastructure of evidence, the region becomes more governable. Not safer in any naive sense. More governable.

This is where the argument turns from diagnosis to conditions. Across the preceding chapters, the same pattern has appeared in different guises: weak information produces caution; uneven enforcement produces pricing penalties; thin infrastructure enlarges ordinary failures; contested attribution widens disputes; poor disclosure corrodes trust; strategic controversy hardens appetite. None of these problems is solved merely by announcing ambition. They are solved, if at all, by institutional achievements that reduce the room in which uncertainty can multiply. That reduction is the real currency of access.

The central tension is therefore not whether Arctic expansion will happen or fail in some absolute sense. It is whether the region will become more insurable through shared disciplines that lower uncertainty across the system, or whether it will remain a place where every advance in activity produces a matching advance in exclusion, suspicion, and fragmented control. One path makes risk more comparable and therefore more financable. The other leaves operators trapped in a cycle of episodic optimism followed by market hardening, political friction, and renewed arguments about whether the venture was ever properly governable in the first place.

The stakes are practical. If governance improves in ways that matter to claims, underwriting, and operations, Arctic access may widen without pretending the region has become ordinary. If it does not, the most likely result is not dramatic closure but selective viability: a few well-capitalised operators able to survive thick documentation, expensive redundancy, and narrow tolerances, while everyone else faces a corridor that is open in law and brittle in commerce. That difference matters not only for cost, but for power. A region governed by quiet institutional thresholds will reward those who can read and satisfy them, and punish those who still look only at the chart.

The stakes are intellectual as well. Arctic debate is easily captured by headlines, symbolic disputes, and sweeping geopolitical claims. Yet much of the real governing work has been shown to occur elsewhere: inside exclusions, survey recommendations, terminal interfaces, consultation records, monitoring plans, renewal files, claims correspondence, and the routine hesitations of institutions deciding whether a project feels legible enough to support. If future analysis keeps ignoring these quieter sites of power, it will continue to mistake spectacle for structure. The most consequential forms of Arctic governance are often boring on purpose.

That is the path of inquiry from here. It begins by asking what kinds of developments would make Arctic risk more insurable in institutional rather than merely technical terms, then turns towards the competing futures that could emerge from different combinations of standardisation, fragmentation, and market-led discipline. It ends by pressing on the gaps that still matter most: opaque claims, uneven enforcement, and the stubborn difficulty of tracing how standards, finance, and political pressure interact in the actual documents and disputes through which the region is governed. The folder thickens.

The image that best suits this closing movement is the filing cabinet. Arctic access is often sold through ships, routes, and ice maps, but its future may depend more on what fills the drawers: incident records good enough to compare, responsibilities clear enough to defend, monitoring data strong enough to narrow argument, enforcement patterns consistent enough to price, and market signals readable enough that operators can tell whether the next tightening reflects genuine risk or merely another turn of institutional unease. Without that cabinet, every proposal arrives half-blind. With it, even a difficult region becomes easier to govern.

The harder question, then, is not whether the Arctic will continue to attract ambition. Plainly it will. The harder question is what kind of institutional world must be built before that ambition stops relying on exceptionalism and starts meeting a sterner test: whether the quiet governors of access can finally compare, trust, and constrain activity well enough that the region becomes not simple, not safe, but insurable on terms that do not depend on forgetting everything this book has shown about how power really works there.

What would make Arctic risk more insurable

In August 2018, when the *Venta Maersk* completed its trial transit through the Northern Sea Route, many observers reached instinctively for the wrong lesson. They treated the voyage as evidence that access would widen if only ships became strong enough, forecasts sharp enough, and ice windows favourable enough. But a single successful passage never answers the question that matters most to insurers, charterers, financiers, and infrastructure owners: can this kind of operation be made legible enough, repeatable enough, and governable enough that the next file looks less like an exception and more like a category? One voyage proves possibility. It does not prove insurability.

That is the hard distinction this subject demands. Arctic risk becomes more insurable not when nature turns generous, but when institutions become better at reducing surprise. Markets do not ask only whether a ship can survive. They ask whether incidents are reported honestly, whether responsibilities are distributed clearly, whether shore-side systems can absorb disruption, whether inspections behave predictably, and whether later disputes can be argued from records rather than from speculation. The sensor matters. So does the ledger.

This is why the developments that genuinely lower Arctic uncertainty are usually less glamorous than the rhetoric of frontier commerce suggests.

Better incident reporting does not stir the imagination like a new vessel design. Stronger local infrastructure lacks the romance of an opened route. Consistent enforcement sounds bureaucratic beside the drama of geopolitics. Clearer allocation of responsibility looks like paperwork rather than progress. Yet these are the changes that make underwriters less defensive, claims less chaotic, and contract chains less brittle. The quieter the improvement, the more likely it is to matter.

The first of these improvements is better incident reporting, because almost every other judgement in this market depends on what institutions can learn from things that have already gone wrong. Arctic files are still too often shaped by sparse comparators, delayed reconstruction, inconsistent terminology, or a reporting culture that softens awkward facts until the claim begins. Insurers do not merely dislike loss. They dislike not being able to compare one loss with another, to tell near miss from structural weakness, or to distinguish an unlucky event from a pattern hidden inside thin records. When reporting improves - faster, fuller, more standardised, more candid about conditions and decisions - the market gains something more valuable than public transparency. It gains a basis for comparison. The notebook thickens.

This is an institutional achievement, not just a data one. A better sensor suite does not guarantee better reporting if masters fear punishment, owners fear commercial embarrassment, counterparties fear litigation, or authorities collect facts in incompatible ways. Reporting improves when organisations decide that the long-term value of credible disclosure outweighs the short-term temptation to keep the file clean. It improves when clubs, insurers, ports, and regulators reward candour rather than merely weaponising it. It improves when incident categories mean roughly the same thing across systems that must later share risk. In other words, it improves when governance chooses legibility over cosmetic calm.

A second development is stronger infrastructure, and this too is often misunderstood as merely physical investment. More ports, more tugs, better repair access, stronger communications, and more credible medical response plainly reduce severity. But infrastructure only makes risk more insurable when it is dependable enough to change how a claim would unfold in practice. An underwriter does not care about a harbour on a map in the abstract. It cares whether that harbour can receive a damaged vessel, support response under seasonal constraints, interface with terminals and authorities coherently, and shorten the chain by which modest disruption becomes major loss. Concrete without coordination remains thin security.

That is why stronger infrastructure is partly a matter of organisation. A response asset no one can mobilise quickly, a yard whose capabilities are ambiguous, or a terminal whose private rules intensify friction can leave a region looking better equipped on paper than it behaves under stress. By contrast, even modest infrastructure can materially improve insurability if roles are clear, access is realistic, and the service chain is tested in ways the market can trust. Operators and insurers are not asking for perfection. They are asking whether interruption is likely to stay interruption, or whether every setback still threatens to expand into salvage, pollution, delay, and dispute because help remains too improvised to believe in fully.

A third improvement is more consistent enforcement. This sounds dry. It is not. Arctic markets pay heavily for uneven interpretation. When operators cannot predict how flags, port states, terminals, class actors, auditors, and insurers will read similar facts across similar trades, uncertainty becomes self-multiplying. The cost does not arise only from the chance of sanction or detention. It arises from the difficulty of building a commercially durable operating model when the meaning of compliance shifts from place to place or from file to file. Consistency lowers this tax. It allows participants to distinguish genuine tightening from mere variance, and it reduces the temptation to treat every new demand as either arbitrary or politically charged.

Still, consistency should not be confused with leniency. A strict regime can improve insurability if it is intelligible, repeatable, and backed by institutions capable of applying it with reasonable discipline. Markets can price hard rules more easily than erratic ones. This is why governance improvements that matter most are not always those that make Arctic operations easier in the immediate sense. Some make them more demanding. But if those demands are stable enough to compare and credible enough to trust, the region becomes more insurable precisely because the cost of surprise falls. Predictability is a form of access.

The fourth development is clearer allocation of responsibilities. Arctic ventures still too often rely on optimistic ambiguity: charterers expect owners to absorb one category of disruption, owners expect terminals or service providers to carry another, insurers assume operational controls existed that claims later reveal were blurred, and public authorities presume that emergency roles were more settled than they prove to be under pressure. The result is that when incidents occur, losses widen through argument as much as through damage. Clearer allocations do not eliminate conflict, but they reduce the territory in which conflict can grow. The contract stops wobbling.

This too is institutional rather than technological. Better software will not resolve responsibility if counterparties prefer vagueness while the project is profitable and clarity only after the loss. Markets become more comfortable when roles are stated plainly enough that routing authority, response obligations, reporting duties, inspection consequences, and liability pathways can be followed without heroic reconstruction. A project whose documentation shows who decides, who reports, who responds, and who pays for what under stated contingencies looks more insurable because it promises a narrower, more manageable aftermath if the voyage goes wrong. The wording holds.

A credible limitation should be admitted. None of these developments abolishes Arctic difficulty. Better reporting will not stop storms. Better infrastructure will not remove remoteness. Consistent enforcement will not eliminate politics. Clearer responsibilities will not prevent every dispute. The region will remain severe, costly, and occasionally unforgiving. It would be foolish to present institutional improvement as a route to normality in any lazy sense.

And yet this limitation sharpens the real lesson. The question is not whether Arctic risk can be made ordinary. It cannot. The question is whether it can be made more governable, more comparable, and less vulnerable to the sort of cascading uncertainty that causes markets to retreat even from technically capable projects. That is the right test for future proposals. Do they make later incidents easier to understand? Do they reduce the distance between event and response? Do they narrow interpretive variance? Do they clarify responsibility before the claim rather than inside it? If not, they may still be innovative. They are not yet meaningfully more insurable.

This gives the reader a practical way to judge Arctic optimism. When a proposal boasts of stronger ships, smarter routing, or new commercial openings, the real question is whether the surrounding institutional world has thickened alongside the technology. Is reporting likely to improve or remain selective? Will infrastructure truly shorten severity, or merely decorate presentations? Are enforcement patterns becoming more coherent, or simply harsher in scattered ways? Does the contract map responsibility more clearly than the last generation of ventures, or is it still gambling on goodwill under stress? These are the quiet indicators that separate genuine progress from another cycle of enthusiasm waiting to be corrected by claims.

The image that best captures the issue is the drawer in the filing cabinet. If Arctic risk is becoming more insurable, the drawer should become easier to organise: incident reports fuller, comparisons cleaner, responsibilities clearer, response assumptions more credible, and institutional reactions less erratic. If the drawer is still a jumble of opaque claims, thin records, inconsistent treatment, and improvised blame, the apparent progress on the water may be telling a flattering story that the market will eventually refuse to keep funding.

The harder question, then, is not whether future Arctic proposals will promise greater capability. Plainly they will. The harder question is whether they also promise the slower institutional gains that let insurers believe the next incident will generate less confusion than the last - or whether the region will keep producing technically impressive ventures that fail the sterner test of insurability because the governance around them remains too thin to carry the weight of success.

Competing governance futures

What would a more governable Arctic actually look like: one rulebook, many guarded local rulebooks, or a commercial order held together mostly by insurers, terminals, financiers, and private standards bodies? The question matters because the region's future will not be decided by a single dramatic event or one triumphant technology. It will be decided by the shape of the institutions that make activity legible, punishable, financeable, and defensible after things go wrong. The chart is only the beginning.

That is why scenario thinking matters more than headline thinking. Headlines reward spectacle. Governance futures turn on quieter structural drivers: whether states converge or diverge in their appetite for standardisation, whether ports and regulators interpret common texts in comparable ways, whether claims remain too opaque to build shared learning, whether insurers continue to price uncertainty conservatively, and whether private actors become more comfortable writing the practical rules of access themselves. These are not competing predictions so much as competing logics. Each produces a different Arctic commercial order even if the same ships continue to sail through the same water.

The first plausible future is tighter standardisation. This is the scenario in which formal rules, technical expectations, reporting habits, and enforcement practices become more comparable across the institutions that matter most. Not identical in every detail, but sufficiently aligned that an operator can move from design to underwriting to port interface to claims handling without discovering that each stage uses a different grammar of prudence. The appeal is obvious. Standardisation reduces interpretive variance. It makes risk easier to compare, incidents easier to categorise, and responsibilities easier to defend after the fact. In insurance terms, that usually means a better chance that Arctic activity can be priced as difficult but governable rather than exceptional and unstable.

The costs of this future are more ambiguous than its advocates sometimes admit. Tighter standardisation raises entry barriers because it demands more documentation, more disciplined systems, and more willingness to operate inside a narrower range of accepted practice. Smaller or newer entrants may struggle first. Some local flexibility would be lost, and operators used to exploiting ambiguity between flags, ports, class practices, or insurance interpretations would find less room to manoeuvre. Yet incident response under this future would likely become more orderly because expectations about reporting, command responsibility, evidence preservation, and minimum preparedness would be easier to align before the emergency rather than argued into existence during it. The form is stricter. The aftermath may be cleaner.

The second plausible future is fragmented regionalism. This is the Arctic as a patchwork of partially overlapping but increasingly distinctive regimes, shaped by local political priorities, strategic sensitivity, infrastructure unevenness, community pressure, and divergent administrative cultures. In such a future, operators would not face one Arctic problem, but several. A route, terminal, or project acceptable in one region might attract a very different reading in another because consultation expectations, strategic sensitivities, inspection intensity, sanctions exposure, or evidentiary habits would no longer be loosely converging. The same rule text might survive on paper while its lived meaning diverged markedly from one jurisdictional or institutional setting to the next.

Fragmentation offers some advantages. It allows local conditions to matter more directly. It may produce rules better fitted to specific coastlines, communities, infrastructures, and security concerns. It can preserve room for political discretion where states do not wish to surrender local control to a wider discipline. But it is a harder world for insurers, charterers, and operators because cost rises with unpredictability. Fragmented systems are difficult to compare, difficult to model, and difficult to insure gracefully.

Entry barriers increase in a different way here: not through one high common standard, but through the need to master multiple partial standards at once. Incident response also becomes more awkward, because a casualty moving across institutional boundaries or touching several authorities may encounter competing assumptions about responsibility, disclosure, and acceptable remedies. The folder thickens unevenly.

The third plausible future is market-led self-regulation. In this version, private actors do much of the practical governing work through insurance terms, class requirements, terminal rules, financing conditions, charterparty language, audit systems, and reputational thresholds. States remain present, of course, but the decisive operational discipline increasingly comes from institutions that decide whether a project is insurable, bankable, berthable, or commercially tolerable. This is not a fantasy. Much of the Arctic already works this way in practice. The question is one of degree. If formal governance remains partial, politically contested, or too slow to generate stable confidence, private governance may continue filling the gap.

This future can be efficient in a narrow sense. Markets can move faster than states. They can tighten clauses after claims, demand stronger evidence after public controversy, and condition access on practical safeguards without waiting for a diplomatic consensus that may never come. For sophisticated operators, a market-led order may even feel clearer than a politically fragmented one because the signals are immediate: the premium rises, the exclusion appears, the terminal checklist lengthens, the financier hesitates. But this clarity has a price. It tends to privilege those with capital, administrative depth, and the capacity to satisfy thick private requirements. It can also produce uneven accountability, because private actors govern through contract and appetite rather than through public obligation. Incident response in such a system may be well disciplined for those inside the preferred tier of operators and much rougher for everyone else. The market can be orderly and exclusionary at the same time.

A credible limitation should be faced squarely. These futures are ideal types, not sealed boxes. No real Arctic order will belong neatly to one alone. Elements of standardisation can coexist with regional fragmentation. Market-led discipline can flourish inside formally harmonised systems. States may deliberately leave some matters to insurers and terminals while hardening others under public control. The value of the typology lies not in pretending reality will choose one pure form, but in clarifying the structural pressures that pull governance in different directions. Scenarios are tools for comparison, not oracles.

That is why the real drivers matter more than the labels. Standardisation grows where claims learning thickens, where institutions trust one another enough to compare practices, and where the cost of variance begins to outweigh the value of discretion. Fragmentation deepens where sovereignty concerns, strategic rivalry, local political pressure, and uneven infrastructure make common treatment harder to sustain. Market-led self-regulation expands where private institutions are asked to manage risk faster and more concretely than formal public systems can. These are not passing moods. They are durable tendencies. They help explain why the same event can be read as an argument for more harmonisation in one setting, more local control in another, and more private caution in a third.

A brief example makes the practical distinction clearer. Imagine a future Arctic project proposing a terminal upgrade, associated shipping service, and specialised support arrangements. Under tighter standardisation, the decisive questions would concern whether the project can satisfy a clearer common framework and generate evidence comparable enough to reassure multiple markets. Under fragmented regionalism, the same project would succeed or fail largely on its ability to navigate place-specific political, regulatory, and contractual conditions that resist easy translation. Under market-led self-regulation, the decisive test would likely be whether insurers, financiers, and infrastructure owners regard the file as governable enough to support despite the absence of fully settled public consensus. The asset remains the same. Its governing universe changes.

This is why the typology matters for costs, entry barriers, and incident response. Standardisation raises costs up front but can lower the price of interpretive chaos later. Fragmentation may preserve local authority while imposing repeated translation costs on every participant. Market-led self-regulation can accelerate adaptation yet entrench private thresholds that are difficult to challenge publicly once they become normalised. None of these futures abolishes Arctic difficulty. Each redistributes it. The question for serious readers is not which future sounds most elegant in theory, but which structure would most likely narrow avoidable uncertainty without merely pushing cost and discretion into darker corners of the system.

The image that best captures the choice is the drawer in the filing cabinet. In one future, the files become easier to sort because institutions gradually agree on what counts as a good record, a material incident, a credible response, and a defensible allocation of responsibility. In another, the drawer fills with papers organised differently in each subfolder, forcing every new entrant to relearn the filing logic region by region. In the third, the drawer is managed less by public rule than by the quiet preferences of whoever controls access to cover, finance, berths, and continuation of trade. The papers still govern. They simply do so under different custodians.

The harder question, then, is not whether the Arctic will continue to be governed. Plainly it will. The harder question is what mixture of public standard, regional divergence, and private discipline will come to define the next phase of access - and whether those who speak most confidently about Arctic opportunity are reading the slow institutional drivers carefully enough to recognise which future they are already helping to build.

A research agenda for boring power

In March 1989, after the *Exxon Valdez* grounded in Alaska, the visible disaster was easy to narrate. The harder story sat elsewhere, in the quieter institutional machinery that later decided what the event would mean for underwriting, regulation, liability, monitoring, infrastructure planning, and the market memory of northern operations. The spill was public. Much of the governing work that followed was not. That imbalance has never really gone away.

It is tempting to treat Arctic governance as a field best understood through summits, treaties, naval movements, strategic speeches, or dramatic casualties. Those things matter. But they rarely explain enough. The deeper and more durable forms of control often sit in what looks, at first glance, too dull to command attention: claims files that do not become public, inconsistent inspection habits, survey recommendations, private standards, renewal negotiations, exclusions, financing conditions, terminal checklists, consultation records, and environmental data whose absence becomes visible only when something goes wrong. Power here is often boring because it works best when it appears routine. The drawer stays shut.

That is why a serious research agenda has to begin with humility about what is still poorly known. The Arctic is not merely under-observed in the scientific sense. It is under-described institutionally. Too much analysis still leans on formal rules and public statements while leaving the quieter governing mechanisms comparatively unexamined. We know that insurers matter, but often not enough about how they change appetite after a dispute that settles privately. We know that enforcement varies, but often not enough about how that variance is experienced across flags, ports, and markets. We know that standards shape access, but often not enough about how they interact with finance, reputational thresholds, or the practical willingness of counterparties to carry a file. The gaps are not decorative. They are where explanation fails.

Claims opacity is the first and most obvious deficit. Marine and Arctic-related disputes frequently disappear into arbitration, negotiated settlement, club correspondence, internal market memory, or fragmented legal process. The result is a peculiar asymmetry. Markets learn. Outsiders often do not. Underwriters, brokers, surveyors, lawyers, and major operators may absorb lessons from a difficult incident even when no clear public precedent emerges. Scholars and policy analysts, by contrast, are left to reconstruct institutional change from policy wording, anecdote, and indirect shifts in behaviour. This matters because claims are one of the main places where Arctic governance is rewritten. If the event record remains opaque, we struggle to know whether later tightening reflects actual loss experience, reputational panic, reinsurance caution, or some combination that no public document fully discloses.

This opacity matters for practitioners as much as for researchers. An operator trying to assess a new route, a new terminal, or a new service structure needs more than legal permission and technical optimism. It needs a way to infer what the market has already learned from the hidden archive of previous incidents. If claims remain hard to study, serious commercial actors may end up relying too heavily on broker folklore, whispered precedent, or selective memory. That can make the Arctic look more mysterious than it is while also making it easier for private thresholds to harden without explanation. A market can govern most effectively when the reasons for its caution are only partly visible.

Enforcement variance is the second major gap. Formal standards may be public and widely cited, yet their lived meaning can differ sharply across ports, flags, terminal cultures, auditing styles, and political contexts. This variance is often acknowledged and rarely measured well. Too much writing still assumes that once a code or standard exists, the main question becomes whether actors comply. In practice, the more revealing question is how different institutions interpret, prioritise, intensify, or relax similar requirements under different pressures. A strict but intelligible inspectorate may reduce uncertainty more effectively than a lighter and more erratic one. A terminal that adds predictable private requirements may make a route easier to insure than a formally permissive environment where expectations remain unclear until the vessel arrives. Without close attention to these differences, analysis mistakes legal text for institutional reality.

The consequence is serious. Enforcement variance does not merely produce administrative inconvenience. It shapes cost, appetite, routing choices, infrastructure use, and the relative advantage of large or experienced operators over smaller entrants. It also affects incident response. If evidence preservation, deficiency treatment, survey escalation, and reporting expectations differ across settings, a casualty crossing or touching multiple jurisdictions becomes harder to classify and settle. The resulting uncertainty is then priced back into the market. A research agenda that neglects variance will therefore miss one of the main channels by which public administration becomes private cost.

The third thin area is the interaction of standards with finance. This is perhaps the least glamorous and one of the most important. Standards are often studied as technical or legal devices. Finance is often studied as an external source of capital. In Arctic practice the two are tightly entangled. Standards do not simply tell operators what safe conduct looks like. They also help lenders, insurers, charterers, and infrastructure owners decide whether a project is governable enough to support. A requirement that appears technical may also function as a financing threshold. A monitoring plan may matter because it improves claims defensibility. A class notation may matter because it reduces information asymmetry. A consultation record may matter because it lowers the likelihood of costly delay or controversy. Research that splits standards from finance misses the mechanism by which quiet rules become access conditions.

This is where a durable method begins to emerge. To study Arctic expansion seriously, one must read documents not only for what they declare, but for what they quietly redistribute. The policy should be read for where uncertainty is carved out, priced, or pushed back onto the operator. The survey recommendation should be read for what weakness has become newly legible to the market. The terminal checklist should be read for how infrastructure owners allocate disruption and liability. The consultation record should be read for whether local knowledge has altered operating assumptions or merely decorated them. The environmental monitoring plan should be read for how an operator prepares for the future argument about causation. The dispute should be read not only for who won, but for what later market caution it may have seeded. The file teaches.

A named example shows why this method matters. After the *Exxon Valdez* catastrophe, the most important changes were not exhausted by public law or public memory. They also appeared in underwriting habits, response expectations, environmental baseline logic, and the market's altered willingness to take northern pollution narratives at face value. Anyone studying only the visible legal aftermath would have missed much of the governing afterlife of the event. The same logic applies now to less famous incidents, private disputes, and seemingly minor administrative shifts. Quiet governors rarely announce their importance. Their importance must be inferred from repeated traces.

Still, a limitation should be faced openly. Boring power is difficult to research precisely because it resists spectacle and often resists disclosure. Some documents are private. Some negotiations are inaccessible. Some institutional memories are carried in people rather than in archives. There is a real danger of overinterpreting fragmentary evidence or of mistaking an isolated commercial choice for a durable governing pattern. Care is needed. The antidote is not to retreat into only what is publicly indisputable. It is to compare patiently across policy language, inspection practice, claims handling, financing behaviour, infrastructure conditions, and the timing of market shifts. The method must be cumulative.

That caution also protects against overclaiming the coherence of the system. Arctic governance is not a single machine humming in perfect coordination. It is a layered and often improvised arrangement of states, insurers, class societies, ports, terminals, financiers, communities, sanctions screens, auditors, and political pressures. Their incentives overlap without fully matching. Their actions sometimes align, sometimes clash, and sometimes simply accumulate. The value of focusing on boring power is not that it reveals a hidden master plan. It reveals how many small, defensible, procedural decisions can produce a commercial order whose total effect is larger than any one actor intended.

This matters for practitioners because it changes where attention should go. The serious operator, lender, or analyst cannot afford to read only the headline event or the public rule. The more revealing signals may lie in a new exclusion, a changed terminal form, a slower compliance review, a sharper survey emphasis, a shift in what counts as adequate consultation, or a claims file that settled too quietly for public confidence but loudly enough to alter market behaviour. These are not side details. They are the medium through which Arctic expansion is governed in practice. To ignore them is to mistake visibility for importance.

The image that best captures the whole agenda is the filing cabinet. The Arctic is full of striking pictures, bold maps, and geopolitical language, but its future may depend just as much on what accumulates in those drawers:

reports that are never widely read, checklists that quietly harden, disputes that teach without becoming precedent, monitoring records that narrow later argument, and financing conditions that translate soft concern into hard threshold. The cabinet is boring only to those who have not yet understood that this is where access is often won, narrowed, or lost.

The harder question, then, is not whether more research is needed. Plainly it is. The harder question is whether scholars and practitioners are willing to follow Arctic power into the places where it becomes least theatrical and most effective - and whether they can learn to read the next document, dispute, inspection, or renewal not as administrative debris, but as evidence that the real governors of the region have been at work again, quietly altering what expansion will mean.

About the Author

Nuno Valcorte is a nonfiction writer interested in how large geopolitical shifts are enabled or halted by institutions that rarely appear in heroic narratives. His work focuses on the practical machinery of modern power: standards, contracts, audits, and the administrative routines that translate uncertainty into rules. Rather than treating the Arctic as a stage for exceptionalism, he approaches it as a place where familiar tools of governance are tested by distance, cold, and imperfect information.

Valcorte writes in an academic nonfiction mode that values clarity over slogans. He is drawn to the boundary where public authority meets private ordering, especially in domains where decisions are made through technical language that can exclude non-specialists. That interest makes insurance, classification, and liability more than specialist topics: they become a way to see how access is granted, how responsibility is assigned, and how behaviour is disciplined without overt coercion.

A quiet historical thread runs through his approach: major maritime disasters have repeatedly forced societies to renegotiate what they will tolerate in exchange for commerce, and which organisations are trusted to certify safety. From iconic ship losses to pollution crises that reshaped public expectations, these episodes show how "routine" paperwork can suddenly become political. Valcorte's aim is to help readers recognise that dynamic before the next Arctic incident turns a technical dispute into a global argument.

www.ingramcontent.com/pod-product-compliance
Lightning Source LLC
Chambersburg PA
CBHW031320230926
51848CB00001B/21
9789377940249